LAST TSAR

S. S. OLDENBURG

LAST TSAR

Nicholas II, His Reign & His Russia

❧

Volume 2

YEARS OF CHANGE, 1900-1907

Translated by Leonid I. Mihalap and Patrick J. Rollins
Edited by Patrick J. Rollins

❧

ACADEMIC INTERNATIONAL PRESS

1977

THE RUSSIAN SERIES / Volume 25-2

Sergei S. Oldenburg **Last Tsar! Nicholas II, His Reign and His Russia**. Volume 2: **Years of Change, 1900-1907.** Translation of *Tsarstvovanie Imperatora Nikolaia II,* Volume 1 (Belgrade, 1939), Part I-II, Chapters VII-XII.

ISBN: 0-87569-068-8

Maps by Richard D. Kelly, Jr.
Composition by Susan D. Long
Title page by King & Queen Press

Illustrations from Thomas Michell, *Russian Pictures* (London-New York, 1889); Count Paul Vassili[pseud. Juliette Adam?], *Behind the Veil at the Russian Court* (London, 1914); S.S. Oldenburg, *Tsarstvovanie Imperatora Nikolaia II* (Belgrade-Munich, 1939-49); A.J. Sacks, *The Birth of the Russian Democracy* (New York, 1918); *Stikhotvornaia satira pervoi russkoi revoliutsii (1905-1907)*, (Leningrad, 1969).

Printed in the United States of America

ACADEMIC INTERNATIONAL PRESS
POB 555 Gulf Breeze FL 32561

CONTENTS

☙

❧

THE   EMPIRE

NORWEGIAN   SEA

BARENTS SEA

KARA

BRITAIN

NORTH
SEA

BALTIC SEA

Helsinki

GERMAN - EMPIRE

Riga

St.Petersburg

Archangel

Vilno

Warsaw

Pechora

Ob

AUSTRIA-
HUNGARY

Smolensk

Moscow

Dnieper

Kiev

Nizhni - Novgorod

RUMANIA

Kharkov

Kazan

Odessa

Volga

Ufa

Tobolsk

BULGARIA

Don

Samara

Cheliabinsk

Ural

Omsk

Tomsk

Irtish

Novosibirsk

BLACK   SEA

OTTOMAN
EMPIRE

Semipalatinsk

Batum

CASPIAN SEA

Tiflis

Baku

ARAL
SEA

Lake Balkhash

Khiva

Amu

Syr

GeoK-Tepe

Tashkent

KULDJA

IRAN

Bukhara

Kokand

Kushka

AFGHANISTAN

LEGEND

Boundary of the Empire

Great Siberian Railway

Chinese Eastern Railway

South Manchurian Railway

Annexed 1858-1860

Annexed 1864-1895

Occupied 1871-1881

NEPAL

INDIAN
OCEAN

INDIA

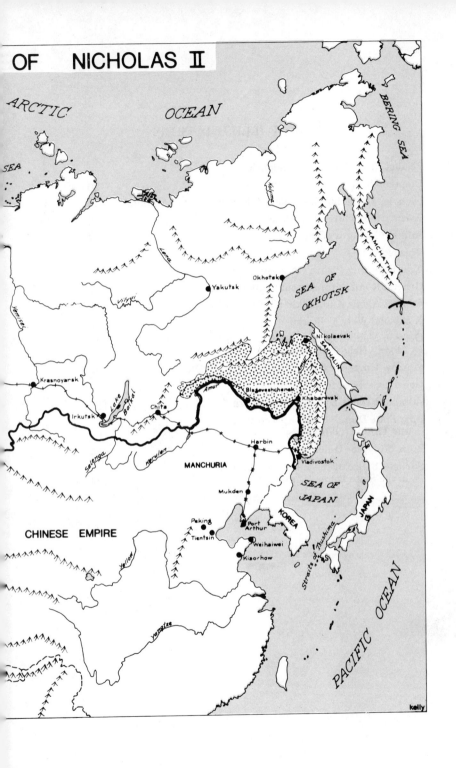

ARCTIC OCEAN

SEA

BERING SEA

KAMCHATKA

SEA OF OKHOTSK

Okhotsk

Yakutsk

Lena

Vilyui

Kolyma

Nikolaevsk

SAKHALIN

Krasnoyarsk

Yenisei

Lake Baikal

Chita

Irkutsk

Selenga

Kerulen

Amur

Blagoveshchensk

Khabarovsk

Harbin

MANCHURIA

Vladivostok

SEA OF JAPAN

Mukden

JAPAN

Peking

Tientsin

Port Arthur

KOREA

Straits of Tsushima

CHINESE EMPIRE

Yellow

Weihaiwei

Kiaochow

Yangtze

PACIFIC OCEAN

kelly

LIST OF ILLUSTRATIONS

✺

CHAPTER SEVEN

THE CRISIS IN RUSSIAN AGRICULTURE

The eve of the twentieth century found the Russian economy in a generally healthy state. Industrial expansion continued despite a recession that followed the initial period of rapid industrial growth. State revenues continued to rise. Development of the rail network pushed ahead, and construction of the Siberian railway moved forward at a remarkable pace. The agricultural picture was bleak, however, and eighty percent of Russia's population made a living in agriculture. Advanced ailments of various descriptions were gnawing away at the agricultural sector. Spokesmen everywhere were calling attention to the ominous conditions in Russia's villages.

Russia was regarded as the granary of Europe. Its vast chernozem (black earth) zone was noted for its amazing fertility. In the preceding decade Russia's economy overall had taken a major step forward. Nevertheless, in the central districts of Russia—at the very heart of the realm—every poor harvest threatened a famine and required government assistance. Western Europe had not experienced such conditions for decades. Russians took little comfort from the fact that conditions in India and China were far worse, for by every other standard Russia had risen above any classification as an "Asiatic" country. Foreigners were prone to ascribe the precarious state of agriculture to the Russian system of landholding. They obstinately clung to the myth that all land in Russia belonged to noble landlords who, they claimed, confiscated nearly all of the peasants' harvest! That picture in fact was perfectly inaccurate. Almost the complete opposite was true. In the fifty provinces of European Russia, which contained over three quarters of the empire's population, peasant landownership and land tenure predominated overwhelmingly. Statistically the peasants possessed about forty percent of the land, but actually their holdings were much greater. The discrepancy arose from the fact that state lands consisted primarily of forest and wasteland. If those lands were excluded from the total, then only about one million desiatins [2,660,000 acres] of arable land belonged to the state. Crown lands [*udelnye zemli*] were appreciable only in the single province of Simbirsk. More than half of all arable land had been transferred to the peasantry at the time of the abolition of serfdom, and for forty years the land had been passing steadily from the nobility to the peasants and other classes. By the beginning of the twentieth century peasants had possession of more than 160,000,000 desiatins [over 426,000,000 acres], or more than three-fourths of all arable land. The nobility owned 52,000,000 desiatins [over 138,000,000 acres], but roughly half of that was forest and wasteland. All other landowners combined (merchants, foreigners, municipalities, joint-stock companies, etc.) owned about 30,000,000 desiatins [about 80,000,000 acres], consisting mainly of land suitable for cultivation.

In twenty-two provinces located almost entirely in the black earth region more than half of the land belonged to peasants. In some localities peasants held eighty percent of the land. Moreover, arable land belonging to the state and the crown as well as a significant portion of privately owned land were leased to peasants. So great a preponderance of small-peasant farming over large-scale agriculture was not to be found either in England or Germany or even in post-revolutionary France. Russia was a land of small-peasant farming. Great estates were merely islands in a sea of peasants. Only in the Kingdom of Poland, the Baltic region, and the province of Minsk did the nobility own more land than the peasants.

A whole series of legislation protected peasant landownership. Once land came into the possession of peasant communities, it became their inalienable property. The peasant domain could only grow and actually did grow year by year. The government had created a special agency, the Peasant Land Bank, to provide privileged conditions under which peasants could purchase land from private landowners.[1]

Even so, peasants were the least productive landowners in Russia. The average yield on private estates was roughly one-third greater than the yield obtained by the peasantry. On

private estates that utilized advanced agricultural technology
the yield was substantially greater than that. During the dispute on the influence of harvests on grain prices, it was alleged that a vast majority of peasant holdings (91 percent was
given, but that was an exaggeration) did not produce grain
for the market. Therefore, in order to feed the cities, factories,
and even the peasantry of those provinces where grain production was inadequate, the state had to depend primarily on
privately owned lands. That land already produced the surpluses that were shipped abroad and formed the chief item
in the Russian balance of trade. It was that surplus that in
years of famine went to feed the peasantry victimized by
local crop failures.

The greatest suffering from poor harvests occurred in the
provinces with the greatest percentage of peasant holdings:
Kazan, Samara, Ufa, Voronezh, Penza, Tambov, Riazan, and
others. Those were all rich fertile lands, but nevertheless
everything clearly indicated that agriculture in that area was
going through a serious crisis. The peasants usually attributed
the crisis to a shortage of land or an excessive burden of taxes.
Both the salt tax and the poll tax had been repealed, however,
in the 1880s. Land taxes were insignificant and, strictly speaking, the only important direct tax borne by the peasants was
the redemption payment for land received with emancipation.[2]

THE ROOT OF THE PROBLEM

The basic cause of the agrarian crisis was the peasants' method
of farming and above all the system of land tenure. The great
majority of peasant lands belonged to the obshchina [land
commune] in which peasants owned land collectively and
not as individuals. The land was the property of the commune, which not only periodically reapportioned it among its
members but also laid down the rules and procedures for
working the land. The obshchina prevailed throughout all of
central, northern, eastern, and southern Russia as well as the
northern Caucasus. Peasants owned land privately as households only in the western territories, chiefly in the area that
had been under Polish rule until the late eighteenth century.
East of the Dnieper River property owned privately by households predominated only in the province of Poltava and in

Peasants Threshing Grain

parts of the provinces of Chernigov and Kursk. Significantly, not one of the western provinces, where ownership by households prevailed, experienced hunger as a result of crop failures that periodically wrought havoc in central and eastern Russia. This pattern existed even though peasant allotments were much smaller in the west. On the other hand, the percentage of peasant landowners was much lower than in other parts of Russia.

For the emancipated peasant in the obshchina the authority of the village assembly took the place of the authority of the former landlord. The obshchina had numerous partisans who advanced both economic and social arguments in its defense. They maintained that it offered a uniquely Russian solution to social questions. They argued that because of the obshchina the Russian villages contained scarcely any landless proletarians: migrants to the cities retained their ties with the obshchina, for even though the relationship was difficult to preserve, the desire to preserve it was very strong. Every peasant was a joint owner of the general allotment. When a family increased in size, it could count on an additional portion from the holdings of other less populous families. Peasants who had departed to work in factories could return to their homes and once again receive land to till. The obshchina offered an unquestionable advantage to the state in that its members were responsible collectively for the payment of taxes. Therefore, since every departure from the commune increased the tax burden of those who remained behind, the obshchina was reluctant to release its members "to freedom."

Worshippers of socialist economics long had regarded the obshchina as "their very own," for they considered it the most practicable manifestation of socialism in rural Russia. In truth they could not be bothered by the fact that that system led to individualism, and they dismissed cultivation by artels as an exception.[3] The populists—agrarian socialists—without exception, and with them the liberal intelligentsia, wholeheartedly endorsed the obshchina. So too did the Slavophiles and also, among the governing elite, those adherents of "demophilism" whose chief spokesman was Pobedonostsev. On the left the only opposition to the obshchina came from the Marxists, who believed that it impeded the development of capitalism, which to them was an essential precondition for socialism.

As time passed, however, the deficiencies of the obshchina became more obvious. By protecting the weak, it hindered the progress of the strong, confident peasantry. It promoted equality but stood in the way of any general improvement of rural conditions. Russia's population grew incomparably faster than the people's income from the land, and that was the single most important factor in the decline of economic productivity. The 1890s formed the critical period in that respect. Agriculture clearly lagged behind the general growth of the national economy, and gradually rural stagnation turned into depression. Even in the middle of the nineties there were many who disputed that. The populists still found it possible to claim that peasants, existing at the level of a natural economy, could save themselves from disaster in an agrarian crisis. That crisis—revealed chiefly in the collapse of grain prices—at first struck more severely at the private estates.

THE IMPOVERISHMENT OF THE LANDED GENTRY

The competition of overseas [North and South American] grain in European markets delivered a grave blow to Russian agriculture, and the loss of established markets staggered the landowning nobility. Only the wealthiest landowners were able to endure the new ordeal. The Nobles Bank absorbed debts of almost one billion rubles. Characteristic of the mood of depression that gripped the gentry during this period was a speech in 1896 by A.P. Strukov, marshal of the nobility of Ekaterinoslav province. Strukov called for a *temporary moratorium on the indebtedness of nobles' property*. Citing a decline of more than 50 percent in nobles' landholdings in Ekaterinoslav in thirty-five years, he explained that income from the land more often than not failed to cover interest payments. He suggested that the Nobles Bank take all the property under its own management but allow the owners to continue to reside on their estates and at the same time provide financial assistance for them to raise their children. Strukov's proposal was an expression of utter desperation. Nevertheless he raised a legitimate question as to the ability of the bureaucratic managers of the Nobles Bank to earn a greater profit from those estates than their traditional proprietors.

In the fall of 1897 the chairman of the Committee of Ministers, I.N. Durnovo, formed a special commission to look

into the needs of the landed gentry. The commission pondered the question for five years but produced little in the way
of realistic assistance to the nobility. One result of its efforts
was a law of temporary entailment, passed in 1899. That legislation gave the nobility the right to declare their estates indivisible and inalienable for two generations and to bequeath
the property to any of their sons. Another law passed in the
summer of 1901 provided favorable terms for private persons
to purchase (and the nobility to lease) state lands in Siberia.
Guided exclusively by its consideration for the common good,
the government found it impossible to provide the gentry with
substantial subsidies from general funds.

The intelligentsia did not conceal their malicious delight
at the distressed condition of the landowning nobility. Where
the interests of the peasantry and gentry were concerned, the
intelligentsia sincerely believed that the deteriorating position
of the gentry somehow would produce a corresponding improvement in the position of the peasantry. As the collapse
of grain prices painfully depressed Russian agriculture, many
persons facilely contented themselves with the notion that
only the big landowners and "kulaks" [rich peasants] suffered, while the peasant masses stood to profit from the low
level of prices! Meanwhile the decline of large estates was re-
ducing still further the general economic level of the villages.
The breakup of large estates deprived landlords of the opportunity to make efficient use of improved agricultural technology, and it deprived the peasantry of sources of supple-
mentary income. Moreover, the decline of large landowning
began to diminish those local "grain reservoirs" which sustained the peasants in lean years. The impoverishment of the
landed gentry together with communal landownership served
only to deepen the agricultural crisis in the villages.

GRADUAL ACKNOWLEDGMENT OF THE CRISIS

Following the sombre warning of 1891, poor harvests—with
all their fatal consequences—struck again in 1897 and 1898.
The same areas were affected, though not as seriously as in
1891. The voices of optimism grew silent and yielded gradually to the universal recognition that something was seriously
wrong with the entire agricultural sector in Russia.

Witte—the erstwhile minister of the entire national economy in the early years of the reign of Emperor Nicholas II—possessed a versatile mind, but he was only dimly aware of the needs of agriculture and he regarded the landed gentry with a certain disdain. He vigorously pursued the industrialization of Russia and his sympathies lay with the city and factory rather than the village. He once declared that it was his "deep conviction that no economic problem is more important in Russia, embracing as it does all sides of our economic life, than the fundamental improvement of the economic welfare of our rural population in the strict sense of the word."[4] That declaration was merely an adroit plea for protectionism as a spur to the industrial development that eventually would create a market for Russian agriculture. Writing in *Novoe vremia*, V.I. Gurko criticized Witte's policy of favoring industry over agriculture.[5] Gurko argued that everywhere else industry grew as a result of demand: "Are we really capable of reversing that order—first to create industry and only then to provide a market for its products by increasing the well-being of the masses?"

The emperor had a deep abiding interest in the welfare of the villages. He expressed his feelings at the time of his coronation when he addressed the delegations of gentry and peasants. Nevertheless, in the first years of his reign he did not concern himself with the complex and controversial problems of the economy.

The loudest protests against the deterioration of agriculture came from the ranks of the gentry who had witnessed the decline of the villages firsthand. Throughout the nineties, prominent Saratov landlords had decried the impoverishment of Russia's central provinces, the reduction of herds of cattle, and other signs of deterioration. "No!" protested Count A.A. Bobrinsky[6] in 1897, "we are *not* a particular group of landowners! We are representatives of agriculture throughout all of Russia. We represent the interests of ourselves, the peasants, and the entire country!" Even though the intelligentsia, steeped in "class" prejudice, refused to admit it, the landed gentry truly did speak less for their own special interests than for the general interests of rural Russia. Interestingly enough, the Marxists paid close attention to the agricultural crisis, though for quite different reasons. In their view the "proletarianization" of the peasantry was an essential prerequisite for the development of capitalism in Russia. The Marxist journal *Nachalo* observed in the spring of 1899 what was "at first glance a paradoxical development—that the peasants suffer most in those provinces where they possess the most (and also the best quality) land and where the obshchina predominates. . . ."

To acknowledge the existence of a serious crisis was one thing: to find a solution was another. The populist intelligentsia was inclined toward a program that would grant full political rights to the peasantry, spread education to the villages, and distribute among the peasants the land owned by the state, the monasteries,[7] and the nobility. Those measures, they maintained, would eliminate the crisis. Even liberal economists recognized that elimination of middle and large estates could prove disastrous, if only because the harvest of the larger estates was much greater than that of the peasant sector. The large estates consequently provided the surplus wheat that found its way abroad and became a major factor in Russian finances. Feodor I. Rodichev, a well-known zemstvo constitutionalist, had argued in the debate on the relation of harvests and grain prices that "the acquisition of more land by the peasants will not help. . . . All this talk about enlarging [peasant] strips is nothing but an abstract fantasy. . . . The problem is not land starvation. There is enough land but it is being cultivated inefficiently."

AN OFFICIAL INQUIRY

In the spring of 1899 the Assistant Minister of Finance, Vladimir I. Kovalevsky, formed a small commission of experienced men to investigate the depression in the central black soil region. That action made news, because it signaled the government's open admission of the problem. The populist press was willing to concede the impoverishment of the central areas but not only the central provinces: the entire country suffered because of the general political environment. Conservative critics maintained that the crisis resulted from profligate expenditures in the outlying regions which in turn placed an excessive tax burden on the Great Russian provinces. Almost alone among the critics it was the Marxists who put the finger on the obshchina: "It represents the mass ruination of the small independent peasant proprietor," wrote *Nachalo* in 1899. "In the first place, it is not simply a question of the central region, and in the second place, it is not a question of the impoverishment of the entire center but only of a certain sector of the economy . . . . Nevertheless, in the granary of Russia the grain producer himself has no grain. The root of the problem lies in that very obshchina over which we have pondered for so long, as a mother lingers over the cradle of her infant and ponders its future. At the moment scarcely anyone will admit that the contemporary commune is falling rapidly into ruin."

That was an isolated opinion at the time. During the reign of Alexander III, the government had taken decisive steps to bolster the obshchina. On 14 December 1893, in the very last year of his reign, the tsar had issued a series of reinforcing regulations. Hitherto peasants had been free to leave their communes after discharging their debts for the land. The new regulations required that two-thirds of the members of the commune had to consent to the departure of any peasant. The government looked upon the commune as part of the structure of the state and defended it on that basis. But most enemies of the regime also defended it. Thus the obshchina provided common ground on which antagonists stood together. Even Prince Meshchersky approached the question obliquely and implied that he merely was restating someone else's opinion when he cited the "naked and distinct" view that it would be desirable for Russia to divide the rural population into landowners and tenants "like the rest of the world." But, he continued, abolition of the commune was in itself inadequate. It was also necessary to repeal the laws that restricted the sale of peasant land only to other peasants and prohibited its sale to "outsiders."

Throughout 1899 and 1900, Kovalevsky's special commission compiled interesting material on conditions in the central provinces. The evidence confirmed the collapse of agriculture in that region. Even so, the commission failed to outline any way to escape the crisis. It recognized that one cause of the problem was the continuous repartition of communal lands, but it accepted that process as an unavoidable evil. The commission report fatalistically concluded that "the relative decrease of the amount of land possessed by peasants, as a natural consequence of population growth, requires no proof. It follows from the very nature of things."[8]

After two bountiful years, crop failures recurred in 1901. Once again they struck mainly in the central and eastern provinces. Overall, forty-two provinces experienced below average harvests. The disaster precipitated another round of controversy between the liberal and conservative press, for it offered the first test of a reorganized system of handling grain reserves. A law of 1900 had removed this responsibility from the zemstvos and placed it in the hands of the central administration. Government authorities, however, drew a different conclusion from the new catastrophe. They decided that urgent measures were needed to improve conditions in the countryside. In its New Year edition of 1902 *Novoe vremia* noted the widespread opinion that the crop failure of 1901 was "not simply an accident but the result of the state of agriculture which is unsatisfactory in every respect."

Educated society, which formed a somewhat organized element in national life, was incapable of helping the government, for society saw the agricultural crisis only as another manifestation of the general deficiency of autocratic government. The liberal and socialist press interpreted the agricultural crisis as one of the deterrents to industrial growth. The peasants, who were unable to see the entire national economy in perspective, either dreamed of acquiring more land or sought to escape by migrating; between 1894 and 1901 more than 1,200,000 peasants did migrate to Siberia. The government, however, was well aware of the limits of the land fund, and it recognized the importance of high yielding private landownership to the national economy. As for migration, the capacity of Siberia was much less than a glance at a map would indicate; the lands of Central Asia required extensive irrigation, and Manchuria had not yet been consolidated into the Russian Empire.

On 12 November 1901 the government announced the formation of a new, expanded commission "for a comprehensive analysis of the question of the economic decline of the center in comparison with economic conditions in other parts of the empire." The agenda of the commission included the investigation of the status of landownership and land use, the tax structure, seasonal occupations, the income of private and peasant households, and the like. Vladimir N. Ko-kovtsov,[9] assistant minister of finance, held the chairmanship of this commission. Invitations to participate in the commission were extended to representatives of various departments and to experts and landowning members of the zemstvos. Responsible for a comprehensive investigation of only one aspect of the agricultural problem, the commission nevertheless was unable to act with dispatch. It busied itself with assembling a mass of statistical data and only in October 1903, after two years, did it convene a plenary session to summarize the results of its labors.

THE EMPEROR "GOES TO THE PEOPLE"

In order to move the agrarian question off dead center, Nicholas II moved decisively in January 1902. On 23 January he formed the Special Commission on the Needs of Agricultural Industry and charged it to determine the requirements of agriculture and also to draft "measures for the benefit of this branch of the national economy." Finance minister Witte presided, even though he was always cool toward the needs of the countryside. Sipiagin and Ermolov were involved intimately in the work of the commission, which consisted of twenty of the highest officials. In addition, several members of the State Council and Prince Alexis G. Shcherbatov, chairman of the Moscow Agricultural Society, were drawn into the commission. The commission met on 2 February to determine its basic structure. Witte pointed out that the commission would have to deal with general matters whose solution would require the participation of the emperor. Sipiagin observed that "many problems basic to the agricultural industry could not be resolved exclusively from the standpoint of agriculture" but that other national interests also had to be considered.[10]

The commission next decided to turn directly to the most interested segments of the population and to inquire how they themselves perceived their needs. Such an inquiry was a bold step. A survey of the intelligentsia hardly could be expected to yield practical results. Their views were understood well enough, and their perspective always led to demands for a reform of the entire political system in the spirit of the most radical contemporary theory. In this case, however, the question was to be put not to urban but to rural Russia—to that segment of the population, gentry and peasants, in whose loyalty the emperor had the utmost confidence. Neither the traditional policy of his father—the policy of devising every conceivable protection for peasant agriculture and the commune—nor the theories prevalent in Russia's educated society offered any solution to the agrarian problem. Nicholas, therefore, turned to the land itself, to the men of experience, in order to learn what they thought about the most complex issue in Russian life.

The problem, then, was to determine who represented "the land." The zemstvo assemblies were comprised of elected representatives who were suspected, and frequently with good reason, of fundamental opposition to the regime. Relations between the government and the zemstvos were strained. Two years earlier Witte himself had argued that the zemstvos were incompatible with autocracy. Sipiagin, too, harbored no sympathy for elected institutions. A broad decentralized referendum provided the solution.

In all the provinces of European Russia the special commission created provincial committees to assess the needs of agriculture. Subsequently, similar committees were formed in the Caucasus and Siberia. The provincial governors-general served as chairmen. The committees [eighty-two in all] were comprised of representatives of the provincial gentry, based on their status, of representatives and officials of zemstvo boards, of several high ranking officials of the provincial administration, and of other persons whose participation the chairman deemed useful. Similar committees [a total of 536] functioned at the district level, where the district marshals of the nobility presided. In provinces without zemstvos the government organized committees of local landowners. Approximately six hundred committees operated throughout the whole of Russia.

The chairmen possessed broad authority, which they exercised without uniformity under varying circumstances. Generally the district committees were more independent and more "public" in character, while the provincial committees tended to be more formal and bureaucratic. In several instances the chairmen invited all members of the local zemstvos to serve on the committees. Some, therefore, were rather large and diverse in their composition. Their agendas included several practical questions on which the government sought advice. On the whole the members of the committees came from an environment relatively untouched by political propaganda, and rarely did they abuse their rights by advancing political demands. Sipiagin's recommendation concerning the composition of the committees proved fortunate, for they proved to be competent, business-like organizations.

THE MURDER OF SIPIAGIN

Sipiagin, however, did not live to see the special commission complete its work. On 2 April 1902, at the very height of the enterprise, he was struck down by the bullet of the Socialist Revolutionary Stefan V. Balmashov. Disguised in an adjutant's uniform, Balmashov came to the Mariinsky Palace where the State Council was in session. He gained entrance by declaring that he was delivering a package from Grand Duke Sergei Alexandrovich. He then mortally wounded the minister with one pistol shot. An hour later, Sipiagin died, fully conscious: "I have loyally and faithfully served His Majesty the Emperor and have wished evil upon no one," he said before he succumbed. And indeed in Sipiagin the emperor lost a dedicated and faithful associate and a man difficult to replace. Like Bogolepov before him, Sipiagin too perished because he represented a regime detested by the revolutionary movement. A gentle and deeply honest man, he could not have aroused personal hostility in anyone.

Sipiagin's assassination had a fateful effect on Russian life. The deed created an unbridgeable chasm between the emperor and oppositionist social elements. The murder left Nicholas deeply shaken and outraged. Within two days he appointed State Secretary for Finnish Affairs Viacheslav K. von Plehve[11] to succeed Sipiagin as minister of internal affairs. Plehve was known to favor harsh repressive measures. The decision was made to try the assassin, Balmashov, before a court-martial, that is, to impose the death penalty. Civil courts could not impose a death sentence. Thus Bogolepov's murderer had received a sentence of twenty years' hard labor (and soon escaped). Balmashov conducted himself courageously and correctly at his trial. To his sister he denied all the rumors that he had been tortured, and he told her that he had no cause to complain about his treatment by the authorities. When the death sentence was passed, he refused to apply for a pardon. His execution [by hanging] in May 1902 was the first political execution in the reign of Emperor Nicholas II. It widened the gap: the emperor saw Sipiagin as a martyr slain in the line of duty; to the intelligentsia Balmashov became a hero.

REBELLION IN THE CENTER

Peasant riots in Poltava and parts of Kharkov provinces erupted almost simultaneously with Sipiagin's assassination. In the middle of March 1902, peasants in the Poltava provincial districts of Poltava and Konstantinograd began to invade the estates of the gentry and demand free grain for themselves and fodder for their cattle. Raids in broad daylight grew more frequent. "What's the difference?" asked the plunderers. "It will soon be ours anyway." On 28 March a crowd of peasants appeared with carts at Karlovka, the estate of the Duke of Mecklenburg-Strelitsky, and seized all the potatoes in the storehouses. The scene was repeated for the next three days as mobs of peasants with three or four hundred carts made the rounds of the estates and carried off the produce. Members of the crowd were heard to shout: "Take it! You must do what it says in the books!" The governor of Poltava entered the troubled area with three battalions of infantry, and on 1 April he came upon a mob plundering a mill only ten miles from Poltava. At first the crowd, armed with stakes and pitchforks, tried to resist, but they dispersed after the first volley. Three peasants were killed, and four were wounded. In the more distant parts of the province the rioting continued for two more days.

In the province of Kharkov (in the Valkov and Bogodukhov districts) the riots were more violent. Not only did the peasants plunder granaries but they also carried away agricultural equipment, drove off cattle, and set fire to estates. During the looting of a hospital, they even pulled the mattresses out from under the patients. They literally took apart one manor house and carried off the lumber. In Kharkov, as in Poltava, the disorders continued for several days. All in all rioters plundered sixty-four estates in Poltava province and twenty-seven in Kharkov. In the villages the authorities discovered anti-government literature written in the Ukrainian language. It called on the peasants to rise up and seize the property of the landlords. The authorities arrested the leaders of the movement; the less important participants were flogged and released. To the victimized landlords the government awarded state funds, and it levied additional taxes on the villages that had participated in the rioting.

The cause of the disorders, which affected four districts populated by Little Russians [Ukrainians], was propaganda skilfully designed to take advantage of special local conditions. At the time of emancipation many of the peasants of this area had received "free" title to their lands. That is, in return for accepting smaller allotments they were not required to make redemption payments.[12] This produced a number of genuine dwarf farmsteads. Nevertheless, since these farms were owned by households [rather than communes], these peasants were more prosperous than those in central and eastern Russia. Animosity toward the landlords or "pans" probably was more pronounced, however, than in Great Russian areas.

During the emperor's visit to Kursk on 29 August 1902, he received peasant deputations from the neighboring provinces and told them: "This spring the peasants in some parts of Poltava and Kharkov provinces looted estates. The guilty will receive the punishment they deserve, and I know that the authorities will not permit such disorders in the future. . . . Remember, you do not get rich by stealing someone else's goods, but by honest labor, thrift, and by living according to God's commandments. I shall not cease to look after your real needs." Speaking to landlords at the Kursk railway station, Nicholas hinted at forthcoming reforms: "I know that rural life demands special attention. The landed gentry are going through a difficult period; there is also disorder among the peasants. On my orders the ministry of internal affairs is working out measures to deal with the latter. In due course we shall ask the provincial committees, assisted by the nobility and the zemstvos, to participate in this work. And as for the landed gentry—the bulwark of order and the moral vitality of Russia—it will be my constant concern to strengthen it."

RURAL RUSSIA SPEAKS

The local committees on the needs of agriculture began their work in the summer of 1902, first at the provincial and then the district level. The problem was stated in broad terms. The special commission distributed a list of questions to which it sought answers. In sending its inquiries to the district committees the commission explained that it "had no intention to restrict the opinions expressed by the local committees, since the general question concerning the needs of our agricultural industry allowed great latitude in the expression of opinion." The government dominated the proceedings in so far as it discarded the elective process in the selection of committees. Local chairman had the authority to invite every zemstvo assemblyman, but the zemstvos themselves were not permitted to elect representatives to the committees. The committees were formed in various ways. In Orel, for example, the provincial committee was created according to the general guidelines, but two brokers from the grain exchange were also invited to participate. The Lokhvitsk district committee (Poltava province), on the other hand, included every zemstvo member as well as more than sixty other "experienced persons." In Arzamas [Nizhni Novgorod province] twenty-five peasants from the local districts were invited to participate. In most cases the participants were vocal. The committees met in public, and closed-door sessions were rare. Discussion of the needs of Russian agriculture went on simultaneously in six hundred centers.

The committees considered a variety of subjects—public education, reorganization of the courts, "the small zemstvo unit" [an all-class zemstvo at the district level]—and in some committees (and rarely) discussion turned to the desirability of political reform and the establishment of some form of popular representation. Nicholas A. Khomiakov, the son of a well-known Slavophile and godson of Gogol, published a long article critical of the government's policy. He asserted that "the needs of Russian agriculture have been ignored completely." The government has legislated against agriculture, he wrote, with its railroad tariffs, state monopolies, and protective tariffs favoring industry. The district committees completed their work early in 1903, and the provincial committees

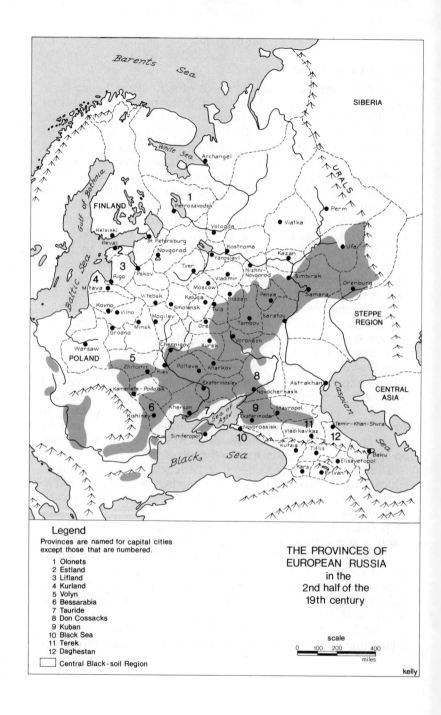

THE PROVINCES OF
EUROPEAN RUSSIA
in the
2nd half of the
19th century

Legend

Provinces are named for capital cities
except those that are numbered.

1 Olonets
2 Estland
3 Lifland
4 Kurland
5 Volyn
6 Bessarabia
7 Tauride
8 Don Cossacks
9 Kuban
10 Black Sea
11 Terek
12 Daghestan

Central Black-soil Region

scale

0   100   200   400
miles

kelly

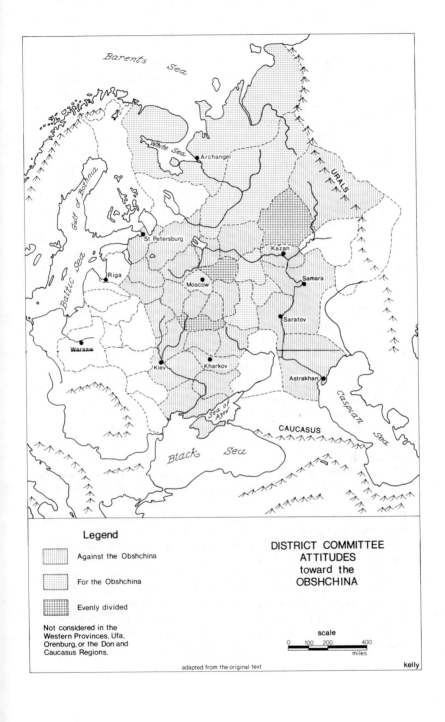

Legend

Against the Obshchina

For the Obshchina

Evenly divided

Not considered in the
Western Provinces, Ufa,
Orenburg, or the Don and
Caucasus Regions.

DISTRICT COMMITTEE
ATTITUDES
toward the
OBSHCHINA

scale

0   100   200   400
                     miles

adapted from the original text

kelly

then compiled the results. In some provincial committees the chairmen deleted from further discussion several matters forwarded from the districts. That was the case in Kharkov, Tver, and Tambov—provinces where liberalism seemed most prevalent. In other provinces, especially where zemstvos were lacking and there was no animosity between governors and elected organizations, the provincial committees even supplemented and extended the work of the district committees.

In general, however, the committees concluded their work in an atmosphere quite remote from conditions at the start. In a period of eight to ten months the differences between the government and society, including the more moderate circles, had grown sharper. The interior ministry applied repressive measures against individual committee members whom it accused of anti-government agitation. This policy inhibited the work of the provincial committees. Fearful of complications, some governors-general withheld permission to publish some reports. The governor of Kharkov, for example, suppressed Nicholas N. Kovalevsky's report, the tone of which can be judged from one of its concluding statements: "We cannot begin to battle the mosquitoes until we have dealt with the vampires. . . . The agricultural industry cannot be improved to any appreciable degree without first eliminating the main causes of the present condition of the villages. . . ." In Tula and Tambov a large number of members refused to participate further in the provincial committee as a protest against constraints imposed by the chairman (who was simply following the instructions of the minister of internal affairs). The Moscow provincial committee split when the majority rejected a proposal of a liberal minority, which then withdrew from the committee. Fortunately the essential work by district committees on the local level proceeded in a more harmonious atmosphere devoid of political wrangling and repression. Thus the task which the emperor had assigned to the special commission basically was achieved.

What were the results of so great an effort, this survey of rural Russia? The proceedings of the committees filled dozens of volumes.[13] They reflected every shade of opinion, and consequently the more agile and energetic intelligentsia hastened to extract what best suited their political aims. Even before the official publication of the committee reports, a group of

zemstvo liberals obtained manuscripts of materials prepared
by about a third of the committees and published their own
report titled *The Needs of the Villages*.[14] Paul N. Miliukov
provided an introduction. On questions such as the foundations of law and order, self-government, peasant rights, and
public education the authors used whatever supported their
opinions. They rejected or briefly noted as abnormal or exceptional everything that they found disagreeable. Therefore,
although only two or three dozen committees had touched
even remotely on political themes, *Needs of the Villages* conveyed the impression that rural Russia seethed with political
demands, adding "if not this, then nothing"—that is, unless
our demands are met, there is no salvation for agriculture.

The opinions of six hundred committees naturally provided
grist for almost any position. The committee reports contained some statements by zemstvo liberals recalling addresses
made by the emperor at the time of his accession. The reports
were almost unanimous in their support of the zemstvos,
and in non-zemstvo provinces many committees appealed for
their introduction. Society in general, but also members of
the government, favored legal equality for the peasants with
other classes, and they were nearly unanimously in favor of
the extension of public education. Work on the revision of
statutes affecting the peasantry was renewed on 15 January
1902, a week before the tsar established the Special Commission on the Needs of Agricultural Industry.

CONDEMNATION OF THE OBSHCHINA

But the committees reflected something else which the liberal
press and literary monthlies either ignored or mentioned only
casually. A great number of committees had touched upon
the very root of the agrarian problem—the question of the
obshchina. Even more remarkable, a considerable majority
of them took positions against the commune or at least went
on record as favoring the right of peasants to depart freely
from the communes. A report edited by Alexander F. Rittikh
indicated that 184 committees in forty-nine European provinces (excluding the Don region) had taken up the question
of the commune, and 125 opposed its retention. (Opinion
ranged from compulsory liquidation to easy withdrawal for

individual members.) Forty-two committees favored retention
of the commune with modifications, and seventeen came to
no conclusion, deciding either "to let nature take its course"
or deferring the question "for further investigation." Based
only on the district committee reports, opponents of the
commune had a substantial majority of 113 to 32. The provincial committees reflected the influence of the administration: 12 opposed the commune, 10 favored it, and 6 took no
position.

Those figures acquired even greater significance in that the
question was not raised at all in provinces where the obshchina
did not exist. No one anywhere suggested the introduction
of the obshchina as a cure for the ills of agriculture! In the
entire western region of Russia only the Uman district in the
province of Kiev raised the question of communal tenure and
that was to express the desire "to *eliminate* communal property that still existed in fifty-five villages of the district."
Furthermore, in ten provinces where the two types of peasant
tenure were intermingled [communal and private household],
every committee opposed the commune. In only two of those
provinces did a minority of committees (four out of eighteen)
favor it.

District committees expressed support for the obshchina
in only six provinces.[15] Unanimous support for the commune
appeared in the provinces of Moscow, Nizhni Novgorod, Tambov, and Vologda.[16] Majority support in favor of the commune emerged in the provinces of Vladimir, Viatka, and Tver.[17]
The influence of the liberal zemstvos, which endorsed communal tenure for social and political reasons, apparently was
quite effective. Only one committee, Arapulsk in the province
of Viatka, recommended that the obshchina be strengthened
and transformed into an agricultural artel for cultivation of
the land. Other defenders of the communal system suggested
various remedies to improve it: to make repartition[18] more
difficult, to leave the land in the hands of those who cultivated
it efficiently, to set limits on the size of allotments, and
other measures. However, all opponents of the commune did
not necessarily favor its liquidation. Only 52 of 125 committees proposed legislation to abolish the commune or to
place a total ban on repartition. The other 73 recommended
either an easy transition to household ownership without

compulsion or the right of peasants to leave the commune and convert their holdings into private property.

Recognition of private landownership by peasants raised another fundamental problem, namely the peasant's right to sell his land. Russian law held that peasant lands constituted "property in dead hands"—property that could not be sold. On the one hand this prevented the alienation of peasant lands, but on the other hand it deprived peasants of normal profits in real estate. Of the 83 committees that considered this problem only 7 went on record in favor of preserving the inalienability of peasant land; 27 recommended that peasants be given full title to their property, and 49 endorsed conversion to private property with some restrictions, usually the stipulation that the land could be sold only to other peasants. The Kiev district committee most ably expressed the argument for the right to dispose of land freely:

The Kiev district committee could not fail to take note of the frequently expressed fear that the peasants' freedom to alienate their property would enable wealthy persons to buy up the land and that this would lead to the creation of a landless proletariat. The district committee, however, does not share this concern for the following reasons:

First, the development of a landless class from the ranks of the peasantry appears in all events to be an inevitable fact of life, for the population grows while property has reached definite and relatively limited proportions.

Second, if the government should attempt to preserve the villages' right to communal possession, *a much greater danger* will appear—the danger that the mass of the population will be transformed into a land-starved proletariat through the division of the land into such small plots (the pulverization of the land) that it will become impossible to maintain a healthy agricultural economy.

The Kiev committee also warned that a prohibition against the sale of peasant land to members of other classes would work only to the benefit of kulaks and not to the sellers of the land. Most other committees, however, did not support the Kiev committee on that issue. However, in a book on the land question published in 1903, A. Voskrensky[19] forcefully expressed similar views on the consequences of retaining the obshchina: "As long as the peasants lack the good sense to end the repartition of the land, and as long as the government adheres to its policy of non-interference . . . communal tenure will wipe out all distinctions among the peasantry. Reapportionment will make them all equals. No one will have sufficient grain to carry him over to the next harvest. No one will be able to keep a horse or cow on the land allotted to him. Is it really necessary to bend every effort to maintain a system that reduces the peasantry to such straits? Can we afford any longer to respect the inviolability of such a system?"

WAS ANYBODY LISTENING?

Since the views of the various committees did not correspond to the social elite's pet theories on rural life, the Russian press by and large ignored the committees' reports. At the same time those reports were something of a surprise to the government. Nicholas A. Pavlov, an energetic member of the committees, wrote: "A special commission is formed at the initiative of the emperor . . . and close to six hundred committees discuss a single idea (while only eight committees babble about a constitution). The committees are conservative. They call for the abolition of the obshchina, for private ownership, for credits, for separation from the communes, for the right to migrate, and so forth. To the greatest act of the emperor—to his appeal to the people of the soil—rural Russia responds with one single, clear, and thoughtful answer. Regardless of whether the answer was persuasive, the fact that fifty thousand peasants and townsmen responded to the emperor demonstrates the wisdom and loyalty of the country." Nevertheless, Pavlov was forced to the bitter conclusion that "the emperor's historic and most significant effort was wrecked . . . . The commune stood at the brink, but once again the bureaucracy and society came to its rescue."

The aggravated political struggle forced the vital agrarian question into the background, and yet the work of the committees was not in vain. It bore fruit over the course of three or four years. The final report of the commission remained unfinished, but the efforts of the district committees were published in fifty-eight volumes within about a year. Wishing not to be delayed by the final report, Nicholas II relied partly on those preliminary reports and initiated the first step toward reform in his Manifesto of 26 February 1903: "To Our deep sorrow the discord, which has been spread partly by intentions hostile to governmental order and partly by enthusiasm for principles alien to Russian life, prevents Our general efforts to improve the well-being of the country." After this ominous introduction, however, the manifesto listed a series of projected reforms. The decree ordered the administration to adhere unremittingly to the *ordinances on toleration*. Even the opposition press remarked that this was the first time that word had appeared in an imperial manifesto. But religious toleration came naturally to the emperor and, however discreetly, he had expressed his will in this matter more than once. The tsar ordered that the reexamination of legislation on rural conditions be continued and "transferred to the localities for further discussion and coordination with local conditions by the provincial committees, which shall draw on the closest participation of distinguished public figures invested with public confidence. The committees shall base their deliberations on the inviolability of the commune. In addition, they shall investigate temporary means to facilitate the withdrawal of individual peasants from their communes. They shall seek urgent measures to abolish the system of joint responsibility which constrains the peasantry."

In addition to the other provisions of the manifesto was a critical directive to reform local government "in order to satisfy the diverse requirements of rural life through the efforts of local citizens guided by strong legitimate authority." This was identical to the administrative reform that Witte had cited as the expansion of local self-government in his memorandum on *Autocracy and Zemstvo*. In 1903 the government formed a commission under the chairmanship of the distinguished historian Sergei F. Platonov; it was called the "Commission on Decentralization," since its objective was to strengthen local government.

The manifesto's insistence on the inviolability of the commune may seem strange in view of the local committees' negative attitude toward that institution. The explanation was that the government could not embark easily on a new course when public opinion overwhelmingly favored the existing system. It was difficult to work against a patently necessary reform, but the government needed absolute assurance that it was essential. The committees' recommendations had not been summarized and, moreover, only a fraction of the committees had insisted on the need for immediate and decisive measures against the obshchina. The government, nevertheless, did take into account the condemnation of the obshchina when it agreed to make it easier for peasants to depart from them. The government's chief concession, however, was to sacrifice its own interests by agreeing to abolish the system of joint responsibility which held punctual peasant taxpayers responsible for the debts of their less reliable communal associates. A law disposing of joint responsibility followed two weeks after the Imperial Manifesto of 12 March [1903].

The emperor found it difficult to overcome the inertia of the state machinery. Nevertheless, the issue had been joined, and a revised attitude toward the obshchina began to take hold. Nicholas must have found hopelessly naive a letter that he received about this time (early 1902) from Count Leo Tolstoy. "With death not far away, I am writing to you as though from another world," he said. "Autocracy is an obsolete form of government . . . . A hundred million people will proclaim that they want free use of the land—that they want to see the abolition of the right to private landownership. I believe that its elimination would bring the Russian people a high degree of independence, prosperity, and contentment." But even as Count Tolstoy composed his letter, agriculture languished in stagnation and depression for the very reason that private property did not exist in the most fecund areas of Russia.

The last link of that great project undertaken by the Russian government in the first three years of the twentieth century as preparation for the solution of the agrarian question was the plenary session of the commission created in 1901 to investigate the decline of the central provinces. For two years the department of indirect taxation[20] had been assembling a mass of statistics on conditions in central Russia in comparison with other parts of the empire. The situation overall was even more critical than when the Special Commission on the Needs of Agricultural Industry completed its work. From 10 to 24 October 1903 the commission met under the chairmanship of Kokovtsov to summarize its findings. Fourteen representatives of various agencies (from the ministries of finance, agriculture, interior, and district boards) and eighteen zemstvo representatives comprised the commission. The very first issue was whether the question could be confined to the decline of the central region. The zemstvo members insisted that it was a problem affecting all Russia, but a majority finally resolved that "the depression was manifest more distinctly in the central provinces."

The aggravated conflict between society and government adversely affected the work of this commission. The zemstvo representatives reached a private agreement among themselves and submitted a memorandum declaring that strictly economic measures were pointless. They insisted that a solution required an overhaul of the legal and social relations in the villages. The first step, they maintained, was to revise the legal regime that governed the peasantry by limiting the authority of the superintendents of the peasantry[21] and by abolishing corporal punishment. The zemstvo representatives also stressed the desirability of extending public education, easing the restrictions on departure from the communes, and converting the land to household ownership. Finally, in what was at that time an unacceptable political demand, the zemstvo members insisted on permission to hold regional zemstvo congresses, and they called on the government to empower the zemstvo assemblies to legislate in matters that affected local economic life.

Kokovstov, the chairman of the commission, insisted that the conference limit its discussion to matters within its jurisdiction. He stressed that the commission was charged to investigate the economic impoverishment of central Russia and that it hardly would be "proper to attribute the depression of that area to universal causes . . . for to do so would deny the possibility of determining effective measures to satisfy local needs." After that, the commission adopted a few harmless platitudes—financial assistance for the zemstvos, the development of cottage industries, regulations on migration, and the reduction of redemption payments—and adjourned.

The memorandum of the zemstvo representatives prompted only restrained journalistic comment. The caution of the press reflected the rigorous censorship then in effect. The socialist journal, *Russkoe bogatstvo*, bitterly noted that "the fate of the zemstvo members is instructive. Hopefully that lesson will not be wasted on those to whom it is most applicable." On the right, *Moskovskie vedomosti* simply observed that the members of the zemstvos had offered the peasants "a book instead of bread."

CHAPTER EIGHT

THE REAL MASTER OF RUSSIA

In its New Year's edition of 1903 *Novoe vremia* declared that "the significance of what we now are experiencing can be described this way: We have reached a critical juncture, a turning point in favor of agriculture, the moment at which the wheel of our economic policy is turning toward the interests of the village." During the past year, the condition of the villages indeed had become the central concern of the government. For ten years every effort had been made to maintain the status quo in the villages while Witte satisfied the priorities of industry. In the end only the emperor himself could have brought about such a momentous reorientation of Russian economic policy.

In the ninth year of his reign the personality of Emperor Nicholas II remained practically as great a mystery to society and the people in general as it was at the time of his ascension to the throne. Or to put it more accurately, his true character remained shrouded in fabrications created in circles hostile to the regime. That distortion may have been a conscious maneuver or simply the result of misperception, like underestimating an opponent (for assuredly the emperor was the enemy of revolution!). Still, the attitude toward Nicholas II differed substantially from the hatred tempered by fear and involuntary respect that enemies of the Russian monarchy had displayed toward the tsar's autocratic predecessor.

A mien of gentleness and affability rarely marred by temper concealed the emperor's forceful will from all but his intimates. As a result the nation regarded him as a benevolent but weak ruler, easily swayed by all sorts of contradictory propositions and currents. The popular view also held that the emperor was readily susceptible to the claim that "this is the way it was done in the reign of the late tsar."[1] Moreover, whenever some new and unexpected decision was taken, a search began instantly to uncover "the influence behind the scenes."

That characterization of the emperor had little relation to the truth, for it confused appearance with reality. The truth was that Emperor Nicholas II, having listened to various opinions, ultimately relied on his own judgment and acted on the basis of conclusions framed in his own mind. Frequently his decisions ran directly counter to the advice he had received. At times he surprised his associates, because his reserve allowed no one to penetrate to the source of his decisions. But no one stood "behind the scenes"—except the emperor himself! In fact, during the first years of his reign, Nicholas gradually came to dominate his ministers even more than Alexander III who was, after all, only "his own foreign minister." Nicholas went beyond his father when he turned the wheel of economic policy in favor of the villages and thus extended his influence directly into the realm of national economic policy.

Nicholas himself established the basic objectives for both the foreign and domestic policies of Russia. In foreign affairs he embarked upon the "great Asian program" while simultaneously devoting every effort to maintain the peace of Europe. In domestic policy he corrected the imbalance created by rapid industrialization, a development that had left rural Russia trailing in the wake of the cities. In carrying out the reforms of his predecessors, he insisted on one indispensable condition—to preserve inviolate the autocratic power that guided the reforms. The emperor believed that the inviolability of autocracy was essential to Russia's might as a great power and to its domestic prosperity. In 1899 Nicholas rejected any further extension of local self-government, because he feared that the process would strengthen aspirations to limit the power of the tsar. Thereafter he seemed to adhere to a new guideline: to satisfy insofar as possible all demands for reform that were *non-political* in nature. The emigre journal *Osvobozhdenie* characterized that policy as an attempt "to bribe every influential segment of the population"—the merchantry, landed gentry, and workers. The list should have included the peasantry, for the improvement of their personal welfare acquired top priority in 1902. Inadvertently, however, this exile journal paid the government the highest compliment by recognizing how it endeavored to satisfy the needs of all sections of the population!

Emperor Nicholas II

ZUBATOV'S POLICE UNIONS

By the end of the nineteenth century industrial workers had become a special concern of the government. Their need for association, self-education, and the organized defense of their interests clashed with official fear of the emerging revolutionary movement and with the economic potentialities of a nation still in the early stages of industrial development. But then a clever and energetic representative of the administration conceived a bold plan to satisfy the workers' needs while simultaneously protecting the interests of the regime. The creator of this scheme was a former chief of the Moscow Okhrana [Secret Police], Sergei V. Zubatov.[2] Zubatov proceeded from the wholly accurate assumption that the government's interests were by no means identical to the narrowly defined interests of the factory owners. Therefore, he reasoned that workers could improve their lot without political action. Zubatov concluded that it was worth the risk to unionize those workers on whose "loyalty" he felt he could rely. Up to that point the government had suppressed all labor organizations. Only the socialists had attempted to organize the workers. But to the socialists the proletariat was only an instrument in the struggle against the existing order.

The ministry of internal affairs had no confidence in this venture, but Grand Duke Sergei Alexandrovich, the governor-general of Moscow, supported Zubatov. Thus the first experiment with a legal labor organization took place in Moscow. A mutual insurance system was established, and later the labor organizers assembled several Moscow University professors to lecture on and discuss a range of general educational topics. The basic objective of these lectures was to explain the status of the Russian working class and the methods used by workers in the West to improve their living conditions. Prominent scholars such as the historian Paul G. Vinogradov, professors Ivan K. Ozerov, Alexander A. Manuilov, A.E. Vorms and others generously contributed analyses of British trade unionism (a non-political movement at the time) and Bismarckian labor legislation to the Moscow program. The movement spread from Moscow into the western provinces where a Jewish Independent Labor Party had been formed as a counterweight to the socialist Jewish Bund.[3] The major figures in this organization were not "paid agents" but rather leaders who believed that workers had more to gain from cooperation with the system than from struggling to overthrow it. Most prominent among the leaders of this movement were Shaevich in Odessa and Mania Vilbushevich in Minsk.[4]

On 19 February 1902 the Moscow workers, led by the so-called Zubatov unions, staged an impressive demonstration in support of the monarchy. More than fifty thousand people singing "God Save the Tsar" gathered in the Kremlin at the monument to Alexander II to offer prayers on the anniversary of the Emancipation. At nearly the same time the new organization played an active role in strikes against several Moscow factories. Opposition to the "Zubatov Plan" came from two different quarters. Muscovite factory owners complained to Witte against the Moscow police for "encouraging strikes." Simultaneously the intelligentsia mounted a bitter campaign against those who took part in "police directed" worker organizations. They inspired rumors that the government bribed lecturers to speak at labor meetings and that the Zubatov organizations were traps for snaring "undesirable" elements in the labor movement.[5] Professor Ozerov was singled out for denunciation. He responded to those charges by asserting that "we [Russians] have no respect for opinions that differ from our own. Our answer to a different opinion is slander, filthy slander." Nevertheless the moral pressure of the opposition succeeded. Most of the lecturers hastily withdrew from further activity. Instead of Moscow University professors the labor groups had to be content with clergymen and a few nondescript lecturers like V.P. Nazarevsky, the chairman of the Moscow censorship committee.

With the death of Sipiagin and his replacement by Plehve in the spring of 1902, the official attitude changed somewhat. The new minister was opposed to "risky experiments." He preferred the older well-tested method of straightforward suppression. Nevertheless the Zubatov organizations survived. Although their influence diminished in Moscow, they successfully continued to combat the Bund in the western provinces, and a Zubatov-type Assembly of Factory Workers was established in Petersburg.

THE REFORMS OF 1903

In June 1903 the government introduced two new pieces of legislation for the protection of workers. The Law of 2 June made factory owners liable for industrial accidents, while the Law of 10 June created a system of factory elders and provided for elected representatives to communicate with employers and government authorities.[6] Before adoption of the Law of 2 June, owners were held accountable for workers' injuries only if their culpability could be established in a court of law. Under the new law employers were absolved from liability only if they could prove that the worker himself was at fault. Workers who were injured and unable to work were eligible for pensions amounting to two-thirds of their wages, and a sum equal to fifty percent of their earnings was allocated to medical treatment. The number of industrial workers (2,373,000 in 1900) exceeded two and a half million in 1903.

The government made an even greater effort to improve Russian education. General P.S. Vannovsky's appointment as minister of public education (in March 1901) led to the drafting of projects for a comprehensive educational reform at all levels. In the end, in truth, the emperor rejected a radical plan for "unified schools" (whose usefulness still is being debated in the West), and after a year General Vannovsky was dismissed and retired. His successor, Gregory E. Zenger [Sänger], was a classicist known especially for his translation of Pushkin into Latin. Although his appointment reduced the tempo of reform, significant changes nevertheless took place in education. The secondary schools broke with the tradition of Count D.A. Tolstoy and the system predicated on the study of classical languages. In the fall of 1901 the ministry abolished the compulsory study of Greek and considerably shortened the Latin course. (The ministry retained the old curriculum in only five secondary schools.) The authorities also took steps to eliminate the overly burdensome course load of the students. They allowed students to form scholarly and literary societies, and (during Zenger's tenure) created student government by permitting students to elect class elders, or leaders.[7] At the request of the government a commission of professors actively considered the need for further reforms, especially the desirability of dispensing with the educational inspectorate.[8]

The expenditure for public education increased steadily from year to year and more than doubled during the decade 1894-1904. The budget of the ministry of public education increased from 22,000,000 to 42,000,000 rubles; credits for church-operated parish schools grew from 3,500,000 to 13,000,000 rubles; and government appropriations for schools of commerce (which had not existed previously) reached 2-3,000,000 rubles a year. Zemstvo and municipal appropriations for education increased in about the same proportion during that decade. By 1904 the combined expenditure of all government agencies (the holy synod and the ministries of public education, finance, agriculture, war, navy, etc.) and local governments produced an annual educational outlay of more than 100,000,000 rubles.

Work on drafting new peasant legislation began in 1902, and in 1903 the government completed the compilation of a new criminal code. In the opinion of most the new code was far more liberal than the statutes then in force, but even though the new code was published, no date was set for it to take effect.

LITERARY FERMENT AND LIBERAL CENSORSHIP

The first years of the new century witnessed the revival of Russian literature. Chekov had turned to drama, and Gorky the writer was beginning to be overshadowed by Gorky the public figure. In their places as writers of prose fiction appeared Leonid Andreev, an unquestionably gifted writer with an inclination for morbid, torturous experiences, and then Ivan A. Bunin and Alexander I. Kuprin (whose novel *The Duel*, based on life in the officer corps, was an outstanding success). Besides the writers grouped around [Gorky's] Marxist publishing house *Znanie* [Knowledge], the schools of modernism and symbolism also grew and flourished. Their vehicles were the journals *Novyi put* [The New Way], after 1903, and *Vesy* [The Scales], after 1904, and the Scorpion publishing house, established somewhat earlier. Briussov, Hippius, Merezhkovsky, and Feodor Sologub published their best poetry during this period. These years also witnessed the publication of Andrei Bely's *First Symphony*[9] and Alexander A. Blok's poetic debut in *Novyi put*.

A new interest in religious questions—an unusual occupation for the Russian intelligentsia—developed during the winter of 1901-2. A conference in St. Petersburg on religion and philosophy brought together an extraordinary combination of ecclesiastics, religious authorities, divinity professors, the rearguard of Slavophilism (like General Kireev),[10] and writers and journalists associated with *Novyi put*. The conferees discussed aspects of Christian dogma, freedom of conscience, marriage, and Tolstoy's doctrines. For bravely acknowledging that the holy synod was right in excommunicating Count Tolstoy, Merezhkovsky came under bitter attack from intelligentsia circles. Their wrath led him to protest that "a second censorship more real and more cruel than the first has arisen in Russia—the censorship of 'public opinion.' " This "second censorship" even penetrated the field of literary criticism. "What am I to do?" asked Anton Krainy[11] in *Novyi put:* "In our country literature, journalism, and writers are sorted and bundled in two sacks. On one is written 'Conservatives,' and on the other 'Liberals.' Scarcely has a journalist opened his mouth before he finds himself dumped into one of these sacks. Certain burning issues and persons are excluded from discussion—one dares not express his thoughts on them, for no one will listen. They listen for only one thing: Do you approve or condemn? If you condemn, you go into one sack; if you approve—into the other. And just sit there, and don't complain about the unsuitable company, for you have brought it upon yourself. . . . Our literary bigotry—unseemly even in a cultural illiterate like our contemporary 'writer' [i.e., Gorky] —is a great misfortune!" Krainy's exegesis laid bare the essence of Maxim Gorky's writing: "It is still possible to live and breathe—a man is still a man. It takes a violent thrust to project someone into oxygen-free space and thus put an end to human suffering. That thrust—which brings man his final mortal liberation by drowning him in a sea of carbon dioxide— that is what Maxim Gorky and his disciples preach."

THE REVOLUTIONARY PARTIES

The objections of that minority, which stood apart from the struggle, clearly revealed Russia's tragic derailment from its

historic course. With minor exceptions Russia's entire educated elite became consumed by its acrimonious, implacable,
and blind opposition to the regime. It was precisely at that
moment that society took up the curt categorical battle cry,
"Down with Autocracy!" In legal publications that slogan became a cudgel for assaulting "the bureaucracy." Among the
organized forces of revolution two movements had emerged—the Populist-socialists who dreamed of a peasant insurrection (extending to the army which consisted mainly of
peasants) and who relied on terrorism, and the Marxian-so-
cialists who looked to the labor movement and who hoped
through propaganda and strikes to "agitate" the cities into a
more active response to their program.

The Battle Organization of the Socialist Revolutionary Party tried to terrorize the government by murdering its unpopular representatives. In this way the Battle Organization hoped
to ignite the spirit of revolution throughout society. It claimed as its first victims N.P. Bogolepov and D.S. Sipiagin.[12]
That same organization attempted to assassinate the governors
of Vilna and Kharkov, General Victor K. von Wahl and Prince
I.M. Obolensky, against whom it openly pronounced "death
sentences."[13] The revolutionary leaflet that condemned the
governor of Kharkov, declared: "The Battle Organization
is compelled to fulfill its civic duty and to remove Prince
Obolensky by the only means at its disposal—death." The
inscription on the pistol fired at Obolensky melodramatically
proclaimed "Death to the Tsarist Henchman, Enemy of the
People!"

The Social Democrats, as the Marxists were known after
1898, regularly published abroad a journal called *Iskra* (The
Spark). Their doctrine was more precise than that of the Populists, and in general their cadres were more numerous. They
held their second party congress in Brussels in the summer of
1903. The Russian delegation included representatives of
about twenty illegal local committees, and they were joined
by party leaders from the centers of emigration in Europe.
Members of the Jewish Bund took part in the congress but,
refusing to abandon their special "national" program, the
Jewish delegates eventually withdrew from the congress
(which subsequently moved from Belgium to London). It was
at this second congress that the Social Democrats split into

Bolsheviks and Mensheviks. After the withdrawal of the Bund, a group of extremists led by Lenin (Ulyanov) formed a majority. The "veteran" of the movement, George V. Plekhanov, a well-known emigre, supported Lenin at that point, but the other leaders—Martov (Tsederbaum), Paul B. Axelrod, Vera Zasulich, Leon Trotsky (Bronstein) (a newcomer at the time) —wound up in the minority.[14]

The basic difference between the factions was that Lenin wanted to transform the party into a strictly centralized organization obedient to the will of the center. That meant that the party would be less numerous, but for that reason also more tightly knit. The Mensheviks, following the example of West European socialists, sought to swell the ranks of the party from the broad working masses. They objected to an excessive concentration of power in the central committee. Within a brief time Lenin broke with Plekhanov, resigned from the editorial board of *Iskra*, and formed his own journal, *Vpered* [Forward].[15]

THE LIBERATION MOVEMENT

These organized revolutionary movements would have been powerless at the time if the social mentality of the Russian intelligentsia had not condoned revolution as a means of struggle. The illegal appearance in 1900 of Professor Boris N. Chicherin's *Russia on the Eve of the Twentieth Century* signaled that ominous development, for at one time the author had opposed any form of illegality. The non-socialist opposition took an even more decisive step in June [July] 1902, when the journal *Osvobozhdenie* [Liberation] made its first appearance in Stuttgart, Germany, under the editorship of Peter B. Struve.[16] The oppositionist elements that gathered around the new *Liberation* journal ranged from moderate socialists to legal zemstvo dissidents. Though its positive ideals were heterogeneous, the Liberation movement was united by a common hostility toward the government and toward "autocracy" and "bureaucracy."

Osvobozhdenie's basic demand was a constitution. Its first-edition editorial declared that it was "impossible to expect, and therefore incongruous to demand, that Mr. Witte institute the far-reaching financial and economic reforms that the country so desperately needs. Only well-organized popular representation can give these things to Russia." Those words sound almost ironical today when even the parliamentary democracies have to resort to emergency powers in order to carry out economic and financial reforms. In those days, however, the idea enjoyed substantial credence.

In contrast to the socialist press, which offered a collage of theoretical discussion and militant slogans, *Osvobozhdenie* was designed to shed light (from its point of view) on all aspects of Russian life. Its "strength" was its chronicle, which carried "correspondence from the localities." With contacts in various circles—not only the zemstvos but also the high reaches of the bureaucracy itself—the *Liberation* staff was able to publish a variety of secret memoranda, notes, reports, and circulars selected for the purpose of exposure. *Osvobozhdenie* reserved much space in its correspondence for political gossip. It was the first to publish Witte's memorandum *On Autocracy and Zemstvo* as well as material on student unrest. To a certain extent the editorial board tried to maintain a tone of relative moderation, and on occasion it even objected to the "drill-master tone" of the socialists. Numerous copies of each edition were printed and mailed to Russia in sealed envelopes that looked like private correspondence. The first issue of *Osvobozhdenie* appeared soon after the assassination of Sipiagin.

PLEHVE, AN UNINSPIRED BUREAUCRAT

V.K. Plehve, named by the emperor to head the ministry of interior after the murder of the former chief, was an intelligent and energetic man. But he apparently had little confidence in those principles which he was called on to defend. He express-ed his misgivings more than once in private conversations. Convinced that autocracy was outmoded and yet having ac-cepted the duty to preserve it, Plehve could conceive of noth-ing better than new forms of repression. Uninspired retrench-ment was the essence of his policy. Whether it was the Com-mission on the Needs of Agricultural Industry, Zubatov unions, zemstvos, or professorial university boards, Plehve perceived everything negatively. To him everything represented a threat. The tragedy for the crown was that Plehve frequently was

right. Every one of those organizations could have been sub-
verted by the government's enemies, and naturally they did
not miss a single opportunity to do so! Every effort, therefore, demanded an extra exertion, and yet the regime gained
only imaginary relief by not stirring at all. "The uninter-
rupted and ceaseless expansion of administrative and bureaucratic tutelage beyond all previous experience undermines
civic vigor," wrote Lev A. Tikhomirov in a contemporary
work on *Monarchical Statesmanship.* "A nation educated in
such a manner gradually must lose its political sensibility and
steadily degenerate into a 'mob.' And without fail the democratic principle of leadership will dominate the mob."

At the very beginning of Plehve's tenure, on 6 June 1902,
he issued an order to terminate statistical inquiries in progress
in the villages of twelve zemstvo provinces. His directive explained that the researchers were on the whole "unreliable"
persons. "Continuous contact with the peasantry affords a
wide field for anti-governmental propaganda, which is very
difficult to combat because of the weakness of police surveillance in the villages." Official sources provided the interesting
information that although twenty to twenty-five full-time
statisticians were assigned to each province, the "part-time
staffs" numbered anywhere from thirty to seventy persons.
In Poltava province, however, where peasant riots had taken
place recently, the number of "part-time" statisticians approached *six hundred! Osvobozhdenie* replied that "of course,
the political unreliability of zemstvo statisticians is an indisputable fact, and it would be a mean trick to deny or conceal
it . . . [but in fact] all of the idealistically motivated intelligentsia are unreliable."

That rather typical episode underlined the serious need for
repression. Still, Plehve's order had the effect of admitting
that there were practically no "reliable" people and that the
only alternative was to cease all efforts, even though the
activity was essential. The preparation of the reforms projected
by the emperor went forward, of course, but the new interior
minister exuded a spirit of defeatism. He seemed to concur
with the revolutionaries that the existing system could not
endure any meaningful reform. He tried to convince the emperor that growing disturbances throughout the land made it
necessary to postpone reform. Meanwhile the disturbances

grew more intense. Animosity toward official policy became all the more apparent. The educated society communicated through a prearranged code. At literary evenings or concerts the elite listened to poems about "night" and the "daybreak" that would follow. Or, they were treated to the image of a thunderstorm looming on the horizon. The lines, "They are cutting the forest!—the young, verdant forest," brought noisy applause, for the audience understood that the poet was referring to the [suppression of] student riots.

The work of the Special Commission on the Needs of Agricultural Industry came to a halt. N.A. Pavlov alleged that "Plehve requested permission to end the commission's activity, and he got it." That was not quite true inasmuch as work continued for another year on a series of problems. The most pressing questions, however, were removed from its agenda.

A serious labor disturbance erupted in Zlatoust [Ufa province] in early March 1903. It began because of dissatisfaction over new pay books, but it soon took a more ominous turn. The police were unable to control the throng of workers who besieged the offices and apartments of the factory managers. On the fourth day of the strike, 13 March, a detachment of troops moved into the factory. The appeals of the military authorities were ignored. The workers began to advance toward the soldiers. After three warnings, the troops fired at the mob. The workers threw themselves to the ground, then rose and moved forward again. Only after three volleys did they begin to disperse and run away, but forty-five workers were killed and eighty-three were wounded. Never in the entire reign of Nicholas II had there been such a bloody encounter. Even though the authorities had acted only out of dire necessity, the event prompted a vociferous public protest, and St. Petersburg University once again became the scene of an illegal assembly.

THE KISHINEV POGROM

An event early in 1903 in Kishinev [Bessarabia province]— the Kishinev pogrom—had rather serious consequences. Since many tales sprang up about it, a general reconstruction of the basic facts is in order. Kishinev was a city with a sizable Jewish minority. A diverse mixture of Moldavians, Russians,

Gypsies, and others made up the remainder of the population. The city was free from any noticeable revolutionary ferment. Like most southern Russian cities, there had been friction between the Jews and the other elements of the population, but no major explosion occurred until 1903. The city had an anti-Semitic newspaper, *Bessarabets* [The Bessarabian],[17] but it had no particular influence on the illiterate and predominantly non-Russian majority of residents. In March 1903 the paper reported a ritual murder in the nearby village of Dubosary, an allegation that local authorities refuted in a subsequent edition.

On 6 April 1903, the first day of Easter, an incident involving Jews and Christians took place in the city square. Testimony about the incident was inconclusive. However, within half an hour or so, rioting enveloped a large part of the city. Jewish shops and then Jewish houses were invaded and looted. The police, taken completely by surprise, were paralyzed. The governor, a complacent old man, a retired general named von Raaben, scurried around the governor's mansion calling police stations and army barracks. Unfortunately, most of the officers and a good part of the men were on Easter furloughs. Chaos reigned over the city for several hours. By evening the rioting had subsided, but the excitement had not. Intense passions and bitterness, whetted by all manner of tales about Jewish atrocities, had seized the plundering mob. The rioting resumed on the following morning. The Jews' feeble efforts at resistance only aggravated the viciousness of the attackers. Finally, a massacre of the Jews began. In some houses nearly everyone was murdered—the brutalized mob spared neither women nor children. By midday troops of the local garrison appeared and began to disperse the looters, who discarded their ill-gotten goods as they scattered.[18] By the time order finally was restored, forty-five Jews had been killed. Seventy-four were injured seriously, and about three hundred and fifty suffered lighter wounds or injuries. Seven hundred houses and six hundred shops were destroyed. Three or four dead "Christians" testified to the weakness of the Jewish resistance.

Russia had not witnessed a pogrom like that in more than twenty years. In Shpol (1897) and Nikolaev (1899) mobs had looted Jewish businesses, but no blood had been spilled. Their failure to master the situation until the second day, and then only with the aid of the army, made it abundantly clear that Kishinev's local authorities had displayed neither vigor nor dispatch. The interior minister's circular specifically cited their laxity. The government declared a state of reinforced security in Kishinev and arrested about two thousand people for participating in the pogrom. Governor Raaben was relieved of duty. The vice-governor and the chief of police were transferred to other cities. Plehve's circular of 24 April 1903 declared that "His Majesty the Emperor has been pleased to remind all provincial and municipal chiefs of the duty incumbent upon them, as a personal responsibility, to take all measures for the prevention of violence and the maintenance of tranquility among the populace in order to eliminate the sources of danger to the lives and property of any segment of the population." At first the government provided aid to the victims. Later there was a great flow of private contributions with considerable amounts coming from abroad.

COMPASSION, CONDEMNATION, AND SLANDER

The entire country was incensed, and conservative journals were as indignant and vocal as the liberal press. "Just as after a great battle, the human victims number in the hundreds," wrote *Kievlianin*, "and yet there was not even a struggle. Defenseless people, guilty of nothing, were battered as in mortal combat." *Novoe vremia* observed that "our recent history has been unblemished by a pogrom like that at Kishinev," and it prayed, "God grant that it will never happen again. Ignorance and savagery are always identical, and spite is always to be dreaded for it arouses the beast in man." *Russkii vestnik* also condemned the tragedy: "The infamous and shameful behavior of the participants is well-established, but so is the conduct of those responsible for preventing and then stopping the outrage at the outset."

Bishop Anthony Volynsky (Krapovitsky) delivered a telling sermon against the pogromists in the Zhitomir Cathedral on 20 April: "Under the pretense of spiritual wrath, they served the demon Greed. Like Judas, corrupted by the love of money so that he betrayed Christ with a kiss, so those wretches, hiding behind the name of Christ, slaughtered His kinsmen in order to steal their goods. . . . That is the behavior of savages, who are always prepared to murder simply to satiate their lust and enrich themselves."

Acknowledging that the compulsory concentration of Jews in the cities of the Pale aggravated anti-Semitism, an official ukaz, published on 22 May 1903, opened an additional one hundred and fifty cities and towns to Jewish settlement.

In a different social and political setting such a deplorable outburst of racial strife would have been recognized for what it was and unanimously condemned. The police, inexperienced in dealing with spontaneous demonstrations, would have pulled themselves together and come up with effective measures for quelling riots. The courts would have punished the guilty and compensated the victims as best they could, and this sad chapter would have been closed. But in the poisoned political atmosphere of 1903 the enemies of the government turned the Kishinev pogrom into a potent political weapon. They twisted the local authorities' inaction and confusion into complicity in the crime. Even worse, they charged that the authorities deliberately had permitted the pogrom to take place. Later, they even accused the interior minister of actually having organized the affair.

The foreign press came into possession of a letter, allegedly "intercepted," in which Plehve warned the governor of Bessarabia that a pogrom was imminent but advised that it would be undesirable for him to use weapons against the mob. The Russian government immediately published categorical proof that the letter was a forgery. Then it expelled Dudley D. Braham, the correspondent of *The Times*, who was responsible for broadcasting the lie. Nevertheless, the reputation of the Russian government was slandered irredeemably. Prince Sergei Urusov subsequently wrote in his memoir[19] that he found it necessary "to reject emphatically the accusation that Raaben deliberately approved the pogrom and to dismiss as a fabrication the letter allegedly written to Raaben on that account by the minister of interior." Prince Urusov also commented that Plehve was too intelligent to desire a pogrom, while Raaben was utterly unsuited by temperament to carry one out.

Nevertheless, the idea of official complicity gained credence and caused great harm to the interests of the Russian state.[20]

The ill-effects took various forms. The flow of funds into revolutionary coffers increased. The Bund, in particular, profited immensely under the pretense of organizing self-defense against further pogroms. The Kishinev affair did great damage to the Russian government's prestige abroad. L. Rataev, a prominent member of the secret police (the Third Section), maintained that it prompted the Jew, Evno Azef, who for twelve years had served faithfully as a government informer in the revolutionary movement, to assume that terrible dual role—*okhrannik* (agent of the tsarist secret police) and terrorist—with which his name is associated forever.[21]

Prince Urusov related the extent to which the pogrom led foreigners to false impressions of the Russian system. In the summer of 1903 an Englishman came to Kishinev to look into the pogrom. He was quite amazed to learn that the perpetrators were in jail awaiting trial and that a regular inquiry was underway. On the basis of consular reports which rejected the fantastic allegations, the British government made an official report on the situation in Kishinev to both houses of Parliament. Even so, in December 1903 there appeared in Kishinev an American correspondent who wanted to investigate "the Christmas pogrom."

During the summer of 1903 the government completed its investigation of the "lesser" cases (the looting) connected with the pogrom. Of the 566 persons brought to trial, 314 received prison sentences. In November the government began to process the 350 persons accused of robbery and murder. That inquiry took place behind closed doors in order to prevent specious and inevitably biased press reports from inflaming hot heads. Despite that precaution, reports of the proceedings reached Rumania on the same day and appeared immediately throughout the foreign press. Prince Urusov, who witnessed the trial, recorded two characteristics in the proceedings. First, he noted the tendency of radical lawyers— the representatives of "civic action"—to use the court to "expose" the government with no interest whatsoever in convicting the accused.[22] Second, Urusov remarked at the dubious credibility of the witnesses' testimony: "Witnesses who hid in their cellars through the pogrom testified, nevertheless, to what was going on two blocks away; witnesses to murders identified different persons among the accused." The trial lasted about a year and resulted in a series of convictions.[23]

CIVIL TURMOIL AND QUESTIONABLE POLICIES

On 6 May 1903 in the city park of Ufa terrorists assassinated the provincial governor, N.M. Bogdanovich, "who by his brave death has impressed his service upon the throne and fatherland," as the emperor wrote to his family. Although the murderer escaped this time, Azef's hand was evident. His notorious service in the Okhrana apparently gave wings to the rumor that the ministry of interior had ordered the killing. But the assassination of Bogdanovich was part of the systematic unfolding of the Socialist Revolutionary plan "to punish by death" all representatives of the regime who displayed energy in the struggle against disorder. They shot at Prince Obolensky for suppressing peasant rioters in the province of Kharkov; they murdered Bogdanovich for crushing the strike at Zlatoust. Yet the effort to terrorize official representatives failed, for scarcely a governor was to be found who could be diverted from executing his duties by the threat of assassination at the hands of the revolutionaries. The intelligentsia, however, were enamored of the idea of "revolutionary justice."[24] Society, faithful to its "Hottentot morality" all too evident during periods of sharp political strife, gave vent to its displeasure by justifying and even approving these criminal "executions." Indeed, when the government occasionally reacted to assassination by imposing the death penalty, the Russian educated public even became indignant.

A new wave of unrest erupted in July 1903 with the strike of streetcar workers and longshoremen in Odessa. Since the Independent Labor Party was prominent in the strike, the police considered it unnecessary to interfere. An immense demonstration took place on the 17th—"For a moment the entire city fell under the power of the working masses," according to *Osvobozhdenie.* Sympathy for the strikers spread. A general strike threatened. In some instances the strikers beat up other workers who refused to go along with them. General Kaulbars, commander of the military district, grew increasingly concerned, since the police already were powerless. He summoned troops from the nearby garrisons, and

toward evening they occupied the city. There were no incidents, and the demonstrations ceased the very next day. The
government, however, decided that it was playing with fire
to allow the Zubatov unions to participate in such movements.
Accordingly they exiled Shaevich, the Independent leader,
from Odessa, much to the satisfaction of the Social Democrats.

Demonstrations in Kiev on 21-25 July 1903 were resolved
less smoothly. During a strike at the railroad repair works,
the strikers stopped trains, bombarded police and soldiers
with stones, and smashed windows in parts of the city. Troops
reached the scene only on the third day of the strike, and
they were forced twice to fire on the workers. In the end
four people were killed and several dozens were wounded.
Disorders were controlled without loss of life in Elizavetgrad
(27-29 July) and in Nikolaev (in August).

Besides the workers' strikes, another major round of dis-
ruptions stemmed from the protests of the Armenians against
the transfer of property of the Armenian-Gregorian Church to
the custody of the state. Plehve advised this measure because
Armenian Church property, managed by officials of the Ech-
miadzin Monastery designated by the Armenian Patriarch
(Catholic), provided a substantial income which, according to
the reports of spies, went to support the Armenian national-
revolutionary movement in Russia and Turkey. To prevent
this, Plehve recommended to Nicholas that the property of
the church be brought under the management of the state
treasury. His plan was designed to ensure that all funds allocated for legitimate religious and cultural needs of the Armenian population would be satisfied as before, except under the
supervision of the imperial government. Accordingly, on 12
July 1903, the tsar issued an ukaz to that effect.

The Armenian people interpreted the decree as an attempt
to sequester the property of their church and an encroachment
upon its sacred rights. In every city with an Armenian population the scene was reminiscent of contemporary France
during the inventory of church and monastic property.[25]
Crowds surrounded the churches and refused to permit in-
ventories to be made. They stoned the government's officials,
and clashes, sometimes bloody, took place in Alexandropol,
Elizavetapol, Yerevan, Baku, Tiflis, Kars, and Shusha. (In

Elizavetapol there were seven deaths and twenty-seven people injured.) In the end this measure did scant harm to Armenian revolutionary organizations, but it did turn the loyal core of the Armenian population against the Russian government.

The city of Gomel experienced a unique chain of events between 29 August and 1 September 1903. The Jews, who formed a majority of the city's population, already had proven their ability to defend themselves. In April 1897 in response to rumors of an imminent pogrom the Jews took to the streets and eventually set upon a detachment of Russian troops. Although it was difficult to identify the guilty parties, a court subsequently found that there indeed had been violence, and it imprisoned five Jews for resisting a police patrol. In 1903 reports of the Kishinev pogrom, the spread of the revolutionary movement among the workers, and the influence of the Bund, which began to overcome that of the Independent Labor Party, all created a tense atmosphere in Gomel. Then on 29 August a dispute between Jewish and Russian workers erupted in violence. As *Osvobozhdenie* observed, "In this first skirmish the Jews gained the upper hand." However, seeking to "avenge their defeat," a mob of Russian workers invaded the Jewish quarter on the 31st and began to smash windows and loot homes. They sacked about 140 houses before the Jewish self-defense forces responded, but soon the Jews were fighting and returning shots in earnest.

Just at that moment troops returning from summer maneuvers entered the city. Inflamed by rumors that "the Jews were massacring Russians," the soldiers delivered their first assaults against the buildings from which the Jews were firing. This later inspired the accusation that the government had shown partiality. The Gomel riot, however, was suppressed with dispatch, and the number of victims was moderate: four Russians killed and five wounded, two Jews killed with nine wounded. In contrast to the Kishinev pogrom, the vandals in Gomel ran up against Jewish opposition. The subsequent trial reflected this resistance, for among the accused the number of Russians and Jews was approximately equal.

TSAR AND PEOPLE UNITED IN ST. SERAPHIM

On 17 July 1903—the very same day that the Social Democrats convened their second congress in Brussels and the same

Nicholas II Bearing the Relics of St. Seraphim

day that the mass labor demonstration startled the officials of Odessa—an entirely different spectacle was unfolding at the opposite end of Russia. On that day His Majesty the Emperor arrived at the Sarov Monastery to take part in the transfer of the relics of St. Seraphim of Sarov. Those events at Sarov marked a momentous occasion in the life of the emperor, for Nicholas had developed an intense interest in the life of St. Seraphim, an ascetic monk who had died in 1833.[26] As soon as the holy synod announced his canonization, Nicholas made a huge contribution to refurbish the monastery, construct a shrine for the saint's remains, and prepare for his reinterment. These preparations went on for half a year. The "legal" radical press expressed its opinion characteristically by saying nothing. Foreign emigre journals, including Osvobozhdenie, ridiculed the preparations and went so far as to assert that St. Seraphim's canonization was illegal since his corpse had not lain undecayed [for the required one hundred years].[27]

The Sarov hermitage, nestled on the wooded border of the provinces of Tambov and Nizhni Novgorod, was a hundred versts from the nearest railroad. Anticipating several thousand pilgrims, the government erected temporary barracks around the cloister to house them. Word of the ceremony spread all across Russia, and pilgrims and the ill in search of cures began to flock to Sarov from all parts of the country. Combined with the residents of the outlying districts, at least three hundred thousand faithful converged on the monastery to pray and to catch a glimpse of the tsar.

The emperor, both empresses, the grand dukes Sergei Alexandrovich, Nicholas Nikolaevich, and Peter Nikolaevich, other members of the imperial family, Metropolitan Anthony of St. Petersburg, and the bishops of Nizhni Novgorod, Kazan, and Tambov arrived in the village of Sarov toward evening on the 17th. The next morning Nicholas walked to the remote little cloister to which St. Seraphim often retired. Throngs of pilgrims, mostly peasants, lined the road and lustily cheered their tsar. Later, after a Mass in the Uspensky Cathedral, a procession wound its way into the Church of Zosimo-Savvatiev where St. Seraphim's coffin had been placed. The emperor, grand dukes, and bishops raised the coffin onto a litter and bore it into the cathedral. By then evening had fallen, and the faithful stood in rows holding lighted candles. One of the celebrants later wrote:

Leaving the church we truly found ourselves in another temple. People standing in reverent silence filled the grounds of the monastery; every hand held a candle. Many had faced the cathedral and knelt to pray. As we passed through the wall of the monastery, we came upon the same spectacle, but now even more majestic and awesome. Stretched before us was an enormous multitude. Everyone had a candle, and some even held several. So still was it that the flames did not even flicker. Here, literally, was a pilgrim's encampment—masses of people, carts, and carriages of every description with tethered horses. . . . Chanting voices arose from various places, but the singers could not be seen, and the voices seemed to come from heaven itself. . . . Though the night passed, the singing continued.[28]

Archbishop Dmitry of Kazan celebrated Mass on the third day. He observed that "this secluded cloister of ascetics had become a populous city. The forest of Sarov, perpetually empty and still, is filled at the moment with emotion and with voices, movement, and noise. But these are not the sounds of worldly bustle . . . rather they signal the mighty fervor, and they manifest with irresistible power the vibrant and flourishing spirit of that piety by which Orthodox Rus lives and breathes."

The emperor greeted the nobility of Nizhni Novgorod, led by their marshal, A.B. Neidhardt, and the gentry of Tambov and their marshal, Prince Cholokaev. The tsar shared a brotherly meal with the monks of the cloister. On the fourth day, as the time for departure approached, Bishop Innocent of Tambov celebrated the Mass in a chapel in one of the barracks erected for the pilgrims. He took the occasion to stress the importance of the close contact between the tsar and his people, so manifest during those few memorable days. And indeed, the ceremonies at Sarov did reinforce the emperor's faith in his people. He found himself intimately surrounded by untold multitudes who were overcome by emotions the same as his and who affectionately expressed their devotion to him. He met peasants, clergymen, and noblemen. Subconsciously it came to him that the sedition, which had plagued him for the past year and which posed such a threat to his ministers, was an alien, non-Russian, and distinctively urban phenomenon. In contrast, the heart of Russia was still healthy and it still beat in unison with the heart of the tsar.

This faith in the unity of tsar and people, which inspired Nicholas's every act, was founded partly on truth and partly on self-deception. Part of the populace absent from Sarov was plunging, at that very moment, deeper into its stubborn and twisted contempt for the regime. Yet those people formed a vital component in the structure of the country. Without them there was no intermediate link between the crown and the masses. Without them there were not enough people to execute the tsar's will conscientiously — "not from fear but from conscience."[29]

Efforts to create ideologically conservative organizations met with little success. The Russian Club was revived in St. Petersburg,[30] and unions of academicians opposed to the prevailing views of society enjoyed some support among students. Professors A.S. Biazingin in Kharkov and V.V. Nikolsky in Petersburg organized conservative circles and gave lectures. But the intelligentsia libeled and visited moral terror on isolated "dare-devils" like that. The average *intelligent* sincerely believed that anyone who did not share his opinion was either a traitor, a liar, or at best not quite normal.

THE EASTERN QUESTION IN 1903

No significant change in the international situation occurred during the first three years of the twentieth century. The left coalition government of Waldeck-Rousseau governed France (June 1899-June 1902), Bülow directed Germany, and the Conservatives continued in power in England. The Anglo-Boer War ended in (May) 1902, and no new war or revolution erupted to plague the great powers. However, on 29 May 1903 a coup d'etat in Serbia upset this placid state of affairs. The murder of King Alexander Obrenovich, his wife, and members of his retinue greatly shocked Europe.[31] Every capital considered severing relations with Serbia, but the new Karageorgevich dynasty managed to establish its authority and gain popular support. Of particular importance to Russia was the reorientation of Serbian policy away from Vienna and toward St. Petersburg. The Karageorgeviches had a long history of association with Russia. George and Alexander, the

the sons of Prince Peter, had been educated in Petersburg, George at the Alexander Corps and Alexander in the Corps of Pages of His Imperial Highness. Their mother was the sister of the Russian grand duchesses, Anastasia Nikolaevna and Militsa Nikolaevna.[32]

Russia and France maintained relations appropriate to allies despite their obvious lack of sympathy for each other's domestic regime. In September 1901 the tsar paid his second visit to France. He observed the French naval maneuvers at Dunkirk and the army maneuvers at Rheims, but much to the dismay of Parisians he did not visit the capital. The tone of Franco-Russian relations was changed somewhat under the new (radical) regime: Nicholas expressed no desire to visit Paris, and the French government did not press him. *Revue des deux Mondes* observed that "this second visit of the Russian tsarist couple admittedly did not inspire the same broad popular enthusiasm as the first." In the spring of 1902 (7-9 May) Emile Loubet, the President of France, paid a return visit to St. Petersburg. In speeches exchanged on the occasion the emperor and president mentioned nothing of substance but merely reaffirmed in general the immutability of the alliance.

At the same time Russo-German relations grew rather more complex. For almost three years, from 1898-1901, the British government had pursued a binding alliance with the Germans, which Berlin finally had rejected. Erroneously having concluded that British interests were absolutely incompatible with the interests of Russia and France, Germany then witnessed with some alarm the first steps toward the formation of an Anglo-French entente. The kaiser strived to stay in touch with Russia mainly through his personal correspondence with the tsar. Although during the first decade of his reign the tsar and his family had paid several visits to the empress's relatives in Germany, those holidays had no connection with politics. Beyond that, the two monarchs held only three serious "business" meetings between 1901 and 1903: at Danzig (September 1901), Reval (August 1902), and Wiesbaden (at the end of October 1903).

Prince Henry of Prussia, Emperor William II's brother, spent considerable time with the tsar and tsaritsa at Spala during the autumn of 1901. Henry took home from this extended association with Nicholas an impression of the Russian monarch that was quite different from the view prevalent in German ruling circles. "The tsar is benevolent and courteous but not as mild as frequently thought," he told the chancellor. "He knows what he wants, and he won't yield to anyone (*lässt sich nichts gefallen*). He has a humanitarian outlook, but he intends to preserve the autocratic principle. He is open-minded on religious questions but always avoids public controversy with the Orthodox Church. He is a good military man." Prince Henry also reported that Nicholas "has no love for parliaments." In speaking once of King Edward VII, the tsar remarked that even "in his own country he can do exactly nothing."

Relations with Austria continued within the framework of the 1897 agreement on the maintenance of the status quo in the Balkans. Austro-Russian relations were tested seriously in 1903 by a Macedonian revolt that led to brutal Turkish repression and Bulgarian intervention in behalf of the rebels. The situation deteriorated still further when two Russian consuls were murdered, G.S. Shcherbina in Mitrovits and A.A. Rostovsky in Bitol. In August [1903] Russia dispatched a fleet to Turkish waters, and this action forced the Turks to take speedy and energetic action against the assassins. Then in September 1903 Emperor Nicholas II and his foreign minister went to Vienna. During a hunting trip to the mountain resort of Mürzsteg, the two emperors and their foreign ministers discussed the Macedonian question.

On 19 September 1903 *Sankt-Petersburgskiia* [Peterburzhskie] *vedomosti* reported officially that "from the very beginning of the Macedonian revolt both of the neighboring and friendly empires, faithful to the agreement of 1897 which has served as the basis of their Balkan policies, never ceased to work actively in the interests of peace." In their effort to maintain the status quo, Russia and Austria also took steps against the Macedonian rebels, who were supported by Bulgaria. On 17 September the Russian government had declared that the Macedonian revolutionary committees, "motivated by narrow self-interest, intend to create a 'Bulgarian Macedonia' at the expense of the rights and interests of other Christian nationalities whose interests are equally dear to Orthodox Russia."

The Mürzsteg Program [19 September/2 October 1903] called for the following reforms in Macedonia: first, that Russian and Austro-Hungarian representatives be attached to the governors and participate in the administration of Macedonia; second, that foreign advisors be introduced into the gendarmery [which was to be commanded by a foreign general] ; and third, that the Macedonian courts be reorganized to include equal numbers of Christians and Muslims.[33] Turkey accepted this program, but its implementation left much to be desired.

THE INEVITABLE TEST OF ARMS IN ASIA

It is no exaggeration to record that during the first phase of the reign of Emperor Nicholas II the Far East and the "great Asian program" provided the key to Russia's foreign policy and to some extent its domestic policy. During their meeting at Reval [August 1902] the tsar told the kaiser that he had a special interest in Eastern Asia and considered it the mission of his administration to strengthen and expand Russian influence in that part of the world. At Reval as at Danzig [September 1901] Nicholas agreed in principle that a Russo-German quarrel would serve only the interests of revolution. The tsar, however, was much more interested in another question—the position that Germany would take with regard to the Far East—a matter on which William II evaded any definite commitment. "The Admiral of the Atlantic salutes the Admiral of the Pacific!" So signaled the German emperor in bidding farewell to the Russian tsar at Reval. Actually his greeting reflected more arrogance than flattery, for Russia was approaching superiority in the Pacific, whereas the German fleet of 1902 was not the equal of the British or even the French fleet.

The growth of Russian power alarmed all the other powers, Germany included. "If England and Japan would only act together," wrote the kaiser to Bülow on 5 March 1901, "they might be able to crush Russia. But they will have to hurry, or the Russians will become too strong." Bülow himself outlined the situation even more clearly in an interesting memorandum dated 12 February 1902: "Undoubtedly the gradual emergence of hostility toward Russia, even where least expected [France], is the most remarkable development of our time.... Events of the last quarter of the century adequately explain the growth of Russophobia, which is a confirmed fact." The German chancellor then referred to the rapid expansion of Russian power in Asia and the anticipated collapse of Turkey. Certainly, with a secure front in Asia, Russia could begin to speak with new authority in the Near East. St. Petersburg's curve was rising on the scale, and the other powers regarded Russia with fear and envy.

It was both remarkable and tragic that Russia's Asian policy, which foreign diplomats appraised so accurately, encountered a complete lack of understanding in Russian society. Russian critics babbled about a "Manchurian adventure," and they readily discovered the roots of Russia's Far Eastern policy in the greedy interests of some *aides-de-camp* of the tsar" in timber concessions on Korean territory. Even the Russian Marxists belatedly concluded that "no assessment of the question is more lacking in substance than the view of those bourgeois radicals who attributed the entire affair to the quest for concessions on the Yalu River . . . . The interpretation that relies on the adventurism of various court cliques is not only inadequate but without substance."[34]

Japan, of course, posed the basic obstacle to Russian supremacy in the Far East. Nicholas very early had foreseen a collision with Japan, although the hope always persisted that fear of Russian power might deter Tokyo from an attack. The emperor was aware that in a war Japan's proximity to the theater of operations and the poor communications between European Russia and the Far East would give Japan initial superiority. Therefore, while hoping to avoid war under any circumstances, he particularly wanted to avoid war as long as the Great Siberian Railway was still under construction. "I do not want to seize Korea," he told Prince Henry in October 1901, "but under no circumstances can I allow the Japanese to become firmly established there. That would be a *casus belli*. A conflict is inevitable, but I hope it will not take place in less than four years, for by then we will have achieved naval supremacy. That is our basic goal. In five or six years the Siberian railway will be completed."

Late in the fall of 1901 Japan's leading diplomat, Marquis Ito, came to Russia with the hope of concluding an agreement on a delimitation of spheres of influence. The essence of his proposal was that Russia would retain Manchuria while Japan still was trying to acquire a foothold on the Asian mainland. Thus, the Japanese proposal offered Russia nothing.[35] A.N. Kuropatkin, the war minister, observed that "the complete abandonment of Korea is too high a price to pay for an agreement with Japan." On the report summarizing the negotiation with Ito the tsar wrote that "in no way can Russia abandon its previously acquired right to maintain as many troops in Korea as the Japanese." Once having established themselves in Korea, the Japanese obviously would have come up with fresh demands. Moreover, Russia's prestige in Asia would have suffered a heavy blow if St. Petersburg had forsaken the Koreans, who depended on Russia for protection against the Japanese.

The next move in the game of Far Eastern diplomacy was the conclusion of the Anglo-Japanese Alliance on 17/30 January 1903.[36] England and Japan mutually promised benevolent neutrality if either of them should become involved in war, and they pledged military assistance if either partner were engaged by two opponents. Russia responded immediately to this alliance by pressuring France and Germany to adopt some counter-measure. Berlin, however, refused to take part in any combination, despite the urging of its ambassador to St. Petersburg, Count Alvensleben. The German ambassador stressed the great significance that the tsar placed on such an agreement, and he cautioned that a rejection would cause great harm to Russian-German relations. France, on the other hand, dutifully responded to its obligations as an ally. On 3/15 March 1903 Petersburg and Paris circulated a joint declaration which addressed itself rather vaguely to the Anglo-Japanese Alliance. In the event of "agressive action by third powers" or as a result of "disorders in China," it declared, Russia and France reserved the right "to take appropriate measures."

Korea meanwhile retained its formal independence. During the early years of Russian-Korean friendship, the Korean government had granted a group of Russian officers a lumbering concession in territory situated mainly along the Yalu River, which formed the border between Korea and Manchuria.[37] As conflict with Japan loomed larger on the horizon, this concession afforded an opportunity not only to survey the terrain but also to prepare a kind of forward defensive perimeter—a "screen" in front of the Manchurian frontier.[38] Obviously, a strategic matter of this nature could not be discussed openly. But, as a result, the Russian public gained the wrong impression of the whole affair. Public opinion regarded the concession as a lucrative prize which a "greedy court clique" absolutely refused to surrender to Japan, even though Tokyo threatened Russia with war.

In 1902 Witte toured the Far East and returned full of pessimism. His journey convinced him that Russia's cause there was lost. He was prepared, therefore, to recommend extensive concessions. The emperor, however, sent his own "intelligence officers." One of them, State Secretary Alexander M. Bezobrazov, acquired great notoriety. But having determined already that Russia's Far Eastern policy formed "the basic task of his administration," the emperor could not countenance Witte's negative conclusions. If preparations were incomplete, then efforts had to be redoubled. If the present distribution of forces was unfavorable, then one had to maneuver. Under no circumstances, however, would Russia forsake its historic mission. Admiral Eugene I. Alekseev, commander of Russian armed forces in the Liaotung Peninsula, also warned of the dangerous situation, but he did not advise "retrenchment." Instead he urged immediate measures to bolster Russian defenses in the Far East.[39]

Japan, meanwhile, was preparing strenuously for war. Tokyo was constructing a sizable fleet in England and also negotiating for the purchase of some vessels in South America. The outlook grew ever more menacing. The Siberian railroad opened to through traffic in August 1903, even though the route was unfinished—track had not been laid around Lake Baikal, and trains had to be ferried across the lake on steamships. Therefore, a bottleneck existed at the very center of the route. Of a new class of battleships only one, the *Tsesarevich*, was operational. Nicholas believed that by 1905 or 1906 Russia would be strong enough in the Pacific to have no more fear of Japan. But this was 1903, and the next eighteen months loomed as the period of greatest risk. Although the possibility of war had become quite real, it was impossible of course to predict what might touch it off.

On 25 January 1903 a special conference on Far Eastern affairs reappraised the situation. Baron Roman R. Rosen, Russia's ambassador to Tokyo [1897-99 and 1902-4], warned

of the impending conflict and declared that Japan was preparing for the conquest of Korea—what other purpose could
Japanese armaments have? The ambassador to Peking, Paul
M. Lessar, reported on the Chinese government's new policy
to promote the colonization of Manchuria. War Minister
Kuropatkin declared that any uncontrolled Chinese colonization of Manchuria had to be opposed by "prompt decisive
measures, or the entire area as far as the Amur River will be
populated in no time, and then it will be difficult to stem the
flow of the yellow race into [Russia's] Amur region." Witte
defended the policy of non-resistance. He argued that the
threat of war was exaggerated and that a reasonable agreement
with Japan was possible. Later, on 25 March, at a special
meeting of the defense council Witte again insisted that as-
sumptions presented by General Constantine I. Vogak,[40] military attache in the Far East, "could never take place"—the
general situation was "not as threatening as all that!"

Whether for tactical reasons—to avoid decisive opposition
to the emperor's plans—or because of a genuine misinterpre-
tation of Far Eastern events, Witte's basic position was unique.
Maintaining that in the future Manchuria should either join
Russia or become completely independent, he urged appeasement and opposed a military solution. He argued that the
"completion of this process should be left to historical forces,
without hastening or forcing the natural flow of events."[41]

In the meantime, however, this "natural process"—if Russia
retreated on the Pacific—would have led directly to the consolidation of Japan's position on the mainland in Korea and
to the rapid Chinese colonization of Manchuria. The passive
program that Witte propounded would have caused Russia to
be ejected from the Far East. Even persons as remote from the
government as contributors to *Osvobozhdenie* understood
that. Prince G.M. Volkonsky,[42] responding to another author
in *Osvobozhdenie* (Number 49), wrote: "I could have agreed
with Mr. Martynov if he had convinced me that our economic
and political inactivity in Manchuria would not induce Japan
to occupy successively Korea, Port Arthur, Manchuria, the
Maritime Provinces, and the Amur region." Volkonsky concluded that even if it failed, resistance offered less risk than
passivity.

Witte's stance on the most crucial issue of the day would
have produced his immediate resignation if the Russian cabinet

had been united. For almost a year, however, discord prevailed
and even though it was only moderate, the emperor's influence
could not overcome it. One must conclude that Witte's un-
willingness to accept the need for an active Far Eastern policy
had some effect on Russia's inadequate preparedness for war.
Witte's opposition by no means reduced the *chances of war*:
it only reduced the *chances of a Russian victory*.

THE EMPEROR TAKES CHARGE

Returning from Sarov with renewed confidence in the strength
of the Russian people, the tsar took two steps to consolidate
Russia's position in the Far East and thus to surmount the
government's hesitation. On 30 July 1903 Nicholas created
the Far Eastern Viceroyalty,[43] and on 16 August 1903 he
relieved Witte of his duties as finance minister. To the position
of viceroy the emperor appointed Admiral Alekseev, who for
several years had commanded the Kwantung district. The
viceroyalty was created to unify all organs of Russian authority in the Far East in order to counter the anticipated Japanese
attack. The viceroy exercised authority over all military and
naval forces and the civil administration, including the officers
and territory of the Chinese Eastern Railway.

Witte's dismissal apparently surprised him, although seen in
perspective it is difficult to understand why he was not removed sooner. The form of his removal was quite honorable,
for the tsar appointed him chairman of the committee of
ministers to succeed I.N. Durnovo, who died at the beginning
of the summer. Witte nevertheless took it as a personal insult.
From that moment on, it is fair to state, Witte became a
personal enemy of the emperor, although under the circumstances he invariably tried to conceal his bitterness. The dismissal of Witte perplexed the Russian press. Remote from and
uncomprehending of the nature of Far Eastern problems, the
newspapers focused on the defects of Witte's economic program. But the press was uncertain, and even *Osvobozhdenie*
was unable to decide immediately whether Witte had been
disgraced or promoted. *Grazhdanin* attributed Witte's fall to
the fact that as industry expanded, "the decline of agriculture
became more evident, and the full burden fell most heavily
on two classes—the gentry and the peasantry." *Novoe vremia*
carefully blended editorial praise with criticism.

Meanwhile the internal struggle followed its inexorable course, a route marked clearly by repressive measures against the Tver provincial zemstvo assembly on the eve of the year 1904.[44] In December 1903 that provincial assembly, always one of the most liberal zemstvos, became embroiled with the Tver district zemstvo over the latter's recommendation to transfer the zemstvo schools to the administration of the holy synod. The provincial zemstvo resolved to sever relations with the district organization and, as far as possible, deprive it of funds. At that point Boris V. Stürmer, director of the department of general affairs[45] of the ministry of interior, arrived from St. Petersburg to investigate matters in Tver. On the basis of Stürmer's report, Plehve asked the emperor for formal authorization to institute exceptional measures against the Tver zemstvo. On 17 January 1904 the newspapers carried the announcement that the elected board of the Tver provincial zemstvo (and also the Novyi Torzhok district board) had been dismissed, that the convocation of the provincial assembly had been cancelled, that the government would appoint a new board, and that the minister of interior had been granted authority "to remove from the province those persons whose influence was detrimental to the operations of the zemstvo board."

Those extraordinary measures, which were not part of the general zemstvo legislation, represented the government's response to the revolutionary tendencies that had spread among the zemstvo's employees, particularly in the public schools of the Novyi Torzhok district. Documentary evidence disclosed that the schools were used to propagate anti-religious literature and such "distorted views" as, for example, the sympathetic protrayal of the Pugachev rebellion, and so on. As in the earlier case against the zemstvo statisticians, the substance of the government's charges was well-founded. Socialists claimed a relatively large number of adherents among public school teachers, especially in areas where there were liberal zemstvos. Even at the risk of dismissal, those socialists accepted the duty to spread their doctrines.

The result was a vicious circle: non-intervention gave free rein to propaganda, while repression inflamed opinion, even moderate opinion, against the government.[46] The government could dispense, perhaps, with zemstvo statisticians, but how was it to handle the schools? It could close them, but then what—what would replace them? As on every other question, the government came face to face with the same tragic fact—that it lacked loyal supporters among the literate and semi-literate elements of society. What was true of zemstvo statisticians was equally true among the labor organizations.

THE ROAD TO WAR

At a meeting in Wiesbaden in late October 1903 Nicholas confided to the kaiser his displeasure with the French domestic situation. French irreligiosity absolutely repulsed him, and he attributed the problem to the Freemasons who were influential even in Italy. Nevertheless, he declared, he had to maintain his ties with the French to ensure that they did not defect to the British camp. Bülow recorded the tsar's desire to avoid war with Japan, unless the Japanese themselves attacked Vladivostok or Port Arthur. Nicholas, in other words, did not want war, but he was prepared for it.

By then the real source of the conflict was becoming more apparent. The problem was not Korea, as many had long imagined, but Manchuria itself. After the Boxer Rebellion, Russia had helped China out of its difficulties with no great loss. In return Russia sought through an agreement with China to obtain special advantages in Manchuria. The opposition of all the other powers at the beginning of 1901 forced Russia to remove this question from the agenda. Russia, however, continued to occupy Manchuria although an agreement of 1902 promised that the territory gradually would be restored to China (except for the corridor of the Chinese Eastern Railway). Actually the great powers were reconciled to Russian preponderance in Manchuria. Germany openly declared its disinterest in the question; France was Russia's ally; Japan, through Marquis Ito's diplomacy, attempted to obtain "compensation" in Korea; England and the United States were interested mainly in the policy of the Open Door (equal commercial status) in Manchuria. But as the "critical moment" approached, Japan began to pose as the defender of China's rights and to insist that Russia fulfill the Russo-Chinese agreement of 1902 and evacuate Manchuria by the end of 1903 as specified. St. Petersburg countered by pointing out that China itself had not met the conditions for Russia's withdrawal. At the same time Tokyo protested Russia's enterprise in Korea.

Negotiations continued through almost all of 1903. Russia was prepared to make far-reaching concessions, but St. Petersburg refused to grant Japan the right to become the arbiter of Russo-Chinese relations. Tokyo meanwhile simply awaited the opportune moment to avenge itself, and Japan's timing was most fortuitous. Anglo-Saxon opinion supported Tokyo's demand that Russia get out of Manchuria, although the prospect of a Japanese seizure of Korea was an entirely different matter.

The specific twists and turns of the negotiation are of no particular consequence. Japan made demands; Russia, in general, could not make concessions. The timing of the end of the negotiation depended on Japan, since Russia had no desire to go to war and had no intention to launch an attack. Russia had only one alternative, to prepare energetically to repel an attack. At the end of 1903 the government dispatched the newly completed battleship *Tsesarevich* and the armored cruiser *Bayan* to the Far East. They were followed soon afterward by the battleship *Osliabia* and several cruisers and destroyers. The prospect of an unavoidable conflict became increasingly apparent to the West European governments. Count Johann H. von Bernstorff, the German charge d'affaires in London reported that Japan would have to act promptly, because the British attitude toward the Anglo-Japanese Alliance was cooling and Russia's Far Eastern forces were growing daily. The French government found it necessary to declare that the Franco-Russian Alliance pertained only to European affairs. Germany assured both Russia and Japan of its benevolent neutrality.

In January 1904, without awaiting Russia's reply to its latest note, Japan severed diplomatic relations with the Russian Empire. In response a Russian circular of 24 January/6 February 1904 declared: "The ambassador of Japan has presented a note to announce his government's decision to end any further negotiation and to recall its ambassador. By its action, taken without even waiting to receive the note sent to it by the Imperial Government, the Tokyo government places upon Japan the entire responsibility for the consequences."

Nevertheless, on 26 January/8 February Count Alexander K. Benckendorff, the Russian ambassador to London, approached the British foreign minister, Lord Lansdowne, with a request to mediate in order to avert a conflict. The French ambassador [Paul Cambon], greatly agitated, called on Lansdowne for the same purpose. The English minister refused to do anything, however. It was too late, he said, and besides, "Japan does not wish the mediation of anyone."

Japan had decided long since to break off relations, but it determined the actual date with great precision. The armored cruisers *Nisshin* and *Kasuga*, recently purchased from Italy (or rather repurchased from Argentina), had just passed Singapore and could not be intercepted. Meanwhile the latest Russian reinforcements (*Osliabia* and a contingent of cruisers and destroyers) were still in the Red Sea.

On the night of 26 January/8 February 1904, without an official declaration of war, Japan attacked Port Arthur.

THE SIGNIFICANCE OF THE RUSSO-JAPANESE WAR

Never, since Peter the Great carved out Russia's "window to Europe," was there a struggle more portentous for the future of the empire than the Russo-Japanese War. At stake was Russia's access to warm water, its dominion over the scantly populated expanses of Manchuria, and its predominance over a vast area of the globe. Russia could not avoid this struggle without forsaking every claim to a future in Asia. Sydney Tyler, an American annalist of the Russo-Japanese War, wrote of "two irreconcilable destinies." "Unless all the labor and sacrifices of years are to be in vain, and the great Siberian Empire is to remain a mere gigantic *cul-de-sac*, Russia must establish herself permanently in the Gulf of Pechili, and find in its ice-free ports that natural outlet for her trans-continental railway . . . ."[2] Similarly, D.I. Mendeleyev wrote that "only those who reason without wisdom ask, why this [trans-Siberian] railroad? But every thinking man realizes that it is a great and uniquely Russian undertaking . . . a route to the ocean— to the Great Pacific, a centripetal counterbalance to our centrifugal forces, a route to history yet to be written, to a future to be carved inevitably upon the shores and in the waters of the Great Ocean."

Emperor Nicholas II was fully aware of the historic importance of the "great Asian program." He was convinced of Russia's future in Asia, and he worked, gradually but incessantly, paving the way for the Russian Empire to acquire a "window" on the Pacific. On the threshhold of the twentieth century, having surmounted the resistance in his immediate environs and in the complex precincts of international affairs, Nicholas II was the main bearer of that concept of Russia's imperial greatness. He did not relish war. He was willing to surrender a great deal if the sacrifice would achieve "universal peace." At the same time he realized that capitulation or "passivity" offered little hope of preventing war.

Since 1895, if not earlier, the emperor had foreseen the possibility of a conflict with Japan for supremacy in the Far East. He had prepared for that struggle on both the diplomatic and the military fronts, and his accomplishments were manifold. An agreement with Austria and the restoration of neighborly relations with Germany had secured Russia's western borders. Construction of the Siberian railway and reinforcement of the fleet had given Russia the means to conduct the struggle. But even though the surveyor accurately staked out the dimensions of Russian policy, work on the foundation remained somewhat incomplete. In particular, not enough had been done to strengthen Russia's position in the Far East. Construction of the fortress at Port Arthur, hampered by meager appropriations, proceeded very slowly. Meanwhile the government spent twenty million rubles on port facilities at Dalny, which also was situated on the Liaotung Peninsula. This discrepancy did not stem from deliberate maliciousness. Rather, it reflected Witte's characteristic mode of operation. The finance minister always found a budgetary "surplus" to fund enterprises under his personal jurisdiction, but he routinely made severe cuts in the initial requests of other departments, including the military.

Even so, the war ministry itself, under the direction of General A.N. Kuropatkin, failed to take a vital interest in the Far Eastern program. As late as 1903 the war minister stubbornly insisted that it was impossible to dispatch sizable reinforcements to the Far East, because such action would seriously weaken Russia's posture along its western frontiers. The emperor found it difficult to overcome this administrative resistance which, it should be understood, never took the form of direct insubordination but expressed itself instead in all manner of delays and excuses. The real significance of the "Kwantung-ites"—Bezobrazov and Admiral Abaza, the sometime deputy of Admiral Alekseev—was that they were responsible for reporting every deficiency to the tsar. For that reason they were generally unpopular and particularly detested by the ministers. They were akin to the "sovereign's eyes," supervising the execution of his orders. Or, as Kuropatkin confided to his diary, they were "a weapon that the emperor used to prick us," a "mustard plaster" that would not let the ministers sleep. Those individuals, of course, did not make "grand policy," for the emperor already had determined Russia's basic objectives.

Throughout 1903 military agents without exception reported Japan's energetic preparations. As a result Russia increased its forces in the Amur region by some twenty thousand men, even though State Secretary Bezobrazov insisted that an army fifty thousand strong should be concentrated in southern Manchuria. Kuropatkin used every excuse to avoid that. "For two years I constantly told him that we had to reinforce our positions in the Far East," Nicholas wrote to Kaiser William in April 1904. "He obstinately ignored my advice until it was too late to strengthen our forces." If higher governmental spheres were cool toward Russia's Far Eastern undertakings, Russian society was indifferent and even negative in its attitude.

Japan, meanwhile, was preparing for the struggle with energy born of desperation. The prestige of Europe, based on invincible power, stood very high. But the Japanese were absorbing European technology rapidly, acquiring a European facade, and skilfully adopting Western ways in order to win acceptance among the "whites." The idea of a war with Russia entered Japanese popular psychology long before 1904. A well-known Anglo-Japanese writer, Lafcadio Hearn, described Japanese soldiers returning in 1895 from the war with China and quoted, as quite common and natural, an old Japanese friend's remark about the dead: "There are no Japanese dead who do not return. There are none who do not know the way. From China and from Chōsen [Korea], and out of the bitter sea, all our dead have come back—*all*! They are with us now. At dusk they gather to hear the bugles that called them home. And they will hear them also in that hour when the armies of the Son of Heaven shall be summoned against Russia."[3] That was an idea to which the Japanese people grew accustomed.

Between 1895 and 1903 Japan increased its peacetime army two-and-a-half times (from 64,000 men to 150,000) and more than tripled its artillery. In addition the Japanese trained cadres that eventually enabled them to field an army far in excess of the estimates of any foreign military agent.[4] Naval expansion was even more pronounced. A new Japanese fleet was built practically from scratch and mainly in British shipyards. From a navy numerically inferior to that of the Chinese or even the Dutch, a new fighting force was born and it was equal to the fleet of a great power. Japan purchased its armaments with money paid by China [as indemnities] for the Sino-Japanese War of 1894-95 and in part for the Boxer Rebellion. And as fortune would have it, Russia was guarantor for the punctual payment of China's military debts.

The Japanese made these exertions with a view toward a great struggle, offensive in nature—a contest for hegemony in the Far East—and they chose the most propitious moment to begin the war. It would be hypocrisy to criticize Japan for pursuing its objectives with inflexible consistency. Nevertheless, it must be admitted that in 1904 Japan was in every respect the aggressor. Russia could have prevented the war only by withdrawing voluntarily from the Far East. St. Petersburg made several concessions, including the delaying of the dispatch of reinforcements to Manchuria, but half-measures could neither avert nor postpone the conflict.

THE STRATEGIC BALANCE

Following several decades of peace, the Russo-Japanese War became the first major conflict to witness the employment of modern weaponry—long-range artillery, armored cruisers, and naval mines. However, neither airplanes nor dirigibles were available yet, and wireless telegraph and submarines were still in their infancies and played scarcely any role in this conflict. Although Russia's peacetime army numbered about a million men, by January 1904 total Russian armed forces in the Far East had not yet reached 100,000. A force of 20,000 formed the Port Arthur garrison. About 50,000 were concentrated in the Ussuri region, and fewer than 20,000 were stationed in garrisons in Manchuria. Communication with European Russia depended on the recently completed single-track railway which could handle only four trains a day in each direction. Work was nearing completion on the section around Lake Baikal. The resident population of the Russian Far East, from which reserves could be drawn, was less than one million. Military estimates held that Japan would mobilize an army of 375,000 men. As it turned out, Japan put more than half a million men under arms. Moreover, Japan had sufficient naval transport to deploy two fully equipped divisions simultaneously, and the sailing time between Japanese ports and Korea was less than twenty-four hours.

Port Arthur—Outer Roads

Japan's ability to wage war on the continent hinged on control of the sea, and Russia's Pacific Fleet possessed considerable strength: seven battleships, four armored cruisers, [six protected cruisers] (including the world's fastest cruiser, *Novik*, capable of 25-26 knots), twenty-five destroyers of the newest class, and a sizable array of gunboats, supply ships, and older "numbered" [unnamed] destroyers. The Russian admiralty confidently assumed that Russian naval supremacy was assured. That confidence was premature and would remain so until the beginning or middle of 1905. At that time several ships under construction in the Baltic would be ready to join the fleet, and then the Russian navy would deploy the impressive total of fifteen battleships.[5] When the war broke out, however, the Japanese navy enjoyed a decided numerical superiority based on six battleships, six armored cruisers (augmented within a month by the *Nisshin* and *Kasuga* which were passing Singapore when diplomatic relations were severed), [and sixteen protected cruisers]. Japan had an even greater edge in destroyers [twenty], torpedo boats [eighty-five], and auxiliary vessels.

An abundance of naval bases gave Japan still another advantage, for Russia had only two bases in the Pacific. Almost the entire Russian fleet was concentrated at Port Arthur. The harbor there, with its inner roads guarded on all sides by high hills, once afforded ideal refuge for a fleet, but it was neither spacious nor deep enough to accomodate easily the larger contemporary vessels. Its basic deficiency was the narrow passage to the inner roads which required ships to enter and leave one at a time. The [commercial port of] Dalny had a splendid harbor but was completely unfortified. Russia's second base, Vladivostok, was ice-bound for several months of the year. Nevertheless, four cruisers, three of them armored, were stationed there. In addition the light cruiser *Variag* stood in the Korean port of Chemulpo [Inchon] at the disposal of the Russian ambassador to Korea.

Following the break in diplomatic relations, the viceroy of the Far East received the following instructions [from the tsar]: It is preferable that the Japanese fire the first shot; any landing in Korea is not to be opposed, unless it occurs on the northwest coast; only if their ships cross the 36th parallel are they to be intercepted. Russian authorities apparently still hoped that Japan would decide not to strike first. They also assumed that Tokyo would not abandon the established international custom of a formal declaration of war. But they forgot that Japan had opened the war against China in 1894 with a surprise attack.

The Port Arthur squadron, engaged in frequent training exercises, usually anchored in the outer roads of the harbor. It was lying there on the night of 26-27 January/8-9 February, when it was surprised by Japanese torpedo boats. They hit and seriously damaged the newest battleships, *Tsesarevich* and *Retvizan*, and the cruiser *Pallada*. The Russian sailors recovered quickly, began to fight back, and drove off the attackers. Panic in the city was avoided. When the Japanese squadron appeared again off Port Arthur on the morning of the 27th, the Russian fleet sailed out to meet it and, supported by coastal artillery, promptly forced the Japanese to withdraw.

"GOD SAVE THE TSAR!"

News of the outbreak of the war stunned and stirred Russia. Scarcely anyone had expected it, since the vast majority of Russians had only the vaguest interest in Manchuria. Nevertheless, the reaction was universal: Russia had been attacked. During the initial phase of the war that one idea became paramount: Russia had been attacked, and the enemy had to be repulsed. In Petersburg and other cities patriotic demonstrations, long unwitnessed in Russia, burst forth spontaneously. Especially unusual was the fact that even students took part in them. At St. Petersburg University students concluded a rally by marching to the Winter Palace singing "God Save the Tsar." Those who did not share that feeling— and there were many—remained silent that day and kept out of sight. Only the students of the Women's Institute provided an exception to the general enthusiasm. At a stormy meeting the women students all but unanimously opposed a vigil of prayers for victory which the council of professors proposed to hold in one of the buildings of the institute. That incident gave rise to a rumor, whether true or not, that the women had telegraphed greetings to the Mikado [Japanese Emperor]. In Armenia revolutionaries killed two and wounded several

other persons by bombing a meeting conducted by Armenian
clergy to pray for victory.

Early in January 1904 oppositionist elements had gathered
in St. Petersburg to convene the first illegal congress of the
Union of Liberation and to elect a secret executive committee.[6] They were quite taken aback by the effusion of patriotism. Zemstvo and noble assemblies and municipal dumas
adopted resolutions of support. The zemstvo constitutionalists
who assembled in Moscow on 23 February, also motivated
by patriotic enthusiasm generated by the war, resolved to
withhold any statement or declaration of constitutional demands for at least a few months. *Vestnik Evropy* ventured
that "the war, which has revived the spirit of every segment
of the Russian nation and revealed the full depth of its
devotion to the welfare of the state, must and, we sincerely
believe, will dissolve the many prejudices that have stifled
a wide range of creativity. The mental and moral maturity
of the public, which willingly shares the concerns of the
government, will be recognized. With such a hope the losses
and suffering inseparably associated with the war become
more bearable." While withholding its own opinion, *Russkoe
bogatstvo* ridiculed that statement, which it called a "curious
tirade." "Of course, there is the hope of a better life, but,"
the socialist journal warned, "the very existence of a war
offers no guarantees."

Osvobozhdenie, linked both to zemstvo funtionaries and
to organizations further to the left, found itself in a quandry.
In "A Letter to Students" P.B. Struve wrote: "Shout—Long
live the Army, Long live Russia, Long live Liberty!" But he
was answered on the pages of the very same journal: "We
will not mingle our shouts with their shouts. . . ! At any
rate we will remain true to ourselves and to the slogan, Long
live Russia, but we will not forget to add 'free' each time.
However, since that is too cumbersome to chant in the streets,
the best solution is to replace those three words with the
two which are already familiar—"Down with Autocracy!"[7]

A.N. Hippius admitted that the war had little effect on
literary circles, "probably because it was so remote. Moreover, no one expected it to produce any domestic change—
except for the triumph and strengthening of autocracy—
because at first everyone believed that we would defeat the

Japanese." Only Valery Briussov was moved to write a poem,
"To the Pacific Ocean." Meanwhile a heavy demand for cheap
popular war prints and portraits of war heroes partly reflected
the temper of the masses. Revolutionary terrorists masquer-
ading as traveling salesmen sometimes found themselves selling
those pictures. With bitter anger the terrorist Ivan Kaliaev[8]
complained to his comrade, Egor Sozonov, that "the people
are being driven to the slaughter, and yet there is no protest.
Patriotism has seized everyone—there is an epidemic of stu-
pidity. The people gape at heroes with their mouths wide
open."

Interior minister Plehve was alleged to have said at the
outbreak of hostilities that "a short victorious war" would
be useful to Russia.[9] Such an assessment was justified in
that a short victorious war might have stabilized the climate
of Russia in 1904, but of course there is no reason to infer
from Plehve's remark that he was in some way responsible
for a war started by Japan at a time of its own choosing.
Moreover, there was no way that the war could be either
short or victorious. It began under conditions quite unfavorable to Russia, and only time and dogged efforts could change
them. After the first fit of anger and the impulse to rebuff the
enemy, an entirely different attitude soon began to emerge,
for neither the people at large nor the educated public fully
grasped the significance of the war.

Abroad, attitudes toward the war varied. England and the
United States openly sympathized with Japan. In London
an illustrated weekly war report appeared under the title
"Japan's Struggle for Freedom." President Theodore Roosevelt went so far as to warn Germany and France that if
"under any circumstances" they should take a stand against
Japan, he would "immediately side with the latter" and would
"go as far as necessary." The tone of the American press,
especially the Jewish segment, was so hostile toward Russia
that *Novoe vremia* complained: "Jewish propaganda is practically an accomplice of the war in those countries where Jews
control the press and stock exchange. . . . Without American
and British protection Japan undoubtedly never would have
embarked on a war against us." That observation over-simpli-
fied a very complex international situation.

France, interested in Russia primarily as an ally against Germany, found the war very disquieting. Although the French press (except the extreme left) maintained the tone appropriate to an ally, the Combes-Delcassé government hurriedly negotiated for an understanding with England. In Germany the leftist papers opposed Russia, while those on the right for the most part took Russia's side. The critical factor at that moment was the German emperor's personal attitude toward the conflict. *"Tua res agitur!"*[10] he wrote on the margin of a secret dispatch from Count Arco-Valley, his ambassador in Tokyo. "The Russians are defending the interests and supremacy of the white race against the increasing domination of the yellow race. Therefore, our sympathies must lie with Russia." China, meanwhile, hastened to proclaim its neutrality, hoping in that way to protect itself from reprisals by the victor.

"PATIENCE, GENTLEMEN!"

To fight a great power, as Japan proved to be, required a herculean effort. Russia, however, expected to fight a "colonial war." In his war memoirs[11] General Kuropatkin recalled how "on entering the war with Japan, we considered it necessary to hold our main forces in a state of readiness in case of a European war. Therefore only a small part of the forces stationed in European Russia were selected for deployment in the Far East. The Warsaw Military District, our most numerous garrison, did not contribute a single army corps to the Far East." Relations with Austria and Germany gave no cause to fear an attack from that quarter, but the decision apparently was justified by the terms of the Franco-Russian agreement which prohibited Russia from concluding a pact of neutrality with Germany. The convention of 1892 committed Russia to furnish 7-8,000,000 men in the event of a German attack on France—an eventuality that had to be taken into account.

As soon as the war began, on 7 February, the tsar appointed Minister of War Kuropatkin to be commander-in-chief of the Manchurian Army. This was a popular appointment, for the public remembered Kuropatkin as Skobelev's chief of staff. Cautious and rather indecisive, he was quite unsuited for a command position. As General M.I. Dragomirov put it: "Kuropatkin appointed—that's fine, but where is Skobelev?"

Having calculated the required number of troops and the rail capacity and having considered the inevitability of Japan's overwhelming numerical superiority during the first phase of the war, Kuropatkin secretly leaned toward the "tactic of 1812"—toward a gradual withdrawal into the depths of Manchuria, to Harbin, if not farther. On 27 February he addressed a delegation of the St. Petersburg municipal duma: "I beg you to be patient and, with full realization of Russia's strength, patiently to await further developments. Our initial steps entail the movement of troops through vast spaces.... Patience, patience, and patience, gentlemen!" But Kuropatkin had neither the "nerves of steel" nor the far-reaching authority required to play out the role of Barclay de Tolly [the architect of the strategy of 1812]. He even had to conceal his personal preference for a policy of withdrawal. The day after urging "patience," as he bade farewell to the delegation at the railway station, the commander-in-chief promised that before long he would be sending "good news to gladden the tsar and Mother Russia."

To command the fleet the tsar named Admiral Stepan O. Makarov, one of Russia's finest naval officers.[12] Makarov was immensely popular with the navy. He left immediately for Asia and reached Port Arthur on the 24th of February. However, overall command of military operations remained in the hands of the Far Eastern viceroy, Admiral Alekseev. The emperor was the arbiter of any dispute between senior commanders. Divided authority created scarcely any problem in the navy, but the differences between Kuropatkin and Alekseev did not take long to materialize, for the viceroy favored a plan of action more energetic and more venturesome than the army commander had in mind.

DISASTER AT SEA: MAKAROV LOST

For the first two-and-a-half months of the war military operations centered almost exclusively on Port Arthur. Elsewhere on 27 January a Japanese flotilla attacked the cruiser *Variag* and the gunboat *Koreets* at Chemulpo. Their crews had not even learned that war had broken out before they were engaged and destroyed in an unequal battle.[13] After that skirmish, the Japanese began to land troops in western Korea. They seized control of Seoul and placed the Korean emperor under guard. Advanced detachments of the Russian army, which had crossed into north Korea to reconnoiter, gradually retreated as the strength of the enemy increased. On 22 February Japanese ships appeared off Vladivostok, and the Russian cruiser squadron responded by raiding the northern coast of Japan. Port Arthur, however, remained the center of the conflict, and depression reigned there during the first days after the Japanese attack. The light cruiser *Boyarin* and the mine-layer *Yenesei* exploded when they ran over their own mines. The vessels that had been damaged in the initial night attack were towed into port, but their repair required a long time. On 12 February the Japanese made another effort to exploit the weakest feature of Port Arthur when they tried to block the channel into the inner harbor by sinking "fireships."

Admiral Makarov's arrival buoyed the spirit of the fleet. The new commander raised his ensign on the high-speed cruiser *Askold*, continuously sallied out to sea, engaged the Japanese fleet whenever it approached Port Arthur, and even launched a sortie to locate the nearest base of the enemy squadron. Makarov was optimistic about the quality of the Russian fleet. Even though he had only six battle-ready warships to oppose Japan's fourteen, he refused to be paralyzed by the unfavorable odds. He was not afraid to take risks: he knew that the Japanese hardly dared to meet in a decisive battle since they had no access to replacements, whereas a new Russian squadron equal in size to the first was being made ready in the Baltic.

But on the 31st of March Admiral Makarov was lost together with the battleship *Petropavlovsk* which hit a mine and exploded and sank within two minutes. Makarov's loss was a fatal blow to the Russian navy. A mood of depression descended over the entire country. The tsar usually concealed his emotions even from his diary, but on that day he wrote: "The news was unusually grave . . . . All day long I was unable to collect myself because of this terrible misfortune . . . . God's will be done in all things, but we pray the

Admiral Makarov

Lord to be merciful to us poor sinners." The *Pobeda*, another battleship, was damaged at the same time. Consequently the Russian squadron abandoned the sea for two whole months. Admiral Nicholas I. Skrydlov succeeded Makarov, but he could not even reach the fleet [because the Japanese had isolated Port Arthur].

Only the cruiser detachment based at Vladivostok retained its freedom of action. During the first six months of the war, the cruisers conducted several raids south to the Korean Straits, into the Pacific Ocean, or along the Japanese coast. They sank several Japanese transports laden with troops and heavy artillery for the siege of Port Arthur. Their action delayed the bombardment of the fortress by two or three months. But three armored cruisers[14] could not take on the whole Japanese fleet.

On 30 March/12 April, the day before the *Petropavlovsk* disaster, England and France signed the *Entente Cordiale* in which the French renounced all claim to Egypt in return for British recognition of their rights in (then independent) Morocco. An agreement of far-reaching significance, it laid the foundation of the Triple Entente.[15] The rapprochement of Russia's ally, France, and Japan's ally, England, created a paradox, but their understanding dealt with specific issues and involved no contradiction of their treaties of alliance. The French press suggested that Russia only stood to profit from the agreement, because it gave France the chance to exercise a "moderating influence" on England. Russian diplomatic circles practically ignored the development. However, the April 15th edition of *Novoe vremia* remarked that "nearly everyone noticed a cool breeze in the atmosphere of Franco-Russian relations." The Anglo-French agreement inspired rumors of possible mediation between Russia and Japan. The Russian government quickly dispelled that idea with a curt announcement that any interference in the war that has been imposed upon Russia would be considered an unfriendly act.

RETREAT FROM THE YALU

The next blow to Russia fell in the latter half of April. The Japanese army had concentrated in northern Korea. To the north across the wide valley of the Yalu River stood a small

Russian force which Kuropatkin, in accord with his strategy
of a retreat in depth, designated a "rearguard." It was to delay the enemy as long as possible but not to engage in a
major action. The first land encounter was very important
psychologically, and the Japanese prepared for it meticulously.
They did everything necessary to secure decisive numerical
superiority and eventually concentrated about 45,000 men
against 18,000 Russians. At Chiuliencheng, the focal point of
the battle, the Japanese had a five-to-one advantage.

The Russian forces, commanded by General M.I. Zasulich
[younger brother of the revolutionary, Vera Zasulich], held
an excellent position on the river's elevated right bank. Unfortunately, the Japanese crossed the river above the en-
trenched Russians and hit them on the flank. The Siberian
riflemen put up a stout fight, but the enemy's superiority was
too great. Two battalions avoided capture by fighting their
way out of a Japanese encirclement. Many soldiers carried
away the memory of the regimental priest Shcherbakovsky
leading the breakout of a Russian detachment with a crucifix
in his hands. The battle cost Russia 2,268 dead and wounded
as well as several guns. Japanese losses were half that.[16] The
Encyclopaedia Britannica compared this engagement to the
battle of Valmy in 1792—the "beginning of a new era," Asia's
first victory over the "white race."[17] Of course the battle of
the Yalu would have received less attention if the war had
turned out differently.

On 18 April the Japanese crossed the Yalu River in force.
On the night of the 20th they tried again to block the entrance
to Port Arthur with fire-ships. That effort enjoyed partial
success. On the 21st the Japanese began to land at Pitzuwo on
the northern coast of the Liaotung Peninsula. On 23 April the
viceroy managed to travel from Port Arthur to Mukden, but
that very evening rail communications were disrupted. Mounted detachments succeeded in restoring rail service for two
days, and two trainloads of artillery shells got through to the
south. Then on the 30th the Japanese cut the railway for
good. Thereafter an occasional blockade runner was Port
Arthur's only contact with the outside. That rapid sequence
of events impressed on the Russian public that the situation
was far more serious than originally believed. Port Arthur was
cut off from the Manchurian army, and the Pacific fleet was

practically useless. The slow buildup of reinforcements caused A.S. Suvorin to complain that "we have even less than a stream, we have only a trickle." But recalling Kuropatkin's advice as he left for the front, a lead article in *Novoe vremia* urged, "Patience!"

During the first part of May the fortunes of war turned temporarily against Japan. Two battleships struck mines near Port Arthur. The *Hatsuse* sank in place in fifty seconds in full view of the Russians watching from shore. The *Yashima* was towed away but later sank at sea. The Japanese successfully concealed her loss for a whole year. On the same day two Japanese cruisers collided and one was lost. In addition a supply ship blew up on a mine. After that "revenge" for *Petropavlovsk*, the Japanese fleet did not dare to venture close to Port Arthur.

THE INVASION OF THE KWANTUNG PENINSULA

The Japanese army that landed at Pitzuwo deployed a covering force to screen against the Manchurian Army and then marched south. At one point the Kwantung Peninsula narrows [to about two miles], creating a natural fortress around the town of Chinchou and the Nanshan Hill.[18] The Russians hastily fortified the area and spiked it with heavy guns. Even so, the commander of the Kwantung district, General Anatole M. Stessel, considered the position too remote from Port Arthur. Fearful that he did not have enough troops to protect the coasts between Chinchou and Port Arthur, he gave the local commander, General Alexander V. Fock, an order similar to the order to Zasulich on the Yalu: slow down the enemy but do not take too many chances.

On 13/26 May 1904 the Japanese stormed Chinchou and the Nanshan heights. Attacking under intense fire without cover, they suffered heavy losses. The position was defended only by the 5th [East] Siberian Rifle Regiment supported from the sea by the gunboat *Bobr*. After a sixteen hour battle, the Russians retreated, abandoning their heavy artillery which had been damaged. The Japanese lost about 5,000 men, at least three times the casualties suffered by the Russians, but they had overcome the main obstacle on the road to Port Arthur. Next they seized the port of Dalny without a fight

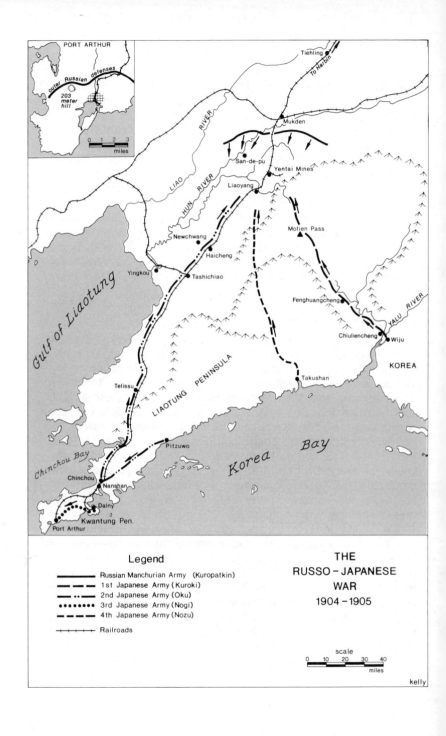

THE
RUSSO-JAPANESE
WAR
1904-1905

Legend

———————— Russian Manchurian Army (Kuropatkin)
— — — — 1st Japanese Army (Kuroki)
—··—··— 2nd Japanese Army (Oku)
●●●●●●● 3rd Japanese Army (Nogi)
— — — — 4th Japanese Army (Nozu)

+—+—+—+ Railroads

scale
0   10   20   30   40
miles

kelly

and began immediately to use its invaluable facilities to land
an entire army.

Then began the siege of Port Arthur. The isolated Kwantung
district contained three senior commanders: General Stessel,
the commandant and military governor of Kwantung Province;
General Constantine N. Smirnov [Stessel's successor as commandant of Fortress Port Arthur]; and Admiral William K.
Witgeft, who commanded the fleet in Admiral Skrydlov's
absence.[19] Cut off from the outside world, the lack of a single
undisputed commander might have been dangerous had it not
been for General Roman I. Kondratenko. Displaying rare ability and tact, Kondratenko managed to reconcile the divergent
views of the various commanders for the common good. Justly
was he considered the soul of the Port Arthur defense.

KUROPATKIN STRIKES BACK

Based on his own last impressions and the alarming communi-
ques from General Stessel, Admiral Alekseev believed that the
fortress was unprepared and would be unable to hold out for
long. But the fall of the fortress would have meant the certain
destruction of the fleet. Consequently the viceroy demanded
that Kuropatkin drive south to raise the siege of Port Arthur.
For Kuropatkin, however, the period of retreat was far from
over. From the east through the mountain passes out of Korea
General Kuroki's army was advancing on Kuropatkin's flank,
and the Japanese were landing still another army [at Taku-
shan] between Korea and the Liaotung. Under those circumstances Kuropatkin regarded a move to the south a dangerous
absurdity, a "strategic folly." The conflicting strategies were
relayed to the tsar for a decision. The result was an indecisive
operation, reluctantly executed by Kuropatkin with inadequate forces—a southward advance of ten-to-fifteen miles, a
battle at Wangfangkou [Telissu] on 1-2/14-15 June 1904, and
then under Japanese counter-attacks a retreat to the original
position.[20] At the viceroy's headquarters [in Mukden] the
sentiment was that "Kuropatkin ought to be hanged." All the
same, the operation delayed the siege of Port Arthur by about
two weeks. The Japanese had recovered the initiative, but
they were in no hurry to advance in the north.[21]

On 10/23 June for the first time since the death of Makarov,
the Russian squadron put to sea from Port Arthur. By then

the ships damaged in the first two months of the war had been repaired. The opposing forces were once again "commensurable," although the Japanese navy remained stronger, despite the loss of the *Hatsuse* and the *Yashima*. Witgeft sailed with the idea of reaching Vladivostok, if he could make it without a fight. However, he ran into the Japanese squadron and returned to Port Arthur by nightfall.

PUBLIC APATHY AND ELITIST DISSENSION

Most of Russia was scarcely conscious of the war. The first partial mobilizations affected only a few districts. After the initial shock, domestic life went on as if impelled by inertia. Senator Nicholas A. Zinoviev investigated the Moscow provincial zemstvo, and as a result the government reversed the election of Dmitry N. Shipov[22] as chairman of the provincial zemstvo board. The press devoted much space to the deliberations of the Commission on Orthography of the Academy of Sciences which on 12 April began to consider some orthographic reforms. Radical circles rejoiced at the military disasters but still saw nothing serious in the situation. The lack of victories disappointed the man in the street and led him to criticize the government. But the average citizen had no idea of the enormous problems involved. To him the Japanese were an enemy of no consequence—just "monkeys."

The emperor continuously visited troops headed for the front. In 1904 he traveled literally all over Russia, because he considered it his duty to greet the men who were going off to die for their motherland. He also visited the shipyards where work proceeded feverishly to ready the ships of the Second Pacific Squadron. Meanwhile the new finance minister, V.N. Kokovtsov, successfully raised a new loan to finance the war. The bonds were sold mainly in France but also in Germany. That loan enabled the government to fight the war without raising taxes and without disturbing the ruble's parity with gold. During the summer, the capacity of the Great Siberian Railway doubled to accomodate eight trains each way daily. Criticism of the war smouldered in high places among those persons most closely associated with Witte. The former finance minister stubbornly insisted that Russia had no need of Manchuria and that "Bezobrazovist" intrigues had caused the war.

He openly declared that he preferred not to see Russia victorious. He expressed this view not only in letters to Kuropatkin,
with whom he remained on friendly terms, but also in a conversation with Bülow, the German chancellor: "As a politician," he told the German early in July 1904, "I fear any
swift and brilliant Russian successes. They only would make
the ruling circles in St. Petersburg too arrogant . . . . Russia
needs to experience a few more military failures."

TWO ASSASSINATIONS: BOBRIKOV AND PLEHVE

On 3 June 1904 Eugen Schaumann shot and mortally wounded
N.I. Bobrikov, the governor-general of Finland, and then committed suicide on the spot. The assassin was a young Finn of
Swedish descent, the son of a [former] senator. For over six
years Bobrikov had placed himself at the emperor's disposal,
and Nicholas felt his loss deeply. "A great loss, difficult to
replace," he wrote in his diary. As Bobrikov's successor the
emperor appointed Prince I.M. Obolensky, the governor of
Kharkov. Six weeks later, on 15 July, Egor Sozonov's bomb
killed interior minister Plehve. The explosion obliterated
Plehve's carriage, killed his coachman, and wounded ten people, including a three-year-old girl. The assassination was the
work of the Socialist Revolutionary Battle Organization,
which had been hunting Plehve for some time.[23]
  Plehve's death was a great shock. "The Lord visits us sternly
with his anger," wrote the tsar. But the assassination produced
general rejoicing among the intelligentsia. Oppositionists kept
silent, for what they had to say exceeded the censorship
restrictions. With some accuracy *Moskovskie vedomosti* noted
that "liberals and proponents of gradualism undoubtedly were
one with the dynamiters in their systematic hatred for V.K.
Plehve, and they sympathized with the results if not with the
organization responsible for the catastrophe." But even conservatives disavowed the fallen minister. Prince Meshchersky
was the first conservative to criticize Plehve's policy openly.
Plehve, he wrote, was responsible for "atrophying the spirit of
the Petersburg bureaucracy . . . for destroying its embryonic
freedom of initiative and its spontaneity." *Novoe vremia* was
more ambiguous: "A year from now perhaps only a few will
recognize V.K. Plehve as a statesman."

Viacheslav Plehve

Egor Sozonov—Plehve's Assassin

Lev Tikhomirov wrote critically of Plehve in his diary: "He had everything—intellect, character, honesty, efficiency, experience . . . . Many people loyal to the sovereign, to Russia, and to order offered him their resources . . . . He listened to everyone, lied, and fooled everyone. Gradually he cast aside all honest people, and he himself became an oppressor and nothing else." Recording his impressions of a journey along the Volga, Tikhomirov wrote: "I heard the assassins cursed but not a word of regret about Plehve himself."[24]

THE BATTLE OF THE YELLOW SEA

In Manchuria the gradual northward retreat of the Russian army continued. Three Japanese armies advanced against it: [the Second Army of General Oku Yasukata was moving north along the railway from Telissu; General Nozu Michitsura's Fourth Army, having landed at Takushan, was moving across the peninsula toward a rendezvous with Oku below Haicheng; the First Army, commanded by General Kuroki Tametomo, after crossing the Yalu had moved through the mountains and concentrated around Fenghuangcheng. General Nogi Maresuke's Third Army, designated to besiege Port Arthur, was landing unopposed at Dalny].

Sharp Russian delaying actions continued throughout July. The Russians inflicted heavy losses on the Japanese at Tashichiao (11 July), but on the following day they pulled back again in accord with the general plan. Meanwhile, reinforcements arrived steadily. Liaoyang was being readied as a fortress, and the consensus was that the withdrawal would end there. Kuropatkin was not fully satisfied that the balance of strength had tipped, but he agreed to make a stand at Liaoyang.

The establishment of a base at Dalny and the Japanese build-up on the Kwantung Peninsula lasted for about two months. Then on 12 July General Nogi began to attack in earnest. After three days of hard fighting the Japanese seized the Russians' forward positions, and two days later they captured the next line on Wolf Hills. By 27 July Nogi's troops were only a few versts from Port Arthur, and the siege of the fortress proper began. Random shells from the heavy Japanese siege guns began to arch across the hilltops and fall on the inner harbor.

Port Arthur's naval command already had decided that little could be gained by putting to sea and that it was better to remain at Port Arthur, help defend the fortress, and wait to be rescued. Consequently some of the middle and small caliber guns had been removed from the ships and mounted in the forts; some of the ships' companies also were detached to reinforce the fortress garrison. But as Japanese shells began to rain on the inner harbor, Nicholas sent explicit instructions for the fleet to break out to Vladivostok. Admiral Witgeft prepared to execute his sovereign's command.

The First Pacific Squadron got underway on the morning of 28 July. Six battleships, four [three] cruisers, and eight of the best destroyers put to sea. The armored cruiser *Bayan*, damaged by a mine ten days earlier, had to be left behind. The Russian fleet was handicapped in that three of the battleships could make only thirteen knots, while the enemy squadron was capable of seventeen knots. Witgeft sent the destroyer *Reshitelnyi* to be interned in the neutral Chinese port of Cheefoo. That was the price to be paid for the opportunity to send dispatches to the viceroy and to the cruiser squadron at Vladivostok so that the northern force would come out to meet the fleet. The Japanese followed *Reshitslnyi* and in flagrant violation of international law entered Cheefoo and seized the disarmed destroyer. Admiral Togo Heihachiro had four battleships, [and three armored and eight light cruisers]. In addition four armored cruisers patrolled the Korean Straits against the Vladivostok cruiser force.

At their first sighting the Russians managed to avoid battle and, leaving the Japanese behind, continued on course for Vladivostok. But superior speed enabled the Japanese squadron to overtake the Russians about ninety miles from Port Arthur, and thus began the first large-scale naval action of the war. Both sides suffered heavy damage, especially the two flagships, Witgeft's *Tsesarevich* and Togo's *Mikasa*. Admiral Togo was prepared to accept the escape of the Russian squadron to Vladivostok, when fortune once again came to the aid of the Japanese. A heavy shell hit the *Tsesarevich*'s bridge and killed Admiral Witgeft. The squadron continued to follow the flagship for several minutes, but then another shell destroyed the ship's conning tower [and the *Tsesarevich* began to turn in circles]. The flagship finally raised a signal transferring command to Admiral Prince Paul P. Ukhtomsky aboard the battleship *Peresvet*. *Peresvet*'s masts had been shot away, and Ukhtomsky had trouble sending signals. Confusion reigned. The cruiser *Askold* signaled "follow me" and sailed off to the south. *Retvizan* headed back to Port Arthur after a desperate effort to engage the Japanese. Prince Ukhtomsky followed *Retvizan*,[25] while some of the cruisers followed *Askold*. "The two chance hits which killed Admiral Witgeft and put the flagship out of commission decided the fate of the battle."[26]

July 28 marked the end of the First Pacific Squadron. Although five battleships, the cruiser *Pallada*, and three destroyers returned to Port Arthur, they never ventured to sea again. The rest of the ships were lost or disarmed. Speedy little *Novik* skirted the entire eastern coast of Japan and on 7 August reached Sakhalin Island. But two stronger enemy cruisers caught and sank her as she was loading coal. *Tsesarevich* and three destroyers reached the German port of Kiaochow.[27] *Askold* and one destroyer made it to Shanghai. *Diana* reached Saigon in Indo-China where it was interned to the great surprise of the crew—French authorities in Petersburg apparently insisted on it in order to avoid complications with England.

England diligently looked after Japan's interests, and France, torn between an old ally and a new friend, tried to follow a middle course by adhering strictly to the rules of neutrality. During the summer of 1904 two ships of the Volunteer Fleet, the *Petersburg* and the *Smolensk*, had a busy time in the Mediterranean and Red Seas intercepting ships bound for Japan with war material.[28] The protests of the European governments quickly terminated that activity. Germany was one of the complainants because of the seizure of the German vessel *Arabia*.

Three days after the battle of the Yellow Sea, the Vladivostok cruisers, which had set out to rendezvous with the Port Arthur squadron, ran into a superior Japanese force in the Korean Straits. The Japanese damaged the slower *Riurik*, and she held up the other two. Finally, having lost a third of their crews, they fled to the north. *Riurik* fought heroically but was sunk. After that battle of 1 August, the northern cruisers remained at Vladivostok.

THE BIRTH OF THE HEIR

During those fateful days and before the naval disaster became known, Russia was blessed by a long-awaited event of great joy: [on 30 July 1904] to the empress was born a son, Alexis Nikolaevich, the tsarevich. In his Manifesto of 1 August 1904 Emperor Nicholas proclaimed that in the event of his death [his brother] Grand Duke Michael Alexandrovich would become regent, but Empress Alexandra Feodorovna would be responsible for raising the tsarevich. Kaiser William, with whom the tsar was on even closer terms since the war, was invited to become godfather to the new heir. To celebrate the christening the Manifesto of 11 August granted traditional privileges and boons, such as the cancellation of debts and the reduction of penalties. The manifesto also contained an important legislative measure—the abolition of corporal punishment when not prescribed by law. The public welcomed this measure with deep satisfaction. Even *Osvobozhdenie* hailed it, though in disparaging terms as "favors from baby Alexis."

LIAOYANG

A two-week spell of rain interrupted military operations in Manchuria, but by 16 August the ground had dried sufficiently, and the first of the war's three general battles began at Liaoyang. Both the Russian army and nation were confident of victory. The opponents were approximately equal in strength.[29] Just before the battle came the good news that the Port Arthur garrison had beaten off General Nogi's first furious assault. The attack had lasted two weeks and cost the Japanese 15,000 men.

Three Japanese armies attacked the semi-circular Russian position: Oku and Nozu, who were moving up from the south, and Kuroki, who was advancing on the eastern flank. In a three-day battle Kuropatkin repulsed the attack south of Liaoyang. Then, having gathered a "fist," he decided to launch a counter-attack against Kuroki. This failed to produce the expected results; indeed, the Japanese pushed the Russians northward into the vicinity of the Yentai mines. At that point Kuropatkin, overestimating the strength of the Japanese and fearing that they might cut the railway north of Liaoyang, again ordered a general retreat. On the morning of August 22nd the Japanese occupied Liaoyang.

The Russians retired in good order without the loss of a single gun. Nevertheless the loss of Liaoyang dealt a serious blow to Russian morale. Everyone had expected that Liaoyang was precisely the point where Kuropatkin would deliver a decisive rebuff to the Japanese. Instead it turned into just another "rearguard action" and a bloody one at that. Russian losses were set at 19,000 killed and wounded, Japanese casualties at 23,000. Only after Liaoyang did Russian society entertain for the first time the possibility that Russia's ultimate victory might not be assured. Nicholas, however, refused to be reconciled to the possibility of Russia's defeat—"I will continue the fight to the end, to the day when the last Japanese has been driven out of Manchuria," he wrote to the kaiser on 9 October. The Russian buildup and the preparation of the Second Squadron proceeded intensely. The emperor also deemed it necessary to appeal to Russian society for cooperation in national affairs. He received the zemstvo representatives who were engaged in caring for the wounded. Their attitude was sincerely patriotic, and at such moments it appeared that their aspirations could be satisfied.

"THE SPRING" OF SVIATOPOLK-MIRSKY

Plehve's office remained vacant for a month and a half during which the assistant minister, Peter N. Durnovo, managed the ministry of internal affairs. After Liaoyang Nicholas decided to name as Plehve's successor the governor-general of Vilna and former assistant minister under Sipiagin, Prince Peter D. Sviatopolk-Mirsky.[30] *Novoe vremia* discussed the appointment in this perspective: "Only the utmost unity and solidarity of government and society can produce the efforts worthy of Russia to defeat the foreign enemy and pacify the diverse domestic malcontents."

The new minister delayed his departure from Vilna for two weeks in order to attend the unveiling of a monument to Catherine II, but he did not hesitate to state his views to a correspondent of the *Echo de Paris:* "We will give the zemstvos the broadest freedom." On the matter of religious toleration and the Jews he was less precise but equally positive: "How can you expect me not to be a supporter of progress?" Prince Mirsky made similar statements to the *Lokal-Anzeiger* of Berlin and to the Associated Press, the American news agency. The Russian press carried these interviews, initially without comment.

On 16 September the new minister received the officials of his department and delivered his famous statement on trust: "Administrative experience has convinced me that to be successful the government must base its efforts upon an attitude of sincere trust in public and class institutions and in the people generally. Only in this way can it hope for mutual understanding, and without that the sound organization of the empire cannot be expected." The tone of Mirsky's statement approximated Goremykin's memorandum of 1899 (to which Witte had objected), and it was received approvingly by conservative slavophiles like General Kireev and Lev Tikhomirov. The statement departed so sharply from the recent atmosphere that it created an immediate sensation.

The tone of the press changed overnight. The censors were at a loss as to what was permissible. On 24 September *Novoe vremia* was exuberant: The speech was "a step forward—for the first time in a hundred years. . . . Truly a breath of fresh air." In his *Kievlianin* of 8 September Professor Pikhno optimistically predicted that "since public elements wholeheartedly aspire to participate in governmental activities, there is no alternative but to expand their participation and also their responsibilities. . . . No longer then will the public blame the government or make unseasonable encroachments upon it." "Are not the minister's words a breath, an unmistakable sign, of spring?" exclaimed A.S. Suvorin. And that moment of Russian life became known as "the Spring" or "the era of trust."

On 26 September in the legal journal *Pravo* Prince E.N. Trubetskoy published a frankly political article. Trubetskoy was one of the few people who could speak both the language of the authorities and the language of the public. He was an example of Count A.K. Tolstoy's caveat that "one cannot be a warrior in two opposing camps." Without actually joining the Liberation movement, people like Trubetskoy sometimes became its spokesmen in influencing the government. The leftists used those people without ever really listening to them.

Prince Trubetskoy's article bore the title "The War and the Bureaucracy." He wrote: "Deep in sleep for many years,

Russia did not see the enemy until he stood before the walls
of Port Arthur. Russian society . . . slept because the authorities ordered it to. . . . In years past Russia resembled the
lock-up of a police station . . . with the all-powerful bureaucracy standing vigil while the nation slept. . . . The army and
navy have not been defeated! The defeats belong to the Russian bureaucracy!" Freedom of speech, he continued, is useful
only to extremists. While moderate men are forced to be
silent, radicals spread their illegal propaganda everywhere,
and that poses a great danger. "The bureaucracy," Trubetskoy
concluded, "should be brought under public control and be
made to govern with and not against society. It should not
be the master of a dumb herd but an instrument of the crown
dependent on society. . . . The throne, gathering the entire
nation unto itself, will become glorious, great, and strong."

The journal *Osvobozhdenie*, which in October moved from
Stuttgart to Paris, took exception to Prince Trubetskoy's
analysis: "As long as the autocratic stronghold remains intact, everything that opposes autocracy is not a danger to be
feared but a great blessing." In the *Kievlianin* D.I. Pikhno
protested that "the Russian public has not been a slave of the
bureaucracy and did not become one in some police station.
It has been working for Russia and creating Russia's strength."
By coincidence, on the day that Trubetskoy's article appeared
the correspondent M. Menshikov expressed almost identical
views in *Novoe vremia:* "The sum of Russia's weakness lies
in the unnatural somnolence of its people, which is being
perpetuated for some purpose. . . ."

Prince Mirsky's statement and the subsequent articles openly critical of the government broke the ice, and Russian society began to speak out. Zemstvo assemblies and municipal
dumas telegraphed greetings to the new minister. Simultaneously the enemies of the government grew bolder. The revolutionary parties had demonstrated little interest in the war as
long as Russia's victory seemed certain. At this point they
sensed that new opportunities were beginning to open up.
Revolutionary agitation spread throughout the country and
also in the army. "Any victory that you achieve threatens
Russia with the disaster of bolstering the regime," declared
a Socialist Revolutionary appeal to Russian army officers.
"Any defeat brings nearer the hour of deliverance. Is it any

wonder then that Russians rejoice at the victories of your enemy?"

SHA HO

Attention shifted for two weeks from domestic matters to the war zone where, unexpectedly, the Russian army launched an offensive. After retreating from Liaoyang, Kuropatkin assumed that the Japanese were about to take Mukden, about sixty miles to the north. Therefore, he was preparing to withdraw to Tiehling [on the railroad about eighty miles north of Mukden] to positions he had selected weeks before. The Russian army had conducted an orderly retreat, and within a month 50,000 replacements had more than compensated for the losses at Liaoyang. On 10 September [Quartermaster General Jacob G. Zhilinsky] telegraphed to announce the formation of the Second Manchurian Army under the command of General Oscar K. Grippenberg.[31] Zhilinsky added, however, that if Kuropatkin managed to give the Japanese a good thrashing, "perhaps the formation of the Second Army would become unnecessary." With that Kuropatkin rather hastily decided to mount an offensive, even though Generals Stackelberg and Sluchevsky recommended against it.[32]

"Yesterday I crossed myself and signed the dispositions for an offensive," read the entry for 16 September in the diary of the Manchurian Army's commander. On 19 September the order was read to the army: "The time has come for us to force the Japanese to bend to our will." Kuropatkin's order, published in the capital's newspapers on 27 September after the offensive was underway, created general excitement and lifted spirits.

Once again the Russian army marched south from Mukden. The Japanese met it head-on. Bitter fighting erupted on 26 September along a broad front of several tens of kilometers. The battle went on for nine full days. The papers wrote that "Tajangshen [Nanshan], Wangfangkou [Telissu], and Liaoyang paled beside it." Positions changed hands many times; guns were lost and recovered. Kuropatkin could neither push through the Japanese front nor outflank it. The bloody fighting subsided on 5 October with a minor tactical victory, the capture of One Tree Hill, and fourteen Japanese guns.

The victorious troops named it Putilov Hill in honor of their general.[33] As the torrential autumn rains set in, the two armies settled into their positions. Russian losses were enormous—42,000 killed and wounded; Japanese losses were about half that—20,000.

The battle of Sha Ho indicated that a relative balance had been established between the two antagonists. Sha Ho was not a defeat—the armies divided the battlefield between them —but the offensive, announced with such ceremony, had been stopped in its tracks at the outset. Nevertheless, the battle solidified General Kuropatkin's position and silenced those who demanded an offensive to relieve Port Arthur. Nicholas appointed Kuropatkin commander-in-chief and recalled Admiral Alekseev to St. Petersburg. "I went through a great inner struggle to arrive at this decision," wrote the tsar. Admiral Alekseev was a consummate proponent for an aggressive policy in the Far East, and he frequently surpassed Kuropatkin in foresight. But for all that, he enjoyed little prestige either with the army or in the country.[34] The problem of unified command was resolved in favor of the former war minister. The emperor requested that he appoint the commanders of the First and Third Manchurian Armies, and Kuropatkin chose General Nicholas P. Linevich and General Baron Alexander von Kaulbars.[35]

A long calm descended over the front.

THE SPREAD OF DEFEATISM

Politics again assumed center stage. The Union of Liberation, acting through its zemstvo wing, began to draft a proposal containing open constitutional demands. What was needed was some basis on which its disparate elements could unite. When the minister of interior learned of the preparations for the national zemstvo congress, his reaction was generally positive, and he foresaw no obstacle to such an assembly. Prince Mirsky's policy of trust initially encountered no dissent. The only resignation came from Prince Alexis A. Shirinsky-Shikhmatov,[36] the governor of Tver province, who explained to the emperor that he opposed the new course. Meanwhile, the press mounted a campaign against the government under the banner of protest against the conduct of the war. The lack of success, because the strength of the enemy had been underestimated and Russia's strength overestimated, created widespread indignation rather than regret. Forgetting that Poltava followed Narva by five years,[37] that England fought three years to crush ten thousand Boers who even lacked artillery, that Russia continued to deploy its main forces on the European frontier—ignoring all that, the average Russian was honestly outraged that in eight months his government could not take care of "some country called Japan."

The government's enemies exaggerated its shortcomings and distorted the facts and thus skilfully manipulated the passions of the naive and uninformed. How was it that a squadron could not be outfitted in eight months? How could it be that the second track of the Siberian railway still was not laid? A notorious war critic, A. Peshekhonov,[38] hypocritically feigning indignation, posed these questions in one of the issues of *Pravo*—as if he were unaware that a battleship cannot be readied for war "on a moment's notice," or that the second track of a five-thousand-mile railroad cannot be built rapidly when military trains are using the route day and night!

The Conference of the Opposition and Revolutionary Organizations of the Russian Empire convened in Paris between 30 September and 9 October [13-22 October 1904]. This was the first organized meeting between the so-called "constitutionalist" and acknowledged revolutionary parties. The participants included: Vasily Ya. Bogucharsky, Prince Peter D. Dolgorukov, Paul Miliukov, and Peter Struve, representing the Union of Liberation; Polish nationalists led by Roman Dmowsky; Polish and Lettish socialists; Armenian and Georgian socialists and federalists; Socialist Revolutionaries represented by Victor Chernov, Mark A. Natanson, and "Ivan Nikolaevich" (Azef); and finally the Finnish activists led by Konni Zilliacus, who was the principal force behind this convention.[39] The Social Democrats (including both Bolsheviks and Mensheviks), preoccupied by their intra-party struggle, were the only leftists not present.

The conference adopted resolutions calling for the "abolition of the autocracy," for its replacement by "a free democratic regime based on universal suffrage," and for the "right of national self-determination" for all the nationalities who populate the Russian Empire. After the conference adjourned, the revolutionary parties met separately without the "constitutionalists," resolved to adopt a definitely defeatist stance, and declared themselves in favor of the general use of terror. According to Miliukov, the liberal oppositionists knew nothing at the time of the convention's extension by the revolutionaries.[40]

THE SECOND SQUADRON BREAKS THROUGH THE NORTH SEA

On 28 September/11 October 1904, with the battle of Sha Ho still raging, the Second Squadron set sail for the Far East. The force included seven battleships, two armored and six light cruisers, and nine of the newest class of destroyers. It was numerically superior to the Port Arthur squadron, but four of the new battleships were inferior in quality to the *Tsesarevich* and *Retvizan*, and two of the battleships (*Sisoi Veliky* and *Navarino*) and two cruisers (*Admiral Nakhimov* and *Dmitry Donskoy*) were older than the ships then at Port Arthur. The squadron commander, Admiral Zinovi P. Rozhestvensky, personally doubted the fitness of his task force.[41] To be sure, as the Baltic squadron set out, five battleships and the cruisers *Bayan* and *Pallada* were sitting at Port Arthur. But the Kwantung Peninsula was a long way off. Fortunately, the squadron's coal requirements during the voyage were amply met as the result of an agreement with the Hamburg-America Line, a German shipping firm.

Passing through the North Sea on the night of 8-9/21-22 October, the squadron came upon a fleet of English fishing boats. The captains of some of the Russian ships thought that they were being attacked. Even now, no one has established beyond a doubt whether Japanese destroyers or submarines were in the area. More likely than not, the Russians were mistaken.[42] At any rate the squadron opened fire on the trawlers and sped off. The Russians were through the English Channel by the time the fishermen returned to their home port of Hull. The British press howled with indignation at this "attack on peaceable citizens," and the intensity of public outrage threatened to explode into an Anglo-Russian war. The Balfour government was in no mood for a war, but public opinion demanded satisfaction in some form or other. Therefore the government hurriedly dispatched a cruiser detachment in pursuit of the Second Squadron, which by then was pulling into the Spanish port of Vigo.

At that critical moment the German emperor told the Russian ambassador, Count Osten-Sacken, that Russia and Germany had to stand together in a conflict with England. Lamsdorf, the foreign minister, interpreted the suggestion as "an effort to weaken our friendly relations with France," but Nicholas replied: "I now favor an agreement with Germany and France. Europe must be delivered from the impudence of England." Accordingly on 16 October he wired William that "Germany, Russia, and France must become allies. Would you draw up such a treaty? As soon as we accept it, France must join her ally. This combination frequently has crossed my mind."

Had the British government, swept along by public opinion, presented Russia with demands that Nicholas regarded as unacceptable—demands that might have delayed the sailing of the Second Squadron or invoked reprisals against its commanders—and had England then tried to stop Rozhestvensky by force, that action would have constituted an attack on Russia by a European power. By the terms of the treaty of alliance France, then, would have been obliged to declare war on England. Under those circumstances Paris hardly could object if Germany also turned up on the side of the Franco-Russian combination. Meanwhile, the emperors of Russia and Austria were negotiating a [secret] declaration to supplement the agreement of 1897. The new agreement committed the two countries to neutrality if either were attacked by "a third party." For Russia the "third party" was England; for Austria it was Italy.[43]

However, on 17-30 October London readily accepted the Russian government's offer to refer the dispute to arbitration by an international commission under the terms of the Hague convention. England wisely refrained from attempting to delay the Second Squadron, and the urgency of a Russo-German accord passed. When the kaiser stipulated that the terms of the alliance be kept secret from France until the treaty was signed, Nicholas would not agree. An exchange of correspondence over the next two months finally concluded with the project being dropped. "This is the first failure that I personally have experienced," wrote William in a pique to Bülow.[44]

The Second Squadron resumed its voyage. The main body of the fleet sailed around Africa, but some of the ships proceeded by way of the Suez Canal. On 16 December Rozhestvensky reached the port of St. Mary on the island of Madagascar. There he learned that Port Arthur had fallen. That raised the question of whether the expedition should continue on to the Pacific or return to the Baltic.

THE ZEMSTVO CONGRESS OF NOVEMBER 1904

After Sha Ho, public attention in Russia focused on domestic issues. The war was discussed only for the purpose of criticizing the government's management of it. Prince Mirsky suggested that the zemstvo leaders allow him to see the agenda of their proposed congress, and he recommended that Nicholas permit the meeting to take place. The emperor was well aware, however, that notorious liberal oppositionists were promoting the congress and that the selection of delegates was "rigged" to favor the organized leftists. Therefore, counter to the advice of his minister, Nicholas insisted that the congress be postponed for three or four months, until the early months of 1905. During the interim, the provincial zemstvo assemblies were to elect genuine representatives to replace the nominees of a few self-appointed factions.[45] By then the zemstvo men were gathering in the capital. The minister of interior informed them that although their convention was prohibited, they could assemble "privately" and he would "look through his fingers." On 2 November a group of zemstvo constitutionalists met in Moscow and agreed that "the absence of official permission only frees our hands" and that the congress still would be a bona fide assembly. The meetings began in St. Petersburg on 6 November 1904, and the delegates took the precaution of holding each session in a different place. One bewildered delegate wanted to know what was up—"we supposedly were summoned with His Majesty's approval, but where is it?" The majority bloc swept aside all protests and set to work immediately to formulate a political declaration. The liberal composition of the congress stood the constitutionalists in good stead, and the assembly unanimously adopted resolutions calling for the abolition of states of emergency, and an end to administrative repression, the expansion of zemstvo liberties, amnesties, and equal rights without respect to social origin, nationality, or religion. On the basic question of limiting the supreme autocratic power the constitutionalists carried the day with a 60-38 majority. D.N. Shipov, the chairman of the congress, objected, however, and the minority's reservations also were recorded.[46]

The congress ended with the signing of the resolutions on 9 November. A delegation presented the document to Prince Mirsky, much to his embarrassment: an assembly, which he had permitted, was tossing the empire a program of constitutional and political reform bearing the imprimatur of the zemstvos! "Mirsky blundered by permitting the discussions," Grand Duke Constantine Constantinovich told his diary. His minister's actions displeased the tsar no end. For the time being, however, Nicholas refused Mirsky's resignation. Instead, he charged him to "straighten out" the government's policy.

The resolutions of the zemstvo congress provided the basis of a systematic and orchestrated campaign. All across Russia well-attended banquets featured political speakers and invariably concluded with the adoption of resolutions calling for a constitution. The crescendo penetrated the imperial study: from Chernigov the marshal of the nobility cabled the tsar personally the text of a constitutional resolution approved by the zemstvo assembly. Nicholas inscribed his reaction on the margin of the telegram: "I find this action insolent and tactless. The zemstvo assemblies, whose jurisdiction is clearly defined by law, have no business to concern themselves with matters of state."

THE MANIFESTO OF 12 DECEMBER 1904

By the first of November six weeks of "spring" had convinced Nicholas that Mirsky's policy was a failure. Designed to unite society and the government in a common struggle against a foreign foe, it was turning society against the war. Prince Trubetskoy's article may have been dictated by a patriotic concern for success in Russia's historic struggle, but after its publication the journal *Pravo* carried more and more propaganda openly demanding an end to the war and a general reorganization of the state system. New newspapers—the Marxist *Nasha zhizn* [Our Life] and the populist *Syn otechestva*

[Son of the Fatherland][47] —brought novel perspectives to Russia's legal press.

"Am I really home?" asked Prince Shirinsky-Shikhmatov, who had just returned from the front. "Part of our society has been seriously infected by the disease of doubt. . . . Are these the same people who only a few months ago stood up for Russia to a man? *Out there,* they do not doubt," he wrote, recalling the army in the field.[48]

All through November the government tried unsuccessfully to bring the anti-war movement under control. But in the Kingdom of Poland mobilization led to demonstrations and riots. In St. Petersburg on 28 November a crowd of several thousand demonstrators carrying red flags disrupted traffic on the Nevsky Prospekt for several hours.

Finally, early in December Nicholas convened a council of higher officials and grand dukes to consider the question of reforms.[49] The council examined a projected ukaz "on improving state administration," which subsequently became known, incorrectly, as the Manifesto of 12 December 1904.[50] The recommendations included an article that summoned public elements to participate in drafting legislation. However, fearing that this would be interpreted as the promise of a constitution, the emperor deleted it from the final version. Among the projected reforms the ukaz mentioned freedom of conscience and a revision of the laws governing the press. The ukaz was accompanied by an official warning that "zemstvo and municipal assemblies and all other types of organizations and societies must not exceed their prescribed limitations." That announcement attracted more attention than the ukaz itself. The provincial assembly in Moscow dramatically interrupted its session. Its leaders explained that a postponement was necessary because of the "distress" of its members upon reading the government's statement.

THE FALL OF PORT ARTHUR

The lull on the Manchurian front entered its third month, but vicious fighting raged around besieged Port Arthur. In an attack on 6-7 September General Nogi's forces seized several outlying forts, but the main defensive line remained intact. On 17 October Nogi unleashed another assault, this

time with the intention of capturing and presenting the
fortress to Emperor Mutsuhito on the anniversary of his
birth.[51] They suffered tremendous casualties but failed. The
Japanese knew that time was working against them—that the
Second Squadron was on its way, that the Manchurian Army
was growing stronger day by day, and that the embattled
defenders had great supplies of food and ammunition. Therefore, oblivious of the cost, they repeatedly hurled themselves
at the fortress and simultaneously tunneled deep under a
cluster of forts north of the old city.

On 13 November Nogi began a new assault; it lasted ten
days and cost Japan 22,000 men. In hand-to-hand combat
in the southeastern sector the Russians literally threw the
Japanese troops off the tops of the hills. On 22 November,
however, the attackers achieved a major victory when they
captured High Hill—203-meter Hill—northwest of the city.
From that vantage they could look down on the broad waters
of the inner harbor. In the next few days Japanese artillery
destroyed the remnants of the First Pacific Squadron. Thus
perished *Retvizan, Pobeda, Poltava, Peresvet, Bayan, Pallada.*
By then most of the crew of each ship was fighting on the
land. Ships that survived the bombardment were scuttled in
shallow water. Only *Sevastopol* put to sea. After repelling
numerous torpedo attacks, the ship exploded on a mine and
sank in blue water as Port Arthur was falling.[52] On 2 December
a Japanese shell killed General R.I. Kondratenko, the most
stalwart leader of the Port Arthur defense. The Japanese
breached the northeastern defenses, which were the strongest,
by digging under and attacking over the fortifications. They
gained the first of the forts in that sector on 18 December,
and with that the fall of the fortress seemed inevitable.

Nevertheless, the next day both attackers and defenders
were astonished when General Stessel, the garrison commander, offered to discuss terms of surrender with General Nogi.
The epic defense of Port Arthur was cut short by an act of
cowardice.[53] The garrison was still strong enough and had
enough supplies to hold out for another two or three weeks
or even a month. Of the 45,000 men surrendered with Port
Arthur, 28,000 were fit to bear arms; the hospitals held 13,000
sick and wounded. The toll for the victorious Japanese was
92,000 men killed, wounded, and diseased.[54]

General Roman Kondratenko

All through the summer in Russia the fall of Port Arthur had been expected weekly. Then the attitude changed, and Russians grew used to the fact that the fortress held out by some miracle. Coming as it did in the midst of quiet, the capitulation resounded through the country like a thunderbolt. Port Arthur seemed to symbolize the whole Far Eastern policy. "The pitiful remnants of our conquering legions laid down their arms at the feet of the victor," wrote *Nashi dni* [Our Days] with unconcealed malice that differed little from the tone of *Osvobozhdenie*. At that point the details of the disaster were unknown. The general impression was that General Stessel had fulfilled his duties to the end, for in a telegram to the emperor he had written: "Judge us, but be merciful .... The men are reduced to shadows."

"And what about the Russian people?" asked Suvorin in a penetrating essay. "Have they or have they not grown up to a consciousness of the fatherland, its honor, glory, and happiness? Have they matured to a comprehension of our problems in the Far East, of the importance of the Great Siberian Railway, and of our need to reach the open sea? Are we or are we not a great people? Is it possible that we have exhausted all our resources—is Port Arthur a mountain that has tumbled down and crushed us? I only ask—ask like one insignificant blade of grass in this great Russian tsardom."

The emperor was in the southwest bidding farewell to troops bound for the front, when he received the report of the surrender. He returned to the capital and on 1 January 1905 he issued the following order to the army and navy:

Port Arthur has fallen into the hands of the enemy. Peace upon your remains and eternal honor to you unforgettable Russians fallen in the defense of Port Arthur! You fell far from your motherland in the cause of your Emperor. . . . Peace upon your ashes, and may your everlasting memory remain always in our hearts.

Glory to the living! May God heal your wounds, cure your illnesses, and grant you the strength and patience to endure your trials.

My brave soldiers and sailors! Do not let this misfortune discourage you. Our enemy is brave and powerful. The struggle against him, which takes place ten thousand versts from the source of our strength, is unparalleled and arduous. But Russia is mighty. Her thousand-year history has witnessed many desperate hours when the trials were even more difficult and the danger even more dreadful, yet each time she emerged from the struggle with new vigor and new might . . . .

Together with all of Russia, I believe that our hour of victory will come, and that the Lord God will bless my precious regiments and ships in their united struggle to crush the enemy for the honor and glory of our motherland.

CHAPTER TEN

RUSSIA'S GATHERING STRENGTH

The first year of the war was ending. It had been a year of disappointments, partly because only a handful comprehended the real problems of waging the struggle. The navy had suffered the cruelest blows; the army was untouched. By the beginning of 1905 about 300,000 men were concentrated in Manchuria. The Siberian railroad was handling fourteen trains a day in each direction compared to just four at the beginning of the war. The war created scarcely any economic or financial problems. The 1904 harvest was plentiful, and industrial production was rising again. Tax revenues flowed at peacetime rates; the gold reserve of the State Bank increased during 1904 by 150,000,000 rubles[1] and more than covered the paper in circulation. Military expenditure in the first year of the war —about 600,000,000 rubles—was covered partly by cash on hand in the treasury (the budgetary surpluses of previous years) and partly by bonds. Both French and German investors heavily over-subscribed to Russian loans.[2] Russia's credit stood high: St. Petersburg borrowed at a rate of 5-6 percent, whereas Japan, despite its many victories, had to borrow at a rate of 7-8 percent.

Time was working in Russia's favor. During the second year of the war, the vitality of the stronger organism would make itself felt—and Russia was the stronger both militarily and financially. Japan had unleashed its energies earlier and still was ahead, but Russia was beginning to catch up. Only one difficulty loomed: in February the army that besieged Port Arthur would join the others at the front and give Japan temporary superiority on the battlefield. By spring or summer, however, a proportionate effort by both sides would tip the scale in favor of Russia. Even those who hoped against that development recognized its inevitability: "If the Russian army defeats the Japanese, which is not as impossible as it may

appear at first glance, then inexorably liberty will be overwhelmed by the clamor and peal of hurrahs and bells across
a triumphant empire," wrote "H. O-V" in *Osvobozhenie*.[3]
Only sabotage in the rear of the Russian army, only civil disturbances in Russia could prevent such a conclusion to the
war.

Despite intense political agitation among intelligentsia and
zemstvo circles, nothing seemed to portend a major revolutionary upheaval. In January 1905 *Osvobozhdenie* somewhat over-
confidently tallied the forces of the Liberation movement: We
have "the whole intelligentsia and part of the people; all the
zemstvos, all the press, part of the municipal dumas, and all
the corporations (lawyers, physicians, and other professions).
All of Finland is for us.... Oppressed Poland and the Jewish
population languishing within the Pale are for us."[4] The empire's non-Russian population was the most openly dissatisfied
with the system. The policy of russification exacerbated minority discontent, especially among the Jews who were the
most painfully aware of their deprivation of rights.[5] Even so,
the first blow did not come from that quarter.

JAPANESE MONEY AND RUSSIAN DISCORD

Civil turmoil in Russia was as essential to Japan as oxygen,
and without question Japan was willing to pay dearly for it.
Did the opportunity present itself to the Japanese government?
To what extent did Japan finance disorder in Russia? In
1904-5 Russian society would have scoffed at such questions.
Now they no longer appear so unreasonable. Nevertheless one
must admit that foreign gold did not inspire the revolution.
Men utterly devoted to the revolution, men willing to give
their lives for that cause, were not revolutionists for the sake
of money, whatever the source. But foreign money was instrumental to some degree in bringing on the revolution. Some
of the regime's native enemies did not spurn the assistance of
Russia's foreign enemies.

A leader of the Socialist Revolutionary Battle Organization,
Boris Savinkov, reminisced openly about one such instance in
1904-5:[6] "From Konnii Zilliankus [Konni Zilliacus], a member of a Finnish revolutionary party, the Central Committee
learned that he received a contribution of one million francs

from a group of American millionaires for the cause of the Russian revolution, on condition that the money be devoted to arming the people, and that it be distributed equally among all revolutionary parties, regardless of programs. The Central Committee accepted the money and gave the Terrorist Brigade [Battle Organization] 100,000 francs. In the spring of 1906 *Novoe vremia* reported that the contribution did not come from Americans, but from the Japanese government. Konni Zilliankus denied this, and the Central Committee had no reason to disbelieve him."[7]

That was not the only contribution. Although allusions to considerably larger sums never were documented, one must remember that neither the donors nor the recipients had any interest in publicity. The British journalist E.J. Dillon, an outspoken critic of the tsarist government, maintained in his book *The Eclipse of Russia* that it was "an indisputable fact" that Japan distributed substantial funds to Russian revolutionaries "of every persuasion." Baron R.R. Rosen, the former Russian ambassador to Tokyo, also testified to that effect in his memoirs.[8] Those were the circumstances in which a labor movement of unrivaled proportions erupted suddenly in St. Petersburg.

FATHER GAPON, THE WORKERS' DEMAGOGUE

Social Democratic organizations had been active among the capital's labor force for about ten years. Even though their adherents formed only a minority among the working men, their numbers were considerable. The Zubatov organizations made absolutely no headway in Petersburg until the fall of 1903, when the Assembly of St. Petersburg Factory Workers was formed. Its leader was Father George Gapon, a priest originally assigned to the deportation jail.[9] Gapon was an extraordinary demagogue and quite unscrupulous to boot. His true convictions remain buried forever; he seems simply to have been swept along by events and dominated by the social environment in which he found himself. An enormous difference existed between Gapon and Zubatov. Zubatov told the workers that the government was not the enemy but the indispensable ally of the working class; Gapon used his official position to spread an entirely different kind of propaganda.

"Little by little Gapon began to contact the more socially conscious workers . . . men who had passed through the [S.D.] party school, but who for one reason or another had not joined any party. Cautiously, but with remarkable single-ness of purpose, he attracted to himself a close circle of sup-porters . . . . His plan was to discover some way to stir up the mass of workers who had not fallen under the influence of the conspiratorial activists."[10] At first he acted with "restraint and care," but by the end of November 1904 he was subjecting the Assembly of St. Petersburg Factory Workers to a program of "systematic propaganda." Gapon attempted to forge an alliance with the left intelligentsia. He promised to prepare the workers for their political debut, but he had to wait, he said, "for some external event; first, let Arthur fall."[11] So little did General Ivan A. Fullon, the governor of St. Peters-burg, suspect Gapon's real intentions that early in December 1904 he spoke at the opening of a new branch of the society and expressed the wish that the workers "always gain the upper hand over the capitalists."

News of the fall of Port Arthur reached the capital on December 21st. On the 28th, immediately after the Christmas holiday, 280 members of the "Gapon society" met and de-cided to go into action. On 29 December 1904 a workers' committee at the Putilov Iron Works, which was engaged in defense work, demanded that the administration fire a fore-man who, they alleged, had dismissed four workers without cause. On 3 January the entire work force struck the factory. The workers' demands already had increased, though they still were economical and not political in nature: an eight-hour workday and a minimum wage. The Assembly of Factory Workers immediately took control of the strike, and its repre-sentatives, headed by Gapon, negotiated with the factory administrators. They also organized the Putilov strike com-mittee and started a fund to assist the strikers. The organiza-tion at that point seemed to have ample financial resources.

By January 5th several thousand workers were striking. In reporting the event to the emperor, V.N. Kokovtsov, the finance minister, noted the economic impossibility of the demands and the harmful role of Gapon's society. That very same evening at a meeting attended by Social Democrats Gapon's organization formulated the movement's political program. Under vague and ill-defined but nevertheless potent slogans—"The Struggle for Justice," "For the Workers' Cause," and the like—the society summoned the workers of the capital to a general strike. The rapid success of the movement indicated that the ground had been well prepared. With that resolution Gapon and his associates suddenly and sharply switched the movement to the political track.

On 6 January twenty-two representatives of Gapon's Assembly drafted a petition to the tsar. On the same day a bizarre incident occurred during the blessing of the waters of the Neva in front of the Winter Palace. During the salute, one of the guns in the battery fired a case-shot. Although neither the emperor nor any of the gathered dignitaries were injured, a policeman was wounded by shrapnel and several palace windows were broken. Rumors immediately spread about an attempted assassination, but an investigation subsequently established a simple case of negligence by someone. That stray shot, however, stimulated the mood of uneasiness and tension. The newspapers made their last appearance on 7 January, for on that day the strike spread to the press. Then the idea of a march to the Winter Palace seized the mass of excited workers.

Gapon and his close associates conceived the idea of a march, and Social Democrats helped compose the petition. That fact alone indicated the fallacy of a "popular impulse to approach the tsar." The content of the petition clearly testified to its socialist origins. Gapon's primitive demagoguery served as the introduction to patent Social Democratic slogans. The opening statements recalled the difficult life of the working people in words that every worker could understand. The rhetoric gradually increased: "We are being pushed deeper and deeper into an abyss of poverty, injustice, and ignorance . . . . We asked [our employers] for little: we seek only what is indispensable to life, those things without which life is nothing but penal servitude . . . . Can one live under such circumstances? Would it not be better for all of us, the toilers of Russia, to die and allow only the capitalists (who exploit the working class) and the bureaucrats (who rob the state and plunder the people) to live and enjoy themselves?"

Then came the demands: "Order immediately that the representatives of our Russian land assemble . . . . Order the election of a constituent assembly on the basis of universal, secret, and equal suffrage. That is our chief request; in it and on it is based everything else; it is the basic and only salve for our wounds . . . ." The petition next listed thirteen points, including the grant of all civil liberties, equality without respect to religion or national origin, ministers "responsible to the people," a political amnesty, and even "the abolition of indirect taxes." The conclusion of the petition read: "Order these measures and swear to fulfill them . . . . If you do not so order and do not respond to our pleas, we shall die here on this square before your palace."[12]

The Russian correspondent of the Paris daily *Humanité* wrote excitedly on 8/21 January that "the resolutions of the liberal banquets and even the zemstvos pale before those which the workers' delegation will try to submit to the tsar tomorrow." And indeed the danger caught the authorities by surprise. The political character of the movement emerged only on the 7th, but no newspapers were being published. Thus Kokovtsov learned of the impending event only on the evening of the 8th, when he was summoned to an urgent meeting at the ministry of internal affairs. The governor of the city hoped to the last moment that Gapon would "take care of the whole affair"!

BLOODY RECEPTION IN ST. PETERSBURG

The threat of a march to the palace by 100,000 people bearing a revolutionary petition confronted the government with a difficult problem. To allow the demonstration would have meant to capitulate without a fight. However, the state's police apparatus was ill-prepared. The gendarmery was more accustomed to catching individuals than to preventing mass demonstrations. This deficiency of the police—already evident in 1903 during the riots in Zlatoust, the Kishinev pogrom, and the disorders in Odessa, Kiev, and elsewhere—became obvious once again in January in St. Petersburg. How was it possible, suddenly on January 8th, to prevent a mass march scheduled for the morrow? In France when authorities of the Third Republic wanted to prevent demonstrations, they rounded up hundreds (even thousands) of suspected leaders twenty-four hours in advance. But in St. Petersburg individual policemen, swallowed up by the teeming masses of the workers' quarters, were absolutely powerless. Moreover, because of the speed with which the movement had developed, the only name the authorities had was that of Gapon. The only way to prevent the crowd from occupying the center of the city was to use cordons of troops to seal off the main thoroughfares that led from the working-class districts to the Winter Palace.

On the night of 8 January official proclamations went up throughout the city. Issued in the name of the governor, they announced that marches were forbidden and warned that it was dangerous to participate in them. The big presses were not working, however. Consequently only small nondescript posters could be printed in the office of the city's governor.

Meantime, the leaders of the movement spent the 8th driving around the city to countless workers' meetings to rally the people to the march on the Winter Palace. Where Gapon was uncertain of his audience, he reassured them by claiming that there was no danger, that the tsar would accept the petition, and that everything would be fine. Where the temper of the audience was more revolutionary, Gapon promised that if the tsar refused their demands, "then we will have no tsar!" —and the assembled workers shouted their approval. "Social Democracy is emerging," wrote Trotsky in his history of 1905.[13] "Meeting hostility, it quickly adapts to the audience and wins it over. Its slogans are taken up by the masses and emblazoned on petitions."

The intelligentsia, like the government, was taken by surprise. They made an effort to persuade the ministers to "avoid bloodshed." Witte was noncommital—"he washed his hands," as *Osvobozhdenie* put it. Assistant Minister of Internal Affairs General K.N. Rydzevsky told the delegation in most reasonable terms that it ought to appeal to the workers not the government: no unlawful demonstration, no danger of bloodshed. But of course the radical intelligentsia hardly could talk workers out of a demonstration which had the intelligentsia's wholehearted approval.

Partly to reassure the more moderate workers and partly to camouflage the true nature of the demonstration from the police and soldiers, Gapon and other leaders recommended that marchers in the front ranks carry icons and portraits of the tsar. That subterfuge apparently was unnecessary in the more progressive districts of the city.

January 9th was a Sunday. Several processions of workers, all scheduled to arrive at the Winter Palace by two o'clock, set out from their districts in the morning. Some of the columns numbered several thousand. The entire body of marchers totaled around 300,000.

One line of march led across the Obvodny Canal to the Narva Gate. There a line of soldiers blocked the way. Despite warnings, the crowd moved forward raising placards that appealed, "Soldiers! Do Not Shoot at the People!" First the troops fired a blank volley. The workers' ranks wavered, but the leaders pressed on, singing and luring the crowd after them. Then came a second volley, this time with live ammunition. Several dozen people were killed and wounded. Gapon fell to the ground—rumor had it that he was killed—but his aides quickly threw him over a fence and he disappeared to safety. The crowd fled home in panic. With minor variations that scene was repeated at several other points: the marchers approached a cordon of troops, refused to disperse, stood fast when blanks were fired, and scattered only when the soldiers used real bullets. Because the cordon was not continuous, isolated groups managed to cross the River Neva and were fired on. Groups of workers mingled with the usual Sunday pedestrians. The small clusters that formed were dispersed by cossacks or musketry. Barricades flying red flags sprang up on Vasilievsky Island, but they were defended lightly. The movement was crushed. Feverish excitement gripped the city until late that night. The tension subsided only after two or three days.

Rumors immediately multiplied the number of victims. An official report eventually set the toll at 130 dead and several hundred wounded. Had the crowd managed to seize the center of the city, the casualties probably would have been much greater. The number of victims was immaterial: what mattered was that a massive popular movement opposed to the government had clashed with troops in the streets of the capital. Undoubtedly the leaders who implied that the movement was not revolutionary and not hostile to the tsar had deceived some of the demonstrators. But equally clear was the fact that a vast number of workers had responded unexpectedly to revolutionary appeals. It appeared then that an ulcer had been lanced on January 9th, and it revealed that not only the intelligentsia but also the "simple people," or at least those in the cities, had flocked in substantial numbers to the banners of the enemies of the regime.

The 9th of January was a "political earthquake." Supporters of the government, understandably, vociferously criticized the government's handling of the affair—that corresponded to the rules of any political struggle. But many of the government's supporters also contended that the authorities had made a fatal error on 9 January—and that is hardly correct historically. Since the government considered it impossible to submit and agree to a constituent assembly demanded by a mob led by revolutionary agitators, no other outcome was possible. Submission before a belligerent mob leads either to the breakdown of all authority or to even worse bloodshed. Of course, with a more effective police force "preventive measures" might have been taken and there would have been no demonstration at all. But by the time the authorities finally realized the seriousness of the situation on the evening of 8 January, it was already too late for prevention.

Enemies of the regime later wrote that all the emperor "had to do was greet the crowd and accept just one of its requests" (namely the demand for a constituent assembly), and with that "the entire throng would have knelt before him." Nothing could have been farther from the truth. George Plekhanov's comment in *Iskra* (18 January) was far more honest: "In crowds of thousands the workers planned to gather before the Winter Palace and *demand* that the tsar appear personally on the balcony to accept their 'petition' and 'swear' that the people's demands would be met. In just such a manner did the heroes of the Bastille and the Parisians who marched on Versailles turn to their 'good king' [in 1789]. They cheered the monarch who showed himself to the mob, as the people demanded, but their 'hurrahs' carried the death sentence of the monarchy."[14] The 9th of January 1905 was a sad and, indeed, a tragic day, but it was not as shameful a day for the Russian monarchy as those events of 5-6 October 1789 in France, which *Iskra* recalled.

The events in Petersburg stunned Russia and Europe. The intelligentsia interpreted the events as a reproach of sorts in that the workers had outstripped the intelligentsia in the radicalness of their demands. The public regarded the intellectuals as too timid. The Social Democrats, who always had maintained that the Russian revolution would come through the efforts of the working class, were especially jubilant. "A decade of Social Democratic efforts has paid off historically," proclaimed *Iskra*. "Social-Democratic workers were influential enough in the ranks of the Petersburg workers to guide this uprising along a Social-Democratic course and to bring the temporary organizers of the movement under the permanent ideological leadership of the proletariat—under Social Democracy."

CONFUSION AT THE TOP

Panic overwhelmed the government. Governor Fullon and, later, Prince Mirsky had to resign their positions. The tsar replaced Fullon with Dmitry F. Trepov, the chief of police in Moscow.[15] Trepov, deeply devoted to the emperor, was a firm man, fearless and full of common sense even though he lacked experience with political problems. Throughout the period of upheaval just beginning, he remained the emperor's faithful aide.

The tension in St. Petersburg did not subside immediately. The strike ended gradually; the first newspapers began to appear on 15 January. Disturbances erupted in a few other cities, notably Riga where the most serious clashes occurred. From Paris General Cherep-Spiridovich's Latin-Slavic Agency cabled that the Japanese were boasting openly about the disturbances created by their money, but neither *Novoe vremia* nor *Grazhdanin* wanted to believe it.

Two of the sovereign's closest advisors, Kokovtsov and Ermolov, the ministers of finance and agriculture, sent him their advice. In a memorandum of 11 January Kokovtsov warned that neither police nor military power could restore the situation. "Your Majesty must speak .... Now that the streets of the capital have been stained with blood, the people will not listen to the voice of a minister or to all of the ministers combined." A.S. Ermolov wrote even more forcefully on the 17th: "Agitation continues and assassinations are being prepared. The disturbances have spread to a majority of the cities, and everywhere they have to be suppressed with troops .... What will happen if they spread to the villages? If the peasants revolt, what forces and what troops will suppress the new Pugachev-style uprising? And are the troops to be trusted?"

The emperor suggested that the ministers convene, and a meeting was held on 18 January under Witte's chairmanship. The ministers proposed a manifesto that would express his majesty's sorrow and shock and declare that he was not duly informed of the seriousness of events in St. Petersburg. Witte even suggested a statement that the soldiers "were not acting on his orders," but Count Dmitry M. Solsky countered that it was "impossible to admit that his majesty's troops could act without his order."[16] Nicholas rejected the idea of a manifesto. He had no desire to shift the blame to others, and he fully shared Count Solsky's opinion with regard to the troops. Instead, he charged Trepov to form a delegation of workers from the various factories. On 19 January he received the working men at Tsarskoe Selo and gave them his opinion of what had occurred: "You allowed yourselves to be deluded and deceived by traitors and enemies of your motherland. . . . Strikes and rebellious assemblies only incite the people to riots—disorder has compelled the government and will compel it to resort to military force, and that inevitably produces innocent victims. I know that the life of workers is not an easy one. A great deal must be improved and put into good order . . . . But to inform me of your needs in a rebellious mob is criminal."

Nevertheless Nicholas released 50,000 rubles to assist the families of the victims of January 9th, and he commissioned Senator N.V. Shidlovsky to form a committee that included elected worker representatives to clarify the needs of labor. The elections turned into political rallies: instead of discussing the needs of the workers, the assembled electors advanced a series of political demands, in particular the reinstatement of the "Gapon society." Consequently the Shidlovsky commission never got off the ground.

Once the term "constituent assembly" appeared in Gapon's petition, even the most moderate zemstvo men and newspapers, such as *Peterburzhskie vedomosti*, *Svet* [The Light], and *Novoe vremia* began to speak openly of a national assembly (a zemsky sobor). On the right only *Moskovskie vedomosti*, edited by V.A. Gringmut, eventually adhered to its former conservative line. Conservative and liberal philosophies clashed head on at a meeting of the Moscow provincial nobility on 22 January. The conservatives, led by the Samarin brothers, mustered a majority of 219-147 and held the upper hand. The assembly's resolution stood as an isolated protest against revolutionary pressures: "A war, a difficult war characterized by hitherto unseen stubbornness, has chained to itself all elements of the nation. But meanwhile, civil rebellion stirs the public and inflames the people . . . . Under such difficult circumstances is this the time to consider any kind of fundamental change in the Russian state structure? Let the storm of war pass, let the rebellion subside. Then, guided by your reigning right hand, Russia will find the way to a secure arrangement of its life . . . . Reign in full awareness of your power, O Autocratic Sovereign." As one might expect, *Novoe vremia* and *Russkii vestnik*, but even *Svet*, reviewed the address unfavorably as, of course, did newspapers farther to the left. At the Russian Club General Kireev and A.B. Vasiliev defended the idea of a zemsky sobor, as a uniquely Russian form of representation, against the idea of a constituent assembly. Their protagonist, Professor B.V. Nikolsky, opposed change in any form.

One after another the institutions of higher learning went on strike "until the convening of a constituent assembly." At St. Petersburg University junior instructors voted 87-4 to suspend classes, even before the students themselves had met. The protests of a few students had no effect. Several hundred of them wrote letters to newspapers urging that classes be continued, but the government itself decided to suspend all studies in higher education until the fall.

MURDER IN THE KREMLIN, CONCESSIONS IN THE CAPITAL

On 4 February 1905 the bomb of the SR terrorist Ivan Kaliaev ended the life of Grand Duke Sergei Alexandrovich.[17] He was, with his brother Grand Duke Vladimir Alexandrovich, regarded as the leader of "the party of resistance." For many years Sergei Alexandrovich had held the position of governor-general of Moscow, and he was indeed a man of strong conservative convictions. At the same time he was capable of bold initiatives. Thanks to his support, Sergei Zubatov was able to organize the monarchist labor unions. The grand duke's death was a heavy blow to the Russian government. Rumors that terrorists were planning to assassinate the tsar himself prevented Nicholas from going to Moscow for his uncle's funeral. Too much depended on his life in those rebellious days. The tsarevich was not yet one year old, and the emperor's brother was too young and too inexperienced in affairs of state.[18]

Father Gapon, who had fled abroad, continually drafted appeals to violence, which even *Osvobozhdenie* ventured to print "only as a document."[19] One of Gapon's manifestoes began with a condemnation of "tsar-the-beast, ministers-the-hyenas," and the "dog-pack of officials." He then urged his followers: "Kill the ministers, the city governors, district police officers, policemen, police guards, gendarmes and spies, generals and officers who gave the orders to fire on you. Know that every measure is being taken to ensure that in time you will have real weapons and dynamite . . . . Refuse to go to war . . . . Rise in arms at the command of the military committee . . . . Destroy the water, gas, telephone, telegraph, and electric lines: horse-trams, street cars, and railroads . . . . We will crush the blood-thirsty spiders who infest the interior of our motherland (the foreign ones we do not fear)." Foreigners believed that a revolution was in progress, and French financiers refused to support a new Russian loan.

On 18 February 1905 the St. Petersburg evening papers carried an imperial manifesto summoning all loyal sons of the fatherland to the struggle against sedition. That manifesto was interpreted as a refusal to grant those reforms that were being demanded with mounting urgency. On the following morning, however, the papers printed an imperial rescript that had been sent to the new interior minister, Alexander G. Bulygin.[20] "I have decided," wrote Nicholas in the most significant part of the text, "to assemble the most trustworthy men, invested with the people's confidence and elected by them, to participate in the preliminary examination and consideration of legislative measures." The tsar was promising to convene representatives of the people in an advisory capacity. Simultaneously an imperial ukaz announced that any person or organization might submit proposals for governmental reform to the sovereign. "With the wave of his scepter the tsar has disarmed the rebellion," wrote Suvorin in *Novoe vremia*, adding that "this is the happiest day of my life." *Osvobozh-denie* had other ideas, however: "The white flag is a symbol of cowardice and weakness . . . . One only has to push with all his might and the wavering autocracy will come tumbling down."

SAN-DE-PU

As Petersburg boiled, major developments were occurring at the front. The three-month interruption of the fighting ended late in December, when General A.V. Mishchenko's cavalry brigade made a bold raid around the enemy's left flank to the port of Newchwang (Yingkou) about a hundred miles behind the front. Japanese reinforcements prevented the cossacks from tearing up the railroad, but Mishchenko nevertheless burned several large warehouses and returned with only light losses. The Russian high command planned to use the month before the appearance of General Nogi's army from Port Arthur to launch a decisive assault against the Japanese. At that time the armies were facing each other across a front of several miles. The eastern flanks of both armies stretched into mountainous terrain. The center along the Sha River was heavily fortified. The western flanks extended into the flat plain of the Liao River and its chief tributary, the Hun.

On 2 January, before the capital's newspapers had resumed publication, Grippenberg's Second Manchurian Army mounted an offensive in the west and enveloped the Japanese left flank. At that point the Russian army enjoyed a decisive numerical superiority over the Japanese, and the initial assault took the enemy by surprise. The battle, fought at temperatures of -20° C., cost about 12,000 Russian and 10,000 Japanese lives, but it produced no decisive result. The consensus of the military experts was critical of Kuropatkin, who ordered a retreat just as the Russians were gaining the upper hand. According to one military historian, "Kuropatkin for no good reason refused to fight."[21] Kuropatkin defended himself by arguing that the offensive was slow in getting started and that a continuation of the battle would have brought unnecessary losses.

The Second Army commander, General O.K. Grippenberg, was so angered by the order to retreat—"that order saved the

Japanese," he later told a newspaper—that he followed the
unusual course of requesting to be relieved of command for
reasons of "ill health." Replying to the tsar's telegraphed demand for "the whole truth," Grippenberg expressed his sincere conviction that no victory was possible under the present
commander-in-chief. He was permitted to return to St. Petersburg to report. With Grippenberg's departure from the army
the press entered the fray. *Novoe vremia* sided with Kuropatkin and labeled Grippenberg's resignation "a desertion." On
the other hand the prominent military expert, General M.I.
Dragomirov, vehemently defended the former commander of
the Second Army. The Third Army commander, General A.V.
Kaulbars, succeeded Grippenberg; General A.A. Bilderling,
soon to be replaced by General Batianov, replaced Kaulbars
at the head of the Third Army.[22]

Kuropatkin, meanwhile, continued to contemplate an offensive. However, the arrival of General Nogi's forces restored
the military balance in Japan's favor. By then over 600,000
soldiers on both sides faced each other along the front—
a number unequalled in the history of warfare, if one discounts
the semi-legendary battles of ancient times.

BLOODY WORK AT MUKDEN

In the middle of February the Japanese began an attack on
the Russian east flank and threatened a deep turning movement. Kuropatkin's forces successfully contained that assault,
but then the Russians discovered a massive Japanese offensive
developing rapidly on the plains west of Mukden. The main
attack seemed to be directed against the right flank. While
pinning the Russian center to its fortified positions south of
Mukden, the Japanese threatened to circle north of the city
and capture the railroad and thus cut Kuropatkin's line of
communications. At the same time the Japanese drove a wedge
between the center and left flank of the Russian front, between the Third and First Armies. Then they concentrated
on a huge encirclement to trap the Second and Third Manchurian Armies in a gigantic pocket around Mukden. The
Japanese pincers, having pushed the First Army into the
mountains to the east and therefore out of reach, threatened
to snap shut.

General Alexis Kuropatkin

Kuropatkin ordered the armies to retreat. In his war memoirs he wrote: "Had we retreated from Liaoyang a day later, Liaoyang would have become a Mukden for us; had we retreated from Mukden a day sooner, Mukden would have become another Liaoyang." The retreat from Mukden was far from satisfactory. The main forces of the Second and Third Armies did indeed escape the Japanese pincers, for when the trap closed, it held no Russian troops. Still, the losses were extremely heavy, and the Japanese took 30,000 prisoners. So badly mauled were the Second and Third Armies that they retreated not to Tiehling as planned but several miles farther north. General Linevich's First Army covered the retreat, and his losses were lighter. The Japanese were so exhausted by the battle that they could not pursue the retreating armies.

Mukden was an outright defeat for the Russian army. The general staff reported the loss of 89,500 men (including prisoners). That represented more than a quarter of the strength of the Manchurian armies. The same source set Japanese casualties at 67,500. The Russians were forced to retreat nearly a hundred miles. Even so, for Russia Mukden was neither a Sedan nor a Waterloo. The Russian army remained a formidable military force; the Japanese army, despite its victory, was practically exhausted. For the last time Japan had taken advantage of its lead in preparedness, and the Japanese commanders had failed to achieve decisive results. The description of Mukden as an unprecedented and shameful defeat was politically inspired to prove the incompetence of the Russian government. Russian society regarded Mukden as a logical episode in the general course of events—any other interpretation would have been surprising. The legal press, and not only *Novoe vremia*, began to discuss peace.

On 25 February 1905 the Japanese occupied Mukden. On 5 March the emperor published his decree announcing the dismissal of General Kuropatkin as commander-in-chief and the appointment of General Linevich in his stead. With great humility and selflessness Kuropatkin requested permission to remain with the army, even in the humblest position. Consequently the tsar appointed him to command of the First Manchurian Army. Thus Kuropatkin and Linevich exchanged places. "The soldiers idolized Kuropatkin to the very end," wrote *Novoe vremia*, and that was true—the former supreme commander had a deep personal concern for his men. Under his command the army always was well-fed and well-clothed. Still, as P.N. Krasnov observed in *Russkii Invalid* [The Russian Invalid], "Everything was done for the soldier's body but nothing for his spirit." Kuropatkin lacked the "divine spark" of a field commander, even though as events later proved, his theory of a strategic retreat according to the plan of 1812 was generally correct.

FERMENT IN THE CHURCH

The Imperial Ukaz of 12 December 1904 contemplated a series of reforms: a new press law, expansion of the rights of national minorities in the areas of culture and education, and religious freedom. Consideration of the latter led to projected legislation for the reform of the Russian Orthodox Church. Ecclesiastical leaders under the direction of Metropolitan Anthony of St. Petersburg proposed legislation to increase the independence of the church from the state. A memorandum drafted by thirty-two priests of the capital appeared on 17 March in *Tserkovnyi vestnik* [The Church Messenger]: "Only a freely self-governing church can express the fervor that burns in human hearts. How would it be if all the adherents of every sect large or small were free to take advantage of unregulated religious life, societies, and unions, while only the Orthodox Church, the custodian of the true Christian faith, remained deprived of the same freedom?" The letter concluded with a demand for a church council.

Constantine Pobedonostsev, the director-general of the holy synod, withdrew almost completely from his duties, avoided the meetings of the ministerial committee, and was overcome by a mood of gloom and futility. "I feel that a crowd gone mad is sweeping me along toward an abyss, which I see before me and from which there is no escape," he wrote to Witte, with whom he continued to maintain good relations. "I am unable to refute an entire ideology." The self-withdrawal of the powerful director-general eased the work of the reformists.

On 22 March the synod unanimously called for the restoration of the patriarchate and an all-Russian church council to

elect a new patriarch.[23] Under the synodal plan the synod itself would become an advisory body to the patriarch.
Churchmen assumed that the Metropolitan of St. Petersburg,
Anthony (Vadkovsky), would be elected. But objections to
this plan came not only from associates of the director-general but also from prominent theologians who earnestly espoused the restoration of self-governing parishes. "The church
must be revitalized, but its rejuvenation must be done correctly and not by repeating the autocratic procedures of
1721," wrote M.A. Novoselov. Criticizing the synod's decisions, he added: "Its haste is truly astonishing; it creates the
image of a 'St. Vitus dance' rather than a serious deliberation
of weighty and holy matters."

Confronted by these differences within the church, Nicholas on 31 March entered the following decision on the report
of the holy synod: "I consider it impossible to accomplish
such a great undertaking in the difficult times that currently
face us. So important a matter as a church council requires
tranquility and careful deliberation. I imagine that when the
propitious moment arrives, following the ancient example of
the Orthodox Emperors, I will put this project in motion and
convene a council of the All-Russian Church for the canon-
ical discussion of religious and church government affairs."

The emperor's decision on that matter did not prevent the
introduction of religious toleration. Although Nicholas had
favored this step since his early years on the throne, he had
been reluctant to act against the wishes of his teacher, Pobedonostsev (whose influence, incidentally, pertained mainly
to religious matters). On Easter Sunday, 17 April 1905, the
tsar issued his ukaz on religious toleration. The decree granted
every adult the right to profess any Christian teaching, it
restored to Old Believers and sectarians their places of worship, and it abolished all previous legislation which denied
those liberties. After the publication of this decree, tens of
thousands of peasants in the western provinces, who only formally were counted as Orthodox, returned to the Uniate
Church.[24]

THE SECOND SQUADRON: FROM MADAGASCAR TO INDO-CHINA

The Second Pacific Squadron, meanwhile, had been anchored
for over two months in the coastal waters of Madagascar.

Naval circles now acknowledged that the Russian fleet was weaker than the Japanese. A newspaper campaign, in which Captain Nicholas L. Klado[25] assumed the leading role, urged the creation of still a third squadron, this one to consist of the old battleship *Nikolai I*, the even older armored cruiser *Vladimir Monomakh*, and three coastal defense battleships designed for service in the Baltic. Admiral Rozhestvensky considered these reinforcements of dubious value because of their slow speeds. However, since his own squadron contained two or three vessels that were no faster, he could not object convincingly to their sailing. Thus the Third Squadron commanded by Rear-Admiral Nicholas I. Nebogatov sailed from Libau [in February].

The continuation of Rozhestvensky's mission posed considerable risk, but his return to the Baltic would have been interpreted as a Russian refusal to fight. Neither the tsar, nor the office of naval operations, nor Rozhestvensky himself wanted the responsibility for such a decision. With "trust in miracles," the squadron was not recalled. It concluded its long stay at Madagascar and resumed its voyage. Early in March it "disappeared without a trace." Then on 28 March the St. Petersburg telegraph office received the surprising report: Rozhestvensky's squadron with its full complement was passing through the Malacca Straits [off Singapore].

The news was sensational. The British, who had a better appreciation of the difficulties of Rozhestvensky's brilliantly executed voyage, were duly impressed. But even the Russians, consumed with projects, constitutions, and electoral laws, took time to recognize a great national achievement. Japanese securities plunged on the European exchanges. "Oh, if God would only grant us a victory, how Russia would take heart, how the smoke and fumes, the choking, the muddle and anarchy would disappear!" prayed Suvorin in *Novoe vremia*. Accordingly, leftists became alarmed at the possibility of a Russian victory that would upset their plans and calculations.

This bright moment was deceptive, however, for it was based on an unattainable hope of victory. The Second Squadron was much weaker, numerically and qualitatively, than the enemy's fleet. Without supporting bases its freedom of movement was restricted. Moreover its commander lacked confidence in its success. Still, the possibility of a Russian victory lived not only in Russia but also abroad. Bülow wrote to William II about it; President Roosevelt considered "the Russian squadron materially stronger" and thought that Japan could hope for victory only because of the fighting spirit and combat readiness of Admiral Togo's fleet.

Rozhestvensky cruised the coast of Indo-China for about a month. To avoid difficulties with England, the French government requested him to depart, but local French naval authorities showed genuine courtesy to their allies in the Russian fleet. Finally, on 26 April Nebogatov's Third Squadron joined Rozhestvensky at Van Fong Bay [near Camranh Bay]. Admiral Rozhestvensky used the occasion to issue his order to the fleet: "The Japanese are absolutely devoted to their emperor and their motherland; they do not tolerate dishonor and they die heroes. But we too have sworn our oaths before the throne of the Almighty. The Lord has strengthened our resolve and helped us overcome the hardships of a voyage such as the world has never seen. The Lord will strengthen our right hand. He will bless us so that we might fulfill our Sovereign's behest and cleanse with blood the bitter shame of our Motherland."

FROM INDO-CHINA TO OBLIVION

The Russian fleet, bound for its only port, Vladivostok (where there were two cruisers and a third under repair), had a choice of two routes. The longer led through the Pacific Ocean east of Japan; the shorter would take the fleet through the Korean Straits between Japan and the mainland. Admiral Rozhestvensky chose the second route. Because of the numbers and speed of the Japanese reconaissance force, the possibility of slipping undetected past Admiral Togo's battle fleet was practically nil. On 14/27 May the Russian squadron entered the Korean or Tsushima Straits. In heavy fog the Japanese nearly missed the fleet; their scouts, however, came upon the last ships in the Russian line. Togo immediately set out to intercept the Russian squadron.[26] From his flagship he hoisted the signal: "The fate of the Japanese Empire depends on the results of this engagement." This time the Japanese were not concerned with the safety of their ships—a victory, whatever the cost, would ensure that no new squadron would sail from Russian harbors for several years.

The superiority of the Japanese fleet began to tell as soon as the battle commenced. In less than an hour the first of several Russian battleships, the *Osliabia*, was sunk.[27] The two squadrons collided and then drifted apart. The battle raged until darkness. Toward nightfall, after heroic resistance, the last of the four new battleships sank—*Suvorov* [the flagship], *Borodino*, and *Aleksandr III*. Two of them were lost with full complements. Admiral Rozhestvensky, seriously wounded by a shell fragment, was transferred from the *Suvorov* to a destroyer.

Torpedo boats sank several more Russian ships during the night. By daybreak of 15/28 May only remnants of the Second Pacific Squadron were still afloat. Individual ships, heavily outgunned, perished one by one—*Svetlana*, *Admiral Ushakov*, and others. The destroyer *Bedovy*, carrying the wounded Rozhestvensky, surrendered. A superior Japanese force surrounded Admiral Nebogatov's detachment, the two old battleships of the line and the two coastal defense battleships, and the admiral surrendered his ships "to save," as he said, "two thousand young lives." Only the light cruiser *Almaz* and two destroyers reached Vladivostok safely; another cruiser, the *Izumrud*, ran aground on the rocks north of Vladivostok. Three other cruisers led by Admiral Oscar A. Enquist fled south and took refuge at Manila in the Philippines. The Russian fleet was utterly destroyed; the Japanese lost but a few [three] torpedo boats.[28] Although Russia's sailors displayed great heroism against hopeless odds, the enemy's superiority was insurmountable.

SPREAD OF THE REVOLUTIONARY MOVEMENT

Russian society reacted to the news of Tsushima with ill-concealed malevolence. Most of the public had grown accustomed to assess all war reports by their effect on the status of the government, as to whether they enhanced or diminished the government's prestige. The government itself was alleged to be following the same policy: "The war drags on only because a victory is needed, desperately needed, to save the autocracy," explained *Osvobozhdenie*. "For that reason Rozhestvensky's fleet sailed to its destruction, and for that same reason does Linevich's army fight and march toward

defeat(?)." For Nicholas the successful conclusion of this
historic struggle was the supreme goal. To Nicholas, then, the
Liberation movement was an obstacle to that vital end, for it
diverted the vast majority of the public into a struggle against
the government for the sake of a radical reorganization of the
entire system.

By that time the excitement of politics had spread to most
sections of society. A "Christian Brotherhood of Struggle"
was formed to illuminate and justify revolution from a religious
point of view. "We are fighting the most godless manifestation
of secular power—autocracy," declared its manifesto. The
symbolists had remained aloof from politics before the war,
and occasionally they had gone so far as to reprove the intelligentsia for its narrowmindedness. But now they too became
imbued with a mystical faith in revolution, and the symbolist
journal *Novyi put* began to adopt a harsher tone. The poet
Viacheslav Ivanov, writing on Tsushima, exclaimed: "Baptize
yourself in fire, Rus! Consume yourself in the flames . . . .
Helms are smashed in the hands of your leaders—The helms-
men of the tsar lead you only to heaven." Several organizations among the "free professions" formed a Union of Unions,
an alliance of the left wing of the Liberation movement's
public elements.[29] One of its principal leaders was Professor
Paul Miliukov, a participant in the Paris oppositionist conference of 1904 but better known at the time as a Russian
historian.

Miliukov's liberal Union called for universal, direct, equal,
and secret elections, and its program was adopted by the
zemstvo congress of April 1905. The zemstvo constitutionalists
worked out the convention's resolutions in advance in a series
of special meetings. Then the congress proclaimed them in the
name of all the zemstvos. The objections of separate groups
of zemstvo conservatives passed almost unnoticed. For example, twenty Moscow provincial assemblymen protested to no
avail the "undesirability of partisanship [party-ness] which
emerged in the private meetings in Petersburg and which is
loudly proclaimed in the all-zemstvo congress, even though
that does not represent the true state of affairs." Zemstvo
constitutionalists, of course, improperly staged those congresses, but it is undeniable that throughout the entire period
of revolutionary expansion those self-proclaimed spokesmen

encountered no notable resistance among the zemstvos. In general they reflected the spirit of the zemstvos, even though they gave it a more radical hue. The moderate elements organized later, but even then the Shipov group remained a minority in the zemstvo movement.[30]

NICHOLAS, BLOODY BUT UNBOWED

The battle of Tsushima impressed the world far more than the fall of Port Arthur. Its decisiveness was taken to indicate Japan's total victory in the war. In fact the Japanese had dominated the sea from the outset, and their control became absolute after the battles of 28 July and 1 August 1904. Tsushima therefore changed nothing as far as the war in Manchuria itself was concerned. Nevertheless, the disaster at Tsushima shocked the emperor, who had believed in Russia's victory to the last moment—"The news weighs heavily on my soul; it is painful and sad," he wrote in his diary on 18 May. The destruction of the fleet again raised the question of whether it was possible to pursue the war. Those closest to Nicholas began to doubt it.

Tsushima also created a new atmosphere in foreign capitals. Washington began to perceive Japan's triumphs as a threat to American interests. Alarming reports from St. Petersburg convinced the German emperor that the Russian monarchy and even the tsar's life stood in mortal danger. On 21 May/3 June William wrote to Nicholas that Tsushima "ends the chances for a decided turn of the scales in your favour." The war has been unpopular for a long time, he continued. "Is it compatible with the responsibility of a Ruler to continue to force a whole nation against its declared will to send its sons to be killed by hetacombs only for his sake? Only for his way of conception of National honour? ... National honour is a very good thing in itself, but only in the case that the whole of the Nation *itself* is determined to uphold it with all the means possible."[31] The kaiser then advised the tsar to make peace.

On that same day William summoned the American ambassador and told him that the situation in Russia was so serious that "the news [of Tsushima] will—when published at Petersburg—create such a commotion that grave disorders, even revolution, are to be expected, if not attempts on the Zar's

life." The kaiser, therefore, requested that President Roosevelt convey through the American ambassador in Petersburg
his offer to Russia to mediate.[32]

On 23 May/5 June Roosevelt cabled his ambassador, George
von L. Meyer, and instructed him to see the tsar personally.
Meyer went to Tsarskoe Selo on 25 May, arriving around 2:00
p.m. It was the empress's birthday and, not wishing to disturb
the family's celebration, the ambassador entered by a side
door and requested to speak to the emperor on an urgent
matter. Despite the inopportune timing, Nicholas agreed to
receive Meyer. The ambassador read Roosevelt's instructions
and spoke at length about the necessity of a quick peace
agreement. Nicholas remained silent for almost the entire
discourse, responding only to Meyer's contention that the
conclusion of peace would be easier while the enemy had not
yet set foot on Russian soil. At the conclusion Nicholas
agreed to peace negotiations on the condition that Japan also
give its preliminary assent. The tsar insisted that no basis be
created for the impression that Russia had sued for peace. The
ambassador reported to Roosevelt by telegram and noted that
he was deeply impressed by the tsar's self-possession.[33]

Also on 25 May Nicholas presided over a council of war
attended by the Grand Dukes Vladimir Alexandrovich and
Alexis Alexandrovich, Minister of War Victor V. Sakharov,
Minister of Marine Feodor K. Avellan, Minister of the Imperial
Court Vladimir B. Frederichs, Commander of the Amur District General N.I. Grodekov, Generals Grippenberg, C.C. Roop,
P.L. Lobko (the State Comptroller) and Admirals Alekseev
and F.V. Dubasov. The emperor posed several concrete questions: Can Kamchatka, Sakhalin, and the mouth of the Amur
River be defended without a fleet? What would be the effect
of a Russian victory in Manchuria on the outcome of the war
in those remote areas? Should Russia enter into negotiations—
if only to discover Japan's demands?

Two men, Grand Duke Vladimir and Admiral Alekseev,
spoke strongly in favor of peace. The latter was very depressed: "The spirit of the army has been undermined," he argued.
General Grippenberg could only recall his old grievances—
"Your Majesty, victory was ours at San-de-pu, if only the
commander-in-chief . . . ." Everyone agreed that Kamchatka
and Sakhalin could not be defended without a fleet.

Admiral Dubasov was the first to speak against a peace predicated on defeat. In January he publicly had recommended that Russia end the war,[34] but now he argued that Russia must not conclude the war at Mukden and Tsushima. After Dubasov's energetic speech, Sakharov and Frederichs also spoke against peace, as did Roop who added, however, that the war could not be continued without convening a national assembly. The meeting ended without a decision. The subject of war or peace remained open, but Nicholas gave his consent to negotiations, if only to determine Japan's conditions.

In a note of 26 May/8 June transmitted simultaneously to St. Petersburg and Tokyo President Roosevelt suggested "that the time has come when in the interest of all mankind [he] must endeavour to see if it is not possible to bring to an end the terrible and lamentable conflict now being waged." Two days later Japan agreed to negotiate, and on the 29th Roosevelt's note was published in Russia. After a brief argument over the site of the conference, Washington, D.C., finally was chosen. Then, because of the unbearable summer heat, the conference moved to the northern sea resort of Portsmouth, New Hampshire.

During this same period, a Franco-German quarrel over Morocco nearly led to war. However, the French council of ministers chose to back down. Delcassé resigned on 24 May, and his successor, Maurice Rouvier, agreed to an international conference at Algeciras to settle the Moroccan question.

DEFEATISTS AND OPTIMISTS

If Admiral Dubasov was indignant that Russia might conclude the war with Mukden and Tsushima, most of Russian society waited precisely for that. Even those who drew no satisfaction from defeat felt that something would be gained in the way of greater freedom. Demands to end the war echoed everywhere. Persons who protested against peace found themselves attacked and slandered. General Kuropatkin demonstrated great civic courage at that moment. On learning that public groups in Moscow were demanding an end to the war, Kuropatkin sent the following telegram to Prince P.N. Trubetskoy, the marshal of nobility: "If Muscovites cannot find within themselves the strength to send us their best sons to help us

speedily subdue the enemy, then at least let them not hinder
us from pursuing our duty to its victorious conclusion on the
fields of Manchuria."

"The depths of servility . . . a malicious prank . . . with
such a patently phoney lackey statement Kuropatkin finally
has destroyed himself in the eyes of zemstvo-Russia," proclaimed *Osvobozhdenie*. Kuropatkin's sincerity, of course, was
beyond question. On that same day (26 May) he wrote to
Witte: "Even now, after the destruction of Rozhestvensky's
squadron, Russia must go on with the struggle; we should not
allow Japan's naval victory to alarm us excessively, because
the Japanese have controlled the sea throughout the war . . . .
We are stronger on the land than ever before, and we now
have the opportunity to be victorious in new and bloody
engagements. By their extreme efforts the Japanese have
strained themselves . . . . They have peaked. We, however,
only have begun to make our strength felt." The general wrote
that he personally would welcome a new battle, for he had
confidence in the success of Russian arms. "And is it not
possible to instill into the Russian intelligentsia some sense
of patriotism for at least a half a year? . . . In any event they
should not prevent us from continuing and completing with
honor . . . our arduous struggle against Japan."

Witte replied on 23 June in quite different terms: "All our
achievements of the past decade must be sacrificed. . . . We
are not to play a leading role in the world—well, we will have
to reconcile ourselves to that." At about the same time Miliukov was writing of the need to bear "in mind that of necessity
our love of country sometimes assumes unexpected forms,
and that its apparent absence in reality represents with us the
very highest expression of true patriotic feeling."[35]

Kuropatkin was not alone in his estimate of the possibility
of a Russian victory. Foreign military experts reached the
same conclusion. "The Japanese have reached the limit of
their endurance," wrote a Colonel Gedke in the *Berliner
Tageblatt* in early June. "They never will get better terms of
peace than now . . . . A victorious army does not sit idle for
three whole months unless it has to.[36] Japan's exhaustion
became more certain as four, five, and then six months passed
and still the Japanese army did not move from the positions
it occupied after the fall of Mukden. Railway construction

around Lake Baikal was completed, and between eighteen and twenty trains a day were passing over the Siberian road. A steady flow of reinforcements from Russia was pouring into Manchuria.

THE ZEMSTVO PETITION AND AN HISTORIC MEETING

Several days after Tsushima, the Union of Unions and representatives of the zemstvos held conferences in Moscow.[37] At first Shipov's zemstvo moderates and the zemstvo constitutionalists met separately, but on 24 May they decided to meet as one body. The difference of opinion was rather sharp at times. The moderates held that it was "inadmissable for the public to proclaim its differences with the government in time of war." They also contended that "the people will not accept a shameful peace." After heated debate the congress decided to draft a petition to the tsar and to select a delegation to present it to him. Prince S.N. Trubetskoy drafted a statement that was acceptable to all. Although the liberals held a majority, they wanted unanimity; Prince P.D. Dolgorukov appealed, "Let us come together on this colorless petition." Fearful that a delegation might lead to a reconciliation with the government, the left radicals moved that the entire assembly call upon the tsar. However, the congress by a vote of 104-90 agreed to send only a regular delegation, and twelve representatives were elected.[38]

The delegation represented a loyalist effort to petition the government. The petition was neither an ultimatum nor a loyal appeal but something in-between. The emperor knew that in addition to moderates the delegation included irrepressible opponents of the order in which he believed. Nevertheless, he decided to receive the delegation.

The historic first meeting between a Russian autocrat and representatives of public oppositionists took place on 6 June 1905 at Petrodvorets. It was a conciliatory affair. Prince Trubetskoy spoke for the delegation, and his language contrasted markedly with the tone of the congresses. "We know, Your Majesty, that this is more difficult for you than for all of us.... Sedition in itself is not dangerous.... The Russian people have not lost faith in their Tsar or in the invincible might of the Russian Empire . . . . But the people are disturbed by the military defeats: they are looking for traitors positively everywhere—among the generals, among your advisors, among us, and among the nobility in general . . . . A bitter and unquenchable hatred is growing and spreading, and it is all the more dangerous because it expresses itself first as patriotism."

Then Trubetskoy turned to the question of a representative assembly: "It is essential that all your subjects, equally and without distinction, feel that they are citizens of Russia; . . . that all your subjects, even though alien to us in blood or faith, see Russia as their fatherland and you as their sovereign. Even as the Tsar of Russia is not the tsar of the nobility, nor the tsar of the peasants or merchants, nor the tsar of social classes, but the Tsar of All the Russias, so persons elected by the entire population must serve not their respective classes but the general interests of the state. Your Majesty," Trubetskoy concluded, "return to the formula of Sviatopolk-Mirsky —that the renewal of Russia must be based on trust."

Nodding in agreement with many points of Prince Trubetskoy's speech, Nicholas replied most cordially that he did not doubt the ardent devotion of the zemstvo men for their motherland. "I grieved and still grieve at the disasters this war has inflicted upon Russia, and at those yet to come, and at all our internal disorder. Cast aside your doubts. My will—the will of your Tsar—to assemble representatives of the people is unchangeable. Let there be, as in days of old, unity between the Tsar and all of Russia and personal communion between Myself and the zemstvo men as the foundation of an order built upon traditional Russian principles. I hope that you will cooperate in this work."

The zemstvo petition referred to the need to assemble popular representatives to decide the question of war or peace, but no delegate's "tongue turned" (as A.S. Suvorin put it) to raise the question of stopping the war when the emperor mentioned more disasters "yet to come." It appeared that a common language had been found, but in fact Trubetskoy did not express the sentiments of the intelligentsia or even a majority of the organized zemstvo representatives. The legal liberal press was caustic but had to restrict itself to murky allusions; journals published abroad, however, came down heavily against Prince Trubetskoy. A certain "Old Zemstvo Man" (the pseudonym of Miliukov) writing in *Osvobozhdenie*

described the speech as "a potpourri of Byzantine phrase-
ology .... It is difficult to sort the wheat from the chaff in
his rambling verbosity."

Shortly after the imperial audience of 6 June, the newspapers published the first details on the representative assembly promised by the Ukaz of 18 February 1905. The early
reports revealed that the assembly was to have consultative
powers and to be called the State Duma. The historic term,
zemsky sobor, discussed since the fall of 1904 was abandoned.
Circumstances had changed too much since the seventeenth
century to permit the resurrection of ancient institutions and
formulas.[39]

During June the emperor received other delegations as well
—representatives of the Kursk nobility, twenty-six provincial
marshals of nobility, and a delegation from the Union of Russian Men.[40] Counts A.A. Bobrinsky and S.D. Sheremetev
urged the tsar not to abandon the principle of election by
estates, or classes. However, on the burning issue of the day
both the Union of Russian Men and the twenty-six marshals
practically reiterated Prince Trubetskoy's appeal: "Your Majesty," read the marshals' petition, "only one thing can pacify
and reassure the public—immediate steps to convene the people's representatives." By that time the tsar already had decided to establish the State Duma. He doubted that the institution would be of any use. Nevertheless, cognizant of the
universal demand developing in support of it, he could do no
more than buttress the "experiment" with certain precautions
designed to hold back the flood tide of revolution.

REVOLUTION BY LAND AND SEA

Several revolutionary outbursts flared up in June. Demonstrating workers and soldiers clashed on 5 June in Lodz, where
strikes and killings had been continuous since the first of the
year. Twelve persons were killed in the June riot that was led
by the Polish Socialist Party and the Bund. The funeral of the
twelve victims precipitated a genuine rebellion. Armed revolutionists fought from barricades and houses for four days, from
the 10th through the 13th of June. Tens of thousands of law-
abiding citizens fled the city. Incomplete official estimates
set the toll at 150 dead and about 200 wounded—the Lodz

uprising claimed more victims than the 9th of January. The Lodz rebellion was just collapsing as rioting erupted in Odessa (12 June). The workers declared a general strike. They refused to allow trains to discharge passengers, and the port district fell under revolutionary control.

On 14 June the crew of the Black Sea Fleet's newest battleship, the *Potemkin-Tavrichesky*, used the pretext of foul meat to revolt and brutally murder most of their officers, including the captain. The mutineers raised a red flag and steered for Odessa, which was still in the grip of rebellion. On the 15th the *Potemkin* entered the port of Odessa. The ship's arrival created an ominous situation, for its heavy guns could level any building in the city. Government troops surrounded the docks and prevented the rebellion from spreading any farther, but looters and arsonists ravaged the waterfront district, where all authority had collapsed.

On 17 June the remainder of the Black Sea Fleet, led by four battleships, approached Odessa. With its superior speed the *Potemkin* knifed through the fleet. The other ships held their fire.[41] The crew of the battleship *Georgy Pobedonosets* also mutinied and set off in the wake of the *Potemkin*. *Georgy's* officers, except for one who committed suicide, were put ashore in a launch. The two battleships were joined by a destroyer in an unprecedented venture—the formation of a "revolutionary squadron."

On the following day, however, the crew of the *Georgy* began to have second thoughts. They had shrunk back from spilling blood and thus were not in as deep as the "Potemkin-ites." It was easier for them to return to the path of duty. The crew of the *Potemkin* threatened to send *Georgy* to the bottom of the sea, but to no avail. *Georgy Pobedonosets* returned to Odessa and the crew opened negotiations with the military authorities. On 20 June the officers resumed command of the ship, and a few dozen of the leading mutineers were arrested.

Potemkin cruised the Black Sea for several more days but the crew found themselves treated like pirates. All harbors were closed to them; coal, water, and food could be obtained only by force. An attempt to land at Feodosia [a Black Sea port in the eastern Crimea] convinced the sailors of the hopelessness of their situation: the local citizens fled beyond the city limits, and troops deployed as skirmishers fired on a landing party when it came ashore for water and coal. On 24 June, the eleventh day of the mutiny, the *Potemkin* returned for the second time to the Rumanian port of Constanza. There the crew disembarked and surrendered the vessel to the Rumanian government, which guaranteed not to repatriate them. After dividing the ship's cash among themselves, the crew of the *Potemkin* scattered all over Europe, and Rumania returned the ship to Russia.

For all their seriousness the June uprisings demonstrated the loyalty of the armed forces. Events revealed that mutineers, even when in possession of so mighty a weapon as the finest battleship of the Black Sea Fleet, soon "gave up" because they lacked the moral certainty that they were right. The example of the *Georgy Pobedonosets*, particularly, was a case in point.

The SR Battle Organization proclaimed that it was still alive by murdering Count P.P. Shuvalov, the mayor of Moscow, on 28 June.[42] On the whole, however, the organization was falling apart. Late in February its leader in St. Petersburg, Maxmillian I. Schweizer, was killed accidentally by a bomb, and the "provocateur" Nicholas Yu. Tatarov exposed and thus terminated a series of assassination plots that were underway.[43]

"Incidents of a reverse character" accompanied these revolutionary disturbances. In Baku in February the city's Armenian and Tatar population engaged in bloody rioting against the government. In Nizhni Novgorod one man was killed and about three dozen were injured when longshoremen clashed with revolutionary demonstrators. In Balashov (Saratov province) townsmen besieged the building in which representatives of the zemstvo and intelligentsia had gathered to draft political resolutions, and the angry crowd threatened to deal with them. Governor Peter A. Stolypin intervened personally to pacify the mob. He recognized, he said, "the indignation" that inspired them, but nevertheless their patriotism was "wild and misdirected." The emperor's attitude toward "illegal" acts against revolutionaries was this: "Revolutionary demonstrations can be tolerated no longer, but at the same time arbitrary mob action is not to be permitted."

PREPARATIONS FOR PEACE AND FOR WAR

Quiet continued to dominate the Manchurian front. Only a minor skirmish occasionally interrupted the calm. A large Japanese detachment marched slowly along the Yalu in northern Korea, but by August it still was many miles from the Russian border. On 21 June the Japanese took advantage of their naval supremacy and landed two divisions on Sakhalin Island. The defenders consisted of some three-to-four-thousand Russian troops, including volunteers raised among the local political and criminal convicts. The uneven struggle dragged on for nearly two months because of the huge area of the island.

The peace conference had been scheduled for the second half of July. After some indecision, Nicholas finally named Witte as chief Russian negotiator. The choice of Witte may seem strange because of his ill-concealed defeatist attitude. But Nicholas recognized that Witte was a gifted man who adjusted rapidly to whatever role he was assigned. Moreover, if the negotiations failed, criticism would be muted if the break occurred under so ardent a champion of peace as Witte. And finally, Nicholas reserved the final decision on peace to himself. Witte left St. Petersburg on 6 July. Passing through Berlin, he met with a friend of his, the banker Ernst Mendelsohn. Witte told him that Russia would have to cede Sakhalin to Japan and also pay a large indemnity. Fearing that Nicholas would resist these demands, Witte asked Mendelsohn to arrange matters so that the kaiser might influence the tsar toward concessions.

Nicholas, meanwhile, did everything within his power to ensure that Russia would continue to fight. He "devoured" any declaration against immediate peace and expressed his agreement and gratitude. Responding to a telegram from a group of Orenburg clergy on 18 July, he wrote: "The people of Russia can depend on me. I never will conclude a treaty of peace that is dishonorable or unworthy of Great Russia." On a wire from the Khabarovsk city duma urging him not to conclude peace without victory he wrote: "I share your view completely." Still, he could not have failed to notice how few resolutions of this kind he received.

The Russian emigre press stubbornly insisted on immediate peace. *Osvobozhdenie* declared that "continuation of the war

Nicky and Willy at Björkö

will cost far more than any indemnity that Japan will agree to .... The government is of the opinion that we will have to reconcile ourselves to the cession of Sakhalin." In Russia the legal journals seconded their compatriots abroad. In May, even before the conquest of Sakhalin, *Nasha zhizn* advised that it be surrendered to Japan, and *Syn otechestva* suggested that the cession of Vladivostok was no more dishonorable than the loss of Port Arthur.

News from the army offered the one bright hope. Rested, replenished with fresh young strength, and revitalized by the consciousness of its growing might, the Manchurian army was again ready to fight. The soldiers were convinced that the only way to get home was to beat the Japanese. Otherwise they would be forced into another retreat, and the immensity of Siberia offered only the prospect of an endless war.

In June the emperor reshuffled the military and naval administrations. On 23 June General Alexander F. Rediger replaced General Sakharov as war minister, and on the 30th Admiral Alexis A. Birilev succeeded Admiral Avellan as naval minister. General Feodor F. Palitsyn became chief of the [newly reorganized] general staff.[44] Two more partial mobilizations, announced for the summer, proceeded without incident. After failing to float a war loan in France, the government concluded a short-term loan of 150,000,000 rubles with Germany.[45] On 6 August the government issued 200,000,000 rubles of war bonds to the Russian public. During the first half of 1905 the Russian gold reserve increased by 41,000,000 rubles.

THE TREATY OF BJÖRKÖ

On 7 July Nicholas invited his cousin the kaiser to visit him off the Finnish coast. The invitation piqued the curiosity of the Germans, and William readily accepted. The meeting of the two emperors took place aboard the imperial yacht *Poliarnaia Zvezda* [North Star] in the Björkö Sound on 10-11 July. After exchanging views on the international situation, William reminded Nicholas of the defensive alliance proposed earlier, when Anglo-Russian relations were aggravated by the North Sea incident. The kaiser observed that Germany was getting along better with France under its new foreign minister.

Nicholas expressed his satisfaction at that and declared that nothing then stood in the way of their treaty. Right on the spot the kaiser presented Nicholas a draft of the treaty, and the two monarchs signed it. In order to stress the solemnity of the document, William asked his adjutant, Heinrich von Tschirschky, to co-sign for Germany. Similarly, Nicholas requested his naval minister, Admiral Birilev, to witness the document without reading it.

The treaty signed at Björkö mutually obliged Russia and Germany to come to the other's assistance if either were to be attacked in Europe. In a separate article Russia agreed to take the necessary steps to draw France into the alliance. The treaty was to become effective as soon as Russia and Japan ratified a peace treaty. The target of this agreement obviously was England.

This treaty in no way contradicted the Franco-Russian Alliance. In both agreements Russia was obliged to render assistance if its ally were attacked. Years before, Emperor Alexander III had wanted to add to the Franco-Russian military convention a special clause that voided Russia's obligations if France became the aggressor. At that time French General Boisdeffre pointed out that such a stipulation was unnecessary since the treaty was defensive in nature. (The obligation to render assistance against an aggressor subsequently formed the basis of the Locarno agreements [1925] as well as several others.) Therefore, when Witte later maintained that the Björkö agreement violated the Franco-Russian Alliance, he was either displaying his ignorance of international law or deliberately misrepresenting the facts. The French obviously would not rejoice over this alliance, but the tsar of Russia had every right to protect the empire's rear—especially when France, for equally legitimate reasons, recently had come to a friendly agreement with Japan's ally in a move that complicated Russia's capacity to make war at sea.[46]

The Björkö treaty, envisioned as an alliance of the three continental powers against England, corresponded fully to views expressed by the emperor since 1895. But in 1905 such an alliance held even greater significance. Nicholas was laying the foundation for the possible prolongation of the war against Japan. The projected Russo-German alliance would take effect only with the conclusion of the war in Asia, but it prompted Germany to favor terms agreeable to Russia. But if the war continued, the treaty practically eliminated the possibility of a German attack on Russia. Nicholas also could depend on the possibility of a German commitment not to attack France, especially since the realignment of the French government. That in turn made it possible to consider the transfer of considerable first-line troops from the western frontier to the Manchurian front. Crack units arriving just as Japanese reserves were being exhausted could decide the outcome in Russia's favor with comparative ease.

Nicholas initially kept the treaty of Björkö completely secret, even from his foreign minister, Count Lamsdorf. The kaiser, however, disclosed the treaty to Bülow, who considered it so disadvantageous to Germany that he threatened to resign. The German chancellor objected to the terms "in Europe only" because he felt that in a war with England Russia had to be committed to an invasion of India. Impulsively but characteristically William wrote that he would shoot himself if Bülow deserted him.[47]

DRIFT TO THE LEFT: THE JULY ZEMSTVO CONGRESS

The fourth zemstvo congress assembled in Moscow early in July. There for the first time the zemstvo delegates heard the conservative voice of Prince N.F. Kasatkin-Rostovsky, who had been elected by the Kursk zemstvo. Nevertheless, the majority of delegates inclined even more to the left than in earlier congresses. The constitutionalists were dissatisfied with what they knew of the "Bulygin project" [the State Duma]. Far from frightening them, the June rebellions only convinced the zemstvo men that they had to adopt a more radical stance. "It is useless to depend on reform," declared Ivan Petrunkevich. "We can depend only on ourselves and on the people. We will spell it out for the people. Discretion is unnecessary . . . [for] the revolution is a fact. We must take our resolutions not to the tsar but to the people!" Petrunkevich's oratory caused three conservative delegates to stomp out of the convention.

The July congress resolved to carry its appeal to the people and the delegates authorized the central bureau "to enter into agreement with other organizations if it becomes necessary."

That brief formula created the most debate and carried by a slender majority of 76-52. The vote paved the way for an alliance between the zemstvos and other, openly revolutionary organizations, first of all the Union of Unions. This resolution came only scant weeks after the tsar had received the zemstvo representatives and heard Prince Trubetskoy's loyal and presumably sincere speech. Nicholas was irritated and alarmed. He commissioned Senator Postovsky to inquire from the zemstvo leaders what to make of such a contradiction of words and deeds. Postovsky was informed that no contradiction existed, a popular appeal was only "a new step along an old road." The "zemstvo-constitutionalist group," which led the July congress, bluntly declared that "the June 6th delegation did not represent the zemstvo constitutionalists but was sent by a coalition within the congress, and its arrangements are in no way binding upon us." In short, the zemstvo men could approach the tsar with elegant speeches, but when he wished to communicate with them, no one was available. This episode seared his soul and convinced him that he could "not depend on those circles." All the same, no one was being insincere deliberately: the zemstvo congresses represented no organized power, they were only the instruments of other more strongly unified groups, chief of which was the Union of Liberation.

THE BULYGIN DUMA: TOO MUCH AND NOT ENOUGH

Deliberations on the organization of the State Duma began at Peterhof on 18 July. Several dozen persons took part—the grand dukes, the ministers, some of the more prominent members of the State Council, several senators, and also the noted historian, V.O. Kliuchevsky. The emperor presided over the discussion. When an article had been discussed thoroughly, Nicholas would announce whether or not he approved it. This procedure took the place of voting. The most extensively debated article proposed that legislation rejected by the State Duma could not be submitted to the tsar for his approval. Opponents argued that its adoption would impose a limitation on the tsar's power. The article was amended. During the discussion of the electoral law, some speakers saw no reason not to allow the election of illiterates who were loyal and capable of speaking in "epic language." Finance minister Kokovtsov, responding with characteristic humor, cautioned: "Do not allow yourselves to be carried away by a desire to hear illiterate old men make epic speeches in the Duma. . . . They will only repeat in epic style what others have told them." The literacy requirement was retained.

The legislation, worked out at Peterhof between the 19th and 26th of July, was published on the Feast of the Transfiguration and was known subsequently as the Law of 6 August or the "Bulygin Duma."[48] It established a consultative assembly elected by the people and empowered to debate projected legislation and official reports. It had the right to interpellate ministers, and its chairman could bring arbitrary actions by the government directly to the attention of the tsar. The existing State Council, recognized as a body experienced in legislative matters, was retained beside the Duma. The emperor could promulgate laws contrary to the recommendations of the Duma or Council. However, the consideration of legislation by both "houses" offered the possibility of obtaining the public's views and made it unlikely that the emperor would act counter to the expressed wishes of the people's representatives without some good reason.

Confidence in the loyalty of the peasantry was the exclusive foundation of the new electoral law. Every peasant and landowner was eligible to participate in the election of electors who, in turn, convened to elect the deputies. The electoral law, on the other hand, severely limited the franchise of urban dwellers. Only householders and persons who paid substantial property taxes could vote. The law almost completely excluded workers and the intelligentsia. *Osvobozhdenie* observed, however, that "having admitted the huge mass of the peasantry to the Duma elections without any qualification, the autocratic bureaucracy has acknowledged that popular representation in Russia can be predicated only on democratic principles."

The Law of 6 August evoked scarcely any enthusiasm anywhere. Most of the public rejected the consultative nature of the State Duma. Much of the nobility was dissatisfied with the abandonment of the principle of election by class; many deplored the preponderence of peasant electors. Some right-wing groups were disturbed that the principle of universal suffrage gave the vote to Jews.

PORTSMOUTH

The Portsmouth Peace Conference opened on 27 July 1905. While granting Witte broad authority in the negotiation, Nicholas also set two conditions: not one kopeck for an indemnity and not a single inch of land. Witte himself was convinced that much greater concessions would have to be made. At the second session of the conference the Japanese presented their demands, which were in sum: (1) recognition of Japan's preponderant influence in Korea; (2) Russia's withdrawal and the restoration of Manchuria to China; (3) cession of Port Arthur and the Liaotung Peninsula to Japan; (4) cession of the southern branch of the Chinese Eastern Railway (Harbin-Port Arthur); (5) cession of Sakhalin and its adjoining islands; (6) reimbursement of Japan's military expenses (in a sum of no less than 1,200,000,000 yen); (7) surrender of Russian vessels hiding in neutral ports; (8) limitation of Russian naval strength in the Far East; (9) grant to Japan of fishing rights off Russia's Pacific coast. (The Japanese proposal originally transmitted to President Roosevelt also demanded the dismantling of the fortifications at Vladivostok.)[49]

Publication of the Japanese demands had a pronounced effect on American public opinion. It was Japan, evidently, and not Russia that wanted to annex Korea. It was for self-aggrandizement and not for "the struggle against annexations" that Japan had bled for Port Arthur. Nevertheless, Roosevelt considered Tokyo's demands quite acceptable.

The negotiators disposed of several items without difficulty. Korea passed from the agenda with a meaningless declaration on the sovereignty of its emperor. Manchuria was to be evacuated simultaneously by Russian and Japanese forces. Japan accepted a section of the Chinese Eastern Railroad to Chengchiatum, about 160 miles south of Harbin or roughly as much of the route as they had conquered. The question of fishing rights presented no problem. The rest of the demands, however, the Russians flatly rejected. By 5 August the conference was deadlocked, and at that point the center of negotiations actually shifted from Portsmouth to Peterhof.

On 7 August the kaiser telegraphed the tsar to advise that he leave the question of war or peace to the State Duma. "If the Duma speaks out for peace, then you would have your nation's's authorization to conclude a treaty on the condition offered to your delegation in Washington. . . . No one in your army, or country, or in the rest of the world could blame you. If the Duma should decide that the offer is unacceptable, then Russia itself, thanks to the Duma, will call upon you, its emperor, to continue the struggle, while the nation accepts the responsibility for any consequences." Nicholas replied: "You know how I hate bloodshed, and yet that is more acceptable than a dishonorable peace, which would crush completely my faith in myself and in my fatherland. . . . I am prepared to accept the responsibilities myself because my conscience is clear and I know that the majority of the Russian people will support me. I am fully aware of the great significance of the times I am living through, but I cannot act differently."

Nicholas believed in Russia, and he was willing to continue the war. Therein lay his strength. He did not believe that Russia had been defeated and, although he agreed to negotiate for peace, he always was aware that the negotiations might collapse. It was essential, however, both in Russia and abroad that the responsibility for breaking off the negotiations fall upon Japan. The public could readily grasp the meaning of an indemnity. According to *Osvobozhdenie*, some peasant superintendents *(zemskie nachalniki)* already were stirring up the villagers by warning that "if we make peace with the Japanese, they will demand an enormous sum and you will have to pay it. That means that taxes and duties on everything will double. . . . [The peasants] one and all wanted to continue the war." Other countries, as well, had little reason to see Japan win a large indemnity. Japan's creditors, of course, would welcome one, but their governments could see that a large sum would go to feed Japan's armaments. And whom would they be used against next time?

President Roosevelt concluded that a settlement had to be reached, and he suggested a compromise. Japan, he proposed, might annex the southern half of Sakhalin, and Russia would make a substantial payment to repurchase the northern half. Japan would get what it needed, and Russian honor would be unsullied. On 10 August the U.S. ambassador, Meyer, again called upon Nicholas and tried for two hours to persuade him

to accept the president's proposal. The tsar informed him
that Russia would pay no indemnity in any form: Russia
was not a defeated nation; Russia was not in the position
of France in 1870, and if necessary he himself would go to
the front. Meyer raised the possibility of new losses of territory in the future, to which Nicholas replied: "Why have the
Japanese not attacked our army in so many months?" The
ambassador argued that Russia had occupied Sakhalin for
only thirty years and that without a fleet a reconquest of
the island was impossible. The tsar answered that, as an ultimate concession, he was prepared to yield the southern
half of Sakhalin, but only if Japan agreed not to fortify it
and to return the northern half without compensation.[50]

Nicholas offered this concession to demonstrate his willingness to meet some of Roosevelt's proposal. But at the
same time he had detailed information on Japan's severe
financial problem and, apparently, he was certain that Tokyo
never would settle without an indemnity. The Americans felt
the same way. Roosevelt, therefore, sent Meyer another cable
suggesting that the ambassador warn Nicholas that he risked
the loss of Vladivostok and eastern Siberia. On 14 August
Roosevelt telegraphed Berlin to urge the kaiser to use his
influence with the tsar. Witte, too, believed that Roosevelt's
compromise should be accepted, and in a conversation on
the 13th with two prominent journalists he reportedly said
that Russia could afford to pay 2-300,000,000 dollars for
the return of northern Sakhalin. On the following day he
hastily retracted that conversation: Nicholas would not budge.

THE TSAR'S FINAL OFFER: PEACE WITH HONOR

At the session of 16 August the Russian delegation presented
its proposal. Russia refused to pay an indemnity; it would
agree to pay only for the maintenance of Russian prisoners
in Japan. Russia would agree to the cession of southern Sakhalin on condition that Japan returned northern Sakhalin
without compensation. Furthermore, Japan had to promise
not to fortify the island and it had to guarantee free navigation
in the Lapérouse Straits [between Sakhalin and Hokaido,
the northernmost Japanese island]. Russia previously had
rejected Japan's demand to turn over those ships that had

taken refuge in neutral ports and also any limitation of its naval forces in the Far East. "The plenipotentiaries of Russia have the honor to declare, by order of their August Majesty, that this proposal represents the last concession that Russia can make with the single aim of coming to an understanding." There was a brief silence. Then Komura Jutaro, the head of the Japanese delegation, announced in a well-controlled voice that in the interest of restoring peace the Japanese government gave its consent to those conditions! Everyone present, including Witte, was stunned.[51]

No one had expected Japan to relinquish both an indemnity and half of a conquered island without compensation. Witte adjusted quickly to the situation and in an ensuing interview with journalists took sole credit for his success. However, the sudden decision of the Japanese delegation only proved how accurately Nicholas had assessed the prospects of both nations. His readiness to continue the war was real; Japan's obstinacy was mainly a bluff. Japan was closer to exhaustion than Russia and far more dependent on foreign assistance. In one year of war Russian imports had decreased while Japan's had risen sharply. The war cost Russia about 2,000,000,000 rubles, and Japan roughly the same—about 2,000,000,000,000 yen. In Japan, however, military expenditures caused taxes to rise about 85 percent, whereas taxes in Russia increased about five percent. These figures indicate how desperately Japan needed an indemnity or, without it, how desperately it needed peace.[52]

The military superiority that Japan enjoyed at the beginning of the war was decisive throughout the siege and fall of Port Arthur, but the advantage was spent completely and still the Russian army was not crushed. A retreat to Harbin, assumed by Kuropatkin at the outset of the war, became unnecessary. In August 1905 the army stood 150-200 miles farther north than the year before, and its lines of communication with the rear were far more efficient. Japan's big "trump" was civil disorder in Russia, but the speedy liquidation of the June riots and the "incidents of a reverse nature" demonstrated that domestic chaos was uncertain. Under those circumstances the Japanese, confronted by the possible collapse of negotiations, understandably hastened to take the tendered half of Sakhalin and drop their other demands.

JAPAN'S JILTED MASSES

The peace made at Portsmouth was not the peace that the Japanese people, intoxicated by victory, expected. When the government published the terms of the treaty, major disturbances erupted throughout Japan. Flags of mourning blanketed the cities, barricades went up in the streets, and the offices of the official newspaper *Kokumin* were set afire. When the government presented the treaty to the Diet for ratification, however, the clamor subsided. Speaking in defense of the treaty, the commander-in-chief of the Japanese armies, Marshal Oyama Iwao declared: "The fact is that after a full year of war, victoriously concluded at Mukden, the Japanese Army paused for five and a half months and dared not launch an offensive."

Perhaps, if Witte had been less pessimistic and stood firm earlier on some other issue, reserving that as the final mark of "good will," then perhaps the cession of southern Sakhalin might have been averted. In 1925 Tyler Dennett, an American scholar, observed that "few now entertain the opinion . . . that Japan was robbed of an even greater prospective victory. A contrary opinion is common. It is believed by many that Japan was so exhausted at the end of May that only the restoration of peace saved her from collapse or ultimate severe defeat at the hands of Russia."[53] Kuropatkin energetically defended that view in his memoirs, when he had little interest in predicting a victory for General Linevich, his successor as supreme commander.

NICHOLAS II—ONE AGAINST THE MILLIONS

Japan's sudden acceptance of his terms surprised Nicholas no less than his envoys at Portsmouth. The only difference was that he hoped that Japan would reject them. "This evening a telegram[54] arrived from Witte announcing that the peace negotiations have come to an end. I walked around all day as though in a trance," wrote the tsar in his diary on the 17th. On the following day he added: "Only today did I begin to grow accustomed to the idea that peace is about to be concluded; it is probably all for the good, for it must be thus." In his diary on 22 August Grand Duke Constantine Constantinovich quoted Olga Constantinovna, the queen of the Greeks: "In sending Witte to America, the emperor was so convinced of the unacceptability of our conditions that he did not even consider the possibility of peace. But when Japan accepted our terms, there was nothing left but to conclude peace. . . .Now Olga, who has seen him and the Empress Alexandra Feodorovna, tells me that they act as if they had been doused with water. Our army in the field was growing stronger, and fortune appeared ready to smile on us."

Nicholas did everything in his power to end the war on honorable terms. Domestic turmoil was paralyzing Russian might. Domestic and international conditions made it impossible not to negotiate, but having begun, he could not reject the cession of Port Arthur and Korea (which Russia had agreed to relinquish even before the war!). President Roosevelt, Emperor William, Russian plenipotentiary Witte—all demanded greater concessions. Only the tsar's determination not to yield prevented peace under less favorable conditions.

Russia did not win the war, but neither did it lose everything. Japan began to sense Russia's might just as Tokyo was preparing to reap the fruits of its victories. Russia remained a great Asian power—an impossibility had Petersburg, in order to avoid war, supinely yielded to Japanese demands in 1903. Weakened by the struggle far more than Russia, Japan was unable to resume its advance in Asia for many years. Then expansion became possible only because of the Chinese revolution, World War I, and the Russian revolution.

In the final months of the war, Nicholas had to lead the struggle against enemies both foreign and domestic. At that point the words of Ivan T. Pososhkov,[55] written two centuries earlier about another tsar whom history knows as Great even though he failed to achieve all his goals, became all too appropriate—"Our great monarch exerts himself, but he will not manage in time for he has few helpers to his liking. He pulls up the mountain with the strength of ten, but millions pull downhill: how will his struggle end?" Although "millions pulled downhill," Emperor Nicholas II still "managed" to end the war in a manner that allowed Russia to remain a great power in Asia.

CHAPTER ELEVEN

PEACE BUT NO PEACE

The war ended but Russia heaved no sigh of relief if only because the nation had carried the burden of war so lightly. Russia had employed only ten percent of its armed might: in a population of 145,000,000 only 1,012,000 men were mobilized.[1] Although the terms of peace were not particularly advantageous to Russia, the public had expected much worse. *Osvobozhdenie* frankly admitted that Russia had gained an "extremely favorable peace" and attributed that outcome to the moderating influence of Great Britain. But *Syn otechestva*, which once had resigned itself to an indemnity and the total loss of Sakhalin, remained dissatisfied and carped that the "bureaucracy is incapable of concluding peace on favorable terms." *Novoe vremia* gratuitously advised that "by exercising more self-control Russia definitely could have obtained more favorable conditions and at least retained all of Sakhalin." The Treaty of Portsmouth had a deleterious effect on the army. Kuropatkin wrote that "no defeat we have suffered has had such a harmful effect on the army as this premature peace which deprived us of our victory." All in all, neither joy nor wrath greeted peace, for Russia, caught up in the vortex of great events, simply forgot the war as soon as it ended.

The revolutionary parties were making active preparations for battle, and weapons began to arrive from abroad. On August 26th the steamer *John Grafton* ran aground near Jakobstadt on the Finnish coast. The crew scattered after blowing up the ship, but part of its cargo—1,780 Swiss-made rifles and ninety-seven crates of explosives—fell into the hands of the authorities. "A nasty business," commented the emperor on receiving the report of this "find." The *John Grafton* was not the only vessel that smuggled weapons to the Finnish and Russian revolutionaries.[2]

Bloody strife erupted once again between Tatars and Armenians in Transcaucasia. At Baku over three hundred people were killed and injured, more than two-thirds of the oil rigs were burned down, and fire consumed several thousand tons of oil. Petroleum production was cut by more than half— a serious blow to Russia's economy. Even bloodier fighting claimed over six hundred lives in Shusha, and fires destroyed a great number of residences.

Twenty-three provinces experienced poor harvests in 1905, and the government anticipated the need for a relief program to feed the population of the afflicted area. Then the first half of September brought a lull in the turmoil. For the first time in many months, Nicholas was able to spend two weeks with his family in the Finnish skerries away from the business of government. Empress Maria Feodorovna went to Denmark where her aged father King Christian IX [reigned 1863-1906] was living out his final years.

Zemstvo representatives convened again on [6-13 November][3] in Moscow, this time openly and without interference from the government. The congress decided to continue its struggle for broader popular representation and universal suffrage, but at the same time it rejected the call from the left to boycott "the Duma of August 6th." The highlight of the congress was the appearance of a Polish delegation. Following the July congress, the zemstvo central bureau had reached an agreement with Polish nationalist leaders, and the September congress was presented a resolution calling for broad autonomous status for Poland. The only strenuous objection to that resolution came from Alexander I. Guchkov,[4] whose opposition brought him his first taste of widespread public notoriety. The congress approved the resolution on Polish autonomy by the decisive margin of 172-1, but the merchants of Moscow sent a special delegation to Guchkov to thank him for his stand.

Sergei Witte returned to Russia from Portsmouth on 15 September. He was acclaimed everywhere on his journey through Europe, for Russia's success at Portsmouth was credited to his skill in diplomacy. Witte always had a knack for maintaining good relations with the foreign press, and during his tenure as finance minister he had established solid connections in international banking circles. Consequently his every public appearance was masterfully arranged. Much was expected of him in Russia, too. A reputation as an oppositionist, gained in the preceding two years, went some way in reconciling the "public"[5] to him. Moreover, his undeniable achievements as director of Russian financial policy brought him the prestige of a true statesman. His victory at Portsmouth reinforced and enhanced that reputation: "All other names pale beside that of Witte," proclaimed *Russkii vestnik*. The tsar gracefully greeted Russia's representative and bestowed upon him the title of Count. Detractors later dubbed him "Count Half-Sakhalinsky."

THE UNIVERSITIES AND THE POLITICAL ILLITERATES

On 27 August 1905 a new law granted autonomy to the universities by transferring all internal matters to academic corporations (boards of professors) and the rectors whom they elected.[6] Classes resumed in the fall under the new regime in which the rectors were in charge. Prince S.N. Trubetskoy was elected rector of Moscow University, and Professor I.I. Borgman was chosen to head St. Petersburg University. Unhindered, the students immediately organized meetings to decide whether to attend classes, since they had decided in February to strike until a constituent assembly met. The revolutionary parties, following the lead of the Social Democrats, seized the opportunity to exploit the situation and began to turn the lecture halls into public forums. Without controls outsiders freely entered the universities now under professorial management.

Politics became the order of the day. The students were told that surely they did not intend to monopolize the right to assembly—would you slam your doors in the face of the people? Meanwhile, agitators were demanding that students, not professors, should control the universities. At St. Petersburg the students proclaimed a boycott of seven professors guilty of "reactionary tendencies." Not only *Novoe vremia* but even *Osvobozhdenie* protested that action. Peter Struve wrote: "The right to haul people into court because of the way they think must never be given to anyone, not even students. . . . I do not want to be compelled to obey any faction whatever its persuasion, whether it wears the double-headed eagle or the Phrygian cap,[7] whether it originates with Peter the Great or Karl Marx."

Prince Trubetskoy, aware that autonomy also entailed a responsibility to the state, announced that if outsiders were admitted to the lecture halls, he would close the university, and on September 20th he did indeed close it. "I guarantee you the freedom to assemble, but as rector, as professor, and as public official, I hereby affirm that this university cannot be used as a public meeting place." Prince Trubetskoy's resolute stand had a decided impact on the student body. Some of the organized student sections declared themselves in favor of resuming classes and called for an end to the meetings.

Then Trubetskoy went to St. Petersburg with the hope of persuading the government to issue a law that would grant freedom of assembly to all. That would discourage outsiders from invading the universities. While meeting with the minister of public education on 29 September, Prince Trubetskoy became ill. He died that same evening of a heart attack. The highest officials of the government accompanied his remains to the Nikolaevsk Station, and the tsar sent a wreath of white orchids. In Moscow the funeral of the university's first elected rector was used to stage a revolutionary protest, and it concluded in the streets in a series of clashes with the police.

BJÖRKÖ ON THE ROCKS

Shortly after the signing of the Treaty of Portsmouth the emperor informed his foreign minister of the existence of the Björkö treaty. Its terms upset Count Lamsdorf, who pointed out that France never would enter into a triple alliance with Germany. He then requested the Russian ambassador in France, Alexander I. Nelidov, to canvass the French government and confirm that its reaction would be negative. Witte previously had advocated precisely such an alliance of the continental powers and he was to do so again. At that moment, however, he unexpectedly sided with Lamsdorf.[8]

On 24 September 1905 Nicholas wrote to William: "The peace treaty will be ratified in a few days. The treaty that we concluded at Björkö ought to take effect . . . . If France decides not to participate, the import of article 1 [to assist one another if attacked by a third power] will change radically.

At the time I did not have all the documents with me. Our
relations with France exclude the possibility of an armed
conflict with her.... If France refuses, the text of the treaty
will have to be amended."

Nicholas, in other words, wanted to save the treaty but
considered an amendment necessary. To defend against what
eventuality? Apparently the Russian government's concern
was the (then) remote possibility of a French attack on Germany. If that were to occur, Russia of course had no obligation
to support France. Close and confidential relations between
the French and Russian general staffs, the result of years of
military collaboration, also made it impossible for Russia to
march against France. At Björkö the two emperors were constructing an alliance against England and they dismissed the
possibility of French aggression as highly improbable. That
remote possibility was the ground on which opponents attacked the treaty. As the tsar was writing to the kaiser, Witte
was writing (25 September) to Count Eulenburg to affirm his
"complete solidarity" with Björkö but also to point out that
"some hindrances had to be put aside."

THE FIRST GENERAL STRIKE

Protests in the universities were only part of the agitation that
began to spread in the second half of September. In Moscow
one strike followed another, first the print shops, next the
bakeries, and then several factories. The strikers staged marches
and on the 22nd and 24th they clashed with the police.
Demonstrators did not invade the streets of St. Petersburg,
where the imperial guards regiments were stationed, but thousands of persons attended rallies at all of the educational
establishments. Throngs of workers crowded the auditoriums.
Revolutionaries spoke freely and enthralled the crowds with
words hitherto prohibited.

Meanwhile top government officials were holding private
conversations with a view toward forming a united ministry in
advance of the State Duma. Witte proclaimed his support of
constitutional reform and arrogantly fulminated against those
who tried to oppose him. He clashed bitterly with finance
minister Kokovtsov. A sizable majority of the upper bureaucracy tended to agree with Witte. The reformist inclinations at

"the top" quickly became known to society, the Union of Liberation, and the Union of Unions and had the effect of increasing the confidence of the opponents of the regime. The opposition called for a boycott of the Duma, because the electoral law guaranteed the government an "obedient" peasant majority. The idea of a boycott was all the more popular with the intelligentsia since they and the workers did not have the right to vote anyway.

The oppositionists' refusal to go along with the Duma meant that they had to adopt other means of struggle. That brought the revolutionary and oppositionist parties together on the general demand for a constituent assembly to write a Russian constitution and on the desirability of taking action before the Duma convened in January. Action—but how? Although the revolutionaries were fairly well armed, an armed uprising seemed hopeless and the potential for terrorism seemed to be exhausted. Therefore, the coalition of parties, groups, and organizations that formed the Liberation movement employed a new tactic, part of the programs of the western socialist parties but as yet untried—the general strike for political gains.

The general strike movement lack a unified command. It drew its strength from the common goal that united each component and from the general commitment that whoever or however a strike might start, everyone had to support it. Consequently the initial scope or significance of the movement was not immediately apparent. Nevertheless, all elements were behind the general strike, and with that general endorsement it developed rapidly into an awesome power that became psychologically irresistible.

The movement appeared without warning and spread with extreme rapidity. The employees of the Moscow-Kazan Railway struck on 7 October. On the following day work stopped on the Yaroslavl, Kursk, Nizhni Novgorod, and Riazin-Ural roads. The strikers felled telegraph poles in order to paralyze traffic on other routes where workers resisted the strike. Obedient to their leaders, the railwaymen halted work without making any demands. "We will present them when all the trains have stopped," they declared. On 10 October traffic came to a halt on the Nikolaevsk Railway: Moscow was cut off from the outside world, and the entire province was without rail service. On that same day a general strike was announced for Moscow.

Representatives of the railroad workers' union met with Witte on the 11th and presented their demands: (1) a constituent assembly based on universal suffrage and direct, equal, and secret elections; (2) abolition of the states of reinforced security and martial law; (3) the freedom to strike, unionize, and assemble; (4) an eight-hour work day on the railroads. Witte replied that he did not like the idea of a constituent assembly—"in America the capitalists buy off the voters"—but he judged the other demands to be acceptable—"martial law is an anachronism." The workers turned to Witte and he responded as though he spoke for the government. That was due less to his official position as chairman of the Committee of Ministers than to the general assumption that he would be the future head of the government.

WITTE'S CONDITIONS

As soon as the strikes erupted, Witte entrusted to his long-standing associate Ilya Ya. Gurland the task of formulating a program. Understandably, Witte's memorandum of 9 October differed sharply from his earlier memorandum on *Autocracy and Zemstvo*.[9] With a tone aspiring at times to the poetic the statement glorified the "liberation movement . . . which smolders like a red-hot coal in a heap of ashes" or "flares up with a bright flame." Its roots were to be found "in Novgorod, in Pskov, among the Zaporozhie Cossacks, among the freemen of Lower Podolia (Stenka Razin!—author) and generally within the nature of every person . . . . Society has set its goal, a goal of great significance and utter indestructibility, for there is truth in its goal. Therefore, the government must accept it. The cry of Liberty must become the slogan of the government. There is no other way to save the country . . . . The tide of historical progress cannot be stayed . . . . We have no choice: either we must stand at the helm of a movement that has embraced the entire country, or we must stand by while the country is torn to pieces by primordial forces. Executions and torrents of blood will only hasten the explosion."

Witte then recommended the abolition of all states of emergency, the introduction of civil liberties and equal rights for all citizens, "a constitution in the sense of communion between the tsar and his people through a division of the legislative power, budgetary policy, and control of administrative functions;" the expansion of voting rights, Polish and Georgian autonomy, and a series of other reforms up to the "expropriation of private lands."

Before transmitting this memorandum to the tsar, Witte added that yet another alternative existed—"to go against the course of events"—but he himself would not attempt it. Basically Witte's program was copied from the resolutions of the two previous zemstvo congresses. He informed Nicholas that he would assume the responsibility of creating a unified ministry only if the tsar accepted his program. Witte sent his memorandum to the tsar on 10 October.

"THE REVOLUTION HAS BEGUN!"

Meantime the general strike had spread to St. Petersburg, and the paralysis of the transportation system was spreading throughout the empire. In Moscow the water system ceased to function, the apothecary shops were closed, and the city's slaughterhouses had shut down. An ever-widening circle of the population was drawn into the maelstrom. Even secondary school students struck and took to the streets. On 12 October troops battled demonstrating crowds in the city of Kharkov. The world's first general strike fed upon itself, and the leaders who organized it lost control of it.[10]

Moskovskie vedomosti called for the establishment of a military dictatorship. Prince Meshchersky protested. A dictatorship, he wrote, in fact meant the abolition of the tsar's power with no guarantee that the dictator himself would not succumb to liberal pressure: "It would be ridiculous—it would be acting like Don Quixote—to battle the forces now sweeping across Russia."[11] *Novoe vremia* declared that "repression can do far more to undermine the idea of tsarist authority than the legalization of liberty." *Slovo* [The Word], a moderate-liberal journal, summoned the government to accept those who desire "sensible liberties: We are slow. We were slow. When it was drizzling, we assumed that the clouds would go away. We were slow then to recognize that the downpour was just beginning, and now we hesitate amid the hollow rumbling of the approaching storm. The pent-up waters have been unleashed; the people are witnessing 'the wrath of God.' " And A.A. Stolypin exclaimed: "It's here! The revolution has begun!"[12] Newspapers appeared for the last time in St. Petersburg on 14 October. *Kievlianin*, which had its own staff of dedicated conservative typesetters, was the only paper to publish despite the strike.

NICHOLAS PROPOSES, WITTE DISPOSES

On 13 October Nicholas sent the following wire from Peterhof to Witte in Petersburg: "I direct you to coordinate the activities of the ministers, whom I instruct to restore order everywhere."[13] At the same time the tsar placed all troops in the Petersburg military district under the command of Governor-General Dmitry Trepov. While charging Trepov to maintain order, the tsar also sought a political solution to the crisis. An ukaz published on 14 October proclaimed the measure that Prince Trubetskoy had requested on the eve of his death: in order to prevent meetings in the universities, the large auditoriums of the cities were opened as meeting places. The result was that public meetings were held in both places.

Witte hesitated and did not immediately accept the tsar's charge to him. He insisted that Nicholas first had to endorse his policy. Witte sought to link his fate with the cause of liberal reform. Perhaps, in addition to the tsar's appointment, he hoped to win the support of other elements with the idea of becoming irreplaceable. When Nicholas replied that such reforms had to be promulgated by an imperial manifesto, Witte was dissatisfied and even tried to object. He preferred to have the reforms made public not as the tsar's decision but as "Witte's program."[14] As the rail strike continued, the ministers were forced to travel by boat to Peterhof to report to the emperor. In a long conference on the 15th Witte again offered the two choices, constitution or dictatorship. Grand Duke Nicholas Nikolaevich, who on returning from his estate in Tula had passed through the countryside gripped by the strike, decisively supported Witte. The draft of a manifesto, prepared by Prince Alexis D. Obolensky,[15] was under consideration. The document promised civil liberties and a State Duma with legislative powers. After an hour's discussion,

Nicholas concluded the meeting by announcing that he would "think about it." Later that same day the former interior minister Ivan Goremykin arrived by carriage from Petersburg. The tsar had summoned him. Having taken his leave from Witte, the tsar next met with Witte's old antagonist to consider a manifesto that he was drafting.

October 16th was a day of uncertainty. Rumor had it that Nicholas had rejected Witte's program and that either Goremykin or Count Alexis P. Ignatiev[16] would be appointed prime minister. Petersburg waited in darkness—the electricity had been turned off, and the streets were empty.

"So the days of ominous quiet began," wrote Nicholas to his mother.[17] "Complete order in the streets, but at the same time everybody knew that something was going to happen. The troops were awaiting the signal, but the other side would not begin. One had the same feeling as before a thunderstorm in the summer! Everyone's nerves were strained to the limit, and of course such a situation cannot last long."

THE BIRTH OF THE COUNTER-REVOLUTION

Complex developments were underway beyond the city limits of the capital. The general strike clearly reflected an elemental mood of rebellion, but it struck most painfully at the vital interests of the general population and in particular the urban poor. The markets were without produce and the butcher shops had no meat. Children went without milk. The druggists were on strike, and in Moscow the water system had been shut off. After about a week of such deprivation, the citizenry grew angry and their irritation was not directed entirely against the government. They began to look on the strikers as their enemies, and they saw the source of all their tribulations in the "instigators" of the strike, above all the students and the Jews. Vendors and merchants from Moscow's Okhotny market, their stalls empty because deliveries had been stopped, were among the first to take up arms against the strikers.

Fighting erupted in Moscow on 14-15 October, not between crowds and the police but between strikers and mobs of people, whom their enemies called the "Black Hundreds."[18] They caught students in the streets and beat them up. The students barricaded themselves inside the university in dormitories and classrooms. The mob chopped down trees and burned them in the courtyard for warmth against the chill of the long October night. The confused authorities interfered neither with the students' barricades nor the activities of the mob.

The changing mood made itself felt most clearly in Moscow. Metropolitan Vladimir in an appeal read in all Moscow churches on 16 October called upon the people to fight sedition. On the morning of the 17th the city's water mains began to function again, the butcher shops reopened, and the trams reappeared in the streets. The employees of three railroads—Kazan, Yaroslavl, and Nizhni Novgorod—decided to call off their strike. Some zemstvos also began to protest. The zemstvo assembly of Yelets adopted the following resolution: "Those who can afford it are on strike, but the destitute people of the black-soil provinces are the ones who will have to pay for it later. Let those who do not want to work leave the railroads and make room for the peasants who need work." In Tver on the evening of 17 October a mob surrounded the building of the provincial board where zemstvo employees had gathered to discuss their strike. Someone set the building afire. As the employees fled, they were attacked by the mob which made no distinction between those who were for or against the strike.

In other parts of Russia the strike began belatedly and so it continued to spread. Without newspapers no one had any idea of what was going on in the nearest town. "Rumors filled the land," each one more incredible than the last.

In St. Petersburg on 14 October a Soviet [Council] of Workers' Deputies began to operate.[19] The Soviet consisted of elected delegates from the factories and representatives of the revolutionary parties. On the 16th a delegation from the Soviet appeared before the St. Petersburg municipal duma with a list of demands. The Bolshevik Radin [Knuniants] spoke for the delegation: "We need the means to continue the strike—appropriate money for it! We need weapons to conquer and defend our freedom—give us the means to organize a proletarian militia!" The city duma, however, turned a deaf ear to these demands, despite the whistling and jeering of the crowd that filled the gallery. On 17 October the Soviet published the first issue of its paper, *Izvestiia Soveta Rabochikh Deputatov*—News of the Soviet of Workers' Deputies.

SOLON OR NAPOLEON?

The tsar continued his conferences through the 16th and 17th of October, but he found no one willing to stand firmly against the events sweeping around them. Goremykin's plan for a manifesto did not differ significantly from that of Obolensky and Witte. Goremykin's draft also proclaimed "civil liberties based on personal inviolability, freedom of conscience and speech, freedom of assembly, and the right to form associations as prescribed by law." It also promised to expand voting rights. Goremykin's plan was somewhat less precise than Witte's in its definition of the power of the State Duma: "We command that rights of popular representation, which we hereby grant to the people of Our Empire, provide a firm basic foundation for the introduction of legislative measures into the Duma."[20] This vague wording was intended to convey a promise to broaden the powers of the future Duma.

The tsar rejected still another alternative that had the advantage of directness and clarity—abandonment of the idea of a manifesto and concentration solely on the struggle against the revolutionary movement. Yet any manifesto had to contain a clear and irrevocable commitment [to reform]. "One of two ways was open to us," wrote the emperor [to his mother on 19 October]: "to appoint an energetic military man and use all available forces to try to crush the rebellion; that would have given us time to breathe, but in a few months we would have to use force all over again. That would mean rivers of blood, and in the end we should be where we had started. That is, the authority of the government would be reaffirmed, but the situation would remain unchanged . . . . The other way was to give the people their civil rights . . . and also have all laws confirmed by a State Duma . . . . That, of course, would be a constitution."[21]

In making his decision Nicholas was not concerned simply to eliminate the immediate danger. He knew that the government could crush the revolution by force, but he wanted to reconstruct Russian life by eliminating the discord that separated the government from the vast majority of society if not also the vast majority of the people. In a final meeting with Grand Duke Nicholas Nikolaevich and Baron Frederichs, the minister of the imperial court, Nicholas announced that he favored the second course. Witte was summoned to Peterhof, and at 5:00 p.m. on October 17th, the tsar signed the manifesto.

"Nearly everyone to whom I turned with the problem gave the same answer as Witte, that there was no other way out," he wrote, adding that it was a "dreadful decision" to make but that he "nevertheless made it in complete good conscience." "After such a day my head began to ache and my thoughts were confused. God help us and comfort Russia."[22]

THE OCTOBER MANIFESTO

The Manifesto of 17 October 1905 proclaimed:

Our heart overflows with great and heavy sorrow at the sedition and disturbances in the capitals and in many parts of Our Empire. The welfare of the Russian Sovereign cannot be separated from the welfare of His people, and the people's sorrow is His sorrow. The disturbances that now arise create profound popular discord and threaten the unity and integrity of Our state.

The great vow of the Tsar's service enjoins us to use every resource of Our wisdom and authority to bring a speedy end to the unrest that threatens Our state. We have ordered the proper authorities to take steps to terminate direct displays of disorder, lawlessness, and violence and to secure the safety of peaceful citizens who quietly seek to fulfill the duties incumbent on all. In order to ensure the successful implementation of measures designed by Us for the restoration of peace to our national life, We find it essential to unify the activities of the central state administration.

We impose upon the government the responsibility to execute Our inflexible will:

1) To grant the people the inviolable foundations of civil liberty based upon the principles of genuine personal inviolability, freedom of conscience, speech, assembly, and association.

2) Without postponing the promised elections to the State Duma and insofar as possible in the brief time remaining before its convocation, to admit to participation in the Duma all those classes of the population which presently are deprived completely of voting rights, and to leave further development of the principle of universal suffrage to the future legislative order.

3) To establish as an inviolable principle that no law shall come into force without the consent of the State Duma, and to ensure that representatives elected by the people shall be guaranteed the opportunity to supervise the legality of the actions of those authorities appointed by Us.

We call upon all loyal sons of Russia to remember their duties to their country, to assist in terminating this unprecedented turmoil, and together with Us to make every effort to restore peace and tranquility to our native land.

A diluted version of Witte's memorandum of 9 October was published in conjunction with the October Manifesto. The emperor's introduction indicated that it was "to be used for guidance." Witte's report stressed the need to raise Russian political life "to the level of the ideas which animate the moderate majority of the people." In concluding, Witte declared: "We have faith in the political wisdom of the Russian people. It is unthinkable that our people should desire anarchy which, in addition to all the horrors of civil war, threatens the very disintegration of the State itself."[23] The manifesto did not indicate that the emperor had relinquished his responsibilities. He remained the final arbiter of all affairs of state. Initially, however, Nicholas entrusted Witte with broad authority, including the power to create a ministry. Only the departments of war, navy, and foreign affairs remained under the sovereign's personal control.

TURBULENT REACTION

The manifesto was published in St. Petersburg and abroad on the evening of the 17th of October. Witte lost no time in making it known. It came as a great surprise to the revolutionary parties, who were concerned that they would lose control of the strike and that it would turn the people against them. Thus the revolutionaries gained no sense of victory from the manifesto. Indeed, the proclamation of civil liberties and a legislative Duma created total confusion in their ranks. What was it—a shrewd maneuver or a surrender? Nothing seemed to suggest the latter.

The St. Petersburg Soviet of Workers' Deputies was in a quandary. Its first reaction was neither to halt the strike nor believe the government. "Witte is given to us, but Trepov remains to us," proclaimed Trotsky in the Soviet's *Izvestiia.* "A constitution is given, but the autocracy remains. Everything is given—and nothing is given .... The proletariat wants neither the police hooligan Trepov nor the liberal broker Witte—it wants neither the wolf's mouth nor the fox's tail. It does not want a *naigaka* [whip] wrapped in a constitution."[24]

The manifesto created a great stir in the provinces. Revolutionaries outside the capital took it to mean the total capitulation of the government, while the masses thanked God

October Manifesto with Superimposed Bloody Hand Print

that the strikes and rebellion finally would end. "The tsar has granted freedom"—there was nothing more to ask. The people interpreted freedom in different ways and understood only vaguely what it meant. Nevertheless, they poured into the streets with portraits of the tsar and national flags to celebrate, not denounce, the publication of the manifesto.

The attendant violent outbreak of civil strife originated in the public reactions of crowds whose politics clashed—those who celebrated the tsar's benevolence and those who celebrated the victory over the tsar's authority. That civil strife later was known as "the wave of pogroms" or "the action of the Black Hundreds." In the west and southwest, where Jews were especially active in the revolutionary movement, they bore the brunt of public anger. But the story was the same in areas with scarcely any Jews.[25] In Petersburg demonstrations of both types took place on the 18th; a procession bearing national flags encountered marchers with red flags and fighting resulted. In Moscow, where the wave of revolution already was receding, strikers welcomed a plausible excuse to end the struggle. Demonstrators marched with red banners to the governor-general's palace where Paul P. Durnovo greeted them from the balcony.

CIVIL WAR IN THE PROVINCES

The same scene repeated itself in the provinces. In Kiev, Kremenchug, Odessa, and elsewhere on 18 October demonstrators hoisted red flags proclaiming their victory, defamed authority, tore down the tsar's portraits in public buildings, collected donations for "a coffin for Nicholas II,"[26] and urged the people to continue the struggle. On the following day in Nizhni Novgorod, Balashov, and other cities crowds motivated by the same "offended and inflamed patriotism" took to the streets in even greater numbers. Criminal elements later joined them and looting also took place; but generally those outbursts were directed against the revolution. On the 21st at Nezhin, where the Philological Institute was the local center of radicalism, several thousand peasants from outlying villages assembled before the cathedral. They marched to the institute and demanded that the students take the tsar's portrait and follow them. Then they forced the students and Jews, whom they met on the way, to kneel in front of the cathedral and swear an oath "not to rebel and to honor the tsar."[27]

On 20 October at Tomsk in another corner of the empire a large crowd besieged demonstrators sporting red banners in the city theater. There was shooting on both sides, the building was set afire, and about two hundred people burned to death. In Simferopol, Rostov-on-Don, Saratov, Kazan (where the confused governor promised to disarm the police and withdrew the troops from the city), Poltava, Yaroslavl, Tula, Kishinev—it is impossible to name all the cities—an anti-revolutionary tide surged in reaction to the triumphant displays of the parties of the left. As with all spontaneous popular movements, it was marked by cruelty. The tide of reaction quickly crested and receded in two or three days, between the 18-19th and the 20th-21st of October.

Allegations that the police organized this movement are quite absurd. Events of the previous two years had demonstrated that the police were powerless to control any popular movement. Even if they had wanted to, the police were incapable of organizing a mass movement. "These are not the Black Hundreds but the black millions," exclaimed A.A. Stolypin in *Novoe vremia*. Even the more profound intellectuals who supported the revolution understood that. Writing in *Russkoe bogatstvo*, S. Elpatievsky observed that the lower classes retained their "traditional love for their fatherland and their national pride .... Old beliefs formed over the centuries cannot be removed from life in an instant by bombs, proclamations, or Japanese artillery. Let the people of Petersburg wait to celebrate their victory—there is no victory yet! . . . An ignorant man stands at a Russian crossroad and wonders which way to go." *Kievlianin*'s analysis appeared on 19 October:

The blood of the hapless victims and all the horrors of uncontrolled rampaging fall on the heads of those madmen who caused the explosion in the first place and thereby ignominiously blasphemed the sanctity of the nation .... Say not that the Russian people are enslaved. They are a great and loving people. You do not understand their faith; you do not understand their love—just as they do not understand you. But you forced them to learn the meaning of revolutionary violence; you forced them to comprehend how you were desecrating their most sacred beliefs. Then their contempt for blasphemers erupted in pogroms against the Jews whom they considered your accomplices.

The grandiose funeral of an obscure veterinarian, the socialist Nicholas Bauman,[28] took place in Moscow on 20 October. Bauman was killed on the 18th by the [Black Hundred] worker Mikhalin, who threw himself on "a man with a red flag." Bauman's funeral was the occasion for a show of force by the revolution—the first "civil funeral" in Russia. One hundred thousand marchers, singing the *Marseillaise* and the *Funeral March* and carrying countless red banners, paraded in rows protected by squads of armed workers. Hostile groups studied the procession from the sidewalks and made the revolutionaries uneasy. Returning from the cemetery in the evening the armed guard saw or thought it saw the Black Hundreds waiting in ambush in an unlit street near the riding school. The workers opened fire. Cossacks stationed at the riding school thought they were being attacked. They poured out of the building and began to return the fire in volleys. The workers dispersed, but six were killed and about a hundred were wounded.

SCLEROSIS OF THE BUREAUCRACY

The authorities seemed to have disappeared while these events unfolded. Mobs clashed with one another, but neither police nor troops were involved. Only in Minsk on 18 October did troops fire on demonstrators who were advancing toward them. In Petersburg, however, no demonstrators left or right were permitted to take control of the streets. On the 18th a crowd attempted to release students arrested at the Technical Institute in connection with a bomb thrown at a cossack patrol. Energetic measures by the military authorities dispersed the attackers. The Semenovsky Imperial Guards Regiment, commanded by the able and courageous General George A. Min, formed on Zagorodny Prospekt, and its presence alone was sufficient to nip in the bud the feeble revolutionary urge.[29] As a result of firm action, Petersburg suffered far fewer casualties than other cities. The Soviet, seeking to follow the Moscow example, planned to stage a great funeral for its revolutionary martyrs, but Dmitry Trepov announced that "when one section of the populace is prepared to rise in arms against another section," demonstrations cannot be allowed. Trotsky himself recommended, and the Soviet decided, to cancel the funeral demonstration.

Finally the strikes ceased, calm returned to the streets, and five days after the publication of the manifesto one could again begin to account for events. Public opinion generally held that the liberation movement had achieved a great victory. As V.V. Rozanov put it, "the government has departed." The boundary between the prohibited and the permitted was wiped out. Revolutionaries gathered openly to discuss how to spread their propaganda among the troops and how to foment an armed uprising. The censorship collapsed, and extremist papers began to appear one after another. In *Novoe vremia* Menshikov glorified the "freedom fighters." The holy synod decided to censor Metropolitan Vladimir's popular appeal against sedition. Eight ministers and directors resigned,[30] less from disagreement with "the new course" than to make room for Witte's candidates. A new ministry for trade and industry was created. D.F. Trepov moved from the post of governor-general of St. Petersburg to the less prestigious but especially important position (particularly in those days) of commandant of the palace, which made him responsible for the personal safety of the emperor and the imperial family.

THE BELEAGUERED HELMSMAN

The October Manifesto created an entirely new situation. It diverted the previously unified revolutionary torrent into separate channels, which occasionally smashed into each other. It awakened the popular forces loyal to the tsarist government, who finally saw with their own eyes how serious the situation had become. At the time of its publication, the manifesto had few critics, even on the right. But those early days also signaled the downfall of the man whom many had been willing to recognize as the savior of Russia; Count Witte had miscalculated grievously.

General Kuropatkin first learned of the manifesto on 23 October, and he wrote in his diary: "Sergei Witte triumphs. He has his vengeance, oh, how he has taken his vengeance against the emperor!—more than he himself ever imagined possible." But by the 23rd Witte scarcely had triumphed. Russia's chaos gave no indication of either the "moderate majority" or the "political wisdom" that Witte had praised a few days before. In an interview with the newspaper editors on the 18th he pleaded: "You, gentlemen, must see to it that the sovereign realizes that good measures get results. That is the best way. Support me on that." But in response Witte heard only fresh demands: Remove the troops, organize a people's militia, proclaim an amnesty, abolish the death penalty. The zemstvo representatives, whose program he had adopted and for whom he was holding vacant ministerial portfolios, called on the 22nd. Now they insisted on a constituent assembly. In desperation Witte reportedly exclaimed: "If Christ had been head of government in these circumstances, they would not have believed even Him!"[31]

Court and especially military circles were critical of Witte's actions for different reasons. His program, they alleged, satisfied no one and only increased sedition. "It is strange that so intelligent a man should have erred in his calculations to restore calm swiftly," wrote Nicholas who, leaving political matters to Witte, himself undertook to safeguard the police and military apparatus from the threatening disintegration. On 23 October the tsar appointed P.N. Durnovo as manager of the ministry of internal affairs. On the 27th Grand Duke Nicholas Nikolaevich, whose disappointment with Witte developed quickly, assumed command of the imperial guards and the Petersburg military district.

EX UNO PLURA

One of the immediate consequences of the October Manifesto was the rapid intensification of the revolutionary movement on the outskirts of the empire. Mass demonstrations in the Kingdom of Poland demanded autonomy and even independence. In two or three days a general strike swept across Finland. Governor-General Prince I.M. Obolensky, fearful of being taken prisoner, moved out of Helsinki to the battleship *Slava* anchored at the Sveaborg Fortress. Nicholas decided that in the case of Finland concessions were necessary. His Manifesto of 22 October 1905 suspended all legislation to which the Finns had objected, beginning with the Manifesto of 3 February 1899. "Upon concluding Our examination of the Seim's petition of 31 December 1904, We recognize that it is worthy of attention," declared the new manifesto. It summoned the diet to convene in extraordinary session on 7 December and restored the Finnish constitution to its former status.

Scarcely had *Novoe vremia* detected a "little hint of things quieting down" on 25 October—the reopening of the secondary schools—than disorder erupted at Kronstadt. The crews of several ships revolted and the movement spread across the city. Killing, looting, and general drunkenness gripped Kronstadt and left it for two days in the hands of a horde of drunken sailors. On the morning of the 27th General Nicholas Ivanov landed with two battalions of the Preobrazhensky Regiment and quickly restored order. The sailors were too drunk to resist. Similar events occurred on 30 October in the other corner of the empire at Vladivostok. The only difference was that there the rebels were mainly reservists waiting to return home. After some hard drinking and looting, the mob began to beat up Chinese and Koreans. The city suffered heavily for two days, and then the drunken mob, having had its fun, settled down again.[32]

The zemstvo leaders refused to join Witte's cabinet. Therefore by the end of October Witte filled the "vacancies" originally prepared for them with other liberal officials whom he selected.[33] Meanwhile, parallel with the old machinery, government began to grow new "heads." The Soviet of Workers' Deputies issued orders and they were obeyed. The typesetters union established its own system of censorship by refusing to print newspapers that adhered to the old regulations. It refused to publish the appeals of right-wing organizations, and it even vetoed the publication of the program of the Union of October 17.[34] The "Octobrists" were political moderates who formed around the nucleus of Shipov's group in the zemstvo congresses. The Union of October was strengthened by the addition of many prominent public figures who took the position that the promises of the October Manifesto achieved the goals of their movement.[35]

The new "bosses" behaved more and more imperiously. They began by forcibly seizing private publishing houses for a few hours at a time in order to print their own *Izvestiia*. They found supporters among newly organized and openly revolutionary papers like *Novaia zhizn* and *Nachalo* and among older extremist papers like *Syn otechestva* and *Nasha zhizn*, now surpassed in their radicalism by the overtly revolutionary press. *Novaia zhizn*, run by the symbolist poet Nicholas Minsky and Maxim Gorky, was the mouthpiece of the

Bolsheviks. Many contemporary poets—Minsky, Balmont, Bely, and others—wrote for it. Minsky composed poetry to the
stanzas of the *Internationale*—"Proletarians of all countries,
unite . . . he who is not with us is our enemy, and he must
fall"—while Balmont proclaimed, "Worker, you are Russia's
only hope."

Two weeks after the publication of the October Manifesto,
the government took its first decisive action, although it
affected only a corner of the empire. On 31 October the government declared a state of martial law in the Kingdom of
Poland: "The government will not countenance encroachments upon the security of the state," read the decree, which
then proceeded to enumerate a series of seditious actions in
Poland. On the same day Pikhno inquired in the columns of
his *Kievlianin* whether

"readers of the government's decree reluctantly might not ask if the
same abuses are not also occurring in the cities of Russia? . . . Was
not the Manifesto of 17 October followed by the same displays in
an unchecked revolutionary orgy? All the rebelliousness of the past
two years, the terrible civil war of recent days, and all the disorders
in far distant parts of the empire came about because the flag of
Russia wavered and bowed. . . . Count! Neither you nor anyone else
in the world can replace that banner. Once again it must be raised
high, high so that all of Russia, Europe, and Asia can see and bow
before it. . . . Then this irrational storm will end."

THE SECOND GENERAL STRIKE

The revolutionaries' response to martial law in Poland was
to call a new general strike. To that demand they added
another calling for the abolition of the death penalty for
the Kronstadt mutineers. The revolutionaries hoped that this
demand would give soldiers and sailors confidence that if
they rebelled they would find defenders. The strike began
on 2 November, and Witte issued a personal appeal: "Brother
workers, resume your work, abandon rebellion, spare your
wives and children. Do not listen to evil counsel. Give us
time, and everything possible will be done for you. Listen
to a man who is well-disposed toward you and who wishes
you all good." The Petersburg Soviet answered: "We proletarians share no kinship with Count Witte. . . . The Soviet of
Workers' Deputies has no need of favors from the favorite
of the tsar."

The second general strike, aimed at particular objectives, did not inspire the same elemental enthusiasm as the first. The railroads obediently came to a halt, and the newspapers suspended publication for four days, but even in Petersburg about half of the labor force reported for work as usual. On 5 November the government gave the strikers a plausible reason to return to work. An official announcement declared that no death penalty threatened the Kronstadters—they would be tried for drunkenness and looting but not for mutiny. As for Poland, the government promised to suspend martial law as soon as calm returned. "Let's speak frankly," Trotsky told the Soviet, "we will have to tell the Petersburg workers to call off the strike anyway. . . . It is obvious that political demonstrations are subsiding everywhere in Russia."

Witte pinned great hopes on the zemstvo congress that convened in Moscow on 6 November, and the delegates heard several speakers call for cooperation with the government. Prince Eugene Trubetskoy complained about the "impression in the government that the manifesto has satisfied neither revolutionaries nor zemstvo progressives." Alexander Guchkov insisted that it was essential to spurn the revolution. Nevertheless, the congress could not bring itself to proclaim its support for Witte's cabinet, even in the tentative form proposed by Peter Struve—support for the government in return for the government's endorsement of the congress's program.

The press began to speculate in terms uncomplimentary to Witte. "I would not be surprised in the least," wrote A.S. Suvorin, "if those brave fellows arrested Count Witte tomorrow and threw him and all of his ministers into a cell in the Peter and Paul Fortress."[36] M.S. Menshikov attributed the government's inaction to a devious plan: "I assume that Count Witte indulges the revolution only to be more certain of killing it. . . . It is not the government but society that primarily suffers from anarchy. It is not the ministers who suffer from the doubling and tripling of meat prices. . . . The very same people, those very same workers . . . will take on the revolution and kill it like a wild animal sprung from its cage."

On 10 November Nicholas wrote in despair to Empress Maria Feodorovna: "Everyone is afraid to take courageous action. I keep trying to force them—even Witte himself—to act more energetically. . . . You write to me, dear Mama, that I should trust Witte. I can assure you that on my part I do everything I can to ease his difficult situation. . . . I cannot conceal from you some disappointment in Witte. Everyone thought he was a terribly energetic and authoritative man and that he would begin at once to establish order."[37] Meanwhile the inactivity of Witte's cabinet was creating "a strange impression of fear and indecisiveness."[38]

SIC TRANSIT BJÖRKÖ

Having turned domestic policy over to Witte, Nicholas resumed his correspondence on the Björkö treaty with William II. "There is little chance of drawing France into our alliance," he wrote on 27 October. "Russia has no reason to drop her old ally or to commit violence against her. . . . Therefore, it is necessary to add the following declaration: 'In view of the difficulties which hinder the immediate accession of the government of France, Article I of the treaty is declared herewith to be void in the event of war with France; the mutual obligations which bind the latter with Russia are to be retained in full until the conclusion of a triple alliance.' "

William, however, insisted on the original text, and he maintained that legally the treaty already was in effect. That at least was debatable, since the conclusion of a treaty always required two steps. The monarch's personal involvement in formulating a treaty (the "initiation") did not preclude the need for the more formal act of ratification. As long as Bülow held reservations about the treaty, the German government itself considered it proper to demand revisions of the text. But at this point the Germans flatly refused to admit any alteration. From the aspect of cordial Russo-German relations, that clearly was a mistake. By insisting on the original text on a technicality, the kaiser's government actually destroyed the treaty that would have erected a German-Russian bloc against England. The German refusal to accept the amendment convinced Nicholas that the entire treaty would become a dead letter. Some two years later, Germany too was compelled to accept that conclusion.

REBELLIOUS SAILORS AND POSTMEN

The zemstvo congress still was in session in Moscow when Sevastopol exploded with a rebellion that was particularly serious because it included military and naval units. On 11 November some shore-based naval units mutinied, and part of the Brest Regiment joined them. Unrest became noticeable in the fleet. The local corps commander, General Baron Alexander N. Meller-Zakomelsky, subdued the Brest Regiment, but the sailors held out. The cruiser *Ochakov* raised the red flag. During the night of the 14th a former naval lieutenant, Peter P. Schmidt,[39] took it upon himself to lead the mutiny. On the *Ochakov* he ran up the signal: "I am in command of the squadron—Schmidt." He next sent a telegram to the tsar announcing that the Black Sea Fleet "refuses to obey the government." When emissaries sent ashore to rally other troops were arrested, Schmidt gave orders that the officers held prisoner were not to be fed until the sailors were released.

Nevertheless, the general rebellion that seemed imminent collapsed with the first gun shots. The *Ochakov*, wrapped in flames, hoisted a white flag, and the remaining ships surrendered without a fight. Schmidt was arrested; tried later before a naval tribunal, he was condemned to death and shot. The Brest Regiment, one of the original defectors, played an active role in seizing the naval barracks which were the last stronghold of the mutineers. By the morning of the 16th it was all over, but casualties on both sides numbered thirty dead and seventy wounded.

On the day the Sevastopol mutiny collapsed, the postal and telegraph workers went on strike. They cited the October Manifesto and announced their desire to form a union. The authorities informed them that even foreign governments did not permit state employees to unionize and suggested that they wait for the State Duma to consider the problem. At that, the convention of postal and telegraph employees declared a national strike, and the Petersburg Soviet endorsed it. A great part of the population viewed this strike without sympathy. The most liberal elements were puzzled as to the reason for such a blow to the national economy over a particular matter that had no urgency. Professor F.F. Martens published an appeal in a newspaper in which he called for resistance to the strike "not by word but by deed." Hundreds of volunteers reported to the St. Petersburg post office to sort and deliver mail, and in other parts of the province the same thing occurred. The active movement in reaction to the strike quickly disposed of it, and by 23 November the strike was over in St. Petersburg, though it went on in other parts of the province. The employees were rehired with a month's wages deducted as a fine.

THE MILITANT RIGHT AND THE EXPECTANT LEFT

Right-wingers who championed the preservation or restoration of unlimited tsarist power began to organize during this period. Vadim Gringmut, editor of *Moskovskie vedomosti*, took the lead in forming a monarchist party in Moscow. In St. Petersburg, Dr. Alexander I. Dubrovin organized the Union of Russian People. Its first meeting on 21 November attracted several thousand people to the Mikhailovsky Riding Academy. The Union of Landowners, which convened in Moscow on or about the 20th, adopted a similar program and resolved on an appeal to the tsar "to replace the present government with another, since the present one is unable to establish firm authority and deal with rebellion."[40]

The failure of isolated uprisings did not embarrass the revolutionaries. "The revolution acts with spontaneous wisdom and the spontaneous cruelty of nature," explained *Nachalo*. "When it requires some particular result, it performs tens and even hundreds of experiments. It advances by degrees, building on its individual defeats and setbacks." *Nasha zhizn* had a somewhat broader view: "The Russian revolution is a signal, the summons of an alarm. The revolutionary storm will accelerate and push with ever-growing force from Petersburg to Paris, from Paris to Berlin and Vienna . . . . And where will you weak-kneed rats of the Russian bourgeoisie flee? To Turkey, Persia, or Tibet, to the Saharan Desert, or into the canyons of Cordillera? . . . In time the great revolution will get there too, for it is the master of the world; its realm is the entire universe, from the peaks of the Himalayas to the bowels of Vesuvius."[41] The leftist press exulted over the mutinies of the armed forces: "Kronstadt, Vladivostok, Sevastopol, Voronezh, Kiev, Reval[42] . . . like a fiery serpent mutiny crosses

Russia from garrison to garrison. The call to victory: The
Army joins the Revolutionary People! One military insurrection after another! One blood-bath after another! Dying abso-
lutism cannot stop the avalanche of revolution. It will roll on
to the end!"[43]

In November the central committee of the Socialist Revolutionary Party voted to end isolated terrorism and to concentrate exclusively on tactics of mass struggle. However, that
decision by no means reduced the number of individual terrorist attacks. Swept along by their own rhetoric, the Socialist
Revolutionaries and the Social Democrats apparently mis-
judged the ground slipping from beneath their feet. They
seemed oblivious to the increasing exhaustion and satiety of
the public during the second month of "freedom." When the
government arrested its chairman, George S. Khrustalev-Nosar,[44] the Petersburg Soviet on 26 November decided to prepare
for an armed uprising.

The news of "freedom" also animated the villages. Unusu-
ally violent peasant rebellions broke out in parts of Chernigov,
Saratov, and Tambov provinces. The tsar sent his adjutants—
General Sakharov, Admiral Dubasov, and General Alexander
Panteleev—into those provinces. The appearance of the army
was enough to quiet the disorders, and force was unnecessary.
All the same, the terrorist Anastasius Bitsenko shot and killed
Sakharov in the home of the governor of Saratov, P.A. Stolypin.[45] The goal of the terrorists was not so much "to avenge
cruelties," as most people believed, as it was to murder gradually but systematically the most energetic and able government
officials in order to facilitate the victory of the revolution.

The most serious displays of the agrarian movement took
place in the Baltic, where Latvian national animosity for the
German landlords merged with the strong influence of the
Social Democrats. Rebellion completely embraced Lifland and
Courland. Latvian revolutionary societies convened openly.
The jacquerie destroyed 573 estates with losses mounting to
about 12,000,000 rubles. Great cruelty attended these events.
On the night of 30 November Latvians attacked sleeping
dragoons in the city of Tukkum; they stabbed to death twenty
or so and then set fire to the building. They made a similar
surprise attack on the Provodnik Works in Riga, where they
killed eleven dragoons. The government decreed martial law

and sent reinforcements from Petersburg. Nevertheless, the Baltic rebellion lasted more than a month and claimed numerous lives.

WELCOME FACES AT TSARSKOE SELO

During November the emperor busily strengthened his relations with the troops. Beginning on the 21st, the guards regiments came in turn to Tsarskoe Selo. The imperial couple and the young heir attended receptions for the officers, and the tsar reviewed parades and addressed the regiments. Following the disciplined ceremonies at Tsarskoe Selo, the regiments returned to Petersburg with its strikes, revolutionary leaflets, and audacious poseurs. The contrast intensified their loyalty to the tsar and their hatred for the revolution. Alexander A. Polovtsev,[46] a high-ranking official of the court, wrote that in November the officer corps of the guards appealed for Witte's arrest and the establishment of a dictatorship. Grand Duke Nicholas Nikolaevich, however, restrained the guards for fear that he himself might have to lead a military dictatorship. Direct contact with the emperor convinced the guardsmen that Nicholas was and would remain master over the Russian land.

Representatives of the right first visited the emperor on 1 December. V.A. Gringmut represented the Russian Monarchist Party, Prince Alexis Shcherbatov the Union of Russian Men, and Nicholas Pavlov and others the Union of Landowners. It was not a successful meeting. Proceeding on the assumption that Nicholas was easily influenced, some of the delegates took a sharp tone and practically demanded that he personally confirm the inviolability of his autocratic power. Nicholas replied: "I have no doubt that you will choose no other path than the one I have outlined .... The manifesto that I issued on October 17th is a complete and conscientious expression of my inflexible will; it is an act not subject to change." The emperor considered it impossible to have his name used in a struggle with a government that he himself had confirmed. The conservative delegation left in frustration.

A second reception on 23 December produced an entirely different conclusion. The tsar received a delegation from the Union of Russian People, led by A.I. Dubrovin and P.F.

Bulatsel, but consisting mainly of workers, coachmen, and peasants. Dubrovin spoke: "We impatiently await the convening of the State Duma which will give us, the Russian people, the opportunity to elect representatives loyal to you, Sire, and to the Fatherland." Nicholas agreed to accept the emblem of the Union for himself and the tsarevich, and he replied: "Unite the Russian people—I am counting on you." One of the delegates asked: "Are we right, Sire, to remain loyal to autocracy?" The tsar gave a delphic answer: "Soon, soon the sun of truth will beam over the land of Russia, and then all doubts will disappear."[47]

THE GOVERNMENT BEGINS TO STIR

The Soviet was "preparing" an armed uprising, but its leaders knew that the presence of the guards regiments made an attempt in Petersburg quite impossible. The Soviet decided instead to employ a different tactic—a strike against the state's finances. It published its "financial manifesto" in eight of the capital's newspapers. After a gloomy description of the state of the nation, the proclamation concluded: "The government must be cut off from its last source of survival, its financial revenues." To accomplish that, the Soviet urged the people to (1) refuse to pay taxes; (2) demand gold or silver as payment in all transactions; (3) withdraw funds from all savings accounts and banks demanding payment in full in gold; (4) refuse to pay loans issued by the government while it blatantly made war on its own people. The Soviet's intention was to deplete the treasury's gold reserve, thereby depreciating the ruble and simultaneously depriving the government of access to foreign loans.

This time the government reacted swiftly to counter the Soviet's plan. That same day the authorities closed all the newspapers that had printed the manifesto, and on the following day, 3 December, the government arrested the entire Soviet of Workers' Deputies. Shadow "deputies" and a presidium reconvened and passed resolutions, but the history of the Soviet as an autonomous authority, a second "boss," concluded with those arrests. With the disappearance of the Soviet so too disappeared the uncensored press. The extremists, sensing that the paralysis of the government was coming to an end, decided to wage a general battle—a general strike that would be transformed into an armed uprising when the army rallied to the revolution. Moscow seemed the most suitable center to begin the final struggle, for the governor-general, P.P. Durnovo, had remained completely passive and thus facilitated the activities of the revolutionary organizations.[48] Moreover, discontent had infected the Moscow garrison (especially the Rostov Regiment); the troops had submitted demands to their officers and refused to obey until they were met.

On 5 December, however, a new governor-general arrived in Moscow. Admiral Feodor Dubasov immediately outlined a forceful new policy to the representatives of his administration: "Criminal propaganda has built a nest for itself in this city of Moscow, where once Russia's heart beat with deep love for the motherland. Moscow has become a convention and hotbed of individuals who impudently aspire to destroy the very foundation of order.... Under such circumstances, my appointment to the post of Governor-General of Moscow takes on special significance. It is an appointment to a military command.... I am convinced of the victory over rebellion, but revolution cannot be defeated simply by musketry and bayonets—victory also depends on the moral influence of the best public forces. At this moment sedition confronts the lawful government with insolent demands and bids defiance with raised weapons. That is why I shall not hesitate for a moment to employ the most extreme measures: I shall do what duty requires me to do." The Rostov Regiment returned to duty that same day: the soldiers "rocked" their commander and cheered him with hurrahs.

ARMED INSURRECTION IN MOSCOW

An "order of revolution," as *Novoe vremia* called it, appeared on 6 December and called for the general strike to begin at 12:00 noon on 8 December. "The proletariat will not be satisfied with some partial reshuffle of politicians among the government's personnel. It will not cease its strike until local authorities surrender their power to the institution of the provisional revolutionary government elected by the local population." The announcement was signed by the Social

Moscow Uprising—Barricade of Streetcars

Admiral Feodor Dubasov

General George Min

Democratic and Socialist Revolutionary Parties, the Union of Railroad Workers, the Postal and Telegraph Workers Union, and the Soviets of Workers' Deputies of Moscow and St. Petersburg. In vain did Miliukov warn against this step in his newspaper [*Narodnaia svoboda* (The People's Freedom) published briefly in December 1905].

Meanwhile, from the 5th to the 9th of December, officials met at Tsarskoe Selo to discuss a new electoral law. As in the Peterhof conference of the previous summer, the emperor's decision took the place of a vote. Invited as representatives of the political moderates, Alexander Guchkov and Dmitry Shipov defended the principle of universal suffrage but without success. The emperor did not want to upset the electoral law of 6 August, and he decided simply to supplement it with the addition of new electoral classes. The law was amended to give workers 206 electors, separately elected. It also extended the vote to all private and public employees living in cities and to all tenants. (In St. Petersburg these provisions increased the number of voters from approximately 10,000 to about 100,000.)

The third general strike began on the 8th, as ordered, but it was destined to failure from the start. Many railroads refused to go along, and in St. Petersburg only an insignificant part of the labor force walked out. "The orders said to strike, but they were not obeyed," *Novoe vremia* smugly noted, and on the second day of the strike, 9 December, it reported that "the all-Russian strike has failed miserably."

Nevertheless, except for the Nikolaevsk Railway which was under heavy military guard, all the railroads operating out of Moscow struck, and about two thousand armed workers assembled in Moscow. The revolutionary parties decided to proceed according to plan. Their aim was to get the troops to defect to the revolution, but the movement functioned in a climate of popular indifference. There was no "psychological contagion" whatsoever. Consequently the staff of the militant forces decided to begin a guerrilla war inside the city limits of the old capital. The armed workers received the following "technical instructions":[49] "Operate in small detachments. Use one or two riflemen against a hundred cossacks. It is easier to score a hit by shooting at a hundred than by shooting at one, especially if the one [sniper] fires quickly and then

disappears into nowhere . . . . Let our fortresses be the courtyard passages and any place from which it is easy to shoot and
easily escape." The idea was simple: the soldiers could not fire
at armed workers without hitting innocent people; that would
infuriate the populace and cause them to join the uprising.
Barricades went up all over the city. They consisted mostly
of over-turned sledges or wagons or gates torn from their
hinges and set in foundations of snow. Although the barricades
were numerous, they were not defended at all. Their function
was to hinder the movement of troops and to make it easier
to snipe from windows. Those tactics enabled the workers to
fight almost without casualties. Workers fired at the soldiers
and then hid in the labyrinths of inner courtyards. They
wounded individual policemen standing their posts. At first
the government could not deal with those tactics. The dragoons and cossacks initially had no taste for that kind of
fighting, but then they became enraged and began to pursue
the elusive enemy through the city with real zest. "Could one
regard firing from a corner, a gateway, or a window an act of
bravery?" asked "a Muscovite" in *Novoe vremia* on 23 December. "First they fire and then they flee over fences and
through connecting courtyards, leaving the peaceful citizen
to pay with his own life's blood for their acts of 'courage.'
That sort of 'heroism' is beyond description."

The government ordered porters to keep all gates bolted.
Armed detachments of workers received a counter-order: porters who bolted their gates were to be beaten, and if they did
it again, they were to be killed.[50] Several buildings that concealed snipers were battered by artillery. The uprising did not
spread, but neither did the guerrilla warfare cease. It continued
from 9 December to the 14th. Physical exhaustion noticeably
sapped the cossacks and dragoons, and then Admiral Dubasov
appealed to the tsar by direct wire to Tsarskoe Selo. He
described the situation and underlined the importance of the
outcome of the struggle in Moscow. Nicholas ordered the
Semenovsky Imperial Guards Regiment to Moscow.

The troops were weary, but the Muscovites too were tired
of the shooting. The workers found it increasingly difficult to
get help in raising barricades. With greater frequency they
began to run into hostility or to encounter the volunteer
militia organized by the Union of Russian People. The arrival

of the Semenovsky Regiment on the 15th decided the fate of
the uprising. The workers' detachments began to retreat beyond the city limits. Before their departure, however, they
broke into the apartment of Voiloshnikov, the head of the
Moscow Okhrana, and shot him, despite his children's pleas
for mercy.
The revolutionaries' main line of communication was the
Moscow-Kazan Railroad, and a detachment of the Semenovsky
Regiment commanded by Colonel Riman moved along that
route, occupying stations and shooting workers arrested with
arms in their possession. The shooting in the city ended,
except for the Presnia district, a workers' quarter rising high
above the banks of the winding Moscow River. Revolutionaries
in that section held out for another two or three days. Finally
after an artillery bombardment, the Semenovsky Regiment
occupied the district on the 18th without a fight. The attempted armed insurrection collapsed when confronted by
energetic action of Admiral Dubasov and General Min without
an excessive number of victims: in ten days of struggle the
total number of killed and wounded was less than two thousand. The general strike came to an end before the Moscow
uprising was crushed; another revolt began in Rostov-on-Don
on 19 December, but it was suppressed in two days.

RECONQUEST OF SIBERIA

The next problem was to restore order in the periphery of the
country. Siberia presented the most serious challenge. Since
the first general strike, strike committees actually controlled
the Siberian railway, and several revolutionary strongholds
were established along its route. Rumors magnified their power
and importance. The strikers allowed trains carrying reservists
from Manchuria to pass, but only after subjecting them to
revolutionary indoctrination. The Far Eastern command lost
its head. General Linevich negotiated an agreement with the
strike committee by which reservists could be evacuated. Fed
by rumor, the Manchurian Army smoldered with unrest, and
officers and soldiers held meetings. In his diary on 23 December Kuropatkin wrote: "The reactionary forces are nominating
[A.P.] Ignatiev and breaking Witte. Nicholas Nikolaevich is
striving for a military dictatorship." Reporting a conversation

with his commanders, Kuropatkin recorded that Linevich "does not consider it necessary to combat the extremist parties. He repeated several times that order will not be restored until Russia has her own Napoleon, capable of smashing everything and everyone. . . . Could it be that he imagines himself in that role?"[51]

On 28 December the commander of the Manchurian Army received by way of Shanghai a telegram from Nicholas. The tsar had commissioned General Paul K.E. Rennenkampf to restore order along the Siberian, Trans-Baikal, and Chinese Eastern Railways. Generals Linevich and Kuropatkin were perplexed. Their first thought was "to let Rennenkampf travel as a tourist" [have nominal command]. Kuropatkin thought that Rennenkampf's activities "should be regulated by decrees of the State Duma (?)," but it was difficult to refuse a direct order from the tsar.

At that point Nicholas found an even more efficient executor in General Meller-Zakomelsky, who accepted the assignment of clearing the Great Siberian Railway of revolutionaries. With a detachment of only two hundred men, specially selected from guard units in Warsaw, he left Moscow by special train on New Year's Eve. It appeared to be madness: a strong revolutionary army of several thousand was believed to have occupied Chita, and tens of thousands of reservists returning from Manchuria were completely without discipline. But a handful of men with a determined leader proved stronger than those anarchic elements.

Meller-Zakomelsky operated sternly. At Uzlovaia he ran into the first train-load of undisciplined reservists. He lined up half of his detachment on the platform, while the other half used rifle butts to clear the train of troops who had occupied the officers' compartments. At another station two agitators burst into his car; they were thrown off the speeding train. News of two or three such incidents spread by telegraph were sufficient to ensure that other approaching trains of reservists put themselves in order, and there were no more attempts to agitate among the ranks of his detachment.

A revolutionary band barricaded itself in the depot at Ilan and made an effort to defend itself. Meller-Zakomelsky's detachment, firing in orderly volleys, killed nineteen, wounded seventy, and then the rest surrendered. That was the last

attempt at resistance, although at two other stations Meller-
Zakomelsky's firing squads executed the strike committees.
The two-hundred-man detachment moved swiftly across Siberia, and the revolutionaries scurried out of its path without
a thought of resistance. Chita was the main Siberian center
of revolution. The Reds had been masters there for nearly
three months, and the local governor referred to the Social
Democrats as "the party of order." Although the revolutionary council had access to 30,000 rifles in railroad cars, so
great was the fear of Meller-Zakomelsky's detachment that
the revolutionaries hastened to surrender without a fight
to General Rennenkampf (who was approaching from the
east from Manchuria). That way they did not fall into the
hands of the "dreadful" detachment. Meller-Zakomelsky's
expedition demonstrated how sometimes firmness applied
at the proper time can prevent great bloodshed.

Chita surrendered on 20 January. The Siberian route was
liberated. Generals Kuropatkin and Linevich had committed
no offense but neither had they been able to handle the
situation. An imperial decree early in February relieved them
of their commands. The tsar appointed General N.I. Grodekov
to the command of Russian forces in the Far East. On 8
February 1906 General Meller-Zakomelsky introduced his
detachment to the emperor at Tsarskoe Selo.

INTELLIGENTSIA IN CONFUSION

Russian society experienced a deep psychological crisis in
December. The third general strike and the abortive uprising
in Moscow did not win the unanimous support of the intelligentsia. The imperious tone of the revolutionary organizations had begun to annoy them, and the violent character
of the extremist parties alienated them. On 15 December
Peter Struve wrote in *Poliarnaia zvezda* [The Polar Star]:[52]
"We are sworn enemies of violence of any kind, whether it
stems from the government or from anarchy." Prince Eugene
Trubetskoy was even bolder in his criticism of society's
conduct: "How was freedom of speech used? In truth, no
one hesitated to criticize or denounce the government. The
caliber of speakers and journalists in that regard was mediocre,
but then as everyone knows, even timid animals venture to

attack a toothless lion. . . . Still, how many resolute and courageous speeches were made against that new power, which everyone trusted and worshipped because it brandished the whip long familiar and dear to the heart of the man in the street? Was there no awareness that the people had cast off the old tattered livery and that they were rushing pell-mell to don the bright shining chains of slavery and to set upon their heads numbered caps bearing the inscription 'freedom'?" D.S. Merezhkovsky warned against the danger of mob rule in an article titled "The Approaching Boor," though the boors that he saw were the Black Hundreds.

However, with the collapse of the revolutionary movement, the restoration of order, and the return to normal, Russia's society also reverted to its accustomed role. It developed a sympathy for the defeated revolutionaries and an ardent indignation for the official measures employed against them. The moderate *Vestnik Evropy* complained about the government's "excessive self-defense." The left-wing press daily published "condemnatory evidence" and denounced the executions of armed workers and the destruction of homes, quite forgetting that for a week the revolutionaries had hunted policemen and ambushed soldiers. Society hungrily devoured the slightest accusation. During the peasant riots, a mob in the village of Sorochinsk murdered a district policeman. The councilor Filonov, who was sent to investigate, ordered the peasants to kneel and repent. That form of repression provoked the well-known writer Vladimir Korolenko to send a strange denunciatory letter to the local paper, *Poltavshchina.* A few days later, an unknown assailant murdered Filonov. Korolenko then wrote in embarrassment about "the intervention that I could neither desire nor foresee. . . ."

Even more sensational was "the Spiridonova case." G.N. Luzhenovsky, a provincial councilor, was sent to Tambov to quell peasant unrest. There in the city of Tambov Maria Spiridonova,[53] a young girl of about eighteen, shot him in the stomach, a wound that proved mortal. An enraged crowd beat her severely before she was driven off to jail. While imprisoned, she wrote an hysterical letter accusing the arresting officers of inflicting all sorts of tortures and indignities. An investigation failed to verify those accusations, and Spiridonova herself did not repeat them in court. "How is it possible to print and credit as evidence the hallucinations of a sick, seriously injured person?" asked the *Peterburzhskie vedomosti*. But as in the case of Filonov, Spiridonova's accusations cost human lives: both of the officers whom she accused were killed within the next few months, and the murderers vanished without a trace. Nationwide, the number of terrorist acts increased dramatically in early 1906.

BANKERS AND BISHOPS

The government ran into financial difficulties toward the end of 1905. Tax collections practically ceased, and the gold reserve of the State Bank began to dwindle. The cause was less the "financial manifesto" of the St. Petersburg Soviet than the panic that seized the wealthier classes. Kokovtsov was sent to Paris to raise a foreign loan. His mission, undertaken with Moscow in open rebellion, might have appeared hopeless, but the emperor was also following international events. The Algeciras Conference was scheduled to begin early in 1906, and France needed diplomatic support. Nicholas's promise that Russia would support France on the Moroccan question was sufficient to persuade the French premier to make every possible effort to meet the financial needs of his ally. Russia obtained a short-term credit of 150,000,000 rubles and the promise of a more substantial loan after the Moroccan settlement.[54]

Count Witte nominally retained power for more than four months after the December victory over the revolution, but after the first of December the tsar in fact resumed control of events. His direction became apparent in all areas. The military and police administrations functioned completely apart from the Council of Ministers, and the prime minister himself, having abandoned any independent policy, simply "swam with the tide." On 12 January 1906 Nicholas wrote to his mother: "As for Witte, since the events in Moscow he has radically changed his views; now he wants to hang and shoot everybody. I have never seen such a chameleon of a man. Because of this aspect of his character, scarcely anyone believes in him anymore; he finally has sunk in the estimation of everyone. . . . I like the new Minister of Justice [M.G.] Akimov very much . . . Durnovo is excellent. . . . The rest of the ministers are people of no importance!"[55]

On 17 December the emperor received the three Russian metropolitans to discuss the convening of a church council. On the 27th he sent a letter to Metropolitan Anthony of St. Petersburg. Recalling that the idea of a national council had been proposed the previous spring, Nicholas wrote that he now considered "the time propitious to introduce some changes into the structure of our country's church," and he suggested that Anthony set the date for a council. An organizational meeting to prepare for the national assembly began its work on 6 March 1906. About fifty persons, including ten bishops, took part in the preliminaries. Metropolitan Anthony presided, and the new director-general of the holy synod, Prince A.D. Obolensky, took an active part in the proceedings.

THE SIMMERING QUESTION OF LAND REFORM

In January 1906 Nicholas found it necessary to address himself once again to the question of agrarian reform. That problem, perhaps the most irritating issue in Russian life, had been on the agenda for four years, but war and revolution had pushed it into the background. Redemption payments, the only major direct tax on the peasantry, had been abolished in 1905. Rumor had it that before the elections to the State Duma the emperor would promise to distribute landowners' property to the peasantry; that measure would punish the zemstvo activists for supporting sedition and at the same time ensure peasant support for the struggle against the Liberation Movement. The emperor had no such intention, and it never occurred to him that he might "buy the votes of the peasantry" by violating the principle of private property. To the contrary, he saw the solution of the problem not in some limitation of private ownership but in its extension to the peasantry.

On 18 January the emperor received a delegation of peasants from Kursk and he told them that "all property rights are inviolable. What belongs to a landlord belongs to him; what belongs to a peasant belongs to him. The landlord's possessions are his by virtue of the same inalienable right that makes your land your own." During the second half of January an interministerial committee rejected a proposal by Nicholas Kutler, who functioned in the capacity of agricultural minister as director of the main administration of land organization and agriculture. Kutler's plan envisioned the compulsory confiscation [with compensation] of land rented by peasants. With the rejection of his proposal, Kutler resigned.

The emperor's position on the agrarian question was, like the government's, open and above-board. However, the promise of expropriation was a dangerous demagogic weapon in the hands of the government's enemies, and they used it in "peasant" elections to the State Duma.

KADETS AND OCTOBRISTS

The revolutionary parties went underground. Members of the Union of Liberation, the zemstvo constitutionalists, and segments of the Union of Unions formed the Constitutional Democratic Party. The Kadets[56] held their constituent convention at the time of the first general strike. The party played no role whatsoever in November and December, and only the ebbing of the revolution pushed it into the foreground. At their convention in January 1906 the Kadets proclaimed their allegiance to a constitutional and parliamentary monarchy—a question left open in October—and they began to mobilize for the Duma elections. By contrast, the more radical parties called for a boycott of the elections.

The Union of October 17th—the Octobrists—convened early in February. The convention revealed that the provincial delegates were considerably more conservative than the liberal center. While the spokesmen for the central committee, Michael Stakhovich and Alexander Guchkov, criticized the government for its actions and demanded the revocation of the state of emergency, the provincial representatives took quite the opposite position. "In doing so we will be signing the authorization for a second revolution," exclaimed Chigirev, a delegate from Minsk. Others argued that "only under martial law can peaceful citizens breathe freely." The resolution calling for the repeal of the state of emergency garnered 142 votes, but 140 votes were cast against it. To avoid splitting the organization the central committee dropped the matter. Another resolution calling upon the government to convene the State Duma no later than the end of April received quick approval. On 14 February 1906 the government announced that the Duma would open on April 27th.

The Imperial Manifesto of 20 February 1906 further developed, supplemented, and specified the general promises of the October Manifesto.[57] The manifesto declared that the tsar retained all powers except those specifically shared with the State Duma and the State Council. Half of the members of the latter were to be appointed, and half were to be elected. "Isn't it a pleasant surprise," wrote Struve in *Poliarnaia zvezda*, "to find in the Manifesto of February 20th a juridical affirmation that the autocracy is abolished beyond all question."

On 4 March the government published temporary regulations on unions and associations. On 8 March a decree defined the basic jurisdiction of the State Duma with regard to the budget. A great part of the budget was, in contemporary parlance, "reserved." Repayment of the state debt and the budgets of the imperial court and war and naval ministries could be revised only by legislative procedures, that is, with the consent of the Duma and Council and the approval of the tsar. If the Duma and Council failed to agree on a budget, the amount closest to the previous year's budget was to be adopted. If a budget was not approved on time or rejected, the budget of the preceding year remained in force automatically.

The press engaged in an animated discussion of the meaning of the word *autocracy*. Some held that it meant limitless, while others appealed to history and asserted that it only meant independence from some other foreign power. On 18 February the tsar told representatives of the Ivanovo-Voznesensk Autocratic-Monarchist Party that they should "inform those who sent you that the reforms which I announced on October 17th will be realized without change and the rights which were granted by Me to My people are inalienable, but My Autocracy will remain as it was in former times."

The Russian Assembly[58] issued a special pamphlet that conveyed its point of view: "At times circumstances may arise which place the Russian Tsar under a moral obligation to act outside the State Duma for the welfare of all the people: he may even be compelled to repeal the Manifesto of October 17 . . . . Let no one transform this manifesto into an obligation externally imposed upon the tsar; let no one interpret it as some kind of contract or bilateral agreement."

A FINANCIAL TRANSFUSION FROM FRANCE

The Algečiras Conference concluded successfully, and in March Kokovtsov returned to Paris to negotiate a billion-ruble loan necessary to liquidate the war (mainly the repayment of short-term debts) and to cover deficits incurred during a year of revolution.[59] Leftists conducted a campaign against the loan. Several Russian liberals went to Paris to combat it, but their efforts were unsuccessful—a fact that they later preferred to have forgotten.

For its part the French government acknowledged the demise of the revolution, and it hoped to revitalize the Franco-Russian Alliance, badly shaken by events of the preceding two years. The Algečiras Conference proved the value of Russian support. Therefore, even though the Rouvier government fell and was succeeded by the cabinet of Jean Sarrien at the height of the negotiation, the discussions proceeded. Even the new interior minister Georges Clemenceau raised no objection to the loan but went so far as to tell the Russian ambassador that attacks against "tsarism" in the French press "should not be taken too seriously," for irresponsible journalists write all sorts of things! The loan, concluded in April, was a great success for Russia.[60] Gorky was furious: "*La belle France*, I spit in your eye!"

DISASTER AT THE POLLS

Elections for the State Duma began in March. The initial results did not offer a clear picture, but as the elections proceeded the decisive victory of the Kadet Party became apparent. It was farther to the left than any party participating in the election, and it attracted the votes of the discontented non-party populace. The moderates, led by the Union of October 17, and the rightists, banded under the title of "Monarchists" or the Union of Russian People, could not compete with the Kadets. In St. Petersburg the Kadets won 40,000 votes, the moderate bloc 18,000, and the Monarchists 3,000; in Moscow the Kadets received 26,000 votes, the Octobrists 12,000, and the Monarchists 2,000. The results were the same in the provinces. Only in the cities of the south and west were the Monarchists significantly stronger, but even there Jewish and Polish voters ensured Kadet majorities.

When the electors assembled in the provincial capitals, the two tactics of the peasantry became clear: first, to elect as many of their own deputies as possible, and then to support those candidates who promised land to the peasantry. Nearly every province elected Kadets and non-party peasants, among them the Trudovik group which subsequently proved more radical than the Kadets.[61] The question inevitably arose: What happened to the many thousand who opposed the revolutionary movement in October? Monarchist assemblies probed that question in April, but no answer was discovered. Several explanations are possible. Persons without individual residences were excluded by the electoral law. Others simply weren't interested in elections. Still others detested the revolutionaries' tactics but had nothing against the "alluring prospects" portrayed by Kadet speakers. Whatever the reasons, the electoral results were a heartbreaking disappointment to the government and to the moderate and conservative parties.[62]

AN AUTOCRAT, BUT WHAT KIND?

Discussion of a new code of Fundamental Laws began at Tsarskoe Selo in April. The Manifesto of 20 February provided the point of departure. The conference was unique in that reconsideration of the Fundamental Laws was permissible only on the initiative of the sovereign. The usual officials attended the conference. The most difficult question was the text of Article 4 of the projected code: "The supreme autocratic power belongs to the All-Russian Emperor." The existing code contained the words "autocratic and unlimited."

At the meeting of 9 April Nicholas expressed his own thoughts on the problem: "This is the fundamental question.... It has been on my mind for a full month. Incessantly the question gnaws at me: do I have the right before my ancestors to alter the prerogatives of the power that I received from them .... I was fully conscious of my action of October 17, and I am firmly resolved to pursue it to the end. But even so, I am not convinced of the need to renounce my autocratic rights and change the definition of the supreme power, as it has existed for 109 years in Article 1 of the Fundamental Laws. Perhaps the accusation of duplicity is directed not at the government but at me personally? I accept those reproaches from wherever they come. I am convinced that eighty percent of the people would be on my side. It is a matter for my own conscience, and I shall resolve it myself." The emperor's statement created an unusual stir:

Count Witte: This question will decide the entire future of Russia.

The Emperor: Yes.

Count Witte: If Your Majesty finds it impossible to renounce the principle of unlimited power, then nothing further must be done. The Fundamental Laws must not be reissued.

Count Pahlen:[63] I did not agree with October 17th, but it exists. You, Sire, were the one who desired to limit your power.

M.G. Akimov: To retain 'unlimited' would be to throw down the gauntlet. If the laws that are issued ruin Russia, then you will have to lead a coup d'etat, but for the moment one cannot admit that.

(Other members of the State Council—A.A. Saburov, Count Solsky, and E.V. Frisch[64] —gave similar opinions.)

Grand Duke Nicholas Nikolaevich: The word 'unlimited' was erased by Your Imperial Highness in the Manifesto of October 17.

P.N. Durnovo: After the acts of October 17th and February 20th, the unlimited monarchy has ceased to exist.

Prince A.D. Obolensky: Having stricken 'unlimited,' retain 'autocratic.'

The Emperor: I shall announce my decision later.

(The discussion continued on the 11th and 13th of April. When the deliberations finally concluded, Count Solsky turned to the emperor and asked: "What is your desire—to retain or exclude the word 'unlimited'?")

The Emperor: I have decided to retain the wording of the Council of Ministers.

Count Solsky: Therefore the word 'unlimited' is to be deleted?

The Emperor: Yes—exclude it.[65]

NICHOLAS "DROPS THE PILOT"

The Kadets convened on 21 April 1906 to formulate the party's tactics in the State Duma, and the question precipitated a struggle between leftists and moderates. While still in session, the convention received a telegram that an attempt had been made on the life of Admiral Dubasov. The delegates burst into applause. As it turned out, Dubasov was not injured, but his adjutant, Count Konovnitsyn, and the assassin who threw the bomb were killed.

On 23 April the press announced the retirement of Count Witte and the appointment of his successor, Ivan Goremykin. With Witte departed not only "his" ministers but also P.N. Durnovo and Count Lamsdorf, the foreign minister. A completely new government would greet the State Duma.

Struve's liberal journal *Svoboda i kultura* [Freedom and Culture] published a "political necrology" of the former prime minister. "Count Witte is certainly no reactionary. He is simply a man without any convictions. . . . In order to occupy the top spot in October, he had to proclaim himself a firm champion of reform. In order to stabilize his position, he decided to form a close alliance with P.N. Durnovo. If the highest circles hatched a plot to revert to autocracy and if, in Witte's opinion, it was not promptly doomed to failure, he of course would not hesitate to place himself at the helm of such an enterprise. . . . And after what has happened, that is the only role that could restore Witte to power." That was a prophetic estimate, for Witte more than once offered himself for such a role. Nevertheless, he always encountered one insurmountable obstacle: "As long as I live, I will never trust that man again with the smallest matter! The experience of the past year has been quite enough for me," wrote Nicholas to Empress Maria Feodorovna on 2 November 1906.

The new Fundamental Laws of the Russian Empire, forged so painfully in the crucible of the Tsarskoe Selo conferences, were made public on 26 April 1906. At Miliukov's prompting, the convention of Constitutional Democrats in its final session resolved on a sharp reply: "On the eve of the opening of the State Duma, the government has decided to hurl a new challenge at the Russian people. It now attempts to reduce the State Duma, which is the focus of the hopes of a country which has suffered so much, to the role of servant to a bureaucratic government. No obstacles created by the government will prevent the people's representatives from fulfilling the duties which the people have entrusted to them."

CHAPTER TWELVE

AUTOCRAT AND CONSTITUTION

Novoe vremia carried an unusually perceptive article on the day that the First Duma convened: "Our sovereign, wounded by numerous events, has suffered grievously. The mice emerged from under the ground, nibbled some cheese, and scurried away. But the emperor endures, even though the events of 1904, 1905, and 1906 have been more agonizing for him than for anyone else." Those were without question arduous years for Nicholas, because of the great responsibilities that were his and because of the struggle that he had to wage at home and abroad. His every decision was attacked, frequently from opposite ends of the spectrum. Irresponsible conservative critics berated him for weakness, while the regime's enemies read their own ideas into his proclamations and then denounced him for breaking his word. Nevertheless, rebellion was crushed and the Duma came to life.

"The emperor's vision is greater than ours," continued *Novoe vremia.* "The throne towers over all and from it is visible much that cannot be seen from benches, platforms, and rostrums. . . . The emperor is much better informed than any of us. Let us be thankful for him. If the present generation, nurtured in the turmoil of these restive times, cannot appreciate his greatness and individuality, then will historians, setting straight the record of our time, raise his name all the higher."

Emperor Nicholas II obviously was no admirer of representative government, and he had no illusions about the temper of society. Toward the end of 1905 Sergei Kryzhanovsky was present during a conversation between Nicholas and Witte. He recorded how "with irritation he [the tsar] brushed aside Witte's sugary remark to the effect that the people's representatives would support and sustain the throne and government: 'Do not tell me that, Sergei Yulievich, for I understand perfectly well that I am creating an enemy not an ally. Nevertheless I console myself with the thought that I may nurture a national force that will prove useful in the future in securing Russia along a path of peaceful development without any marked destruction of those foundations on which it has rested for so long.' "[1]

Ideally the emperor regarded unlimited autocracy as the most perfect form of government. However, the early years of his reign had convinced him that in twentieth-century Russia, and especially among Russia's educated elite, the autocracy would not find enough dedicated agents to carry out his monarchic will from conscience rather than from fear. The opposition of the zemstvo camp, the failure of the Zubatov movement, the strikes, and the inefficiency of the state administration during the Japanese war—all those failures ultimately could be attributed to one single factor: the empire lacked educated people ideologically committed to the autocratic system. The loyal masses of the people, in whom the emperor's confidence remained unshaken, could not compensate for that deficiency.

Therefore, to make it easier for Russian society to work for the welfare of the nation, the emperor embarked upon the path of reform, the pitfalls and liabilities of which he was keenly aware at all times. Not for a moment did the consciousness of his personal responsibility for Russia's fate desert him: he was responsible not only for his own errors but also for the failures of others. The irresponsibility of a constitutional monarch, as propounded in liberal doctrine, seemed to Nicholas a criminal washing of the hands. That was why he unfailingly reserved to himself the option to make all final decisions. The October Manifesto did not violate that principle. In essence it promised that no law would be issued without the consent of the State Duma. The manifesto did not define precisely the authority that would be delegated to the Duma, and on that point the interpretation of the lawgiver himself was more authoritative than the opinions of the government's opponents. In general the Fundamental Laws of 1906 created a system similar to that created by the Prussian constitution of 1848.[2]

It was the emperor's desire to incorporate the people's representatives into the tsarist government. He assigned to

the Duma an impressive home, the Taurida Palace, built at
the end of the seventeenth century by [for] Gregory Potemkin, the Prince of Taurida.[3] The emperor and empress together
planned the opening ceremony. Nicholas received and rejected
several proposals for an inaugural statement; he composed
his own words of welcome to the deputies of the people.
The opening of the Duma was a national holiday, and the
peal of church bells across Russia proclaimed the momentous
event. Nicholas knew perfectly well that the deputies' ranks
contained unappeasable enemies. Even so, he deemed it essential that the throne greet the assembly with an appeal for
for mutual service to the fatherland. In his own mind he
did not associate the people's representatives with the bloody
guerrilla warfare that the revolutionary parties, defeated in
open battle, continued to wage against the government. It
was up to the Duma to prove itself: Nicholas intended to
judge the deputies by their own actions and not by the reports
filed by his governors or ministers.

COMPOSITION OF THE FIRST DUMA

At the time of its formal opening the Duma contained about
450 deputies.[4] Nearly two hundred of them were semi-literate
peasants; almost all of the rest had received a higher education.
It was a Duma of intellectuals and peasants. The left extremists had boycotted the election, and therefore the Socialist
Revolutionaries and Social Democrats were not represented.[5]
Nevertheless, more than a hundred deputies considered themselves farther to the left than the Kadets; they formed the
Trudovik [Toilers] group. Deputies from the western region,
headed by a Polish delegation, formed another separate group-
ing. Only 30-40 rightists and moderates were elected, and
only a few of the moderates were recognized political figures—
M.A. Stakhovich, Count P.A. Heiden, and Prince N.S. Volkonsky. None of the right-wing leaders entered the Duma.

Elected as an opposition to the government, the deputies
regarded themselves as tribunes of the people's will, which
in their opinion was the true source of power. To them
the existing laws were irrelevant. What counted were their
own programs and their own broad interpretation of the October Manifesto. Most of them accepted terror as a manifestation

First State Duma—Tsar's Speech From the Throne

of the legitimate wrath of the people, and they regarded the government's anti-terrorist repression as unconscionable violence.

THE DAWN OF A NEW ERA?

April 27th was a bright spring day. Not once during the winter had the emperor left Tsarskoe Selo, where he remained in relative safety under the watchful protection of D.F. Trepov. The imperial yacht brought him to Petersburg on the morning of the 27th, and he went first to the Fortress of St. Peter and Paul. There [in the Cathedral of Peter and Paul] he prayed for a long time at the tomb of his father. Waiting in the Georgievsky Hall of the Winter Palace was the imperial throne canopied in red and gold. Draped over the throne was a mantle of imperial purple trimmed in ermine. A wide passage divided the room, and space was reserved for the members of the two legislative bodies along its white and gilded walls—the State Council stood on the right. Standing with the members of the council were the highest officials of the court and government in their gold-laced, medal-bedecked court and military uniforms. Members of the Duma arrived a little later wearing frock coats and peasant garb.

The distant strains of the national anthem heralded the arrival of the emperor. Footmen in ancient livery led the procession into the throne room. They were followed by dignitaries bearing the state regalia, which had been brought from Moscow for the occasion: the state seal and sword of state, the orb and scepter, and the imperial crown blazing with diamonds. Then came the tsar wearing the uniform of the Preobrazhensky Regiment.[6] Next came the two empresses dressed in white gowns and pearl-studded headdresses. The grand dukes and grand duchesses and officials of the imperial court followed the empresses, and the procession ended with the entry of the ladies-in-waiting and the tsar's aides-de-camp.[7]

A prayer was read, and then the tsar "slowly mounted the steps, turned to face the assembly, and with a deliberateness that served to stress the historic occasion, he solemnly took his place upon the throne. He paused silent and motionless for about half a minute, reclining lightly against the left arm of the throne. The hall was absolutely silent with anticipation."[8] Then the minister of the court passed the emperor a sheet of paper, and Nicholas in his porphyry uniform, rose from the throne to deliver his welcoming address:

Concern for the welfare of our native land, which Divine Providence has entrusted to Me, has prompted Me to call upon the people's elected representatives to assist in the legislative process. With an ardent belief in the brightness of Russia's future, I welcome you, the best people, whom the nation at My bequest has elected to speak in its behalf.

Difficult and complicated tasks lie before you. I believe that love for our motherland and a sincere desire to serve it will inspire and unite you.

For My own part, I shall protect as immutable the course that I have set. I do so in the firm conviction that you will devote all your strength in selfless service to the nation so as to clarify the needs of the peasants, who are so dear to my heart, and to identify those things necessary for the enlightenment and welfare of the people, while always bearing in mind that the spiritual greatness and prosperity of our land requires not only freedom but also order based on law.

I pray that my earnest desire to see My people happy and to pass on to My son the inheritance of a strong, orderly, and enlightened state shall come to pass.

I pray that the Lord will bless the work which awaits Me together with the State Council and the State Duma. May this day signify the renewal of Russia's morality—may it mark the rebirth of Russia's best forces. May you approach with reverence the task to which I have summoned you. May you justify the confidence which the Tsar and the people have placed in you. God help Me and you.

The tsar's address had a great effect. "The more he spoke the greater the emotion I felt," wrote Grand Duke Constantine Constantinovich. "His words were so good, so true, and so sincere that nothing could have been added or taken away." The Kadet leader Feodor Rodichev later recalled that "it was a well-written speech. It was read beautifully with correct emphasis, with full understanding of each phrase, clearly and sincerely . . . . It was without question much-admired." S.A. Muromtsev, the president of the First Duma, similarly observed that "the emperor is a true orator . . . his voice is extremely well-modulated." At the conclusion of the address cheers were raised not only on the right but also, though somewhat less enthusiastically, among the Duma members on the left. As the deputies left the Winter Palace, they still were under the spell of the greatness and grandeur of Imperial Russia, which many of them beheld for the first time.

But once outside the palace the deputies were again in a different world much closer and more familiar to them.

Crowds of intelligentsia and workers covered the banks of the Neva, and they shouted to the deputies from the bridges and embankments: "Amnesty! Amnesty!" As the ferry that carried the deputies passed the Krestov, a large jail in the Vyborg quarter, the prisoners hailed them from all the cell windows. Crowds lined the route from the quay to the Taurida Palace and greeted the deputies with the same cries for amnesty. Not all the representatives were present for the inaugural prayer in the Taurida Palace, since many of them began immediately to discuss how they might express "the demands of the people." One prominent deputy, Maxim M. Vinaver, noted that "persons normally self-possessed ran around flapping their arms."

The vice-president of the State Council, Edward Frisch, took the podium, called the assembly to order, and delivered a short welcoming address. The first order of business was the election of a president and by a nearly unanimous vote the Duma chose Sergei A. Muromtsev,[9] a Kadet and professor of Roman law. Having occupied the president's chair, he immediately recognized Ivan Petrunkevich, who delivered a brief speech on amnesty: "It is a debt of honor, a debt of conscience which demands that the first free word pronounced from this platform be dedicated to those who sacrificed their lives and freedom to win political liberty for Russia .... Free Russia demands the liberation of all who have suffered for freedom!"[10]

Only after Petrunkevich's appeal did Muromtsev make his own inaugural address. He referred to the need to "respect the prerogatives of the constitutional monarch" but also stressed the "rights of the State Duma which are inherent in the principle of popular representation." The first session of the Duma ended on that note. It revealed that the government and the deputies spoke a different language—"spoke past one another," as the expression goes. The Duma's first concern was to obtain amnesty for those who still continued to conduct a bloody civil war against the regime. That was scarcely what the emperor had expected from "the best people."

THE AMNESTY ISSUE

The revolutionary parties immediately understood the profit to be gained from the mood of the deputies, and the entire leftist press constantly repeated the necessity of a total amnesty. Revolutionists harangued meetings of workers and the intelligentsia. Leftist enemies of the Duma demanded "at least" the release of all political prisoners. With no thought at all of ceasing their revolutionary struggle, they looked forward to swelling their ranks with "liberated hostages."

Only members of the Kadet Party were elected to executive positions in the First Duma—Muromtsev, Prince Peter Dolgorukov and Nicholas A. Gredeskul (first and second vice-presidents), and Prince Dmitry Shakovskoy [secretary]. Even so, the more radical element in the assembly began to make its presence known from the very beginning. Thus the Duma resolved to compose a "speech to the throne" as a response to the "speech from the throne," as the emperor's welcoming address came to be called. Furthermore, the Duma's reply was to embody a complete program headed by a demand for "total political amnesty." The deliberations on the response inspired bitter attacks against the government. "We know how many crimes have been committed in the sacred name of the Monarch," declared Rodichev, "and we know how much blood is concealed beneath the ermine robe that covers the shoulders of the Sovereign Emperor." Arguing that punishment would not end terrorism, Rodichev exclaimed that "those people can only be punished with forgiveness." That remark insulted the radicals, who countered that amnesty was "an elementary act of justice."

More moderate speeches scarcely could be heard over the radical din. The only statement from the right on this question was the correction suggested sarcastically by Kontsevich, a priest from the province of Volynia. When the assembly voted to delete the expression "Russian people" from the response so as not to offend other nationalities, Kontsevich proposed adding a statement that "the State Duma is anxious to see Russia lose its identity and even its name." Nicholas grew increasingly irritated as he followed the Duma's deliberations. Meanwhile the terrorism continued. On the 1st of May an assassin murdered the chief of the port of Petersburg, Admiral Kuzmich, and dispatches from the provinces continued to report the murder of policemen.

During the evening session of 4 May, Michael Stakhovich,[11] one of the few persons who like Prince S.N. Trubetskoy had the ability to understand both camps, attempted to mediate and provide wording on amnesty that would be acceptable to the emperor.

The peasants who elected me to the Duma gave me these instructions [he said]: do not touch the Tsar, help him bring peace to our land, support him . . . .
Amnesty covers a broad range of trust and charity. But passing a law is not an end in itself. There still remains the matter of responsibility for the consequences of our action, and that responsibility rests ultimately with the emperor. I turn to those of you who remember the hour of the tsar's annointment ten years ago, when Nicholas stood before the opened holy gates and swore an oath to God in the Cathedral of the Assumption. He cannot ignore his solemn promise 'to bear all for the welfare of his people and the glory of God.' . . . He knows that he is not responsible for what happens in this place . . . but that does not absolve his soul of the knowledge that it is not the Duma but he who must answer to God for everyone tortured in the dungeons or shot down in the streets.
I understand, therefore, why he hesitates and does not commit himself as quickly as we do. He needs help to find the answer. We must explain to him that the previous struggle was terrible, that it was attended by such illegality and unremitting violence that the people abandoned the law and their consciences were drained of mercy. The goal of amnesty is the future peace of Russia. The State Duma must not fail to pledge itself to that end and to commit its support to the sovereign. Criminal means of struggle and contention must be abandoned along with the former absence of civil liberties. Henceforth no one must dare to engage in bloody strife. Hereafter let everyone live, be ruled, and pursue his ends not by violence but by the law. Therefore, let us dedicate ourselves to the Russian law, whose renewal we share and to which we subscribe, and to the law of the Old Testament, thunderously proclaimed four thousand years ago to all people for all time—Thou Shalt Not Kill!

Stakhovich then proposed that the Duma's response to the throne include this statement: "The State Duma expresses the firm hope that now with the establishment of a constitutional system there shall be an end to political murder and all other acts of violence, which the Duma most strenuously condemns as detrimental to the morality of the people and to the very idea of popular representation." Some deputies suggested that the Duma's condemnation should extend only to future terror, since the amnesty applied fully to the past. Prince Eugene Trubetskoy[12] expressed that idea in an article published that very day, and Bishop Baron Roop, a deputy from Vilna, supported the idea in the Duma.

The mentality of the Duma majority, however, was too firmly anchored in the revolution. Rodichev took the podium to assail Stakhovich's position: "This is not the pulpit of a church! Is it our business to make moral judgments on those actions? . . . Gentlemen, we are intermediaries between the sovereign and the people. In us stand the people before the tsar. . . . In Russia there is no legality! In Russia law becomes a mockery! In Russia there is no justice! During the past year, Russia suffered as it had not suffered since the days of Batu."[13] The deputy Shrag was even more frank: "No, we cannot condemn those who gave their lives for others— those who became folk heroes, those whom the people regard as victims and martyrs in the cause of their freedom."

In vain did Stakhovich argue that if there had been, as reported, ninety executions in the last few months, so too were 288 Russian citizens killed and 388 wounded—representatives of the government and mostly simple policemen. ("Not enough!" shouted the deputies in the benches on the far left.) "The Russian people," Stakhovich concluded, "will not see this as a service to them or their welfare. They will recognize it as murder, and the people do not want it." Stakhovich's amendment, however, was rejected, and only thirty-four deputies subsequently attached a minority report to the protocol.

THE DUMA ADDRESSES THE THRONE

The response to the throne was approved unanimously, because several moderate and rightist deputies departed and a small group of Social Democrats abstained. The adoption of that statement in effect determined the fate of the First State Duma. The French journal *Revue des deux Mondes* was puzzled by the demand for political amnesty—"And what about the crimes, the looting, the killings? The Duma had an opportunity to denounce them, but it refused." If a moderate French journal responded in that way, it is easy to imagine the emperor's reaction stemming from his deep concern for his loyal servants, victims of duty, who were being murdered in the streets.[14]

The Duma's "address to the throne" contained demands which violated the Fundamental Laws. It called for a ministry responsible to the Duma, abolition of the State Council, and the compulsory expropriation of land. But the critical provision, in the emperor's mind, was the demand for amnesty and the refusal to denounce murders committed in the future.

Nicholas did not hesitate to make his position known. He refused to receive the presidium of the Duma which was to deliver the statement, and he instructed Goremykin to inform Muromtsev that the document should be handed to the minister of the imperial court. On the following day, 5 May, telegrams to the emperor from rightist organizations sharply critical of the Duma began to appear in *Pravitelstvennyi vestnik*. Finally, the emperor instructed the Council of Ministers to work out an answer to the Duma's program. Nicholas wanted a firm, precise response, but Goremykin in typical fashion "rounded off the corners." The government also concluded that it was useless to introduce legislation into the Duma, except in those cases required by law and budgetary allocations in particular. Thus the first bill introduced into the Duma was a request from the education ministry for funds for a greenhouse and laundry at the Yurievsky University. The tsar's refusal to entertain its leaders somewhat confused the Duma, but it decided that "the form (by which the sovereign received the document) was of exceedingly little importance." The socialists, however, were quick to note that "the Kadets' answer to a slap in the face is silence."

Nicholas regarded the cabinet that functioned during the First Duma as a transitional government. Goremykin, the chairman of the Council of Ministers, was an intelligent and intensely loyal official who carried out the emperor's instructions to the letter. Among the other ministers were old associates of the emperor—V.N. Kokovtsov [finance], A.S. Stishinsky[15] [agriculture], I.V. Shcheglovitov[16] [justice], and Prince A.A. Shirinsky-Shikhmatov,[17] who had assumed the post of director-general of the holy synod. The two "new people" were interior minister P.A. Stolypin[18] and foreign minister A.P. Izvolsky,[19] who came to head the ministry from his post as ambassador to Denmark. The emperor explained Goremykin's selection to Kokovtsov in this way: "To me the most important thing about Goremykin is that he will not make concessions detrimental to my power behind my back." Goremykin, who was the same age as Ivan Petrunkevich, was portrayed maliciously as a senile old man. The fact that he ostentatiously snored during noisy Duma debates may have created that impression.

The government announced its position on 13 May. Promising its "complete cooperation in settling all matters that do not exceed the rights of the Duma," the Council of Ministers stressed that any solution of the land question on the basis proposed by the Duma was "absolutely inadmissable." As for the questions of ministerial responsibility and abolition of the State Council, the government noted that such proposals could not originate with the Duma. Amnesty, the government observed, was the prerogative of the monarch, but for its part "the Council of Ministers is of the opinion that the welfare of the country would not be served in the present troubled times by pardoning criminals who have taken part in murders, looting, and violence.

The Duma reacted angrily to the government's statement. Vladimir D. Nabokov[20] concluded his attack on the government by urging that "we must declare that we never will permit the existence of such a government which seeks not to execute the will of the people's representatives but to challenge and nullify that will. There can be but one solution: the executive power must bow to the legislative power!" The Duma immediately and with all but eleven votes of concurrence passed a vote of censure. From then on, whenever ministers attempted to speak, they were shouted down with cries of "Resign!" The ministers, however, adhered to the Fundamental Laws and ignored the Duma's "gesture."[21]

CAPITAL PUNISHMENT AND LAND REFORM

The struggle between the Duma and government then focused on land reform and the death penalty (once it became clear that an amnesty would not be granted). The Duma launched an inquiry into all death sentences imposed by the various courts and demanded in every case a stay of execution. The government, again appealing to the Fundamental Laws, maintained that no law had been violated and that the Duma's oversight extended only to legislative actions of the government. The Duma then entertained a bill for the abolition of the death penalty, and the government took advantage of its prerogative to demand one month to prepare its position.

Attitudes on the question of murder and executions followed strictly partisan lines. On 14 May eight persons, including two children, were blown to bits by a bomb explosion
in the cathedral square in Sevastopol. Scores of bystanders
were injured as well in this attempt on the life of the Sevastopol commandant, General Nepliuev.[22] When the Duma took
up the case, its only concern was to intercede in behalf of
the terrorists—"A military court has been convened already.
We must avoid bloodshed!" argued one of the deputies. The
leftist press sedately declared that "when the initial shock
wears off, even the wounded and the relatives of the dead
will understand that they were victims of an accident and
that the blow was not directed against them."[23] Given that
attitude toward murder, the deliberation on the death penalty
lost any fundamental humanistic content and became in the
emperor's view nothing but a ploy to save terrorists from
the consequences of their crimes.

On the land question, which was the key issue as far as
the peasantry was concerned, the Kadets advanced a plan for
the compulsory expropriation of rented land. As the need
arose, the plan also envisioned the expropriation of privately-
owned land that exceeded the "toiler's norm" [land that an
individual could not till by himself]. The Trudoviks simultaneously proposed confiscation without compensation of
all privately-owned land. On 19 May Stishinsky, head of the
land organization and agricultural administration, and assistant interior minister V.I. Gurko appeared before the Duma
and spoke in detail in behalf of the government. Gurko's
speech, in particular, was brilliant both in content and deliv-
ery, and it had some effect on the peasant deputies. Gurko
pointed out that the confiscation of all private estates in
Russia would add only insignificantly [about one desiatin—
2.7 acres] to the holdings of each peasant, while at the same
time the peasantry's opportunity for supplemental earnings
would disappear. He criticized the Duma projects, stressing
that their solutions would affect not only the holdings of
the gentry but also of the more prosperous peasants.[24]

The Duma's specialist on agriculture, Professor Michael
Ya. Herzenstein could reply only by referring to agrarian
disorders—". . . or is the May conflagration, which destroyed
150 estates in the province of Saratov, insufficient proof

for you?" He concluded his rebuttal by warning that "if you do not give it to them, the people will learn soon enough where the land is." Nicholas Lvov delivered a lengthy and forceful speech against compulsory expropriation, and he eventually withdrew from the Kadet Party over that issue.

THE GOVERNMENT AT BAY

Events in Bialostok on the first and second of June gave the Duma another issue to use against the government. That city with its predominantly Jewish population had experienced a particularly virulent wave of terror. The first five months of 1906 witnessed several dozen murders, attempted assassinations, and bombings. On 1 June several shots were fired at a Catholic procession, and that touched off a pogrom. In two days 75 Jews were killed and 84 were wounded, while the toll of Christians was seven dead and eighteen wounded. Several times, troops summoned to restore order exchanged fire with Jewish self-defense squads, and this led to accusations against the army.

The Duma sent three of its members to investigate the Bialostok pogrom first-hand. The deputies interviewed Jews almost exclusively and returned with an extremely one-sided and biased view. Their report repeated the old shibboleth that the government, of course, was responsible for organizing the pogrom. At one point in the discussion the deputy Yakubzon declared that the troops were afraid to venture into streets held by the Jewish self-defense forces, because "Russian soldiers have learned to run away from gunfire— the Russo-Japanese War has intimidated them." Angry protests in the conservative and moderate papers, a challenge to a duel from a young officer (Lt. Smirnsky), and a sharp rebuke from deputies Stakhovich and Sposobny prompted Yakubzon to reconsider. He finally admitted that the soldiers held back because they did not want to fire on the people.

The unfettered attacks on the ministers and the repeated demand for their resignation reflected adversely on the prestige of the government. *Russkii vestnik* complained about "the timidity, passivity, and humility of Mister Goremykin's cabinet." Incidents of unrest in the army increased, extending even to the First Battalion of the Preobrazhensky Regiment

encamped at Krasnoe Selo. Agrarian disturbances flared up
again in the provinces. The open conflict between the Duma
and the government created a dangerous "psychological insta-
bility." People began to wonder where the real government
was. Meanwhile the revolutionary terror continued una-
bated.[25]

The State Council, which was intended to be a pillar of
support for the government, sat passively and pondered. When
the Duma, to demonstrate its lack of confidence in the government, reduced from 50,000,000 to 15,000,000 rubles the
request for aid to victims of famine, the State Council, against
Kokovtsov's insistence, approved the Duma's reduction. (That,
incidentally, was the first and only legislative measure passed
by both chambers during the existence of the First Duma.)

The May congress of the [United] Nobility also avoided
any attack on the Duma. Moderates dominated the conference
which adopted and sent to the emperor a statement stressing
the need to expand private property among the peasantry.
The congress elected a Council of the United Nobility, which
subsequently acquired great prominence.[26]

TREPOV'S PLAN TO SNARE THE KADETS

During the second half of June rumors persisted about the
possible formation of a Duma ministry. Nicholas himself
hardly could have agreed to such a step, since he already had
made up his mind about *that* Duma. Nevertheless he did not
discourage those close to him, including D.F. Trepov, from
making "a reconnaissance in depth into the enemy's camp."
Trepov went even farther than parlays with the Kadet leaders:
he openly aired his views in the foreign press. On 24 June/7
July British papers carried an interview that a Reuter's correspondent conducted with the palace commandant. Trepov
frankly admitted that Goremykin's government was not in
control of the situation: "The alliance between the Duma
center and the Trudoviks will be shattered once the center is
called to power. Therefore, I consider it highly desirable to
form a new cabinet from the Duma center."

"That means the Kadets?" asked the correspondent.

"Yes," replied Trepov, "the Kadets. They are the strongest
party in the Duma. Neither a coalition ministry [from the

Duma and the bureaucracy] nor a ministry organized outside the Duma will appease the country." According to press reports, Trepov's comments met with general approval in England. Evidently Trepov calculated that a Kadet ministry would force the liberals to break with the left or else compel them to discredit themselves through weakness or repression. Either result would make it easy to dispose of them. The Kadets took the formation of a ministry quite seriously; both Miliukov and Muromtsev discussed the possibility.[27]

Meanwhile, an open break between the Duma and government drew nearer. On 19 June the deputies and ministers clashed sharply on the question of the death penalty. General V.P. Pavlov, the chief military prosecutor, appeared in order to answer questions on a bill calling for the abolition of the death penalty. The Duma shouted him down, and he found it impossible to speak. A stern man devoted to duty, Pavlov had prosecuted several cases involving revolutionary killings. The deputies jeered him as a "murderer" and "butcher." Before that incident, Minister of Justice Shcheglovitov had taken the rostrum to remind the Duma that the incidence of terrorism had increased after the amnesty of 21 October 1905. "Outrageous political murders occur daily across the vast spaces of Russia," he said. "They drag honest, dutiful civil servants into their graves . . . . To abolish the death penalty under these circumstances is equivalent to a refusal by the state to give every possible protection to its loyal agents." The Duma responded to that plea by passing unanimously and sending to the State Council a bill to abolish the death penalty.

On 20 June the newspapers carried an official announcement explaining various steps that might be taken to improve the condition of the peasantry. At the same time the government rejected any compulsory expropriation. The government's formal statement was intended to stifle rumors that a seizure of private property was in the offing. Those rumors, which originated in the Duma, had precipitated a new wave of agrarian riots in many parts of the country. The Duma received the announcement as a challenge. Vladimir Kuzmin-Karavaev, who was considered a moderate, "became enraged" on reading the statement. The Duma's agricultural committee was charged to draft a response.

Attacks against the Duma began to mount. On the left the Bolsheviks met with workers to denounce the "treason of the

Kadets" and the cowardice of the Duma majority. For the first time large audiences made the acquaintance of the distinctive figure of Lenin.[28] On the right dozens of telegrams begging the tsar to disperse the Duma as quickly as possible continued to fill the columns of *Pravitelstvennyi vestnik.* "The main position occupied by the revolution is the State Duma," wrote A.A. Stolypin in *Novoe vremia* on July 1st. "Truly obscene appeals for the destruction of private property and the ruin of the state are heard there, and they grow more insolent and less restrained from one day to the next. Voices threatening the supreme power itself ring with increasing frequency from its unassailable walls, as from a mighty fortress."

Even so responsible and moderate a man as the historian Sergei Platonov suggested that what Russia needed was "not the dispersal but the dissolution of the Duma on legal grounds. That would be a salutary measure."[29] Most of the ministers shared that opinion, but some saw things differently. Trepov, for example, believed that first the Duma and the Kadets should "discredit themselves even more."

THE END OF ACT ONE

The Duma finally provided a valid reason for its dissolution. On 4 July it decided to offer the nation its "explanation" of the agrarian problem, and its manifesto declared that it would "not retreat from the expropriation of private property and would reject any proposal not consistent with that stand." Prince N.S. Volkonsky vainly objected that "we are in the same position as the ministers, because we too cannot pass a law by ourselves." Miliukov grew very alarmed when he learned of this development, because he realized that the declaration could enable the tsar to dissolve the Duma. At the session of 6 July the Kadets beat a hasty retreat. Petrunkevich offered a revised declaration which advanced the Duma's program without threats. "The time for struggle has not yet arrived," he declared. "When it does come, we will begin to use a different language. But it is unthinkable, of course, to send the people against machine guns while we enjoy the privilege of personal inviolability." Nevertheless, the Trudoviks and Marxists as well as many of the Kadets did not correctly perceive the imminent danger. Only after a long and confusing debate did the Duma adopt the diluted version and then only by a margin of 124-153 with 101 abstentions.

The revolutionary press, resurgent during the period of the Duma (though less frank than during the "days of freedom")— *Ekho* [Echo], *Mysl* [Thought], *Volna* [The Wave] and others —caustically ridiculed the Kadets. But even in its watered-down version the agrarian program of the Duma, designed "to give the land to the people," contrasted sharply with that of the government, which refused to accept that principle.

The decision to dissolve the Duma was taken during a long discussion between Nicholas, Goremykin, and Stolypin. The governor of St. Petersburg, V.F. Schmidt von der Launitz, assured the emperor that the dissolution would create no serious disturbance in the capital. On Sunday, 9 July 1906, Nicholas signed the manifesto that prorogued the Duma. The Taurida Palace was locked and surrounded by troops so that the deputies could not create a show of resistance that might set off disorders. The move surprised the members of the Duma. Once they learned of their dismissal, many of them departed for Vyborg [Finland], beyond the reach of the Russian police, there to discuss their next move. On the eve of the Duma's closure, 7 July, the tsar had approved the new Finnish constitution and a new electoral law which guaranteed universal suffrage and proportional representation. The Finns, therefore, had little inclination to support any move against the government.

ENCORE AT VYBORG

Late in the evening of 9 July some 178 former members of the Duma assembled in the Hotel Belvedere in Vyborg. Miliukov, who was not present, had advanced the idea of a popular appeal for passive resistance—non-payment of taxes, refusal to accept military service, and non-recognition of debts incurred by the government during the period of conflict. Several members raised strong objections. Professor L.I. Petrazhitsky warned that such an appeal was unconstitutional. Herzenstein argued that it ran counter to the convictions of many deputies and could not be supported unanimously. Some noted its futility inasmuch as Russian finances depended mainly on indirect taxes; Professor Gredeskul suggested that in that case the people should boycott the state's liquor shops. The Poles immediately announced that they could not sign the appeal, because their constituents would follow their advice and that would lead to bloodshed.

The question still was not settled when the governor of Vyborg appeared at the hotel to ask the deputies to end their meeting in order not to compromise Finland's autonomy. A majority approved the manifesto, and the minority subscribed to it out of loyalty. Only Prince George Lvov refused, although the Polish representatives issued their own statement to the effect that their adherence would have to conform "to the special conditions prevailing in the Kingdom of Poland."[30]

The members of the defunct Duma expected to be arrested when they returned to St. Petersburg, but the government decided simply to ignore them. More than a year later, the signers of the Vyborg manifesto were prosecuted in the courts.[31] That deprived the "vyborgets," as they came to be called, of the right to stand for election to future Dumas. Other than that, their manifesto was of no consequence, and it affected neither tax receipts nor military recruitment. The Vyborg manifesto was clearly a revolutionary act, an illegal response to the legal act of proroguing the State Duma. It demonstrated how little the law meant to parties of the far left and to the Kadets.

The radical parties issued their own manifesto, a document signed by the Trudovik and Social Democratic fractions of the Duma, by the peasant and railway unions, and by the Social Democratic and Socialist Revolutionary parties: "The toiling peasants must take matters into their own hands. They were not given land and liberty. They must conquer liberty for themselves by overthrowing the entire state administration. They must seize all the land immediately." That manifesto was noteworthy in that it proclaimed the agrarian movement as the final phase of the revolution. *Russkoe bogatstvo* offered a reminder, however, that "before striking a match to set a fire, one must be certain that there will be a wind." The manifesto of the radical left had no more effect than the Vyborg manifesto.

To say that the First Duma was unworkable is not to imply that the deputies were lazy or particularly ignorant. The problem was that the Duma set itself outside the system. It ignored the Fundamental Laws and adhered to its own special conception of the nature of popular representation. According to the historian Professor Vladimir I. Gere: "It took its stand on the basis of a new law, so aptly phrased in the language of the simple folk, 'the law of seizure.' The emperor was to be given a place of honor like a statue curtained off in a temple, while in his name the priests proclaimed their will to the people." The Duma sought to extend the revolution by other means. Having no desire to revoke what he had granted, Nicholas at the same time saw no reason to give in to this new form of revolutionary pressure.

PETER ARKADEEVICH STOLYPIN

The dissolution of the Duma raised the problem of what action to take next—to continue the experiment or to admit that it was a failure, as the rightists demanded? The emperor came down firmly in favor of the first alternative, and he found within the government itself the very man best suited to carry on the job. That man was Peter Arkadeevich Stolypin. Stolypin's task was two-fold: to conduct a merciless struggle against the violent and bloody recurrences of revolution and to bring to fruition those reforms acknowledged as necessary. The latter included the establishment of popular representative institutions that would afford society the opportunity of political participation and yet not become institutions that could be transformed into weapons against the state by the enemies of monarchical government.

Stolypin was precisely the person to fill that role. He possessed great personal courage. He could make prompt decisions and act energetically. He was an effective orator who had impressed even the hostile First Duma. And he was a monarchist absolutely loyal to the emperor. He did not resort to ultimatums to impose his views on the sovereign. As the former governor of the province of Saratov, Stolypin was well-informed on zemstvo and agrarian questions and with the mechanics of the state administration.

He became premier, while retaining his post as minister of internal affairs, on the day of the Duma's dissolution. His first circular (11 July) elicited praise at home and understanding abroad. "Anarchy must be met by relentless countermeasures," it read. "Revolutionary initiatives must be combatted

with every legal means .... Our struggle is not against society
but against the enemies of society. Therefore, indiscriminate
repression cannot be condoned .... The emperor's intentions
remain unchanged . . . the former system will be renovated.
Order must be maintained to the fullest."

Stolypin wanted to emphasize the reformist character of
his program, and therefore he invited several public men to
join his cabinet: Nicholas Lvov for agriculture, Guchkov for
trade, and Feodor Samarin for the holy synod. Nothing came
of these conversations, however, for the moderates demanded
too high a price—five ministers from the public and the publication of their program over the signature of the entire
cabinet.[32] The more conservative Samarin disagreed with the
general thrust of Stolypin's program. After meeting with
Guchkov, Lvov, and Samarin, the emperor wrote to Stolypin:
"I have spoken with each man for an hour. They are not fit
to be ministers now. They are not men of action." To his
mother he wrote: "They set their own opinions above patriotism and they are unnecessarily timid and fearful of com-
promising themselves."

THE CLIMAX OF THE REVOLUTION

Although the first days after the closing of the Duma passed
quietly, on the night of 17 July a revolt erupted in the island
fortress of Sveaborg near Helsinki. An artillery regiment mutinied and began to exchange fire with the shore batteries. A
revolutionary Finnish "red guard" tried to assist the mutineers, but they were opposed by a "white guard" which came
into existence at the same time. The mutineers held out for
three days, but after the explosion of their powder magazine
and the arrival of a fleet which began to bombard the fortress,
they lost spirit and capitulated on the 20th. There were few
victims—nine dead on both sides, including eight who were
blown up with the magazine.

A briefer but bloodier mutiny broke out at Kronstadt on
19 July. It began with the ghastly murder of two officers and
their families, including a ninety-year-old woman. The Yenesei
Infantry Regiment crushed the revolt on the same day. A mu-
tineer described how it happened: "We went to the arsenal,
but soldiers of the Yenesei Regiment were in front of us.

There were machine guns on the sides and more soldiers behind us, so we ran away."

The crew of the cruiser *Pamiat Azova* also mutinied on the 19th. The officers saved themselves by swimming ashore under fire. Soon, however, the mutineers split into factions and, as in the case of the *Georgy Pobedonosets* in June 1905, the loyal crewmen won, returned the ship to Reval, and surrendered. With that flurry of revolts the military mutinies came to an end. An attempt to stage another general strike in Moscow (24-28 July) was a dismal failure, as *Russkoe bogatstvo* admitted. Only revolutionary guerrilla warfare—reflected in a wave of murders and "expropriations" (politically motivated robberies)—reached a crescendo in the first month after the dissolution of the Duma.

Robbery was an important element in the revolutionary plan, for money stolen from banks and post offices was used to pay for weapons and propaganda and to maintain the revolutionary "staffs." Armed robbery supplied the necessary cash as funds from foreign sources began to dry up. Dzhugashvili-Stalin made his revolutionary reputation in one of those big robberies,[33] and Maxim Litvinov (Finkelstein [?]) ran into great trouble when he tried to spend that money abroad.[34] Assassination, however, took precedence above everything in the revolutionary mind.

There was also one case of an assassination by rightists. On 17 July M.Ya. Herzenstein, a former member of the Duma, was killed in Terioki, Finland. The motive apparently had to do with his Jewish background, since, except for his unfortunate reference to the Saratov riots, his activity in the Duma could not have created any personal animosity toward him. At any rate the right-wing denounced the killing even though the assassin obviously was a rightist.[35] Both *Golos pravdy* [The Voice of Truth] and *Russkoe znamia* [The Russian Banner] wrote that the murderer, whoever he was, deserved the death penalty. Nevertheless, right-wing assassinations were exceptional incidents against the general background of revolutionary terror.

August 2, 1906, was known as "Bloody Sunday" in Poland, for on that day twenty-eight policemen and soldiers were killed and eighteen were wounded on the streets of Warsaw, six were killed and eighteen wounded in Lodz, five killed and three wounded in Plotsk, and so on. In nearly every case the murderers escaped. In Warsaw soldiers fired several times into crowds in which the terrorists had sought refuge. The civilian toll was sixteen dead and 150 wounded, and among the victims was one known assassin.

On 12 August an attempt was made on the life of Stolypin. Two strangers dressed as gendarmes appeared at his country house on Aptekarsky Island and threw two bombs of great force. Twenty-seven people in the front part of the house were killed, including the two terrorists. Of the thirty-two people injured, six died on the following day. The upper story collapsed with Stolypin's fourteen-year-old daughter and three-year-old son and their nurse. They were injured seriously by flying debris. Stolypin himself was not injured. Instead of killing the chairman of the Council of Ministers, this revolutionary act enhanced his prestige. Those who had been indifferent to him were overcome by compassion for his sorrow and by involuntary respect for his courage. Suvorin wrote that "he is not afraid to die at his post, even if killed in open combat or through base treachery; he leaves an example for the living to follow. Here's to a brave life, gentlemen, and shame to cowards!" *Russkiia vedomosti* warned that "liberty cannot be obtained in this manner, which only confuses the people and creates a mood which benefits reaction and not the friends of freedom."

On 13 August the revolution took revenge against one of its conquerors. General George Min, who had averted bloodshed in Petersburg in October 1905 and who in December had dealt the final blow to the Moscow uprising, was killed at the Novy Peterhof railway station by five shots from the revolver [of Zinaida Konoplianikova]. Min's death was a heavy blow to the emperor, who called in person on the dead general's family and was present also on the next day for the funeral.[36]

STOLYPIN'S OFFENSIVE: REFORM AND REPRESSION

At the emperor's suggestion Stolypin and his family moved into the Winter Palace, and the minister with new vigor resumed his double-edged program of merciless suppression of the revolution and reforms for the country. Two significant documents appeared simultaneously on 25 August. One announced a far-reaching program of legislative measures prepared by the government. The other was a new law on courts-martial. The government's statement accurately declared that "the revolution struggles on not for the sake of reforms, which the government considers its duty to achieve, but for the destruction of the system itself, for the overthrow of the monarchy and the introduction of the socialist system."

The government's proposed reforms included freedom of religion, personal inviolability and civic equality, improvement of the conditions of peasant landownership, improvement of workers' living conditions through a governmental insurance system, reform of local self-government in favor of the small territorial unit, introduction of the zemstvo into the Baltic and western provinces, extension of the zemstvo and municipal self-governing institutions into the Kingdom of Poland, reform of the local court system, reform of secondary and higher education, unification of the police and gendarmery, and the publication of a new law governing the state of emergency. The government announced that it would accelerate preparations for an all-Russian church council. It also indicated that it would examine, with a view toward their immediate abolition, the restrictions on Jews, "which only induce irritation and clearly have outlived their usefulness."

The decree on courts-martial, preceded by a listing of terrorist acts, introduced as a temporary measure special courts composed of military officers. These military field courts were to handle only crimes of revolutionary violence that were "so evident as not to require investigation." The law stipulated that the accused was to be brought to trial within twenty-four hours after the commission of a murder or armed robbery. Investigation of the crime was to last no more than forty-eight hours, and the sentence was to be executed within twenty-four hours. Thus, no more than three or four days was to pass between the crime and the punishment.[37] This was a stern measure, yet it hardly can be considered more inhumane than the situation in Western Europe or America where a criminal awaits his execution for many long months if not years.

Radical circles focused mainly on the law on field courts-martial and they could not find words bitter enough to denounce it. At the other end of the spectrum the rightists vented their disapproval of the projected reforms. *Russkii vestnik* labeled the government's program "another treaty of Portsmouth, a surrender to the domestic enemy: both there and here we settle for a half-Sakhalin" (referring to the abolition of some restrictions on Jews).

GUCHKOV'S HISTORIC RESPONSE

Guchkov, the chairman of the central committee of the Union of October 17, had quite a different reaction. Expressing his "great pleasure" that Stolypin had not shied away from his plans for reform, Guchkov declared that the law on field courts-martial "is a cruel necessity. We have a civil war on our hands, and the rules of war are always severe. Such measures are needed in order to defeat the revolutionary movement. The massacre in Baku probably could have been avoided if persons caught with weapons had been handed over to a court-martial. . . . I have great confidence in P.A. Stolypin."

Guchkov's statement angered some members of the Union. Dmitry Shipov, an old moderate liberal of Slavophile leanings, announced that he would "not stand for it" and withdrew from the organization. Professor Gere, however, praised Guchkov's stand, and the central committee unanimously re-elected him to its presidency. In an open letter to Prince Eugene Trubetskoy, Guchkov wrote: "Not only do I consider the policy of repression toward the revolutionary movement compatible with general, somewhat liberal, and even radical programs, but I am also of the opinion that they are closely connected, for only the suppression of terror can create normal conditions. . . . If society would disavow its ties with the revolution, isolate the revolution, deprive it of public sympathy, disperse its image of success—then the revolution would be defeated."

Stolypin had succeeded in breaking the magic circle. Until then, reforms inadvertently would have weakened the government, while the adoption of repressive measures would have implied a denial of reform. But suddenly Russia had a government that embraced both objectives and also a substantial public following which understood the government's policy. That was the great historical service rendered by Alexander

Guchkov and the Union of October 17. The other founders of the Union who could not renounce their old ideological blinders stumbled into the Party of Peaceful Reconstruction.[38] That group remained nothing but a political club without real importance. The Octobrist Party, however, became a vital political force as the first government party in Russian life. That was the significance of the Octobrists, even though they had no formal connection with the government.

SOCIETY'S RETURN TO SANITY

The parties farther to the right regarded Stolypin's first steps rather coolly. They frequently criticized him, but they never refused to cooperate with the government in the struggle against the revolution, nor at that critical moment did they attempt to become "an opposition on the right." Society clearly was coming around. In zemstvo elections Octobrist and right-wing candidates were elected nearly everywhere, while the Kadets continued to lose one district after another. Many noble assemblies, particularly in Moscow and Kursk, expelled those who had signed the Vyborg manifesto. In the November elections to the St. Petersburg municipal duma the victors were the conservative "old thinkers." The franchise, of course, was severely limited, but even so in 1903 those same voters had cast their ballots for the "renovators." In September 1906 *Vestnik evropy* sadly observed that "it takes a great amount of knowledge and faith in the correctness of constitutionalism not to go over to the side of reaction."

An incident involving a British parliamentary delegation clearly indicated the changing mood of society. A group from the British parliament was planning "to pay a visit" to the State Duma which in July had sent delegates to an interparliamentary conference in London. (That trip incidentally saved Feodor Rodichev from the fate of the "vyborgets.") Since the Duma had been dissolved, the parliamentarians intended to use their visit to honor the First Duma—to honor people under indictment for issuing a revolutionary manifesto to the nation. "How displeased they [the English] would be," wrote Nicholas to Empress Maria Feodorovna, "if we sent a delegation to the Irish to wish them success in their struggle."

Protests against the visit began to mount. The Moscow Monarchist Party acted first by staging a large rally on 24 September and adopting a resolution against "interference in Russian affairs." Electors of the handicraft industry adopted a similar protest. A majority of Octobrists and rightists carried a similar resolution in the Moscow municipal duma on the 29th: the visit of the British delegation is a "political demonstration that is insulting to our national self-respect." The St. Petersburg Union of Professors agreed to entertain the delegation but only by a slender margin of 20-17. The British press—*The Times, Standard, Daily Telegraph*, and even the liberal *Westminster Gazette*—began to refer to the trip as "a sad mistake" and "crazy undertaking," and one spoke of its organizers as "fidgety nobodies." One after another the delegates began to drop out, and finally the trip was cancelled.

The Kadets, who convened in Helsinki at the end of September, decided to renounce the Vyborg manifesto, which in any event had had no success anywhere. To spare the feelings of the "vyborgets," the congress acknowledged the circumstances that inspired the appeal, admitted that it was "an idea" which deserved to be propagated, but at the same time resolved that "out of necessity, its immediate and partial application" cannot be recommended. Prince Eugene Trubetskoy described the resolution as "a box with a double bottom —the Vyborg manifesto exists, but there is no Vyborg manifesto."

DECAY OF THE TERROR

The revolutionary parties felt the increasing weight of a hostile atmosphere. Terrorist acts multiplied. During the second half of 1906, terrorists killed I.L. Blok, the governor of Samara, the governor of Simbirsk, Starynkevich, the governor-general of Warsaw, Vonliarliarsky, Chief Military Procurator Pavlov, Count A.P. Ignatiev (once mentioned as Witte's successor), and the energetic governor of Petersburg, Schmidt von der Launitz. In December a second attempt was made on the life of Admiral Dubasov.[39] Over the course of the year terrorists killed 768 officials and agents of the government and wounded 820. But killing no longer held the terror that it once did; society no longer sympathized with the terrorists but grew increasingly outraged at their excesses.

The distinction between political assassination and criminal murder was becoming obliterated. Gangs of robbers, who shot policemen and stole hordes of money, announced that they were working to "meet the needs of the revolution." Things became so bad that the executive committee of the SDs in Moscow adopted a resolution against "expropriations." The local branch of the Bund in Brest Litovsk declared that "robberies demoralize the masses and cause them to develop anarchistic tendencies and to become indifferent toward the party." Robbery offered a great temptation, and after a successful "expropriation" many "comrades" absconded with the loot rather than depositing it in their party's coffers. The Bolsheviks, unlike the Mensheviks and the Bund, never rejected "expropriations," even though only part of the proceeds found its way into the party's treasury.

The character of revolutionary murder became completely anarchistic. A person's "position" often determined his fate, because terrorists killed those who were easiest to reach. Administrators popular with the people were favored targets. The goal of the revolution became more and more remote. *Vestnik evropy* admitted that "the revolutionary movement has conferred absolute license upon the scum of society." The revolutionary movement itself was becoming more degenerate and corrupt, and its leaders even began to have doubts. This psychological side of terrorism was described vividly by a "super-terrorist," the Socialist Revolutionary Boris Savinkov. In his novel *Kon blednyi* [Pale Horse] the hero first convinced himself that it was proper to kill "for a cause," then justified murder for "personal reasons" (to eliminate the husband of the woman he loved), and finally committed suicide.

Classes resumed in the universities and technical institutes in the spring of 1906 after a break of a year and a half. The revolutionary parties could not stem the spontaneous urge to return to normal, which was evident even among students. The revolutionaries, therefore, "permitted" the student strike to end on the pretext that the interests of the revolution required young people to return to their studies in the cities. The students divided into many parties, and the Kadets played

the role of moderates in the universities. Their policy was to
support the professoriate and to defend academic peace.
Student political rallies gradually diminished, and classes went
on with only an irregular strike against one thing or another.
On 11 October 1906 the emperor wrote to his mother:
"Thank God, everything goes for the best. . . . Immediately
after a storm the heavy seas cannot become calm right away;"
and in his diary on the 17th he noted: "The anniversary of
the wreck[40] and the tormenting hours of last year—thank God
they are all over now."

At about the same time Stolypin was telling a foreign
journalist: "Revolution? No, it is no longer a revolution.
Last fall it might have been accurate to speak of a revolution,
but now it seems to me that lurid words like anarchy, jacquerie, and revolution exaggerate the situation." At another
point he observed: "If in 1900 anyone had said that in 1907
Russia would be living under its present political system, no
one would have believed him. The liberal nature of the present
system has exceeded our wildest dreams."

AGRARIAN REFORM

Finally, the government decided that the political struggle
no longer was serious enough to postpone the introduction
of needed reforms. Under normal circumstances conservatives
would have contested the promulgation of legislation under
the provisions of Article 87 of the Fundamental Laws, which
allowed for the adoption of emergency legislation between
sessions of the Duma.[41] However, during this transitional
period when the new legal order remained unsettled, that
procedure seemed most appropriate.

War and revolution had delayed urgent reforms for over
three years. The basis of new legislation had been prepared
by local committees on the needs of the agricultural industry,
by commissions that dealt with the impoverishment of the
central provinces, and by special conferences chaired by Witte
and Goremykin. Meanwhile the condition of the peasantry
had not improved, and that defect had created fertile ground
for revolutionary propaganda in the villages—the "last stronghold" of the revolution. The preliminary investigations of
1898-1904 furnished voluminous material for legislative action. The basic conslusion drawn from those studies was that

the major source of stagnation or deterioration in the peasant economy was two-fold: the stifling of individualism and the absence of property rights.

The leftists—including the Social Democrats who were the principal advocates of large-scale agriculture[42] —sought to attract peasants to the revolution by promising a wholesale redistribution of the nobles' land. They also used that ploy to "buy" peasant support in elections. The emperor had no intention of competing with radicals as a demagogue. His concern was the welfare of the whole and the future of Russia. A general redistribution of land would lead only to a new and unprecedented crisis. The alternatives were the impoverishment of the entire peasantry or its differentiation into individual units. The system which had maintained the equalization of property and communal authority over the individual peasant had produced the general decline of the peasant economy. The solution was to release the energies of individual peasant proprietors.

Several decrees led to the creation of a land fund. The Ukaz of 12 August 1906 transferred to the Peasant Bank the agricultural lands owned by the imperial family. The Ukaz of 27 August regulated the sale of state lands suitable for agriculture. The Ukaz of 19 September provided for the utilization of cabinet lands in the Altai region (territory under the direct jurisdiction of the emperor). The first two decrees created a land fund of several million acres in European Russia; the third opened to settlement a vast territory in Siberia. In addition, the Ukaz of 5 October removed all [most] remaining statutory provisions which set the peasantry apart as a class. Henceforth peasants were to be equal to members of other classes with respect to government and military service and admission to institutions of higher education. The restrictions abolished by the ukaz dealt mainly with the authority of the mir, the village assembly, over individual peasants.[43] On 19 October still another decree authorized the Peasant Bank to grant loans to peasants with their allotments as security. That measure tacitly acknowledged the peasant's individual title to his landholdings.

BREAKUP OF THE COMMUNE

All of those measures paved the way for the principal reform, the Ukaz of 9 November 1906, which defined the conditions of peasant emancipation from the communes. With this decree the Russian government finally broke with the agrarian policy of Alexander III and the populist defense of communal tenure. Henceforth the government was committed to develop and strengthen private landownership in the villages.

"In accord with Our Manifesto of 3 November 1905 the collection of redemption payments from peasants for allotment lands is abolished as of 1 January 1907," declared the ukaz. "From that time hence the aforementioned lands are absolved of all indebtedness due to redemption payments and penalties. Peasants shall have the right to withdraw freely from the commune. Any householder who holds allotment land by communal right may at any time demand that the parts of that land accredited to him be deeded to him as personal property."[44]

The Ukaz of 9 November repealed the law of 1894 which required peasants who had discharged their redemption debt to obtain permission from the commune in order to withdraw from it. The ukaz gave individual peasants the right to depart the commune at any time. If the commune and one of its departing members disagreed over the allotment he was to receive, the land captain was to decide the issue. A peasant was free at any time to demand the consolidation of the individual strips that he cultivated. [In this event the commune had to satisfy the request on an individual basis or through a general redistribution of the land; if that was not done, the commune had to pay the peasant for his land at a price determined by the district court.][45] However, in order to eliminate strip-farming, the ukaz provided that each peasant could demand the consolidation of his strips into one holding through a general repartition. If two-thirds of the commune agreed, the repartition could be accomplished at any time. Finally, the ukaz established the principle that property was to be owned by individual householders rather than by families collectively.

Thus after four years the government finally acceded to the wishes of the local committees on agricultural needs.

Stolypin was beyond doubt chiefly responsible for the adoption of this reform, but several agricultural experts took part in drafting the text of the law: Alexander V. Krivoshein,[46] Vladimir I. Gurko, Alexander I. Lykoshin,[47] Alexander A. Rittikh,[48] and others. But it was Stolypin—with the full support of the emperor—who took the responsibility of resolving this controversial question.

And so great opportunities presented themselves to the strong and thrifty peasants. Freed from the burden of redemption payments (the only heavy direct tax they paid), freed from legal restrictions and from the constraining fetters of the commune, they now enjoyed the possibility of using their land as collateral for massive credits from the Peasant Bank at favorable rates in order to purchase additional land from the land reserve. The land fund, moreover, contained not only the public and state lands that had been allocated to it but also the estates of numerous proprietors who could no longer maintain them or who, fearing agrarian disturbances, sold out to the Peasant Bank.

Land reform came, then, not in the form of a crippling blow to the viable sector of expansive private agriculture, and not in the form of gratuitous hand-outs to the entire peasantry, but as incentives to the thrifty peasants. The reform favored the interests of the more productive, sounder elements who would form the mainstay of the national economy. Equality and charity were of no consequence.

The results of the reform could not be seen immediately. It was not a campaign tactic designed to win an election. Its aim was basic agrarian reform that would fundamentally alter the way of life in the villages. As the experience of Russia and many other nations has shown, any government would have found it difficult to maneuver such a program through a parliament.

Besides agrarian reform, Stolypin's cabinet invoked Article 87 to introduce several other important measures: freedom for Old Believer communities (14 October); a limit on the workday and prohibition of Sunday labor for sales persons (15 November); repeal of the prohibition against secret instruction in the western provinces (that is, granting Poles the right to offer private instruction in the Polish language). A decree of the ministry of public education abolished quotas as an entrance requirement to higher education, except that "the general question regarding the rights of Jews will be subject to consideration by the State Duma, and because this is a question of national conscience, the State Duma must determine how it is to be resolved." The State Council approved a bill providing for some expansion of Jewish rights, but the rightist press bitterly attacked it, and the emperor refused to sign it.

ANOTHER UNSATISFACTORY ELECTION

The election campaign for the Second Duma began early and was well underway by late November. The extreme left ended its boycott and participated in this election. Four political philosophies competed for votes: the rightists, who stood for a return to unlimited autocracy; the Octobrists, who endorsed Stolypin's program; the Kadets; and the "leftist bloc," which embraced the SDs, the SRs, and other socialist groups. Many pre-election rallies featured debates between Kadets and socialists or Kadets and Octobrists. The rightists remained aloof from such activities and organized gatherings only for their supporters.

Contrary to the passive attitude of Witte's government toward the first elections, Stolypin's government made several efforts to influence the outcome of elections to the Second Duma. Rulings by the Senate made it possible to reduce somewhat the number of electors in municipal and landowner assemblies. Parties to the left of the Octobrists were denied legal status, and only legal parties were permitted to distribute printed guide ballots. That measure, however, had little effect, since both the Kadets and the socialists had enough volunteers to write out by hand sufficient numbers of guides. This electoral campaign took on a new dimension. In the first election no one defended the government. Rather than a struggle between government and society, the second election was a struggle within society. That alone was far more significant than which faction received a majority of the votes. A significant part of society, especially the affluent, had turned almost completely against the revolution.

The election of electors took place in January 1907. The Kadets maintained their leading position in both capitals, although their majorities declined sharply. They also repeated their victories in most of the larger cities. Rightists were able to gain the upper hand only in Kiev and Kishinev, where Bishop Platon and Pavolaki Krushevan were elected. In Kazan and Samara the Octobrists were the winners.[49]

The provinces yielded far more diverse results. Agrarian demagoguery played a significant role, and the peasantry elected only those who promised firmly and absolutely without equivocation, to get the land. Even so, the same sharp reversal that had appeared in the zemstvo elections persisted, and in the western provinces the Union of Russian People enjoyed great success among the peasantry. As a result some provinces sent Social Democrats, Socialist Revolutionaries, and Trudoviks to the Second Duma, while others elected moderates and rightists. The provinces of Bessarabia, Volynia, Tula, and Poltava produced right-wing majorities; the Volga region elected a majority of leftists. The Kadets lost nearly half of their seats; the Octobrists made slight gains. The Second Duma was an assembly of extremists, and the voices raised most often were those of the socialists and the reactionaries.[50] The leftists, however, had no illusions of having been thrust into power by a revolutionary tide. Those who were elected by peasants—"just to make sure," whatever happened, that they "got" the land—had no real support in the country, and even they were puzzled by their strong showing: 216 socialist deputies out of 500! In contrast to the formal ceremonies that marked the opening of the First Duma, the opening of the Second Duma on 20 February 1907 was uneventful.[51] The government had decided in advance that if the Duma could not accomplish anything it would be prorogued and the electoral law amended. The country took little interest in the new Duma.

"THE DUMA OF NATIONAL IGNORANCE"

On the whole the membership of the Second Duma was inferior to that of its predecessor. There were more semi-literate peasants and more pseudo-intellectuals. Count Vladimir A. Bobrinsky called it "the Duma of national ignorance." There were fewer people with higher educations, and most of them were to be found among the rightists and the Polish

Kolo [fraction], which was headed by Roman Dmowsky, the leader of the National Democratic Party. The rightists elected a number of gifted orators—Count Bobrinsky,[52] Vladimir M. Purishkevich,[53] Vasily V. Shulgin,[54] Paul N. Krupensky,[55] and others—who "gave no quarter" to the socialists. As soon as a revolutionary speech began to roll from the rostrum, they harassed the speaker with parliamentary maneuvers or by shouting from their seats; on the other hand, they enthusiastically cheered any representative of the government. The rightists (and the moderates who usually joined them) made up about one-fifth of the Second Duma. The Kadets and their Muslim supporters comprised slightly more than one-fifth, and the socialists formed a bloc of about two-fifths. The decisive balance in the Duma belonged not to the Kadets but to the Polish fraction. When the Poles cast their votes with the socialists, the Kadets and rightists were in the minority.

The Kadets had several prominent speakers, including Feodor I. Rodichev,[56] Vasily A. Maklakov,[57] and Alexander A. Kizevetter.[58] Despite their large numbers and except for the young Georgian Menshevik Irakly G. Tseretelli[59] and the Bolshevik Gregory A. Aleksinsky,[60] the socialists did not boast a single decent orator. But that did not stop them from speaking a great deal. Stolypin, the chairman of the council of ministers, was recognized by friend and foe alike as the most accomplished speaker in the chamber, and his speeches are recorded as the most brilliant in the history of the Second Duma.[61]

STOLYPIN CONFRONTS THE DUMA

Stolypin appeared before the Duma on 6 March 1907 to lay before it the far-reaching reforms planned by the government. The contrast with the First Duma was apparent immediately. No one called for him to resign. The right applauded Stolypin at the end of his speech, but the fractions comprising the majority demonstratively refrained from debate and moved to proceed with the next order of business. The Social Democrats would have none of that, however. Their speakers took the floor to denounce the government, but they were interrupted from the right by shouts of "Sit down!" and "Liar!

Your hands are covered with blood!" The rightists answered every SD speech with two of their own. More than twenty speakers took the rostrum. The majority's display of "contemptible silence" failed completely.

Peter Stolypin

The debate ended with a brief, forceful speech by Stolypin. "The government would be anxious to find that language that would be mutually understandable. The language of hatred and rage cannot serve that end. I will not resort to it." The government, he said,

> must either step aside and yield to the revolution . . . or take action and defend what has been entrusted to it. The government has one object in mind—to preserve those legacies, those foundations, those beginnings which were established as the basis of reform by Emperor Nicholas II. By waging a struggle with exceptional measures in unusual times, the government has led and presented the Second Duma to the nation. I must declare, and I would hope that my words will be heard far beyond the walls of this assembly, that present here by the will of our Monarch are neither judges nor accused, that these benches are not dockets for the accused—but rather the seat of government. (Applause) The government will welcome any public exposure of any irregularity whatsoever, but it must react differently to any abuse which might create a situation giving rise to public disorder. All your attacks are calculated to cause a paralysis of will and thought in the government, and they all boil down to two words: 'Hands up!' To these words, gentlemen, the government, confident in its right, calmly answers with two other words: 'Not afraid!'

Stolypin's words *were* heard "far beyond the walls of this assembly," and they had a tremendous effect not only in Russia but also abroad.

The government did not introduce into the Duma the law establishing the field courts-martial, which were due to expire on 20 April. (During the period in which they functioned, 683 persons were sentenced to death.) The Duma itself nevertheless raised the issue of repealing the law, and the rightists immediately demanded a statement condemning terror. During this debate, Stolypin quoted a resolution on terror from one of the Socialist Revolutionary congresses. He expressed his hope that the Duma would instead speak "words of appeasement." Concluding, he said that Russia "will be able to distinguish between the blood discussed so frequently here— the blood on the hands of executioners—and the blood on the hands of honest physicians, who in extreme cases use extreme measures but always with one hope, one desire—to heal the stricken patient."

Procedural matters, the budget, and the agrarian question consumed several sessions. On 10 May Stolypin spoke in criticism of the bills introduced into the Duma: "At the present time our state is ailing. The peasantry, which is the sickest and weakest member, is growing more feeble and languishing. It needs help. A simple and completely automatic solution is suggested: take and divide all 130,000 estates which presently exist.[62] Don't you ask whether it is proper for the government to do that? Doesn't it remind you of the story of Trishka's kaftan—do you want to cut the skirt in order to make sleeves? Gentlemen, you do not nourish a body with pieces torn from its own flesh. The organism must be stimulated. Nourishment must flow to the afflicted area, and then the organism will overcome the disease."

Stolypin's closing words received wide publicity: "This matter requires a persevering effort; it requires unremitting hard labor. The problem cannot simply be decided—it must be resolved. Western countries took decades to deal with the question. We are proposing a modest but honest course. Our opponents want to follow a radical course, a course of liberation from Russia's historic past, a course of deliverance from our cultural tradition. They need a great upheaval—we need a great Russia"

THE ZURABOV INCIDENT

An unexpected crisis developed on 16 April during the debate on the quota of conscripts for the coming year. The socialists wanted to reject the bill. The Social Democrat A.G. Zurabov[63] spoke critically of the officer corps and eventually insulted the entire army. In the retelling of it Zurabov's speech, made in open session, was embellished considerably. The stenographic account (which, as they say, was a bit toned down) read as follows: "The army will fight splendidly against us and it will disperse you, gentlemen; but it always will suffer defeat in the Far East."

In the First Duma a similar statement by the deputy Yakubzon evoked scarcely any reaction, but Zurabov's speech precipitated a veritable storm on the right. The ministers demonstrated their contempt by stalking out of the chamber. The Duma's president, Feodor A. Golovin,[64] first tried to avoid an incident and began to scold the rightists. Their protests only grew louder—"The issue is not settled!"—"We're leaving!"—"Russia has been insulted!"—"Out with him!" Golovin had to call a recess, and during the break it was rumored that the government took the matter so seriously that Zurabov's arrogant insult to the army might lead to the dissolution of the Duma.

The Kadets and the president were prepared to give the government full satisfaction by expelling Zurabov, but the socialists and more importantly the Polish Kolo refused to go along. When the Duma reconvened, Golovin declared that he had studied the transcript and was concerned about the impropriety of Zurabov's remarks. Therefore, he said, he would deprive him of the right to speak further and would censure him. Golovin then asked the Duma to approve his action. A majority comprised of rightists, Kadets, and Poles carried Golovin's proposal, but in a stormy protest the entire left marched out of the hall.

The Zurabov incident signaled a split between the Kadets and socialists. The radical left could not contain its wrath. *Russkoe bogatstvo* wrote that "the leaves scattered, and the fire has burned out." It bitterly observed that regardless of how the Kadets tried to "depart from the revolutionary path, they are totally and slavishly dependent on it. The time will come when the storm will howl over the mountains, and once again the people will speak with unmistakable eloquence."

The Kadets' reversal of policy was designed to "save the Duma," but it came too late. However unlikely, even a firm Kadet-rightist alliance in support of the government could not have created a majority without the Polish Kolo. That coalition—from Dmowsky to Purishkevich—did emerge to approve the new military quota, but the motley alliance could not hope to hold together on many issues. Moreover, the reactionaries had no desire, nor any reason to desire the survival of the Second Duma.

The Duma's fate was predetermined and could not be postponed for long. "From an objective perspective," wrote Struve in *Russkaia mysl* [Russian Thought],[65] "the revolution has come to an end." Terrorist acts, less and less distinguishable from outright murder, persisted. With the opening of the Second Duma agrarian disturbances flared anew. But even Lenin acknowledged at the SD's fifth congress that "a revolutionary situation no longer exists." The government also

Socialist Satire of the Liberal Intelligentsia in the State Duma

realized that. It was time to close the books on the years of
transition and resume the normal routine of government. A
more peaceful setting was essential to carry out the program
of agrarian reform and to rebuild the army on the basis of
lessons learned from the Japanese war. Tranquility was impossible, however, without disposing of the Second Duma and
the electoral law that had created it.

THE END OF ACT TWO

The Second Duma tried to avoid giving the government a
pretext to dissolve it. When the rightists moved for an inquiry
into a plot to assassinate the emperor,[66] the Kadets expressed
their profound joy over the timely discovery of the plot and
voted for the resolution. The socialists managed to delete a
statement condemning terror, but the Kadets and the Polish
fraction managed to have their disapproval publicly recorded.

The socialists, meanwhile, took every advantage of their
legislative immunity to promote their revolutionary activities.
The SD faction in the Duma entered into an alliance with a
group of soldiers contaminated with radicalism. They hailed
from various regiments and called themselves the "Military
Organization of the Social Democratic Party." Secret police
agents had infiltrated this group and were monitoring its
activities. Consequently the government was alerted immediately to its connection with the Duma. On 4 May during a
search of the quarters of the Social Democrat I.P. Ozol, a
deputy from Riga, the police arrested several members of the
organization. The SDs in the Duma had the audacity to
demand an inquiry into that search, but on 8 May Stolypin
replied that the official investigation had not yet been completed.

On 1 June Stolypin appeared before the Duma and requested a closed session. That granted, he then demanded that the
Duma withdraw the immunity of the entire SD fraction because it was organizing a military conspiracy. Stolypin's demand put the Kadets in a difficult position. They could not
defend a conspiracy and wanted very much to preserve the
Duma. On the other hand the government's proof of a conspiracy seemed very flimsy[67] and at any rate it failed to implicate every member of the SD contingent. The Duma referred

the matter to a committee; the committee deliberated for two days without coming to any conclusion. Meanwhile the government concluded that it could wait no longer to make arrests—some of the accused had fled already—and decided to proceed.

The final session of the Second Duma took place on the second of June. The question of the day dealt with the local courts, but the radical parties repeatedly attempted to set aside the agenda in order to discuss "the government's imminent coup d'etat," to vote down the budget and all legislation enacted under Article 87, and to draft an appeal to the nation. The Duma rejected each of these proposals in turn. As the session ended, Kizevetter appeared to announce that the committee charged with the question of removing the SD's immunity was not yet ready to make its report.

On the following day, 3 June 1907, the government published the tsar's manifesto dissolving the Second Duma. It also published [under Article 87] a new electoral law. On the morning of that same day the government arrested all the Social Democratic deputies who had not gone underground. The country took the dissolution calmly; there were no demonstrations and no attempts to organize strikes. Normal pedestrian traffic filled the sidewalks, and the police had no reason to reinforce their patrols. Foreign opinion, somewhat prepared for the event by Professor F.F. Martens' letter to *The Times* on the need to revise the electoral law, was at first apathetic and later rather understanding.

THE LAW OF 3 JUNE 1907

The electoral Law of 3 June 1907 was principally the work of S.E. Kryzhanovsky, Stolypin's assistant minister of internal affairs. In drafting the law Kryzhanovsky relied on experience acquired from two Duma elections and several zemstvo and municipal elections. The Law of 3 June had one over-riding objective: to create a system of national representation that would function conscientiously within the framework of the existing constitution and with a minimum disruption of legislation then in effect. The new law—and this was its distinguishing mark—deprived no one of the right to vote (except the Central Asians, who were described as "not yet ready" to participate in the electoral process).[68]

The Law of 3 June fundamentally redistributed the electoral impact of the empire's various social groups. In European Russia under the old law the peasantry elected 42 percent of the electors, landowners 31 percent, and burghers and workers 27 percent. Under the new law peasants elected 22.5 percent of the electors, landowners 50.5 percent, and the urban classes the same 27 percent. The law, however, divided urban voters into two curias to be chosen in separate elections. The First Curia (for those who met certain property qualifications) chose most of the electors. The law ensured that 65 percent of the electors would be chosen by those classes which regularly participated in zemstvo and municipal elections and which, therefore, had more extensive experience in public affairs.

The Law of 3 June also reduced the impact of the non-Russian nationalities. The number of Polish deputies dropped from 36 to 12 (including two deputies to be elected by the Russian population of the kingdom). The representation of the Caucasus was reduced from 29 to 10. The Law of 3 June definitely retreated from the principle of imperial equality that was inherent in earlier legislation. The manifesto frankly declared that "the State Duma must also be Russian in spirit. . . . Diverse national groups . . . must not and will not appear in such numbers as to give them an opportunity to decide matters that are purely Russian in nature." That statement was addressed to the decisive position of the Polish Kolo in the Second Duma.

Russia was not the first state to follow the route charted by the Law of 3 June. In 1848 the first Prussian parliament also was dissolved, and its members also appealed to the nation not to pay taxes or furnish recruits. That appeal failed to elicit any popular response. A second parliament met and it too was dissolved (May 1849). Then the government revised the electoral law, and the Landtag elected under its provisions functioned for nearly seventy years, until 1918.

REAFFIRMATION OF THE TSAR'S HISTORIC POWER

The Manifesto of 3 June carried even greater significance than the electoral law which it proclaimed. The manifesto finally established the new order of the Russian state. It completed the process of reconstruction initiated by the tsar's rescript of 18 February 1905. It provided a clear sense of direction so painfully lacking throughout the years of revolution. Although the words of the manifesto were Stolypin's, the ideas were those of the emperor himself.

In 1906 in the diary which he then was publishing openly, Lev Tikhomirov had asked: "What new order is this? What an absolute absence of principle: neither monarchy nor democracy. We never will be free from chaos and revolution until everyone clearly understands and accepts practically without question the exact locus of the Supreme Power—that majesty which can interrupt our disputes and declare, '*Roma locuta— cause fini*,' and would you kindly obey, because if you don't, I'm going to erase you from the face of the earth."[69]

The emperor's Manifesto of 3 June answered that question. Having enumerated the various amendments to the electoral law, it declared:

> These numerous electoral changes cannot be carried out in the *regular legislative process* through the State Duma, whose composition We recognize, because of imperfections in the system by which its members are chosen. *Only the Power that granted the first electoral law, the historic Power of the Russian Tsar, possesses the right to repeal and replace it with a new law.*
>
> Our Tsarist Power over Our people has been received from the Lord God Himself, and We will answer for the fate of the Russian People before His Throne.
>
> For that reason We are firmly resolved *to carry to its conclusion that program of reorganizing Russia, which We began, and to bestow upon it a new electoral law.*[70]

The manifesto proclaimed that the historic authority inherent in the title Tsar of Russia remained the foundation of the Russian state. All laws emanated from that power. The October Manifesto and the Fundamental Laws of April 1906 established a *new legislative order* which limited the tsar's authority to promulgate new legislation. But if normal legislative procedures failed to preserve the state, *the tsar's authority obligated him and gave him the right to find another solution.* Nicholas evoked that supreme sovereignty when he used the phrase, "the autocracy as it was in former times."

The abandonment of normal procedures as defined by the Fundamental Laws was permissible of course only under extreme conditions. Extra-legal measures always weaken respect for the law and inspire seditious ideas in the minds of some. Yet to ignore the possible need for such action is to be blind to reality. No state can countenance its own destruction by binding itself strictly to the letter of the law. Least able to deny the legitimacy of extra-legal action in an extremity were those who clung to the treacherous and illusory idea of "the people."

Emperor Nicholas II was and remained the supreme head of the nation. He had led it out of war and revolution, and with the Manifesto of 3 June he brought to fruition his great program of renovation. He had confirmed the new Russian order—the Duma Monarchy.

NOTES

CHAPTER SEVEN

1. The Peasant Land Bank was established in 1883. Then with characteristic bureaucratic wisdom the government formed the Nobles Bank in 1885 to make loans to the nobility so they would not have to sell their lands to the peasantry. Mortgage rates for the nobility always were pegged lower than the charges on loans to peasants through the Peasants Bank. Nevertheless, it was a losing battle. Property in the hands of the nobility declined by nearly 30 percent between 1877 and 1905, from 73,077,000 desiatins (194,384,000 acres) to 52,104,000 desiatins (138,597,000 acres). During the same period, total peasant holdings (including communal lands) increased by about 25 percent, from 118,181,000 desiatins (314,361,000 acres) to 146,825,000 desiatins (390,555,000 acres). The Peasant Bank assisted the purchase of land privately by peasant households, and the increase of landownership of that type was phenomenal: from 1877 to 1905 privately owned peasant land increased from 6,552,000 desiatins (17,428,000 acres) to 23,642,000 desiatins (62,888,000 acres)—a gain of about 400 percent.

During the last four decades of the nineteenth century, however, the peasant population of European Russia swelled from fifty million to seventy-nine million. Consequently from 1877 to 1905 the average size of a household allotment declined from 13.2 desiatins (35.1 acres) to 10.4 desiatins (27.7 acres). In France in 1884 the average size of all farms was less than nine acres, but French peasants were relatively prosperous in comparison to the less productive peasants of Russia. (Source of figures: Robinson, *Rural Russia*, pp. 94-102, 131, and 268-69.)

2. Redemption payments averaged 92-93,000,000 rubles annually from 1894 to 1903, while in the same period the total state budget increased from 1,145,000,000 rubles to 2,032,000,000 rubles. (Oldenburg's note)

3. The artel, an ancient Russian institution, was an association of private individuals (in this instance, peasants) freely united in some common economic undertaking. The artel was characterized by collective responsibility, fraternal solidarity, and complete equality in that each member had an equal voice in the affairs of the association and received an equal share of its profits. An elected elder functioned as a kind of foreman and business manager in representing the arteliers to the outside world. All members contributed equally to meet his expenses. By the end of the nineteenth century various kinds of artels had developed in Russia: producer artels (peasants, laborers, artisans), consumer artels, and credit and insurance artels. The artel differed from the obshchina in that the artel was a *free* association of laborers or consumers and thus basically individualistic in form and purpose.

4. Quoted from a speech by Witte early in 1899 to a commission considering the regulation of the grain trade. (Oldenburg's note)

5. Gurko's articles appeared in 1901 as a series entitled "Agriculture and the Strikes." (Oldenburg's note)

Witte's strategy of industrialization (see at .ve, Vol. I, p. 198, Note 7) called for the suppression of consumer demand through taxation and low agricultural prices in order to accumulate savings and capital for the foundations of Russian industry.

6. A.A. Bobrinsky cannot be identified precisely in that three Counts Bobrinsky with the initials A.A. were active public figures at the end of the nineteenth century: Alexander Alexeevich (1823-1903) and his two sons, Alexis Alexandrovich (1852-) and Andrei Alexandrovich (1860-). Oldenburg probably referred to Alexis Alexandrovich, who served for some time as marshal of the nobility of the province of St. Petersburg and also in the Petersburg municipal duma of which he was president for a time. In connection with Oldenburg's preceding reference to "prominent Saratov landlords," the text specifically mentions Prince V. Kudashev (a member of an ancient princely family but otherwise unidentifiable), N.A. Englehardt, who cannot be identified precisely, and Nicholas A. Pavlov, a publicist and self-styled expert on agrarian and peasant questions. Pavlov frequently contributed to *Moskovskie vedomosti* and *Grazhdanin*, always adding after his signature the title "nobleman." He worked as an unpaid official in the ministry of agriculture and was active in conservative salons and politics.

7. Few people realized that monastic lands in European Russia comprised some half million desiatins [about one and one-third million acres]. (Oldenburg's note)

Robinson, however, gives 2,579,000 desiatins (6,680,000 acres) as the total of church and monastic lands in 1905. *Rural Russia*, p. 268.

8. A.D. Polenov, comp., *Izsledovanie ekonomicheskago polozheniia tsentralno-chernozemnykh gubernii. Trudy osobago soveshchaniia 1899-1901 g.* [A Study of the Economic Status of the Central Black-Soil Provinces: Report of the Special Commission, 1899-1901], [Moscow, 1901]. (Oldenburg's note)

Both Polenov and this study are discussed briefly by V.I. Gurko, who was not overly impressed by either of them: *Features and Figures of the Past*, pp. 230-32.

9. Kokovtsov (1853-1943) was a competent, honest, and relatively unimaginative conservative bureaucrat, who throughout his career demonstrated an unfailing aptitude for caution and self-preservation. He entered government service in 1873 as an official in the ministry of justice. He advanced steadily as an expert on the penal system, and in 1890 transferred to the imperial chancellery. In 1896 he became an assistant minister of finance. He ultimately succeeded Witte as finance minister (1904) and Stolypin as chairman of the Council of Ministers (1911). He held both positions until January 1914 when, having run afoul of the empress, he was elevated to the rank of count and fired. After the revolutions of 1917, Kokovtsov fled to Paris, became the head of a Russian bank, published his memoirs (*Out of My Past*) in 1933, and generally prospered as an emigre.

Industrialization maintained its top priority under Kokovtsov's direction of the finance ministry, but the pace of industrialization was reduced as the government allocated a greater share of its resources to agriculture, education, and a general improvement of the standard of living. As chairman of the Council of Ministers, Kokovtsov with conservative support in the Duma cautiously continued Stolypin's domestic and administrative reforms and the tsar's policy of russification. Although Nicholas had high regard for Kokovtsov, the emperor was unable to resist the slanderous attacks of his minister's reactionary enemies who included Prince Meshchersky and the Empress Alexandra.

10. The special commission encountered a serious jurisdictional problem at the very outset. Two weeks before establishing the special commission, the tsar had ordered Sipiagin and the peasant section of the ministry of internal affairs to undertake a major revision of peasant legislation. Sipiagin therefore wished to reserve the peasant question to his ministry. Witte in turn was anxious that the commission stay away from fiscal matters in the domain of the ministry of finance. More than bureaucratic rivalry was involved, however. Sipiagin favored the preservation of the obshchina, while Witte had reached the conclusion that agricultural productivity depended on abolishing the communal system.

11. Plehve (1846-1904) won his reputation as a staunch gendarme over nearly two decades of police work in the ministry of internal affairs. Most recently he had demonstrated great energy in prosecuting the russification of Finland. Although Plehve's reputation as a bloody reactionary was well-deserved, the other side of his regime generally has been ignored. The murder of Sipiagin, who wanted to retain the obshchina as a means of state control over the peasantry, cleared the way for the new interior minister to prepare the dismantling of the village communes and the final liberation of the peasantry. V.I. Gurko actually directed the preparation of the first projects for the abolition of the obshchina, a policy brought to fruition in 1906-11 under P.A. Stolypin. Plehve's initiative in agrarian reform ultimately enabled him to undermine Witte's dominant position in the government.

This came about because of the active role of zemstvo representatives in connection with the work of the Special Commission on the Needs of Agricultural Industry and the peasant disturbances of 1902, both discussed below by the author. Plehve was able to convince the emperor that peasant unrest was a natural consequence of Witte's industrial policy. Moreover, Witte's frequent consultation with zemstvo leaders allowed Plehve to link Witte with the ambitions and demands of the zemstvos for a significant if not major, constitutional role in governing Russia.

12. One of the provisions of the statutes on emancipation allowed peasants to receive free land apart from the communes if they agreed to accept an allotment only one-fourth the size of the standard minimum allotment for their district.

13. The reports of the district committees were published in fifty-eight volumes; the summary and final report was prepared under Witte's direction: *Zapiska po krestianskomu delu predsedatelia vysochaishe*

*uchrezhdennago osobago soveshchaniia o nuzhdakh selsko-khoziaist-
vennoi promyshlennosti, stats-sekretaria Vitte* [Report on Peasant Affairs by State Secretary Witte, Chairman of the Special Commission
on the Needs of Agricultural Industry] (St. Petersburg, 1904).

14. *Nuzhdy derevni po rabotam komitetov selsko-khoaziaistvennoi
promyshlennosti* [The Needs of the Villages according to the Findings
of the Committees of Agricultural Industry], published by N.N. Lvov
and A.A. Stakhovich with the assistance of the editorial staff of *Pravo*
[The Law] (St. Petersburg, 1904). (Oldenburg's note)

15. In two of those provinces, Penza and Arkhangel, one hardly
could speak of a majority, since only one committee in each province
considered the question, while the rest ignored it. (Oldenburg's note)

16. Although the author wrote "Vologda" province, he apparently
meant Penza.

17. Here the author apparently meant Orel rather than Tver.

18. Under the repartitional regime common to the obshchina each
household received its land allotment in several scattered strips. The
village assembly periodically repartitioned and redistributed the land
in order to equalize the holdings of its members. Strip farming was
inefficient and wasteful of both land and labor, and repartitional tenure
deprived the individual of the incentive to improve the land (which
he might lose at the next redistribution). In the obshchina the only
privately owned property was the peasant's home and a small adjoining
garden plot.

19. Neither book nor author can be identified. A zemstvo physician,
Alexander Petrovich Voskresensky (1854-), wrote on questions of
public health in the villages around the turn of the century.

20. In 1896 the ministry of finance reorganized its department of
indirect taxation (*Departament neokladnykh soborov*) as the main administration of indirect taxation and liquor trade (*Glavnoe upravlenie
neokladnykh soborov i kazennoi prodazhi pitei*).

21. The *zemskii nachalnik*, or superintendent of peasantry, exercised
both administrative and judicial control over his charges. Known also
as land captain.

CHAPTER EIGHT

1. That was the opinion, by the way, of the well-known German
historian Otto Hoetzsch. (Oldenburg's note) Hoetzsch (1876-1946) was
Germany's leading authority on Russian history, a subject on which
he wrote prolifically. For many years Hoetzsch held the chair of Professor of East European History at Berlin University. In the 1930s
he was denounced by the Nazis and dismissed. But he survived both
the Nazis and the war, and in the summer of 1945 the university
invited him to return to his old post. Oldenburg probably referred
to Hoetzsch's characterization of Nicholas in *Russland: Eine Einfuhrung
auf Grund seiner Geschichte vom japanischen bis zum Weltkrieg* [Russia:
An Introduction to its History from the Japanese to the World War]
(Berlin, 1917).

2. S.V. Zubatov (1864-1917) participated in radical and revolutionary groups as a youth but subsequently became an informant and undercover agent for the police. He prospered in his new career. In 1889 he was promoted to assistant chief of the Moscow secret police (Okhrana —see below, Note 21); in 1896 he became chief of the Moscow Okhrana and held that position until 1902, when he was placed in charge of a special section of the ministry of interior responsible for organizing and directing the police or "Zubatov unions." Plehve, thoroughly hostile to the Zubatov plan, finally managed to rid himself of Zubatov in 1903. Accused of "intriguing" against the minister, Zubatov was dismissed and exiled to Vladimir. He was released from exile in 1904 and eventually settled in Moscow. Fearful of arrest and trial at the hands of the revolution, Zubatov took his own life on 2/15 March 1917.

3. The Jewish Independent Labor Party, founded in Minsk in 1901, derived much but not all of its inspiration from Zubatovism, with which it was closely associated. The Independent program also reflected the alienation of Jewish workers from the intelligentsia, and a provision calling for a democratic party organization was directed against the intelligentsia who hitherto had dominated the labor movement in the Pale of Settlement. The party's basic aim was to improve the material and cultural condition of the working class. Therefore it rejected an alliance with the intelligentsia who, it felt, all too frequently directed the workers into a senseless political struggle that only frustrated the workers' aspirations for economic and cultural advancement.

The Independents enjoyed only moderate and short-lived success. In Vilna, the stronghold of the Jewish Bund, the Independent Party collapsed in 1902 after only a year. In Odessa, where socialists offered little competition (the Bund had little influence beyond the Pale), the movement flourished until a massive strike in 1903 got out of hand; the local authorities had never been enthusiastic about Zubatovism, and without police support the Independents were unable to continue. In Minsk, its strongest center, the Jewish Independent Labor Party dissolved itself in June 1903. By then the ministry of interior under Plehve had withdrawn its support from Zubatov's experiment. Popular support diminished, especially after the Kishinev pogrom (discussed below), because of the Independents' close identification with an increasingly repressive regime. For an excellent survey and analysis of this and the larger question of Jewish disaffection and opposition see in particular Ezra Mendelsohn, *Class Struggle in the Pale: The Formative Years of the Jewish Workers' Movement in Tsarist Russia* (Cambridge, 1970).

4. In Odessa many of the two thousand workers who enlisted in the party were non-Jews, and the party therefore omitted the adjective "Jewish" from its title. The leaders, however, were predominantly Jewish, and the head of the organization, Shaevich (sources provide no further identification) was also a Zionist. According to Mendelsohn, Vilbushevich persuaded Zubatov that Zionism might be used effectively against the revolutionary movement, and a Zubatov-Zionist movement made some progress until 1903 when the government turned

against both Zionism and the Independent Party. Vilbushevich herself eventually settled as a pioneer in Palestine. One of the founders of the Independent Party, she began her activities in Grodno. In Minsk, the chief of police, Captain Vasiliev, was the enthusiastic leader of the Zubatov experiment. (Ibid., pp. 143-50.)

5. According to V.I. Gurko, however, the "rumors" were not without foundation: "Educational activity among the workers was combined with police measures. . . . At meetings organized in Moscow labor districts by the secret police not only opponents of socialism spoke but also its leaders; frequently, however, the latter would be arrested after the meeting adjourned." *Features and Figures of the Past*, p. 117. Gurko was quite critical of Zubatovism.

6. Part of the struggle between Witte and Plehve centered on control of the department of factory inspection, an agency established in 1882 to see that employers observed the labor laws. The ministry of finance originally controlled the department. Under Witte lax enforcement was the rule, since he looked first to the interests of industry. Zubatovism, however, stressed the government's paternal interest in the welfare of the workers. Moreover, the police department doubted the anti-revolutionary alertness and zeal of the factory inspectors and sought control of the inspectorate in order to ensure its conservatism and reliability. Plehve, therefore, wanted to bring the department of factory inspection into the ministry of interior. An Imperial Ukaz of 30 May 1903 subordinated the factory inspectors to their local governors. This in effect meant their control by the ministry of interior, but it also meant that the original purpose of the factory inspectorate was lost in that it became an extension of the police whose chief interest and function was to preserve order in the empire. In 1905 the department of factory inspection was transferred from the ministry of finance to the interior ministry.

7. Vannovsky, "dug out of the archives and appointed Minister of Education" at the age of seventy-nine (Gurko, p. 98), was so infirm that he had to be carried up and down stairs by two aides. Nevertheless, he moved energetically, building on foundations laid by Bogolepov, to rejuvenate the Russian educational system. In May 1901 Vannovsky formed a commission to investigate and revise the secondary school curriculum. Since much of the preliminary work already had been accomplished by his predecessor, the commission quickly concluded its deliberations. In June the tsar approved the projected reform and ordered its gradual introduction beginning in the fall of 1901. The goal of the plan was to create a unified school; that is, to bring the curriculums of the gymnasiums (which prepared students for universities) and the *realschulen* (vocational secondary schools) more into line with one another. This would make higher education, both traditional and technical, more accessible to Russian students. The study of Latin and Greek was de-emphasized. Reduction of the classical core afforded more time to emphasize contemporary subjects—Russian language, science, geography, and especially modern European languages.

Vannovsky's ministry marked the culmination of Witte's influence on general education in Russia and the effort to make modern secondary education more accessible and more attractive to young Russians. Vannovsky ended a twenty-year moratorium on the construction of new gymnasiums. Moreover, between 1885 and 1895 only three *realschulen* had been opened; but by 1905 an additional fifty-one had been built, and their enrollment tripled (from 17,535 in 1895 to 51,502 in 1905). Social democratization accompanied this expansion of education. At the beginning of the reign of Nicholas II commoners made up 44 percent of gymnasium enrollment; by 1904 they were 59 percent of that population. However, within a week of Plehve's appointment as minister of interior Vannovsky resigned as minister of public education. Witte's influence over affairs declined. Vannovsky's successor, Gregory Zenger, generally followed the lead of the new interior minister.

Plehve believed that imperial stability and order depended on the aristocratic principle and the preponderant influence of the landowning nobility. That meant separate schools for the noble and non-noble classes, the preservation of academic formalism, and resistance to the dilution of entrance requirements that would lead to further democratization of Russian higher schools. In July 1902 a commission under Zenger's direction met to solidify the structure of the gymnasiums and *realschulen*. Greek was eliminated from all but a few schools. Latin was eliminated from the first two years of the gymnasiums but not added to the curriculum of the *realschulen*. (The "maturity examination" mandatory for entrance into the universities required a knowledge of Latin.) The gymnasiums retained an eight-year course, the *realschulen* six, and only the first two years of each were coterminus.

The authoritative history of education in Imperial Russia is *Education and the State in Tsarist Russia* by Patrick L. Alston (Stanford, 1969); the information and interpretation summarized in this note appears on pages 160-71. Alston's work supersedes two earlier studies: Nicholas Hans, *History of Russian Educational Policy (1701-1917)* (1931; reprinted 1964), and William H.E. Johnson, *Russia's Educational Heritage* (Pittsburgh, 1950; reprinted 1969).

8. The activities of student organizations were curtailed almost immediately. In May 1903 Plehve called Zenger's attention to the spread of political propaganda from the universities into the secondary schools. On 29 June 1903 the minister of public education ordered school authorities to adopt more stringent measures against propaganda. The discussion of further reforms ran counter to the growing policy of repression. Zenger could not keep up with the government's policy, and in 1904 the tsar fired him.

9. Bely's *First Symphony (Northern, Heroic)* of 1904 followed his *Second Sympathy (Dramatic)* by two years and thereby provided a partial glimpse of the humor of these musically organized prose works. "Symphonies" three and four appeared in order (1905 and 1908). Bely, the pseudonym of Boris N. Bugaev (1880-1934), was the most original and probably the most influential symbolist writer.

10. Probably Lieutenant General Alexander A. Kireev (1833-1910), a publicist associated with the Slavic Benevolent Society, a Pan-Slavic organization more devoted to politics than charity. His sister Olga Alexeevna (1840-1925) was the famous Mme. Olga Kireeva Novikov or

"O.K.", noted for her efforts in behalf of Anglo-Russian friendship and the subject of a biography by W.T. Stead—*An M.P. for Russia,* 2 vols. (London, 1909).

11. This was the well-known pseudonym of Zinaida N. Hippius. (Oldenburg's note)

12. The text is slightly in error in that Bogolepov's assassination in February 1901 was undertaken independently by Peter Karpovich, a Socialist Revolutionary who joined the Battle Organization only after escaping from prison for this crime (see above, Chapter VI, Note 22). The Battle Organization (or BO) was organized early in 1902, and its first victim was Sipiagin in April 1902. The BO was the semi-autonomous arm of the Socialist Revolutionary Party. It operated independently but with the general approval of the party's executive committee and with party funds. The BO reflected the resurgence of the nihilism that characterized the revolutionary movement in Russia.

The Socialist Revolutionary (SR) Party was formed during 1900-2 by the fusion of various Populist groups in Russia and abroad. An assorted collection of representatives met secretly in Kharkov in the summer of 1900 and hammered out a general agreement on principles of policy and organization. Organizational work in various localities then followed, while the party's leadership established its center and a new journal in Geneva. The original SR executive committee consisted of Michael R. Gotz (M. Rafailov, 1866-1906), Victor M. Chernov (1873-1952), and Gregory A. Gershuni (1870-1908).

Gotz was the party's leading politician and organizer. The son of a Moscow millionaire, he joined the Populist movement in 1886 but was arrested and exiled to Eastern Siberia in 1888. Amnestied in 1895, Gotz finally settled in 1900 in Paris where with two other Populist revolutionaries he edited and published the revolutionary journal *Vestnik russkii revoliutsii* [The Herald of the Russian Revolution]. In 1902 he moved to Geneva, which then became the headquarters of the SRs. He served as co-editor with Chernov of the party's new journal, *Revoliutsionaia Rossiia* [Revolutionary Russia]. Gotz died in Berlin during surgery to remove a tumor caused by a blow to his spine by a rifle butt when he was a prisoner in Siberia.

Victor Chernov was recognized as the party's leading theoretician. He began his revolutionary career around 1896 by forming the first revolutionary peasant organization in the province of Tambov. The revolutionary task, as he saw it, was first to destroy the peasants' faith in the tsar and then to lead the peasantry through revolution to a socialist republic. Chernov basically rejected the Marxian formula that insisted on capitalism, industrialization, and a revolutionary proletariat as the preconditions of a socialist revolution. Grudgingly he was forced to admit that capitalism was becoming a Russian reality. The SRs, therefore, did not ignore the urbanized peasantry who constituted the industrial labor force. By 1905 the SRs had emerged as the party with the greatest mass appeal. Chernov himself operated abroad from 1899 to 1917. He returned to Russia at the outbreak of the revolution and served from May to September 1917 as minister of agriculture in the Provisional Government. He was elected chairman of the short-lived national Constituent Assembly (January 1918) and subsequently joined the anti-Bolshevik opposition. He fled from Russia in 1921, joined the Second International, and continued to fight Bolshevism with his pen.

Gershuni, the third member of the original SR executive triumvirate, was a pharmacist by training but a conspirator and terrorist by profession. Revolutionaries recognized him, together with Zhelyabov (the chief assassin of Alexander II), as Russia's greatest "artist in terror." Gershuni organized and led the Battle Organization from 1902 until his arrest in May 1903 following the assassination of the governor of Ufa. A court-martial condemned him to death, but the sentence was commuted and he was transported to Eastern Siberia (Akatuisky Prison). In October 1906 he escaped in a barrel of cabbage and returned to Europe by way of Japan and the United States. Along the way he collected substantial donations "to the Russian Revolution." Anticipating his own arrest, Gershuni had entrusted the BO to Evno Azef, the notorious double agent (see below, Note 21). On his return to Russia in 1907 Gershuni assisted Azef as a consultant on terrorism and advisor in a plot to assassinate Nicholas II. His health was failing, however, and he died in Paris in March 1908. Under the leadership of Gershuni and Azef the Battle Organization between 1902 and 1908 assassinated about 140 tsarist officials, including two successive ministers of interior and one grand duke.

The SRs were the heirs of the earlier Narodniks, but unlike their predecessors they attempted to combine an effective agrarian program with terrorism. They never worked out a specific or practical political program, however. Clinging to the Populist illusion of instinctive socialism among the peasantry, the SRs called for the socialization of property while simultaneously proclaiming the peasants' exclusive rights to the land. It was the latter principle that the peasants heard.

The student riots at the turn of the century provided the impetus for the formation of the Socialist Revolutionary Party, and of all the revolutionary organizations the SRs were the party of young Russia. Youth was at once its great strength but also its basic weakness. The SRs never freed themselves from the romanticized fantasies of youth to concentrate on the more serious and practical side of the business of social change. Although the SRs became Russia's majority party, they ultimately lost Russia to the less numerous but better organized Bolsheviks.

The best account of the Battle Organization and the formative years of the party is Boris Nikolajewsky, *Azef, the Spy* (London, 1934; reprinted, Academic International Press, 1968).

13. Though very active, the Battle Organization was not responsible for the attempt on von Wahl. Hirsh Lekert, a Jewish worker in Vilna and a member of the Bund, made that attempt on his own. Von Wahl had ordered the public flogging (in his presence) of a number of Jewish workers who had staged a May Day demonstration. In retaliation Lekert tried to kill the governor, but his aim was bad. Nevertheless, he was sentenced to death by a court-martial and promptly executed. He became a revolutionary and Jewish martyr. In the aftermath of Lekert's

attack local authorities made mass arrests and imprisoned or exiled several hundred workers.

Gershuni (above, Note 12) organized the attempt on Obolensky and selected as the assassin a local worker named Foma Kachura. The Battle Organization deemed Obolensky a candidate for assassination because he had ordered the mass flogging of peasants who participated in the rioting and pillaging in Kharkov province in the spring of 1902 (see Chapter VII). Kachura also missed.

The terrorists initially favored pistols, partly because that weapon allowed them to thrust a death sentence into the hand of the intended victim and then to shoot after he had read it. Pistols tended to misfire, however, and despite their resoluteness, terrorists' hands often shook and spoiled their aim. Consequently the BO turned increasingly to bombs, which only needed to be discharged in the vicinity of the target. Moreover, as the wave of terror increased, official security also grew tighter, and it became more difficult to get close to intended victims. Tighter security almost made it impossible to publish "death sentences" in advance of their executions.

14. George V. Plekhanov (1856-1918), a native of Tambov province and son of a well-to-do landowner, was "the father of Russian Marxism." A prominent Populist leader in the late 1870s, he spurned the movement's adoption of terrorism (The People's Will) and in 1879 formed the Black Repartition, a splinter group that included Axelrod and Zasulich. Then, as an emigre in Switzerland, Plekhanov discovered Marxism and in 1883 formed the first group of Russian Marxists, the Liberation of Labor. In the next two decades he published a wide range of theoretical works and numerous polemics (against Populism).

In 1900 Plekhanov and the younger Marxists, Lenin, Martov, and Alexander N. Potresov (1869-1934) founded the journal *Iskra* to serve as the mouthpiece of Russian Social Democracy. Although Plekhanov supported Lenin at the second party congress in 1903, he broke with him soon afterward and joined the Mensheviks. After the Revolution of 1905, Plekhanov still opposed Lenin's leadership but nevertheless supported the Bolshevik position of opposition to the Duma and their stand on the need for illegal revolutionary activity. In 1914 Plekhanov formed a group known as *Yedinstvo* (Unity) with the goal of unifying the Mensheviks and the anti-Lenin Bolsheviks. The Unity movement had little success then or in 1917.

Plekhanov returned to Russia after the fall of the monarchy but stood apart from the Bolsheviks and Mensheviks. The Unity program of 1917 denied the possibility of a socialist revolution and consequently urged full support of the Provisional Government and its policies. By the end of 1918 the new Bolshevik regime had liquidated completely the Unity organization. Plekhanov, meanwhile, had fled to Finland where he died on 30 May 1918.

Martov (Julius O. Tsederbaum, 1873-1923) became a revolutionary in 1891 and was associated first with the Jewish Bund in Vilna. Later he became one of the organizers of the Union of Struggle for the Emancipation of the Working Class, the first Marxist group formed in Russia. Arrested in 1896 and exiled to Siberia in 1897, he escaped in

1901, fled abroad, and joined the editorial board of *Iskra.* He returned to Russia in 1905 and led the Mensheviks in the St. Petersburg Soviet. In 1907 he went abroad again. A representative of left-wing Menshevism, Martov disagreed with the general Menshevik position against illegal activity and, during World War I, he supported the internationalist position of peace without victory ("centrism").

In 1917 Martov returned to Russia and became the leader of a faction known as the Internationalists whose program called for an immediate peace and a socialist government based on a coalition that included the Bolsheviks. After October, he opposed the Bolshevik dictatorship but also refused to support the anti-Bolshevik counter-revolution. In 1920 he left the country and settled in Berlin, where he founded the *Sotsialisticheskii vestnik* (Socialist Courier).

Paul B. Axelrod (1850-1928) represented the rightist tendency among the Mensheviks. Axelrod joined the Populist movement in the early 1870s and was a co-founder of the anti-terrorist Black Repartition group in 1879. In 1880 he moved to Switzerland, adopted Marxism, and joined Plekhanov and others in forming the first Russian Marxist organization. For the next two decades he wrote several tracts and contributed to many socialist journals, including *Iskra.* After 1905 he became a "liquidator"—an advocate of the liquidation of illegal party activity and a proponent of legal propaganda and organizational work among trade unions and other workers' groups. In 1917, as a member of the executive committee of the Petrograd Soviet, Axelrod urged socialist support for the Provisional Government. After the Bolshevik coup, he left the country and endorsed the foreign intervention against Bolshevism.

Vera I. Zasulich (1849-1919), one of the more famous Russian revolutionaries, was first imprisoned in 1869-71 for her association with Sergei Nechaev, the infamous nihilist. In 1878 she shot and wounded F.F. Trepov, the governor-general of St. Petersburg, but was acquitted by a jury. Before she could be re-arrested, she fled to Switzerland. She returned to Russia in 1879 and joined the Black Repartition group. In Switzerland again in 1880 Zasulich helped direct the Red Cross of the People's Will, an organization formed to assist Russian political prisoners. In 1883 she endorsed Marxism with the others, and for the next two decades she furthered the cause of revolutionary Marxism through her writings and organizational work. She returned to Russia during the Revolution of 1905 and settled in the capital. As a prominent Menshevik leader, she supported the "liquidators" and in 1917 joined Plekhanov's Unity group. She died in Petrograd on 8 May 1919, an unreconciled foe of Leninism.

Leon Trotsky (Lev D. Bronstein, 1879-1940) joined the revolutionary movement in 1898, was arrested almost immediately, and exiled to Siberia. He escaped, however, and in 1902 was invited by Lenin to join the *Iskra* board. Subsequently Trotsky opposed Lenin's concept of party organization, but his theory of "permanent revolution" paralleled Lenin's views on Russia's situation and revolutionary potential. In July 1917 Trotsky joined the Bolsheviks and was admitted to the top leadership. He was the principal organizer of the Bolshevik coup of October 1917 and subsequently played a leading role in Soviet affairs until Lenin's death in 1924. Widely regarded as Lenin's successor, Trotsky was defeated by Stalin. He was expelled from the party in 1927, banished from the Soviet Union in 1929, and murdered by a Soviet agent in Mexico City in 1940.

There are English-language biographies of all of these figures except Zasulich, and for some of course there are several: Samuel H. Baron, *Plekhanov: The Father of Russian Marxism* (Stanford, 1963); Israel Getzler, *Martov: A Political Biography of a Russian Social Democrat* (Cambridge, 1967) and Martov's autobiography, *Annals of a Social Democrat* (Berlin, 1922); Abraham Ascher, *Pavel Axelrod and the Development of Menshevism* (Cambridge, 1973); and Isaac Deutscher, *The Prophet Armed: Trotsky, 1879-1921* and *The Prophet Unarmed: Trotsky, 1921-1929* (Oxford, 1954,1959), which should be read with caution.

15. Plekhanov and Lenin edited *Iskra* from August to November 1903. At that point Plekhanov demanded, and Lenin refused, to restore the entire original board of editors. Lenin quit, and thereafter, until its demise in October 1905, *Iskra* was edited by the original board minus Lenin. Lenin meanwhile brought out a new weekly, *Vpered*, also published in Geneva. *Vpered* appeared in eighteen editions from 22 December 1904/4 January 1905 to 5/18 May 1905.

Although fundamental disagreement over party policy and organization lay at the root of the historic split of the Russian Social Democrats, the issue that produced the labels, Bolshevik (majority-ite) and Menshevik (minority-ite), was a resolution on the reorganization of the *Iskra* board. Lenin's faction narrowly defeated Martov's and immediately claimed to represent the majority view. The literature on the rancorous history of Bolshevism is vast, but one of the classics is Bertram Wolfe, *Three Who Made a Revolution: A Biographical History* (New York, 1948; Boston, 1955).

16. *Osvobozhdenie*, the main journal of Russian liberalism, was published first in Stuttgart (July-October 1902) and then until October 1905 in Paris. As the principal organ of the League of Liberation, *Osvobozhdenie* followed a left-liberal line expressing hostility to the Bolsheviks but a willingness to cooperate with the Mensheviks.

17. The editor, P. Krushevan, was a unique type of anti-Semite who believed that Jews who accepted baptism lost their "harmfulness." In the newspaper *Znamia* (The Banner) he once made the bizarre proposal that Jews be given "an ultimatum"—"either be baptized or get out of Russia."

"Become Christians like us," he wrote, "and enjoy with us an equality of rights as brothers and citizens of Great Russia. Jewish Christians will be given the same rights and privileges as the country's native population, including the right to change their surnames into Russian surnames. In proportion to the other classes, Jews will be granted the right to hereditary enoblement, titles, and decorations. These honors will be distributed by lot (!) among the Jewish intelligentsia. In less than a year the damned Jewish problem will disappear, and instead of seven million enemies, we will have seven million brothers in Christ." (Oldenburg's note and exclamation)

18. On the morning of the second day a Jewish delegation called on von Raaben to beg protection. He replied that he had received no instructions from St. Petersburg and consequently could do nothing. At 5:00 p.m. a telegram arrived from Plehve, and around 6:00 troops entered the city. The rioters dispersed without a shot being fired. The historian of Russian Jewry described the carnage this way:

"The Jews were slain in most barbarous fashion. Many of them were not killed at once, but were left writhing in pre-mortal agonies. Some had nails driven into their heads or had their eyes put out. Little children were thrown from garrets to the pavement, and their brains dashed out upon the stones. Women had their stomachs ripped open or their breasts cut off. Many of them became victims of rape. One gymnazium pupil who saw his mother attacked by these fiends threw himself singlehanded upon them, and saved at the cost of his life his mother's honor; he himself was slain, and his mother's eyes were put out. The drunken hordes broke into the synagogue, and, getting hold of the Torah scrolls, tore them to shreds, defiled them, and trampled upon them . . . . Throughout the entire day, wagons were seen moving in the streets, carrying wounded and slain Jews to the hospitals which had been converted into field-lazarettes. But even this sight did not induce the police to step in." S.M. Dubnow, *History of the Jews in Russia and Poland*, Volume III: *From the Accession of Nicholas II until the Present Day*. Trans. I. Friedlaender (Philadelphia, 1920), p. 74.

19. *Zapiski gubernatora* [A Governor's Memoir] (St. Petersburg, 1907). Prince S.D. Urusov, *Memoirs of a Russian Governor* (London, 1908).

Prince Urusov succeeded Raaben as governor of Bessarabia, gained a local reputation as a pro-Semite, and subsequently served as a member of the opposition in the First Duma. (Oldenburg's note, transposed from the text)

20. The Russian government's treatment of Jews afforded little basis to doubt its complicity in the crime. The reign of Alexander III had been inaugurated by a wave of pogroms (1881) and it ended with the systematic expulsion of Jews from the interior. The illiterate Russian population observed the government's incessant persecution of Jews—the deprivation of civil rights, the constant hounding and raids upon "illegal" residents, the quotas, and general discrimination—and seem to have concluded that the ill-treatment of Jews was a patriotic act pleasing to the tsar and the government. In 1881 peasants in Chernigov province were dissuaded from a pogrom only when they received an affidavit affirming that higher authorities would not call them to account for being remiss in their "duty of pogroms." A Ukrainian peasant imprisoned in 1897 for his part in a pogrom in the village of Kantakuzenka (Kherson province) complained: "It was said that one is permitted to beat Jews, but it turned out to be a lie."

Anti-Semitism was rampant among court and government officials, and tolerant officials found it best to remain silent. Among the chief bigots were the tsar's uncle, Grand Duke Sergei Alexandrovich, and Constantine Pobedonostsev, both influential figures. Grand Duke Sergei became governor-general of Moscow in February 1891 and immediately set out to purge the city of Jews. In 1898 Pobedonostsev received a foreign delegation from the Jewish Colonization Association seeking permission to establish Jewish agricultural colonies in Russia. When refused, they asked Pobedonostsev what would result from the government's constant persecution of Jews. He replied that a third would die out, a third would emigrate, and a third would be completely assimilated. Prince Urusov, quoted above by Oldenburg, was a member of a commission convened by the ministry of interior in January 1904 to investigate the Jewish question in the aftermath of Kishinev. He recorded that at the outset the conferees were given to understand that any proposal to mitigate the restrictions on Russian Jewry would be poorly received in "the highest spheres" meaning, presumably, the tsar himself. See Urusov, p. 93, and Simon Dubnow, *History of the Jews: From the Congress of Vienna to the Emergence of Hitler.* Trans. Moshe Speigel (New York, 1973), Vol. X, pp. 517-26, 566-68, 579-87.

21. In 1826 Emperor Nicholas I established the Third Section of His Imperial Majesty's Own Chancery as the highest office of the political police, charged with maintaining internal security throughout the empire. In 1880 the Third Section was abolished as an independent agency and its functions were transferred to the department of state police in the ministry of internal affairs. Within the police administration a security section—*Okhrannoe otdelenie* or, as it commonly was known, the *Okhrana*—was created for the political police, and offices were established in the two capitals and other major cities. The designations, Third Section, Okhrana, and secret police came to be used synonymously.

Rataev was Azef's official contact and immediate supervisor until 1905. Rataev joined the police department around 1880. Intelligent and skillful, he advanced to the post of Okhrana chief. But, a *bon vivant* and Don Juan, his mind usually was elsewhere and he did his work sloppily. Plehve called him a "blot" on the department and in 1903 put him in charge of the foreign division of the Okhrana. That afforded Rataev plenty of time in Paris and other centers of delight, but the demotion rankled and he retired in 1905.

Evno-Meyer F. Azef (1869-1918) was the son of a poor Jewish tailor from the village of Lyskovo in Grodnensky province. In 1893 in order to earn money he began reporting the activities of student radicals to the police. His income allowed him to earn a degree in engineering at the Polytechnic Institute in Karlsruhe, Germany. After graduating, Azef maintained his revolutionary and police connections. In 1903 he succeeded Gershuni as head of the SR Battle Organization (see above, Note 12). His first project was the assassination of Plehve (July 1904), whom he held responsible for the Kishinev massacre. In 1905 Azef organized the assassination of Grand Duke Sergei Alexandrovich and also became a member of the SR central committee. He continued to satisfy the police by betraying SR terrorists. In 1908 he was exposed by Vladimir L. Burtsev (1862-1942), the original historian of the Russian revolutionary movement. Azef went into hiding, and in 1909 as Alexander Neumayer, he became a stockbroker in Berlin. In 1915 the German police discovered his identity, and Azef was arrested and imprisoned until December 1917. He died in Berlin on 24 April 1918. See Nikolajewsky, *Aseff the Spy.*

22. Lawyers for the Jewish community contended that the official instigators of the pogrom were not among the accused. When the court ruled against their demand for a wider indictment, the Jews' attorneys withdrew from the proceedings. Dubnow, *The Jews in Russia and Poland*, vol. III, pp. 90-92.

23. "Scores" of murderers and rioters were sentenced to prison or hard labor. The court, however, dismissed civil actions brought by Jews seeking compensation for damages. A few months later, the Russian Senate (in its role as a supreme court) rejected a suit against the government for damages and thus averted the precedent of compensating pogrom victims with state funds. Ibid., p. 92.

24. Leonid Andreev's novel, *The Governor* [1906], reflected this characteristic. (Oldenburg's note)

25. In 1904-5 the French Chamber of Deputies passed legislation on the separation of church and state. One provision of the new law provided for private corporations to assume title to church properties, which then had to be inventoried.

26. Saint Seraphim of Sarov (1759-1833) was the most renowned and revered Russian holy man of modern times, and his consecration in 1903 was called by some "the greatest event in Russian history of the twentieth century." Seraphim entered the Sarov monastery at the age of nineteen. After fifteen years in the ordinary life of the community, he withdrew and spent the next thirty years in secluded prayer, meditation, and study. He lived at first in a hut in the forest near the cloister and then, when an infirmity made it difficult for him to walk, he immured himself in a cell within the monastery. Finally in 1825 he opened the doors of his cell and from dawn to evening for the rest of his life he received and comforted, advised, and healed thousands who sought his counsel and intercession.

The emperor's "intense interest" in Father Seraphim stemmed immediately from the imperial couple's inability to produce a male heir. Following the birth of their fourth daughter, Anastasia, in 1901, Alexandra and Nicholas came under the influence of a charlatanic French mystic, "Monsieur Philippe." Formerly a butcher's assistant in Lyons, Philippe Vachot was introduced to the imperial couple in 1901 by Grand Duchess Militsa Nikolaevna, daughter of the king of Montenegro, confidante of the empress, and a devotee of spiritualism and the occult. At the emperor's direction Mr. Philippe received a doctorate in medicine from the St. Petersburg Military Academy of Medicine. Then he was appointed a councilor of state and provided quarters in the Winter Palace. His invocations, ministrations, and advice combined with her own anxieties and faith to convince the empress that she was pregnant. During the fall of 1902, she put on weight and went into the customary period of confinement. Only after the appointed date had arrived and passed was she finally examined by the court physician, who found her to be in a quite singular condition. The public was informed discreetly.

To the emperor and empress this misfortune seemed another of the trials visited upon Nicholas who, like Job on whose feast day he was born, had to suffer untold anguish in order to merit rich blessings and rewards. The false pregnancy also convinced Nicholas and Alexandra that they needed a powerful intercessor before the throne of God. Holy Seraphim, who once blessed barren women, was to be their celestial mediator. But to become an effective intercessor, Seraphim first had to gain admission to heaven. Nicholas, therefore, ordered that Seraphim be canonized.

The strange tale of Mr. Phillippe and accounts of the canonization of St. Seraphim appear in various memoirs and in some details in public records. Massie's *Nicholas and Alexandra* curiously overlooks the canonization of St. Seraphim, which preceded the arrival of still another holy man, Gregory Rasputin. There is an interesting if speculative account of these episodes in Essad-Bey, *Nicholas II*, pp. 115-22.

27. Oldenburg refers here to a widespread belief that one of the requirements for canonization was the examination of the remains of a prospective saint after the passage of at least one hundred years. An uncorrupted corpse implied a state of sanctity, since popular opinion and in some cases ecclesiastical authority held that the bodies of true saints did not decompose. The confusion and controversy surrounding the canonization of St. Seraphim stemmed from the ambiguity of Russian canon law and the diverse procedures followed historically by the Russian Orthodox Church in the canonization of saints.

Until the eleventh century the canonization of Russian saints adhered to practice common to the entire Eastern Orthodox Church. By modern times, however, the Russian Church recognized three distinct categories of saints: (1) those venerated throughout the entire church by decree of the supreme ecclesiastical authority; (2) those venerated with official sanction in a particular district, church, or monastery; and (3) those venerated by the faithful with the tacit sanction of the holy synod, even though canonization had not been approved. Authentication of a saint required proof that the venerated person either had been a martyr or had led an exceptionally pious life. In addition, the attribution of a miracle either to the living person or his remains was practically essential. (No miracle was attributed, for example, to St. Vladimir who lived 972-1054 and was canonized in 1240.) Finally, a special inquiry into the incorruption of the remains was an important but not essential part of the evidence.

A month before St. Seraphim's canonization, Metropolitan Antonius of St. Petersburg formally declared in the official journal of the holy synod that uncorrupted remains were not essential to canonization. (*Tserkovniia vedomosti* [Church Messenger], 28 June 1903.) His statement contradicted a pronouncement of 1682 by the Orthodox Patriarch of Jerusalem that proof of incorruptibility was absolutely essential.

The process leading to St. Seraphim's canonization deviated from custom in two respects: it was initiated by a civil authority (the tsar) rather than a bishop, and the period of inquiry and review, normally a minimum of two or three years, was speeded up considerably. Pobedonostsev, as director-general of the holy synod, was responsible for authenticating the saintly virtues and qualities of Seraphim. He apparently did so reluctantly under direct orders from Nicholas.

The standard work on canonization in Russia is E.E. Golubinsky, *Istoriia kanonizatsii sviatykh v russkoi tserkvi* [History of the Canonization of Saints in the Russian Church], (Moscow, 1903); for a concise historical and procedural survey see the *Encyclopaedia of Religion and Ethics*, s.v. "Canonization," by W.H. Hutton.

28. Essad-Bey relates that around midnight the empress, accompanied by an elderly lady-in-waiting, made her way through the woods to the spring in which Seraphim bathed and which, as a result, had acquired curative powers. "Even as the choirs at the nearby monastery sent their last litanies toward the heavens, the Czarina undressed and immersed herself in the miracle-working spring of St. Seraphim." Ibid., p. 122. The author does not relate how or where he came upon this choice bit of intelligence. In any event, within a few weeks of his consecration, St. Seraphim rewarded the devotion of his tormented sponsors, and on 12 August 1904 the emperor and empress and all the Russias received an heir.

29. This phrase was part of the formula on the nature of the supreme autocratic power as expressed in the Fundamental Laws of the Russian Empire.

30. The Russian Club was a patriotic association of wealthy and prestigious noblemen and merchants dedicated to conservative principles. In 1909 the emperor donated 100,000 rubles of his own personal funds for the purchase of a "club house." However, according to V.I. Gurko, the Russian government tended to be "very parsimonious in subsidizing its supporters. The practice of parliamentary states is much more decisive in this respect." *Features and Figures of the Past*, p. 436 n.

31. The Karageorge and Obrenovich families had contended for power in Serbia since the Napoleonic era, when Serbia first became an autonomous Turkish principality. The Obrenovich family ruled from 1817 to 1842 and from 1858 to 1903; in 1882 with Austrian support Prince Milan Obrenovich had proclaimed himself king of Serbia. The pro-Austrian orientation of the Obrenoviches was opposed by Serbian nationalists and especially by the Radical Party, formed and led since 1883 by Nicholas Pashich (1845-1926). On 10 June 1903 radical-nationalist conspirators in the officer corps slaughtered King Alexander (1889-1903), Queen Draga, and twenty members of the court. Five days later, the Serbian National Assembly elected Peter Karageorgevich to the throne. King Peter (1903-21), supported by Pashich, became the leader of the "Greater Serbia" movement which aspired to unite all Serbs and kindred peoples—Bosnians, Croats, Dalmatians, and Slovenes—in one great kingdom. This program required Russia's support, and as Austro-Serbian relations deteriorated, Serbia grew increasingly dependent on Russia. Thus the coup of 1903 and the subsequent shift of Serbian policy from Austria to Russia contributed to the breakdown of Austro-Russian cooperation in the Balkans and set in motion the train of events that plunged Europe into war in 1914.

32. Anastasia Nikolaevna (1868-1935) and Militsa Nikolaevna (1866-) were the daughters of Prince Nicholas (king, 1910-18) of Montenegro and the wives of the tsar's uncles, Grand Dukes Nicholas Nikolaevich and Peter Nikolaevich. The two women were known as the "dark princesses" partly because of their dark hair, eyes, and complexions and partly because of their interest in the occult.

33. British, French, and Italian officers, as well as Russians and Austrians, were to be included in the Macedonian gendarmery. The Mürzsteg Program, which reaffirmed Austro-Russian cooperation, was inspired by the British, and Germany significantly was not a party to it. On the basis of this complete understanding with Austria, Russia was able to withdraw two entire army corps from the Austrian frontier for service in the Far East. (*Grosse Politik*, Vol. 19, Part I, No. 5939.)

34. "Pervye shagi russkogo imperializma na Dalnem Vostoke (1888-1903 gg.)" [Russian Imperialism's First Steps in the Far East, 1888-1903]. Introduction by A. Popov, *Krasnyi arkhiv*, 52 (1932): 34-124. (Oldenburg's note, from the text)

35. Prince Ito's visit took place on 25 November-4 December 1901. Initially encouraged by the willingness of Witte and Lamsdorf (both opponents of an aggressive policy) to make far-reaching concessions in Korea, Ito exceeded his instructions and drafted an agreement with Russia. On 7 December, however, the Japanese government decided to terminate its discussion with Russia and to conclude instead an alliance with England.

Russia's "possession of Manchuria" was in some dispute. In April 1902 Russia had recognized Chinese sovereignty over Manchuria and had promised to evacuate that territory in eighteen months (by October 1903). The Russians completed the first stage of the evacuation but then made any further withdrawal contingent on Chinese "guarantees." England, Japan, and the United States urged Peking to insist on the 1902 convention. When the Chinese therefore refused to make any concessions to the Russians, Russia continued to occupy Manchuria.

36. The British first approached the Japanese on the subject of an alliance in July 1902. The Japanese government pondered the proposal for several weeks before authorizing the negotiation to begin in London in October. The conclusion of the alliance marked England's departure from the policy of "splendid isolation." The treaty, concluded for five years, recognized the independence of China and Korea but also recognized Japan's "special interests" in Korea.

37. The Yalu concession, covering an area of about 3,300 square miles, stretched from the mouth of the Yalu River in the west to the mouth of the Tiumen River in the east. Julius Ivanovich Bryner, a Russian merchant, obtained the concession from the king of Korea in 1896. Julius Ivanovich, grandfather of the American actor Yul Bryner (who added a second "n" to the family's original Swiss name), operated a large import-export firm in Vladivostok and had extensive commercial connections throughout the Far East. In May 1897 Bryner offered to sell his rights. The concession might have fallen into foreign hands, but a few members of the Russian court arranged its purchase by his majesty's cabinet, the department responsible for managing the property of the imperial family.

The inspiration for the enterprise came from two retired guards officers, Colonel Vladimir M. Vonliarliarsky and Captain Alexander M. Bezobrazov. Vonliarliarsky already had squandered his wife's abundant fortune on various hare-brained schemes, and he was anxious to recoup his losses. Bezobrazov, the scion of a distinguished and wealthy noble family, regarded himself as an expert on the Far East, where he had been stationed for a year, and he was consumed by an ambition to make his mark as a statesman. Their scheme was launched with the assistance of Count Illarion I. Vorontsov-Dashkov, former minister of the imperial court and confidante of the tsar, and the tsar's cousin, Grand Duke Alexander Mikhailovich. Although the deal with Bryner was consummated in May 1898, the international climate did not favor the exploitation of the concession. Consequently the "East-Asiatic Company" was put on ice until 1903.

From the start the enterprise was given the character of a "political" institution "directed by the sovereign will of the Russian emperor" to promote "the Russian principle" in Korea and later, Manchuria. Participation in the company was restricted to a handful of "reliable" courtiers whose financial resources were to assist the tsar in his struggle for "purely Russian" interests in Asia. The project posed a clear alternative to Witte's policy and the principle that direction of the commercial and political exploitation and development of the Far East should fall mainly under the auspices of the finance ministry and its front, the Russo-Chinese Bank. That institution, as Bezobrazov put it, was an unreliable and alien agency: "Instead of bringing our own best powers into play, we left the work to Jews and Poles whom S. Yu. [Witte] commissioned to be our color-bearers."

Bezobrazov quickly ingratiated himself with the tsar and remained for five years one of his most trusted advisors. When Plehve succeeded the murdered Sipiagin in April 1902, Bezobrazov found an able and equally ambitious ally. Plehve almost immediately aligned himself with the Bezobrazov clique, and together they tipped the scales against Witte.

See Romanov, *Russia in Manchuria*, pp. 268-86 (quoted, pp. 269-70 and 273). Romanov's work, based mainly on archival material, is the authoritative and indispensable account of this question; unfortunately the translation is too literal and the text is unnecessarily clumsy. An outstanding history of the diplomatic side is J.A. White, *The Diplomacy of the Russo-Japanese War* (Princeton, 1964).

38. Oldenburg's interpretation is a little misleading. Bezobrazov originally (1898) offered three reasons for the enterprise on the Yalu. First, handsome profits would result from the commercial exploitation of the timber. Second, twenty thousand men or more, "garbed as lumberjacks, mounted police, and employees in general" could be deployed as a "military vanguard" along the frontier. They could establish communications, supply depots, and bases to protect the South Manchurian Railway and Port Arthur from a Japanese attack launched from Korea. Third, foreigners already were scrambling for concessions in Korea. If Russia did not act, Korea would be lost forever or, following the military conquest of Korea, Russia would gain nothing but "the job of policing other people's property."

The Russian Timber Industry Stock Company in the Far East was authorized to begin operations in May 1903. By fall, when the Yalu River froze, it had consumed all of its original capital and was bankrupt. With financial disaster and international complications looming,

Bezobrazov began to stress the strategic factor: The Yalu concession was a "military screen" against Japan. "Now, with the evacuation of Manchuria, the screen in the Yalu basin gains special significance in the sense of averting a clash with Japan, and, should a clash occur, in the sense of an obstacle to concerted attack by the Japanese and the Chinese on our railway." Romanov, *Russia in Manchuria*, pp. 13, 269, 282.

39. Admiral Alekseev (1843-1909) had held several responsible commands and apparently owed his successful career partly to his friendship with Grand Duke Michael Alexandrovich. In 1891 Alekseev accompanied the heir-apparent on his tour of the Far East. From 1899 to 1903 he was chief of troops in the Kwantung Region and commander of naval forces in the Pacific. In the critical period of 1903-4 he appears as a naive and somewhat pathetic figure. Anxious to maintain the favor of the tsar but opposed to a war with Japan, Alekseev was for the most part misinformed, deceived, and misled by the adventuresome Bezobrazov and his colleagues.

40. Major General Vogak, a "Bezobrazovist," was the senior military attache in the Far East, concurrently responsible for military intelligence in Tokyo and Peking. He was an unending source of misinformation and optimism. Russian military intelligence was very poor in general. Colonel Samoilov, the military agent in Japan, reported that Japan had an armed strength of no more than 350,000 men and could put no more than ten of thirteen divisions in the field. The naval agent, Captain Rusin, on the other hand, warned that Japanese reserves and auxiliary forces would double the size of the Japanese army. Eventually Japan mobilized 800,000 troops. The ambassador, Baron Rosen, also provided excellent information, but the Russian general staff considered his reports too alarming to be accurate. The general staff assigned only one officer to Japanese intelligence and, as Kuropatkin later lamented, "our selection was bad." Russian officers accepted as fact that one Russian soldier was worth three Japanese. Like every member of the Russian government, including the tsar, they had an inflated view of Russian power and were absolutely confident that Russian prestige in itself was a sufficient deterrent to Japanese aggression: "*Un drapeau et une sentinelle, et le prestige de la Russie fera le reste*" (One flag and one sentry, and Russia's prestige will do the rest). Warner and Warner, *Tide at Sunrise*, pp. 172-73; Gurko, *Features and Figures of the Past*, p. 280n.

41. Witte made this statement at a conference at Yalta on 27 October 1902. (Oldenburg's note)

According to Romanov, Witte's position was basically that Russia should withdraw for the time being from Manchuria (in accord with the Russo-Chinese convention of 1902) but meanwhile gather as many concessions as possible through the Russo-Chinese Bank. Witte, supported by Lamsdorf, believed that a war was economically and technically beyond Russia's means and that it would bring revolution "to the surface." Kuropatkin vacillated but his position was similar. In 1903 he advocated the abandonment of Port Arthur and suggested that Russia might sell back to China the southern half of Manchuria—territory which Russia had recently seized from China. Romanov, *Russia in Manchuria*, p. 14.

42. No G.M. Volkonsky can be identified; possibly Prince Vladimir Mikhailovich Volkonsky (1868-1953), a political moderate who was deputy chairman of the First Duma and assistant minister of interior in 1915-17. The "Mr. Martynov" mentioned further on in the text was probably a liberal zemstvo leader from the province of Voronezh.

43. Although the creation of the Far Eastern Viceroyalty was made public at the end of July, the reorganization was actually put into effect during a flurry of activity on 2-7 May 1903. At that point Nicholas announced his "new course." A month earlier the government had decided to withdraw from Manchuria, restrict activities on the Yalu to legitimate commercial activities, and invite the participation of foreign capital. In May, however, the emperor, following Bezobrazov's suggestions, reversed himself. He ordered that Manchuria was to be kept free of foreign influence and that Russian forces in the Far East were to be increased without regard to cost. Admiral Alekseev was to carry out this program and report directly to the tsar.

At the same time the tsar created a Special Committee for Far Eastern Affairs under the chairmanship of Bezobrazov's cousin, Admiral Alexis M. Abaza. Bezobrazov himself was appointed state secretary and a member of the special committee. The committee absorbed all the lines of responsibility for Russian policy in the Far East and thus displaced the regular state administration. It was at this point, too, that much to the alarm of the Japanese the announcement was made of the formation of the Russian Timber Industry Stock Company in the Far East, a private, closed enterprise to exploit that Yalu concession.

The viceroyalty proved to be a blunder in every respect. It dislocated and impeded Russian diplomacy. Although Alekseev technically was responsible for Russian relations with Japan, he could not act without consulting St. Petersburg, which meant going through Abaza or Bezobrazov. The Japanese interpreted the delays that resulted as Russian efforts to temporize while reinforcing their Asian military and naval establishments. The viceroyalty itself consisted of Kwantung Province in southern Manchuria and the Amur region stretching northward from Vladivostok, two areas separated from each other by the rest of Manchuria. The Japanese logically concluded that the Russians intended to annex the intervening territory. The formal announcement of the creation of the viceroyalty followed by a few days and seemed a deliberate rebuff to a renewed Japanese offer to define our "respective special interests."

44. This and the following two paragraphs appear on pages 221-22 of the text. They have been moved forward and inserted here (following page 219) to avoid interruption of the author's subsequent discussion of Far Eastern affairs.

45. The department of general affairs handled matters concerning the personnel of the ministry of internal affairs. B.V. Stürmer (1848-1917), a career bureaucrat, headed the department from 1902 to 1904. Stürmer achieved his greatest notoriety as head of the Russian government in 1916.

46. Since the legal press could not respond openly to the suppression of the Tver zemstvo, the newspapers (including *Novoe vremia*) remained "eloquently silent." (Oldenburg's note, taken from the text, p. 222)

CHAPTER NINE

1. Chapters IX through XII originally formed Part 2, "The Years of Change, 1904-07" of the original text.

2. Sydney Tyler, *The Japan-Russia War: An Illustrated History of the War in the Far East, the Greatest Conflict of Modern Times* (Philadelphia, [1905]), p. 14.

3. "After the War," *Atlantic Monthly* 76 (November 1895), 604. Lafcadio Hearn (1850-1904), after years of romantic wandering, went to Japan in 1890 as a school teacher. In 1891 he married into an impoverished Samurai family and became a naturalized citizen, taking the name Yakumo Koizumi. He wrote widely on Japanese religion, folklore, and literature and contributed frequently to American journals. He wrote twelve sympathetic, sensitive, and perhaps over-romanticized books on Japan. Some critics hold Hearn to be the greatest master of American prose. See George M. Gould, *Concerning Lafcadio Hearn*, with a bibliography by Laura Stedman (London and Philadelphia, 1908), and also Beongcheon Yu, *An Ape of the Gods: The Art and Thought of Lafcadio Hearn* (Detroit, 1964).

4. The evidence was available to those who were willing to accept it; see above, Chapter VIII, Note 40. In 1895 Lafcadio Hearn, hardly a trained military observer, wrote that Japan's "reserve strength is probably much greater than has ever been acknowledged, and her educational system, with its twenty-six thousand schools, is an enormous drilling-machine." "After the War," 601.
The original text, Vol. I, p. 230, is rearranged slightly to form this paragraph.

5. This included seven battleships of the Port Arthur Squadron, seven of the Second [Baltic] Squadron, and the *Slava* not to mention such older battleships as the *Nikolai I* and *Aleksandr II*. (Oldenburg's note)
The designation of cruisers as "armored" (heavy) or "protected" (light) referred to the location and thickness of their armor. The hull and turrets of an armored cruiser were sheathed in steel 6 to 10 centimeters thick, whereas the hulls of light cruisers were not reinforced but their decks and turrets were "protected" with steel armor-plating up to 3 centimeters. Armored cruisers also carried heavier guns, typically four 8-inch and anywhere from twelve to sixteen 6-inch guns. On Russian light cruisers the biggest weapon was a 6-inch gun, and they sported from eight to twelve of them. On Japanese light cruisers the main armament varied considerably. The *Matsushima*, built in 1890, carried one 12.5-inch gun and eleven 4.7-inch guns; the *Niitaka* and the *Tsushima*, both built in 1902, mounted only six 6-inch guns. The largest naval gun in the Russo-Japanese War was the 12-inch gun which formed the main batteries of the battleships.

6. In July 1903 some twenty liberals hailing from Russian zemstvo and intelligentsia circles met in Schaffhausen, Switzerland, and formed a Union of Liberation dedicated to the "political liberation of Russia." The impetus for the organization came principally from Peter Struve, the editor of *Osvobozhdenie*. On 3-5 January 1904 a constituent congress

was held in St. Petersburg. The purpose of the Union was to organize Russian liberals and especially to bring together the liberal gentry, associated with the zemstvos, and the liberal intelligentsia of the professions, the so-called "third element." In January the Liberationists elected a central council that gave an equal voice to each group. Representing the zemstvo constitutionalists were Ivan Petrunkevich of Tver, Prince Peter Dolgorukov of Moscow, Prince Dmitry Shakovskoy of Yaroslavl, Nicholas Kovalevsky of Kharkov, I.V. Luchitsky of Kiev, and N.N. Lvov of Samara. The spokesmen of the third element came mainly from the capital: N.F. Annensky, V. Ya. Bogucharsky, L.I. Lutugin, V.V. Khizhniakov, A.V. Peshekhonov, and S.N. Prokopovich. Ekaterina Kuskovo, a journalist and the wife of Prokopovich, was the leader of the "St. Petersburg Group" and a particularly active figure in the Union. The Union's organizational meeting was staged under the pretence that it was a conference on technical education.

7. In Russian the expression *Da zdravstvuet* [long live . . .] is considered one word. Thus the writer was objecting to the "three words" *Da zdravstvuet svobodnaia Rossiia!*—Long live Free Russia!—as too cumbersome for political rallies. The "two words" that he preferred were *Doloi samoderzhavie!*—Down with Autocracy!

8. The terrorist careers of these two revolutionists are described below; for Kaliaev see Chapter X, Note 17, and for Sozonov see this chapter, Note 23.

9. "What this country needs is a short victorious war to stem the tide of revolution" was the statement attributed by Kuropatkin to Plehve. While a few historians have questioned whether he actually made that remark, there is no reason to doubt that it reflected his attitude.

10. *Tua res agitur, paries cum proximus ardet* [No time for sleeping, with a fire next door] from Horace, *Epistolae*, I, 18:84.

11. *Zapiska generala Kuropatkina o russko-iaponskoi voine* [General Kuropatkin's Memoirs of the Russo-Japanese War] (Berlin, 1909). An English edition is *The Russian Army and the Japanese War*, ed. Major E.D. Swinton, trans. Captain A.B. Lindsay, 2 vols. (London, 1909).

12. Born in the Far East at Nikolaevsk, the son of a naval ensign, Stepan Osipovich Makarov (1848-1904) attended the Nikolaevsk-on-Amur Naval School. He graduated as a midshipman in 1869 and advanced steadily to the pinnacle of his profession. His genius was recognized in his own time, and his achievement is all the more spectacular because—except for effusive national propaganda—Russia (and the Soviet Union) is a country without naval traditions or an extensive naval history.

In 1876 Makarov received his first ship, the Black Sea cruiser *Konstantin*, which he commanded for the next two years in the Russo-Turkish War. His genius played a significant role in that conflict, for he organized and equipped Russia's first torpedo-boat flotilla and led it in a successful attack on Turkish ironclads. In 1886-89 Makarov sailed the corvette *Vitiaz* around the world, and his observations, published as *"Vitiaz" i Tikhii okean* [*Vitiaz* and the Pacific Ocean], 2 vols. (St. Petersburg, 1894), won him the gold medal of the Imperial Geographic Society.

Promoted to rear admiral in 1890, Makarov became the youngest flag officer in the Baltic Fleet. In 1891 he became chief inspector of naval artillery and in 1894 commander of the Mediterranean Squadron, which he led to the Far East in 1895. He then returned to the Baltic to supervise the training of the fleet. Ever active, throughout the nineties Makarov thought and wrote on nearly every important naval subject. In order to conduct Arctic researches, he designed and supervised the construction of the world's first steam-powered ice-breaker, the *Yermak*, and he commanded her during two Arctic voyages in 1899 and 1901. Appointed commandant of the Kronstadt naval base in 1899, Makarov undertook a variety of technical and theoretical projects. He invented an armor-piercing tip for projectiles, conceived a comprehensive training program for the fleet, and drafted a twenty-year naval construction program. On 1 February 1904 the emperor nominated Makarov to command the Pacific Squadron.

Makarov has been the subject of several biographies both before and since the revolution, although there is nothing of significance in English. The most recent Soviet biography is S.N. Semanov's *Makarov* (Moscow, 1972). See also B.G. Ostrovsky, *Stepan Osipovich Makarov, 1848-1904 gg.* (Leningrad, 1951) and Donald W. Mitchell, "Admiral Makarov: Attack! Attack! Attack!" United States Naval Institute *Proceedings,* 91 (July 1965), 57-67.

13. The Japanese controlled the telegraph station at Chemulpo and apparently also had cut the cable to Port Arthur. Therefore, the commanders of the two Russian vessels did not know that diplomatic relations had been broken. In the early morning of 26 January/8 February a Japanese squadron of five cruisers (soon joined by the *Chiyoda* which had been at Chemulpo for several weeks), two flotillas of torpedo boats, and three transports arrived off the west coast of Korea. Around 2:00 p.m. the *Koreets* put to sea for Port Arthur with mail and dispatches. As she cleared the harbor, she ran into the Japanese, recognized that they were up to no good, and scurried back to Chemulpo. During their chance meeting, however, *Koreets* fired two shots, and Japanese torpedo boats fired three torpedoes. No one hit anything. Tokyo later claimed that *Koreets* shot first and that Russia therefore had started the war. Much later, the official Japanese history recorded that the torpedo boat *Kari* launched a torpedo before the Russians fired. If who fired the first shot was in dispute, who committed the first act of war was quite clear, for on the previous day, 7 February, the Japanese had seized the Russian merchantman *Rossiia* in Fusan harbor.

Under the protection of the Japanese fleet the three transports landed 3,000 men on the 8th. Then at 9:00 a.m. on the 9th the Japanese commander, Rear-Admiral Uryu Stokichi (a graduate of the U.S. Naval Academy), ordered the Russians to get out of Chemulpo by high noon. An American captain, the senior officer present, in behalf of all the foreign ships present protested this ultimatum in violation of Korean neutrality. Admiral Uryu refused to yield. If the Russians didn't leave, he would enter the harbor; the Japanese would aim carefully so as to hit only the Russian ships. Shortly after 11:00 a.m. the two Russian vessels sailed out to certain destruction, leaving behind a third, the transport *Sungari*. As the Russians steamed past the anchored warships of England, France, Italy, and the United States, they were cheered in turn by each of the crews.

The battle lasted slightly more than an hour. The heavier armored and gunned Japanese ships formed a semi-circle and concentrated their fire on the *Variag*. The masts and upper structure of the gallant Russian ship were almost entirely shot away, and her hull was riddled above and below the waterline. Listing heavily and ablaze with several fires, *Variag*, having fired over a thousand rounds, limped back into port. *Koreets*, hit only once but also on fire, followed in *Variag's* wake. (*Variag* probably could have outrun the Japanese and escaped, but she chose to try to protect her slower companion.)

The two hulks returned to their former anchorages, and the European ships took their surviving crews aboard. While Uryu considered whether to enter Chemulpo and finish them off, the Russian officers decided to scuttle their ships. *Sungari* was set afire and burned until the following day. Just after 3:30 p.m. a tremendous explosion and an enormous column of smoke proclaimed the end of *Koreets*. Debris from the ship carried inland for three miles. *Variag* went more quietly. Her seacocks were opened, and she settled into the mud with her riddled funnels above the tide.

The Russian government issued two official histories of the war, one for each service: Morskii Generalnyi shtab, Voenno-istoricheskaia komissiia po opisaniiu deistvii flota v voinu 1904-05 gg., *Russko-iaponskaia voina 1904-05 gg.* [Naval General Staff, Military-Historical Commission on Naval Actions during the War of 1904-05, The Russo-Japanese War, 1904-05], 7 books (St. Petersburg, 1912-18); and Voenno-istoricheskaia komissiia po opisaniiu russko-iaponskoi voiny, *Russko-iaponskaia voina 1904-05 gg.* [Military-Historical Commission on the Russo-Japanese War, The Russo-Japanese War, 1904-05], 9 vols. (St. Petersburg, 1910). Two foreign editions of the latter are: German General Staff, Historical Section, *The Russo-Japanese War*, trans. Karl von Donat, 9 vols. (London, 1909); and French General Staff, *La Guerre Russo-Japonaise de 1905-5*, 4 vols. (Paris, 1911).

An English translation of the Japanese history is: Admiralty War Staff, trans., *Japanese Official Naval History of the Russo-Japanese War*, 2 vols. (London, 1913-14). Oddly enough, the best of the official histories was prepared by the British general staff: Committee of Imperial Defence, Historical Section, *Official History, Naval and Military, of the Russo-Japanese War*, 3 vols. and 3 vols. maps and appendices (London, 1910-20). This was the first project undertaken by the newly formed Historical Section of C.I.D. The editors were able to consult with and profit from the criticisms of the general staffs of both antagonists. Moreover, the history takes advantage of numerous first-hand accounts and memoirs.

Three recent histories attest to a sustained interest in the first of the great wars of the twentieth century: *The Tide at Sunrise: A History of the Russo-Japanese War*, 1904-05 by John and Peggy Warner (New York, 1974) is an outstanding narrative, especially strong on the Japanese side. David Walder, *The Short Victorious War* (New York, 1974) is half as long, more analytical, but somewhat pretentious. John Westwood, *The Illustrated History of the Russo-Japanese War* (Chicago, 1974) is a brief, well-executed sketch by a competent scholar. The first two contain extensive bibliographies.

14. The detachment consisted of the three armored cruisers, *Rossiia*, *Gromoboi*, and *Riurik*; the *Bogatyr*, a light cruiser, ran onto the rocks at the beginning of the war and returned to action only at the end of the war. (Oldenburg's note)

15. The *Entente cordiale* or "cordial understanding" between France and England represented a complete settlement of their worldwide colonial rivalry. Especially important was the composition of their differences in North Africa. France recognized the British occupation of Egypt, while England assured free navigation of the Suez Canal and promised to honor the Egyptian debt. (France was a major creditor.) England recognized France's special interest in Morocco; secret provisions anticipated the collapse of the Moroccan government and committed England to support a partition by France and Spain. The agreement also resolved lesser disputes in West Africa, Southeast Asia, Madagascar, Newfoundland, and the New Hebrides Islands. Anglo-French discussions began tentatively in July and earnestly in October 1903. The outbreak of the Russo-Japanese War hastened the negotiation.

The logical though not inevitable result of the *entente cordiale* was a similar Anglo-Russian understanding that would resolve the outstanding differences between France's ally and its new friend. That agreement came in 1907. The Anglo-French and Anglo-Russian ententes and the Franco-Russian Alliance formed the Triple Entente. Though not a military alliance like the Triple Alliance, these agreements had the same effect in 1914.

Major studies of the formation of the *entente cordiale* are: Christopher Andrew, *Théophile Delcassé and the Making of the Entente Cordiale: A Reappraisal of French Foreign Policy, 1898-1905* (New York, 1968) and George Monger, *The End of Isolation: British Foreign Policy, 1900-1907* (New York, 1963). See also E.W. Edwards, "The Japanese Alliance and the Anglo-French Agreement of 1904," *History*, 42 (1957), 19-27. The latest scholarship is synthesized for general readers in P.J.V. Rolo, *Entente Cordiale: The Origins and Negotiation of the Anglo-French Agreement of 8 April 1904* (New York, 1969) and in Dwight E. Lee, *Europe's Crucial Years: The Diplomatic Background of World War I, 1902-1914* (University Press of New England, 1974), pp. 49-80.

16. The Battle of the Yalu revealed most of the liabilities under which Russia fought the war. All except Kuropatkin underestimated the enemy. General Zasulich, fresh from command of the Warsaw military district, scoffed at Kuropatkin's suggestion that a Japanese soldier was as good as a European. Zasulich's second-in-command boasted that his troops would kill them to a man and take no prisoners: "Our troops carry swords, not ropes." Contempt for the Japanese led the Russians to ignore the necessity of reconnaissance or intelligence. They stretched their forces across a 120-mile front and failed to detect the Japanese concentrating on their left flank. When Zasulich finally realized his perilous situation, his staff fell apart. Colonel Gromov, responsible for

liaison between the commanders of the two flanks, failed miserably. Later court-martialled but acquitted, Gromov nevertheless shot himself. Divided command and disagreement over strategy also plagued the Russians. The mountainous Liaotung Peninsula offered ideal terrain to weak defenders. Kuropatkin planned to use that natural advantage to impede the Japanese advance while he built his own forces. Thus he instructed Zasulich to exercise "firmness and prudence," to avoid a decisive engagement with superior forces, and to "retreat as slowly as possible before retreating again." But Admiral Alekseev, Kuropatkin's superior, favored a decisive stand on the Yalu, an immediate victory, not a prolonged strategic retreat. Most of Kuropatkin's subordinates, like Zasulich, shared Alekseev's view. During the battle, when the hard-pressed commander of the left flank requested reinforcements or permission to withdraw, Zasulich haughtily informed him that "His Majesty has made me a member of the Order of St. George, and I do not retreat." Neither did he send reinforcements, and the flank disintegrated.

According to the British *Official History*, Russia's losses were three times as great as Japan's: 1,400 dead, 3,000 wounded, and 600 prisoners; for Japan—1,036 killed and wounded. The body count, however, had little relation to the significance of the battle. It established Japan as a major military power. In January 1904 Tokyo had been unable to float a loan in London; in May investors in London and New York oversubscribed a new Japanese loan.

17. At Valmy on 20 September 1792 the French defeated the Prussians in an artillery duel. It was the first victory for the new revolutionary government of France.

18. Here Oldenburg refers to the "Chinchou position" and to the battle of Chinchou. Most war histories refer to the Nanshan position and the battle of Nanshan. The Nanshan neck, formed by Chinchou Bay in the northwest and Hand Bay in the southwest, is the point at which the Kwantung Peninsula with Port Arthur at its tip joins the Liaotung Peninsula. The area is hilly, and the hills were steep, rugged, and bare. Nanshan Hill, which the Russians had fortified, commanded the entire area and was the key to the Kwantung Peninsula. About a mile north of Nanshan was the walled city of Chinchou, which formed part of the Russian defenses.

At Pitzuwo the Japanese landed the Second Army—three infantry divisions and an artillery brigade—commanded by General Oku Yasukata. Oku's mission was to cut the line of communication between Kuropatkin and Port Arthur. With that accomplished, another army, General Nogi Maresuke's Third Army, was to land and take Port Arthur.

19. Rear Admiral William Karlovich Witgeft (1847-1904) was an honest but uninspired staff officer with little sea experience. When command of the squadron fell upon his shoulders, he bluntly informed his staff and commanders: "I am no leader of a fleet." Makarov had overhauled the Far Eastern naval command, replacing time-servers with intelligent and energetic officers from his own mold. Unfortunately they were lost with him on the *Petropavlovsk*. Therefore, Witgeft had no able staff officers to compensate for the deficiencies that he so readily recognized in himself. Under Witgeft the naval command followed

the principle that it was better to take no action than to risk the fleet. He determined that the navy would concentrate on the defense of the fortress, undertake no operations beyond the harbor, and wait to be rescued. When his policy became known, one of the wits in the fleet rephrased it: "For the remainder of the war the Pacific Squadron will observe the strictest neutrality."

If the naval command was merely timid, the army was chaotic. Lieutenant General Constantine Nikolaevich Smirnov, sent out from Warsaw to replace Stessel as fortress commander, brought with him a reputation as one of Russia's ablest tacticians. He was much admired in the ranks, and his energy earned him the nickname "Seven Devils." Smirnov's chief problem was Stessel, who not only out-ranked him but also enjoyed the support of Alekseev and indirectly the tsar himself. Although Kuropatkin repeatedly ordered Stessel to take command of the Third Siberian Corps and leave the fortress to Smirnov, Stessel refused. He claimed to be the tsar's personal representative and at one point informed Smirnov: "You will remain commandant, but I shall run the fortress. Whether that is legal or not is my affair. I will answer for it." As a result, Port Arthur fell under two commands that often worked at cross purposes.

Stessel's nominal command, the Third Siberian Corps, consisted of the 4th and 7th East Siberian Rifle Divisions. Major General Alexander Viktorovich Fock (1843-) commanded the 4th; Major General Roman Isodorovich Kondratenko (1857-1904) the 7th. Stessel and Fock were old comrades and had served together in the Boxer Rebellion. At the battle of Nanshan, Fock withheld reserves at a critical juncture, lost the battle, and was mainly responsible for turning the defeat into a rout. Nevertheless, Stessel saw to it that Fock was decorated for his incompetence. After the war, however, a court-martial charged that Stessel "knowingly, deceitfully, and wrongfully presented Major General Fock for the Order of St. George, 3rd class, on the occasion of the battle that he had lost [at Nanshan and] in which this general had demonstrated his complete incapacity."

When the Japanese, pushed the Russian field army back into the fortress, Fock and Kondratenko came, in principle, under Smirnov's command. In August he fired Fock for disobeying orders, and he made Kondratenko commander of all infantry within the fortress. Thereafter Fock, allegedly acting as Stessel's "mouthpiece," took to writing and circulating memoranda critical of Smirnov and his conduct of the defense.

At age forty-seven Kondratenko was the youngest general in the Russian army. He became Smirnov's right hand. An expert at fortifications, he worked indefatigably to prepare and improve the Russian positions and then to direct the defense. One of the few general officers regularly to visit the trenches, Kondratenko was, as Oldenburg writes below, "the soul of the Port Arthur defense." Widely respected, Kondratenko managed to bring about what little cooperation existed between the "camps" of Stessel and Smirnov.

20. Kuropatkin selected Lieutenant General G.K. Stackelberg, commander of the First Siberian Army Corps, to recapture Nanshan and

relieve Port Arthur. Stackelberg maintained his headquarters on a train at Haicheng. Against the rigors of campaigning he maintained his wife, his sister, and a cow. For relief against the summer heat, he maintained a detachment of cossacks to spray the roof of his carriage. Stackelberg was a court favorite and socially prominent in St. Petersburg. His selection to lead the offensive to save Port Arthur was immensely popular and widely discussed by society and the press. By the first of June the Japanese knew as much about the impending campaign as Russian society. Consequently, when Stackelberg reached Telissu, about eighty miles north of Port Arthur, he was surprised to learn that General Oku was marching north from Nanshan with 20,000 men. Through poor reconaissance and faulty staff coordination, Stackelberg lost the initiative. He concentrated his forces on his left flank, where he thought the Japanese were making their main attack. Instead, the main blow fell on his right flank and almost encircled his corps. The Russians had to retreat through three mountain passes. Japanese artillery commanded the passes and turned the retreat into a confused rout. Stackelberg lost 3600 men and sixteen field guns; General Oku reported 1100 casualties.

The forces at Telissu were roughly equal in strength, and the terrain favored neither side. The battle of Telissu convinced Kuropatkin that he needed decisive numerical superiority against the Japanese. Telissu was the first and last attempt to relieve Port Arthur by land.

21. Japan's immediate objective at this stage of the war was Port Arthur, the bastion and symbol of Russian ambitions in the Far East. The ultimate objective was the destruction of Kuropatkin's army. For the time being, however, Kuroki's advance across the Yalu toward Kuropatkin's main concentration at Liaoyang served to hold the Manchurian Army in place.

22. Plehve's reversal of Shipov's election was a purely arbitrary act. D.N. Shipov (1851-1920) was a prominent and popular zemstvo leader and a political moderate. Plehve's action against him apparently was motivated solely by the interior minister's desire generally to curtail and reduce the activities of the zemstvos. Shipov had been active in public and zemstvo affairs since 1877 and had been chairman of the Moscow provincial zemstvo board since 1900.

From 1905 to 1911, when he retired from public life, Shipov was never far from the center of Russian political life. In June 1905 he was invited to form a moderate government, but the plan failed because of the liberal opposition of the Constitutional Democrats. In November 1905 he was one of the principal founders of the Octobrist Party—the Union of 17 October. In 1906 he withdrew from that organization. Elected to the State Council in 1907, he served until 1909. Meanwhile in 1908 he joined the Party of Peaceful Reconstruction.

After the Bolshevik coup in October 1917, Shipov joined the oppositionist National Center. The Communists eventually arrested him, and he died in prison in 1920. His memoirs were published in Moscow in 1918: *Vospominaniia i dumy o perezhitom* [Reflections and Thoughts on My Past].

23. Gershuni, Azef, and two other members of the Battle Organization first discussed the assassination of Plehve in Kiev in October 1902.

The police caught Gershuni in May 1903, and leadership of the organization fell to Azef (see above, Chapter VIII, Note 12). Then in April came the event that determined Plehve's fate as far as Azef was concerned—the Kishinev pogrom. According to Azef's biographer, "though he was not a Jewish nationalist . . . he was at heart a Jew." He "held Plehve responsible and did not conceal his indignation. This he did not confine to revolutionary circles; it was even a subject of his conversations with his police chiefs. . . . Zubatoff records that, in an interview with him, he 'shook with fury and hate in speaking of Plehve, who[m] he considered responsible.' . . . There can be no doubt that this circumstance was the decisive factor in Plehve's fate."

A task force of terrorists assembled in Petersburg in the late fall of 1903. Their first attempt, set for 31 March 1904, was aborted at the last moment. Two weeks later, one of the conspirators was killed accidentally by his own bomb. At that point the terrorists were ready to give up, but Azef arrived to restore their sagging spirits. They decided to try again. Four assassins were on the scene: Egor S. Sozonov (1879-1910) and Ivan Kaliaev, former students expelled during the student riots at the turn of the century, and A. Borishansky and S.V. Sikorsky, workers from Bialostok. Sozonov was designated the chief bomb-thrower; the others, equally armed, were to back him up. To protect his double identity, Azef waited first in Vilna and then in Vienna.

After one more abortive effort early in July (Sozonov arrived late), the terrorists scheduled another attempt for the 18th. This time Sozonov and Plehve kept their appointment, and the others were not needed. The young terrorist ran up to Plehve's carriage and hurled a twelve-pound bomb through the window. Plehve saw him coming and recoiled. That was his last act.

News of the assassination reached a congress of SR emigres assembled in Geneva, Switzerland. An eyewitness recorded the joyful "pandemonium" that broke loose. "I can still see N.: he was standing a little apart; he dashed a glass of water on the floor and, gnashing his teeth, shouted: 'That's for Kishinev!' " Nikolajewsky, *Aseff the Spy*, pp. 58-59, 68-69 (quoted), 76, 81-88 (p. 88 quoted). See also Boris Savinkov, *Memoirs of a Terrorist* (New York, 1931), pp. 58-70; and Sozonov's personal account as quoted in I. Steinberg, *Spiridonova, Revolutionary Terrorist*, trans. and ed. Swenda David and Eric Mosbacher (London, 1935), pp. 123-27; the latter makes use of two collections of Sozonov's letters and papers published after the revolution: *E. Sozonov: Materialy dlia biografii* [E. Sozonov: Materials for a Biography] (Moscow, 1919) and *Pisma E. Sozonova, 1895-1910* [The Letters of E. Sozonov] (Moscow, 1925).

Seriously wounded by the blast that killed Plehve, Sozonov was captured at the scene. Sikorsky was arrested while trying to dispose of his bomb. The rest of the cohort escaped. The two were tried and convicted in a civil court on 30 November 1904. Sozonov's penalty was life imprisonment at hard labor; Sikorsky got twenty years. In Aktuisky Prison deep inside Siberia Sozonov killed himself in November 1910 as an act of protest against the flogging of prisoners.

24. "25 *let nazad (Iz dnevnikov L. Tikhomirova* " [Twenty-five years ago (From the diaries of L. Tikhomirov)], *Krasnyi arkhiv* (1930),

38: 20-69; 39: 47-75; 40: 59-96; and 41: 103-47. Also L.A. Tikhomirov, *Vospominaniia* [Memoirs] (Moscow-Leningrad, 1927).

25. *Retvizan*, on the contrary, was the last Russian ship to leave the battle. For several minutes it was the target of every big gun in the Japanese fleet. The vessel finally escaped under cover of smoke and darkness. Ukhtomsky led the retreat, and his decision was one of the most fateful of the war. The Pacific Squadron was useless in Port Arthur, but even a few ships lucky enough to escape to Vladivostok would have created serious problems for Admiral Togo. The Japanese commander knew that he had to destroy the Pacific Squadron before the arrival of the Baltic Squadron. Most of his own ships needed repair and new gun barrels. If any of the Russian battleships had reached Vladivostok, Togo might have found himself between an anvil and a hammer. Lieutenant Andrew P. Steer of the *Novik* wrote of Ukhtomsky: "Possibly another commander, more brave or better prepared, would have attempted to continue on his road in face of all risks, but Prince Ukhtomski had always been considered a second-rate man. It is quite clear that he ought never to have been made a flag officer . . . ."

A.P. Steer, *The "Novik" and the Part She Played in the Russo-Japanese War* (London, 1913), quoted by Warner, *Tide at Sunrise*, p. 354.

26. So wrote S.K. Tereshchenko in his history of the Russo-Japanese War. (Oldenburg's note) Admiral G.A. Ballard agreed that those two explosions formed "the most critical minute of the war." *The Influence of the Sea on the Political History of Japan* (London, 1921).

27. One of the destroyers smashed on the rocks of the China coast. (Oldenburg's note)

28. Immediately after the Russo-Turkish War of 1877-78 a group of Moscow merchants organized to purchase and operate a fleet of ships. Based in the Black Sea, the vessels were to serve as merchantmen in peacetime. In wartime they were to be converted to armed transports and raiders. The Volunteer Fleet was chartered officially on 5 September 1879 "under the protection of" the heir-apparent, the future tsar, Alexander III. K.P. Pobedonostsev, representing His Imperial Highness, served as vice-chairman of the company and took a keen interest in its affairs, even after 1883 when it was formally transferred to the jurisdiction of the ministry of marine. The fleet plied principally between the Black Sea and the Mediterranean, but its routes and tonnage expanded with the development of the Russian Far East. (It transported those Siberian exiles lucky enough to ride.) In 1909 control of the fleet was moved from the naval ministry to the ministry of trade and industry.

The Volunteer Fleet marked a significant development in Russian maritime history but it has received scant attention. An early Russian work is M. Poggenpohl, *Ocherk vozniknoveniia i diatelnosti Dobrovolnago flota* [A Sketch of the Origins and Activities of the Volunteer Fleet] (St. Petersburg, 1903). The two most prominent recent western histories ignore it: David Woodward, *The Russians at Sea* (London, 1965) and Donald W. Mitchell, *A History of Russian and Soviet Sea Power* (New York, 1974). Western analyses seldom go beyond battles, technology, and tired cliches to examine the political, economic, and strategic considerations that historically influenced Russian naval and maritime development. For essays on that broader perspective see: John A. Morrison, "Russia and Warm Water: A Fallacious Generalization and Its Consequences," U.S. Naval Institute *Proceedings*, 78 (November 1952), 1169-79; and Patrick J. Rollins, "Russia's Fictitious Naval Tradition," *ibid.*, 99 (January 1973), 65-71.

29. Kuropatkin then had 158,000 men and about 600 guns; Russian reinforcements were arriving at a rate of about a thousand a day. Marshal Oyama Iwao, Japan's supreme commander, had 125,000 men and 170 guns.

30. Sviatopolk-Mirsky (1857-1914)—abbreviated hereafter to Mirsky—enjoyed a prestigious education first at His Majesty's School of Pages and then at the Nicholas Academy of the General Staff. He began his career as a young officer in the Russo-Turkish War of 1877-78, after which he entered the ministry of internal affairs where he spent the remainder of his public life. For over twenty years he was a provincial governor, first in Penza and then in Ekaterinoslav. His first position of nation-wide significance came in 1900, when he was appointed assistant minister with the function of commander of the Special Gendarme Corps. He held that post for two years and then, from 1902 until his appointment as minister, served as governor-general of the Northwest Territory (the provinces of Vilna, Kovno, and Grodno).

As a mark of special favor, Tsar Alexander II had granted Mirsky's father, General Dmitry Ivanovich, a Polish nobleman, the right to adopt the name and title of the ancient princely house of Sviatopolk.

31. Jacob Zhilinsky (1853-1919), the army quartermaster general from 1900 to 1904, became chief of staff in 1911 and in 1914 commander of the First military district (Warsaw) and of the Northern Front when the World War began.

Oscar Grippenberg (1838-1916), a Finnish nobleman, was a 66-year-old relic of the Crimean War. He had several defects, including no formal military education. Although he came to Manchuria from the command of the Second military district (Vilna), he never had led anything but a battalion in the field. In addition, he suffered from deafness and apoplexy. He had served as aide-de-camp to Nicholas II, and his rank was that of aide-de-camp general. Grippenberg's appointment was taken as a snub to Kuropatkin, even though the Second Army was not intended to operate independently. The two generals quarreled continuously and openly, until after the battle of San-de-pu (below), when Grippenberg mercifully was relieved and reassigned as inspector-general of infantry (1905-6). Despite his liabilities and infirmities, Grippenberg arrived full of fight. At their first meeting he challenged his troops with an even proposition: "If any of you retreat, I'll shoot you. If I retreat, you shoot me."

32. General Sluchevsky, an engineer, once had commanded a regiment. However, at Liaoyang and Sha Ho he found himself at the head of the Tenth Siberian Corps (two divisions). Despite or perhaps because of that, he did surprisingly well in both engagements. At Liaoyang he failed to hold the mountain passes against Kuroki only after begging repeatedly for and being denied reinforcements.

33. Actually the Russians changed One Tree Hill (its local name) to Novgorod Hill in honor of the garrison town of its captor, the 22nd

Infantry Division. Just to the north was a second hill renamed for Putilov, who was decorated on the spot. In the struggle for the two hills the Russians lost 3,000 men mainly in vicious hand-to-hand fighting.

34. At Harbin on 12 October, to the great satisfaction of the army, Alekseev announced that the tsar had "acceded to my request to be relieved of the duties of Commander-in-Chief." Five days later he left by special train for Petersburg. He arrived on 10 November. There was no ceremonial welcome, and he drove to his residence without an escort. In 1905, however, he received the honor of an appointment to the State Council.

35. Nicholas Petrovich Linevich (1838-1908) had held various commands in the Far East since 1895 and was known as "the Siberian wolf"—apparently a reference to his personality. In 1900 he led the Russian column that marched to the relief of Peking. He was a tough, hard-drinking war-horse, but at sixty-six he was better suited to the pasture than the battlefield. Unlike Linevich, Alexander Vasilevich von Kaulbars (1844-1929) had seen no action since 1878 in the Turkish war; nevertheless he had an insuperable confidence in his own abilities and an insufferable contempt for those of his associates.

36. Prince Shirinsky-Shikhmatov (1862-1930) was an unyielding monarchist. A graduate of the Imperial School of Law (1884), he served for several years in the interior ministry as an advisor to the Esthonian special board. In 1900 he moved to the staff of the holy synod, serving there until 1903, when he was promoted to the post of governor of Tver.

37. Narva and Poltava, major battles of the Great Northern War (1700-21), were separated by nine not five years. In 1700 Charles XII of Sweden crushed the Russians at Narva; in 1709 at Poltava Peter the Great returned the favor. Although the war continued for a dozen years, Sweden never recovered and thus Poltava marks Russia's ascendance over Sweden in the struggle for control of the Baltic.

38. Probably Alexis Vasilevich Peshekhonov (1867-1933), an economist, publicist, and leader of "the third element" in the Union of Liberation. In 1904 Peshekhonov joined the editorial board of the journal *Russkoe bogatstvo.* He served as minister of food supply in the Provisional Government during March 1917 and emigrated in 1924. See above Note 6, this chapter.

39. Working closely with Zilliacus was Colonel Akashi Motojiro, former Japanese military attache in St. Petersburg and since the outbreak of the war the European coordinator of Japanese military intelligence. Late in July 1903, Akashi and Zilliacus went to Switzerland, the center of the Russian revolutionary emigration. There Zilliacus introduced Akashi to most of the prominent revolutionary leaders (including Lenin, who impressed Akashi favorably). Soon afterward, Zilliacus sent out invitations for the Paris meeting, which was attended by representatives of thirteen revolutionary and liberal oppositionist organizations.

Colonel Akashi's wartime intelligence activities are described in Warner, *Tide at Sunrise.* The authors relied mainly on two Japanese works: Lt. General Tani Toshio, *Kimitsu Nichi-Ro-Sen-shi* [Intelligence History of the Japanese-Russian War (Lectures at the War College)], ed. Inaba Masao (Tokyo, 1966) and Komori Tokuji, *Akashi Motojiro* [Akashi Motojiro], 2 vols. (Tokyo, 1928). See also Michael Futrell, *Northern Underground* (London, 1963).

40. Details of this convention appear in the memoirs of P.N. Miliukov, "Rokovye gody" [The Fatal Years], *Russkie zapiski* [Russian Notes], June 1938. P.A. Stolypin referred to the Paris convention of 1904 in a statement that he made during the official inquiry into the Azef affair, and Miliukov offered his explanations to the State Duma on 13/26 February 1909. (Oldenburg's note) The first version of Miliukov's memoirs appeared serially in *Russkie zapiski* in 1938-39. Before his death in 1943, he nearly had finished a second fuller version that was published posthumously: *Vospominaniia, 1859-1917 g.* [Memoirs, 1859-1917], eds. M. Karpovich and B. Elkin, 2 vols. (New York, 1955); part of that work has been translated as *Political Memoirs, 1905-1917*, ed. Arthur P. Mendel, trans. Carl Goldberg (Ann Arbor, 1967).

The revolutionary parties at the Paris meeting agreed specifically to foment demonstrations in Poland in order to tie down as many Russian troops as possible and to intensify the assassination of senior officials in the Caucusus. Colonel Akashi promised money to all who needed it. Warner, *Tide at Sunrise*, pp. 482-83.

41. Russian war councils long debated whether or not to send the fleet, and Rozhestvensky's position never has become clear. His attitude seems to have been that it was a useless gesture. In April 1904 he told the press that "we are now doing what remains to be done, we are defending the honor of the flag. It was at an earlier stage that another course [attack] should have been followed." Still, he seems to have believed that he was the man for the job, either from a sense of duty, which is quite likely, or from ambition, for surely had he destroyed the Japanese fleet he would have become Russia's greatest naval hero.

Zinovi Petrovich Rozhestvensky (1848-1909) went to sea at seventeen and specialized from the outset in gunnery and torpedoes. He was decorated and promoted for bravery during an action in the Turkish war, but later it was discovered that his honors were not merited. He freely admitted his connivance in false reports but offered no further explanation and no official action was taken against him. He held various commands during the 1880s and served from 1891 to 1893 as naval attache in London. In 1894-96 he served in the Pacific Squadron as captain of the admiral's flagship. He returned to the Baltic Fleet in 1896 and took charge of the gunnery school and fleet training. He was promoted to rear admiral in 1902 and in 1903 became chief of the naval general staff. As the Second Squadron was passing the Danish coast, the tsar cabled his promotion to vice admiral.

"The admiral with the terrible name" (*Punch*) is properly spelled "Rozhdestvensky," but the "d" is often dropped to make the pronunciation infinitely easier.

42. The Russians had convinced themselves that the North Sea was crawling with Japanese or British torpedo boats waiting to ambush the fleet. The hysteria was fed by the reports of a Captain Hartling. The naval ministry gave him nine boats and an enormous expense account.

He ensconced himself at a hotel in Copenhagen and then, to make it all seem worthwhile, flooded his superiors with vivid accounts of Japanese torpedo boat activity in the North Sea. By the time the Russian fleet crossed the Baltic, trigger-happy gunners had fired (without damage) at four merchant ships (Swedish, German, French, and Norwegian) and one Danish fishing fleet.

The Dogger Bank incident on the night of October 21/22 began when the decrepit repair ship *Kamchatka*, lagging fifty miles behind the fleet, radioed that she was being attacked by torpedo boats. She fired nearly 300 shots at passing trawlers and merchantmen. The subsequent investigation indicated that the captain and officers of the *Kamchatka* probably were drunk. Nevertheless, her report alerted the entire squadron, and at that point the battleships came upon the British trawlers fishing the Dogger Bank. Indiscriminate firing erupted. Four fishing boats were sunk or damaged; two crewmen were killed and several were wounded. The cruisers *Avrora* and *Dmitry Donskoy* carried on a running battle with each other for several minutes. *Avrora* was hit five times and her chaplain was killed. At the official international inquiry the Russian representatives insisted that Japanese torpedo boats had been present. No evidence, then or now, confirms that contention, but the need to save face explains it. Resting at Vigo, Admiral Rozhestvensky well may have recalled the remark of Nicholas I whose accession in 1825 was marred by the Decembrist revolt: "What a hell of a way to begin a reign."

The tragi-comedy of the Dogger Bank as well as the unparalleled cruise of the Second Squadron has attracted many writers. Richard Hough, a popular writer of naval history, probably has the edge with *The Fleet That Had to Die* (New York, 1958), but equally as graphic is Frank Thiess, *The Voyage of Forgotten Men* (Tsushima), trans. Fritz Sallagar (Indianapolis, 1937). All narrators rely extensively on the accounts of three participants, each in quite different circumstances: Commander Vladimir Ivanovich Semenov, having lost his ship *Diana* to the French in Saigon, made his way to the Baltic in time to ride out again as a supernumerary aboard the flagship *Suvorov*; he wrote three books but his account of the voyage is found mainly in *Rasplata* [The Reckoning], trans. L.A.B. (London, 1909). Chief Engineer Eugene Sigismondovich Politovsky was impressed into service at the last moment and he too sailed in the *Suvorov—From Libau to Tsushima: A Narrative of the Voyage of Admiral Rojestvensky's Fleet to Eastern Seas*, trans. Major F.R. Godfrey (London, 1906). A.S. Novikov-Priboy was an ordinary seaman (and revolutionist) in the *Orel*; his account, written from notes jotted in a Japanese prison camp, won the Stalin Prize for Literature in 1941: *Tsushima, Grave of a Floating City*, trans. Eden and Cedar Paul (New York, 1937). On the arrangements for fueling the ships at sea, see Lamar J.R. Cecil, "Coal for the Fleet that had to Die," *American Historical Review*, 69 (July 1964), 990-1005.

43. Late in November 1904 Nicholas informed the kaiser that "the Emperor of Austria and I have decided to sign a secret declaration . . . of neutrality." The agreement was to cover "the event that one of the two empires should find itself in a state of war, alone and without provocation

on its part, with a third power which seeks to upset the existing status quo." *Correspondance entre Guillaume II et Nicolas II, 1894-1914.* Trans. Marc Semenoff, 9th ed. (Paris, 1924), pp. 131-32; see also Alfred Francis Pribram, *The Secret Treaties of Austria-Hungary, 1879-1914.* English edition by Archibald Cary Coolidge, 2 vols. (Cambridge, Mass., 1920-21), I, 236-39. Nevertheless, given the state of relations in 1904, Oldenburg's speculation on the possibility that France could find itself with Russia and Germany in a war against England is quite tenuous.

44. Nicholas in fact approved the draft treaty, which the kaiser transmitted in a letter of 17 November 1904. However, both Lamsdorf and Witte insisted that it contradicted the French alliance : France had to be consulted in advance and not merely invited to adhere to a treaty in force. In December Russia and Germany concluded a limited agreement that pledged mutual assistance if war broke out with England because Germany was fueling the Russian fleet. See the exchange of correspondence in *Grosse Politik,* XIX (1), nos. 6118-46.

45. The congress was not representative of the zemstvos, and some of the delegates had no zemstvo connections whatsoever. About three dozen "progressive" members of the Moscow provincial zemstvo board formed the nucleus of the assembly, and they invited other like-minded zemstvo and public figures to participate. Only political moderates and liberals were considered, but the 104 delegates who eventually met in Petersburg also represented or were influenced mainly by the Union of Liberation. Nicholas, in other words, accurately read this group: the delegates were essentially private citizens, who could speak only for themselves, and the congress was rigged to advance constitutional demands.

46. The majority resolution called for public participation in the legislative process, in the determination of state budgets, and in safeguarding society against arbitrary administration. Shipov's minority recognized the need for "regular participation of public representatives in legislation" but also called for "preservation of the imperial power, one and indivisible." Quoted by Gurko, *Features and Figures of the Past,* p. 307; see also pp. 304-6 and 308.

47. *Syn otechestva,* published since the early nineteenth century, was acquired by leftists [in December 1904]. (Oldenburg's note) At first its collaborators were populists and members of the Union of Liberation. In November 1905 it became an organ of the Socialist Revolutionary Party, and two weeks later the government suppressed it for good. *Nasha zhizn* was a left-liberal journal published in St. Petersburg in 1904-5.

48. *Novoe vremia,* 24-25 October 1904. (Oldenburg's note)

49. The officials assembled to consider a report and broad recommendations on reform prepared at the direction of Prince Mirsky by Sergei E. Kryzhanovsky, assistant director of the main administration for the affairs of local economy. (Oldenburg's note)

50. An imperial ukaz, or decree, was prescriptive and had the force of law; an imperial manifesto was a public declaration that signaled the emperor's intention, embodied a statement of principles yet to be enacted into law, or accompanied a piece of legislation.

51. In 1904 the Mikado's birthday, his fifty-second, fell on 3 November, or by the Russian calendar, 21 October—the tenth anniversary of Emperor Nicholas's accession to the throne.

52. The brief saga of the *Sevastopol* gave a hint of what the Russian fleet might have accomplished with able leadership. Captain (later Admiral) N.O. von Essen began the war as commander of the *Novik*, but Makarov gave him the *Sevastopol* after her former captain collided with the *Peresvet*. When the Japanese seized 203-meter Hill and began to shell the inner harbor, Essen moved his ship to the outer roads. The Japanese squadron tried desperately to sink the vessel. Admiral Togo wanted to return to Japan for repairs before Rozhestvensky's squadron arrived, but as long as *Sevastopol* survived he had to keep his battleships at sea. Moreover, destruction of the *Sevastopol* was a matter of honor for the Japanese navy, since to that point the army had won all the glory, including most of the credit for destroying the Russian fleet.

For three weeks *Sevastopol* and several destroyers beat off thirty-five attacking destroyers and torpedo boats. She destroyed two torpedo boats and heavily damaged six others; the *Takasago*, an armored cruiser assigned to watch her, hit a mine and was lost with 247 men. The Japanese fired about 120 torpedoes at her. Finally, on the night of 20 December a fusillade of torpedoes mortally wounded the ship. The next day Essen towed it into deep water, opened the seacocks, and allowed the ship to sink.

53. Throughout the siege Russian propaganda portrayed Stessel as the hero of Port Arthur. One of the most popular photos of the day depicted him standing defiantly on a rampart, a symbol of indomitable courage. Later, however, and after the war, a different picture emerged. In 1908 he was court-martialled. The charges were numerous and probably true for the most part. Nevertheless the court decided that most of the counts were unproven or even if true not subject to legal action. On one count, however, Stessel's guilt was confirmed: his surrender of the fortress was premature and unjustified.

In late December Stessel convened a council of war at which the majority of officers opposed a surrender. Nevertheless, he sent Nogi an offer to surrender and did so without convening a second council. That action clearly violated army regulations. Moreover, evidence later proved that even before the surrender had been signed, Stessel had ordered the evacuation and destruction of certain key strongholds. At the same time he telegraphed the tsar that the stores of food and ammunition had been exhausted, when actually the fortress held several more weeks of supplies.

The court sentenced Stessel to be shot to death, but that sentence was commuted to ten years imprisonment, and in the end he served about a year in jail. Stessel was stupid, pompous, overbearing, and probably a coward to boot—in most respects like most of the senior officers who served with and later testified against him. Among all its general officers, the Russian army found only one genuine hero—Kondratenko, who, like Makarov, was the son of a peasant.

Stessel's sycophant, General Fock, was found guilty of spreading subversive reports against Smirnov, but the court ruled that under the circumstances that was not a punishable offense. Nevertheless, Fock was compelled to resign from the army; he later turned up as a volunteer in the Bulgarian army during the First Balkan War of 1912-13. General Smirnov faced the general accusation of responsibility for the improper and premature surrender of the fortress and the specific charge of having failed to assert his authority to control Stessel and Fock. The military court exonerated him on both counts.

54. Japanese deaths were 16,000; Russian 6,000. Japanese wounded totaled 42,000; Russian in excess of 20,000. About 34,000 Japanese soldiers were out of action for illness, mainly dysentery and beri-beri. The Japanese counted 48,325 prisoners including 24,369 soldiers, 8,956 sailors, and 15,000 persons in hospitals. The Japanese also collected 600 guns, 34,000 shells, 35,000 rifles, 2,000,000 rounds of small arms ammunition, about 3,000 edible horses, and another month's supply of rations.

CHAPTER TEN

1. On 1 January 1904 the Russian gold reserve stood at 732,900,000 rubles and on 1 January 1905 at 878,200,000 rubles. (Oldenburg's note)

2. In May 1904 the Russian government marketed bonds worth 300,000,000 rubles in France; early in 1905 it floated a 232,000,000 ruble loan in Germany. (Oldenburg's note)

Japan's credit standing in Europe improved perceptibly in 1904 while, contrary to the author's position, Russia's standing slipped somewhat. On 1 January 1905 the Japanese 4 percent bond stood at 77.75 on the London market, giving a nominal yield of about 5 percent. The Russian 4 percents of 1889 were stronger at 91.50, yielding 4.37 percent. However, the Russian 4s opened the year at 97.50 and were off about 6 percent for the year. The Japanese 4s began the year at 74.50 and had improved about 1.5 percent by year's end. Both securities were weaker than the market in governments in general; an index of European government bonds, compiled by the editor, increased by 5.5 percent in 1904. The Japanese 4s dropped about 15 percent to the low 60s in February, March and April 1904. They recovered in May (after the battle of the Yalu) and until November ranged between 72 and 75. In December with the fall of Port Arthur imminent they made their highs for the year.

In January 1905 a German syndicate, led by the banking firm of Mendelsohn, accepted the 231,500,000 ruble Russian State Loan of 1905 at 90.5 percent of its face value. The loan was sold to the public at 95, giving the bankers a handsome profit. The coupon was 4.5 percent, however, so that even the public "charged" the Russian government a slight premium. By comparison, a year earlier French bankers had accepted the 300,000,000 ruble loan at 94; listed officially as 5 percent State Treasury Debentures, they were sold to the public at an average price of 99. Russian credit was deteriorating rapidly in the estimate of foreign investors.

A basic documentary study of Russian war finances is E.A. Preobrazhensky, ed., *Russkie finansy i evropeiskaia birzha v 1904-1906 gg.*

[Russian Finances and the European Bourses, 1904-1906], documents prepared by B.A. Romanov (Moscow-Leningrad, 1926). A recent study of great importance and merit is René Girault, *Emprunts russes et investissements francaise en Russie, 1887-1914* [Russian Loans and French Investments in Russia, 1887-1914] (Paris, 1973). Also, see below, this chapter, Note 52.

Conservative (and anti-Russian) British financial circles invariably distrusted official Russian statements on national accounts, balance of trade, and the gold reserve. See *The Economist* (London), 1904-6, or practically any other period. The Russian ministry of finance spent considerable sums to bribe the French press in order to create a favorable environment for Russian loans. It was common practice for governments to support the prices of their own bonds, especially in advance of a new loan, and the Russian government did this regularly. A glimpse of the underside of the world of international finance can be found in A. Raffalovitch, *L'Abominable vénalité de la presse francaise . . . d'après les documents des archives russes (1897-1917)* [The Abominable Venality of the French Press . . . according to Documents from the Russian Archives (1897-1917)] (Paris, 1931). Arthur G. Raffalovich was the finance ministry's official agent in France. Some indication of the success of this activity or its lack can be found in Encarnacion Alzona, *Some French Contemporary Opinions of the Russian Revolution of 1905* (New York, 1921).

3. No. 63, 7/20 January 1905. (Oldenburg's note)

4. Ibid. (Oldenburg's note)

5. The commander of the Siberian military district, General N.N. Sukhotin, compiled some interesting statistics on political figures under surveillance as of 1 January 1905. A total of 4,526 persons included 1,898 Russians, 1,676 Jews, 624 Poles, 124 from minority nationalities of the Caucasus, 85 Balts, and 94 of various other descriptions. (This data appeared in *Krasnyi arkhiv*, vol. 32.) (Oldenburg's note)

6. *Byloe*, 1917, No. 3. (Oldenburg's note) See also Savinkov, *Memoirs of a Terrorist*, pp. 126-27; the quotation that follows incorporates both statements, which differ slightly.

7. P.N. Miliukov's memoirs mention Zilliacus's dealings with the Japanese Colonel Akashi, who gave the Finn substantial sums to purchase weapons for uprisings in St. Petersburg and the Caucasus. *Russkie zapiski*, June 1938. (Oldenburg's note)

The transaction occurred at or shortly after the Conference of the Opposition and Revolutionary Organizations of the Russian Empire in Paris in October 1904. See above, Chapter IX and Notes 39-40. In September 1906 Zilliacus attempted to deliver several thousand rifles to revolutionaries in St. Petersburg. Colonel Akashi's money bought both the weapons and the yacht that was to deliver them, the 300-ton *John Grafton*. Russian authorities confiscated most of the weapons, after the *John Grafton* ran aground off the Finnish coast. See Futrell, *Northern Underground*, pp. 66-80.

Zilliacus wrote several works in Finnish, including a two-volume memoir (Helsingfors, 1919-20), and one in English: *The Russian Revolutionary Movement* (London, 1905). A biography is *Konni Zilliacus* (in Finnish) by Herman Gummerus (Helsingfors, 1933).

8. Dillon, *The Eclipse of Russia* (London, 1918); Baron Rosen, *Forty Years of Diplomacy*, 2 vols. (New York, 1922).

9. George Apollonovich Gapon (1870-1906), a Ukrainian priest, began his career working among the poor as a prison chaplain. He was associated with the Zubatov movement since 1902, but only in February 1904 did he receive Plehve's permission to form the Assembly of St. Petersburg Factory Workers. By the end of the year Gapon's organization had eleven branches in the capital, claimed about 9,000 members, and enjoyed some influence over perhaps half of the city's 200,000 industrial workers. Historical evidence permits no firm conclusion as to Gapon's intentions or motives. He worked under the tutelage of the police, collaborated with revolutionaries, and espoused an unfathomable program of nationalist, monarchist, liberal, socialist, constitutional, and revolutionary ideas. The sympathetic view of Gapon holds that all his efforts sprang from a sincere desire to improve the lot of the poor; the less flattering view is that Gapon simply wanted prominence and power and therefore chose the means at hand.

Gapon left an autobiography that has more historical interest than value—*The Story of My Life* (London, 1905), also serialized under the same title in *The Strand Magazine*, 30 (1905): 3-33, 169-80, 304-17, 363-77, and 483-96. One of his assistants, N. Varnashev, wrote a brief memoir: "Ot nachala do kontsa s Gaponovskoi organizatiei (vospominaniia)" [From Beginning to End with the Gapon Organization (A Memoir)], *Istoriko-Revoliutsionnyi sbornik* [Historical-Revolutionary Collection], 1 (1924), 177-208; and there is a biography in Russian, *Georgy Gapon* by D. Sverchkov (Moscow, 1930). The Gapon movement became an aggressive political force by seizing control of the Putilov strike (below), which is covered in M. Mitelman et al., *Istoriia Putilovskogo Zavoda* [History of the Putilov Works], 2nd ed. (Moscow, 1941). See also A.V. Piaskovsky, *Revoliutsiia 1905-1907 gg. v Rossii* [The Revolution of 1905 in Russia] (Moscow, 1966).

The "gaponovshchina" usually is interpreted as the beginning of the 1905 revolution. General works in English include: Sidney Harcave, *First Blood: The Russian Revolution of 1905* (New York, 1964); Solomon M. Schwarz, *The Russian Revolution of 1905: The Workers' Movement and the Formation of Bolshevism and Menshevism*, trans. Gertrude Vakar (Chicago, 1967); Lionel Kochan, *Russia in Revolution, 1890-1918* (London, 1966).

The fiftieth anniversary of the "First Russian Revolution" prompted a great outpouring of material in the USSR, most notably: Akademiia Nauk SSSR, Institut Istorii, *Revoliutsiia 1905-1907 gg. v Rossii: Dokumenty i materialy* [The Revolution of 1905-07 in Russia: Documents and Material], 15 vols. (Moscow, 1955-63). That collection supplements without superseding M.N. Pokrovsky's *1905. Materialy i Dokumenty* [1905: Material and Documents], 8 vols. (Moscow, 1925-28). Important bibliographic guides to Soviet and other monographs and documents are: A.L. Grigorev, *Pervaia russkaia revoliutsiia 1905-1907 gg. i zarubezhnaia literatura* [The First Russian Revolution of 1905-07 and Foreign Literature] (Leningrad, 1956); and G.M. Derenkovsky, ed., *Pervaia russkaia revoliutsiia, 1905-1907 gg.: Annotirovannyi ukazatel literatury* [The First Russian Revolution of 1905-1907: An Annotated Guide to the Literature] (Moscow, 1965).

10. L. Gurevich, "Narodnoe dvizhenie v Peterburg 9 ianvaria 1905 g." [The Popular Movement in Petersburg, 9 January 1905], *Byloe*, 1906, No. 1—an article based on "fresh evidence" from hundreds of documents and accounts of witnesses. (Oldenburg's note)

11. Ibid.

12. The full text of the petition can be found in several places in English translation; two of the most accessible probably are: Harcave, *First Blood*, pp. 285-89; and Basil Dmytryshyn, ed., *Imperial Russia: A Source Book, 1700-1917*, 2nd ed. (Dryden Press, 1974), pp. 380-83.

13. Leon Trotsky, *Die russische Revolution 1905* [The Russian Revolution of 1905] (Berlin, 1923).

14. The author refers, of course, to the "march of the fishwives" in which an angry mob from Paris marched on Versailles and forced King Louis XVI and the royal family to take up residence in the capital. In July 1790 the king accepted a constitution; in September 1792 he was dethroned, and in January 1793 he was executed.

The Russian Social Democrats generally took the position that a petition to the tsar was a futile exercise. Their arguments had little effect on the Petersburg workers, and some local SDs even participated in the march. Gapon's petition included much of what was then the "minimum program" of the Social Democrats, but departed from it in other respects. Gapon's petition, for example, called for ministers responsible to the people; the SD minimum program demanded the destruction of the autocracy and the establishment of a democratic republic, and there were several other differences. Gapon was in touch with Maxim Gorky, and for a time Gorky was credited erroneously with some role in drafting the petition.

The SD minimum program can be found in V.I. Lenin, *Sochineniia* [Collected Works], 2nd ed. (Leningrad, Moscow, 1929-32), 5, 386-87. On Gorky's role in the events of January 1905 see Alexander Kaun, *Maxim Gorky and his Russia* (London, 1931); on Plekhanov's attitude, Samuel H. Baron, "Plekhanov and the Revolution of 1905," in *Essays in Russian and Soviet History*, ed. J.S. Curtiss (New York, 1963), pp. 133-48; see also J.L.H. Keep, *The Rise of Social Democracy in Russia* (Oxford, 1963) and Donald Treadgold, *Lenin and His Rivals: The Struggle for Russia's Future, 1898-1906* (New York, 1955).

15. Dmitry Feodorovich Trepov (1855-1906) was an associate and favorite of the tsar's uncle, Grand Duke Sergei Alexandrovich, the reactionary governor-general of Moscow Province. Trepov had served for nine years (1896-1905) as police chief of the city of Moscow and was one of the chief supporters there of Zubatov and Zubatovism. The post of governor-general of St. Petersburg, abolished in 1880, was restored temporarily to give Trepov the interim powers of military governor and supreme commander of the city and province. Trepov's appointment took effect on 11 January 1905; on the 13th the city was placed under martial law, and within a few days Trepov restored the city to a normal if uneasy calm. Trepov was a relatively capable and efficient policeman, but his education and experience were limited.

He was absolutely devoted to the tsar and the monarchy. Nicholas had great confidence in Trepov and relied on him increasingly over the next several months.

16. Count Dmitry Martynovich Solsky (1833-1910) was chairman of the State Council from 1904 to 1906. He began his bureaucratic career in 1852 and had been a member and functionary of the State Council since 1889. He received his title in 1902. Solsky's argument here was that to admit soldiers could act without a command from the tsar was an explicit denial of the principle of autocracy.

17. Grand Duke Sergei was the first member of the imperial family to be assassinated since 1881, when the terrorist forebears of the Battle Organization murdered his father Alexander II. The circumstances were quite similar except that the grand duke was literally blown to bits and, because he was universally detested, there was little public reaction or sorrow at his passing.

His assassin, Ivan Platonovich Kaliaev (1877-1905), already had participated in the murder of Plehve. Known to his comrades as "the poet," Kaliaev had been a member of the SRs and the Battle Organization since 1903. He joined the party and the organization upon his release from exile, imposed for his role in demonstrations as a student at St. Petersburg University in 1899. Stunned but not seriously wounded by the blast of his bomb, Kaliaev was arrested immediately and tried in a special session of the Imperial Senate on 5 April 1905. After the presentation of evidence, he delivered a stirring "plea," which is one of the classics in the romantic rhetoric of anarchism—"Let not the law, draped in senatorial toga, be our judge. . . . Let the conscience of the people, free and untrammelled, be our judge." Although the "conscience of the people," draped in the mantle of Lenin, eventually extirpated most of Kaliaev's surviving comrades, he himself departed more prosaically. At two in the morning of 10 May 1905 "the law" hanged him in the Schlüsselburg Prison.

Even as they were hounding his associates, the new Soviet authorities were raising monuments to Kaliaev, naming streets after him, and memorializing him in a biography: *I. Kaliaev* by Yu. Sobolev (Moscow, 1924). The details of the assassination of the grand duke are provided by the leader of the organization in Moscow: Savinkov, *Memoirs of a Terrorist*, pp. 76-117; Kaliaev's speech to the court quoted, pp. 112-16.

18. Grand Duke Michael Alexandrovich was then twenty-six years old; Nicholas became tsar at the age of twenty-six. The grand duke played no important role in the councils of state but his name does appear occasionally in the minutes of various councils and committees.

19. This appeal was published in *Revolutsionnaia Rossiia*, the journal of the Socialist Revolutionaries; it was reprinted in *Osvobozhdenie*, No. 67 (5/18 March 1905). (Oldenburg's note) The text of Gapon's message appears in the original text as a footnote.

20. Alexander Grigorevich Bulygin (1851-1919), trained in the law, began his bureaucratic career in the provincial judiciary in 1871. In 1887 he was appointed governor of Kaluga and in 1893 governor of Moscow. There he became one of Grand Duke Sergei Alexandrovich's satraps and became his assistant in 1902. Sergei's influence apparently

made Bulygin minister of internal affairs on 20 January 1905, a post he held without distinction for nine months. Bulygin had no "policy" nor was one expected of him: he remained what he always had been, a faithful executor of the emperor's will. In May Nicholas appointed Trepov to head the police department, in effect removing it from Bulygin's control. Bulygin sent his resignation to Nicholas who curtly informed him that ministers did not tender resignations, they were dismissed. After his dismissal in October 1905, Bulygin served in the State Council. Eight years later the tsar honored him by making him His Majesty's State Secretary for 1913. At the same time he assumed direction of the Fourth Section of His Majesty's Chancellery for Institutions of the Empress Maria (Feodorovna). Bulygin held that post until the revolution. In 1919 a revolutionary tribunal condemned and executed him.

21. That opinion was expressed also by Colonel Novitsky in his lectures at the Nicholas Military Academy, in the German General Staff's commentary on the official Russian history of the war, and by others. (Oldenburg's note)

San-de-pu was a small walled town about 35 miles southwest of Mukden. What actually took place was long since buried in the charges and countercharges in the scandal that followed. One clear result, however, was that the Russians lost 20,000 men, more than twice as many as the Japanese, in what Kuropatkin conceived as a limited engagement to inflict heavy casualties on the Japanese. Grippenberg had a different view of his mission. He began to move forward before general preparations were completed and thus enabled the Japanese to reinforce their threatened flank. Appalled by the initial losses, Kuropatkin ordered Grippenberg to wait until the Russian artillery had time to work over the Japanese positions, but it took more than a day to get the message to Grippenberg's subordinates. The medical transport was in utter chaos, and men with only slight wounds froze to death. The chief medical inspector committed suicide because of the hopeless situation. San-de-pu seemed to confirm the utter incompetence of the Russian army command.

22. Grippenberg's self-serving crusade scandalized the high command in the midst of a losing war, and he should have been censured. Dragomirov, mentioned previously, commanded the Third Military District at Kiev and had served as Nicholas's tutor in military history and tactics. Bilderling commanded the Seventeenth Corps under Kuropatkin at Liaoyang, two corps known as the Western Detachment at the Sha River, and then the Third Manchurian Army, which formed the Russian center at Mukden. His record in all three battles was typical of the Russian commanders, who preferred fixed positions and were extremely cautious when on the offensive. Batianov held no major command during any action in the war.

23. In the Eastern Orthodox Church the patriarch represented the supreme authority of the various confessions, and at that time there were four patriarchs—Constantinople, Antioch, Jerusalem, and Alexandria. An autocephalic Russian patriarchate, established by Boris Godunov in 1589, had been abolished by Peter the Great in 1721. Church

administration subsequently fell to the holy synod, a council of ecclesiastics and its civil administrators headed by the director-general. An authoritative administrative history is Igor Smolitsch, *Geschichte der russischen Kirche* [History of the Russian Church] (Leiden, 1964); see also John Shelton Curtiss, *Church and State in Russia, 1900-1917* (New York, 1940).

24. The Uniate Church represented Orthodox Christians who, by the Union of Brest of 1596, recognized the authority of the Roman Catholic pope but retained the Byzantine rite. The Russian government since the reign of Nicholas I systematically forced the Uniates to worship in Russian Orthodox churches or face condemnation and persecution as heretics. The ukaz on religious toleration did nothing for Muslims, Jews, and other non-Christians living within the empire.

25. Nicholas Klado (1862-) began his naval service in 1880 and had been decorated in 1904 for service in the cruisers operating out of Vladivostok. Though still on active duty, he became the naval correspondent of *Novoe vremia* when he returned to St. Petersburg in 1904. He was one of the first to urge that a new fleet be sent to the Far East and later campaigned for Rozhestvensky's appointment as commander. Klado's ability was as a tactician and his motives and logic elude rational analysis.

He successfully led the campaign to include older vessels, including ships designed for coastal defense, in Rozhestvensky's squadron. His reasoning was that those decrepit vessels would offer attractive targets and by drawing Japanese fire afford the modern ships a better opportunity to concentrate on the enemy. Klado sailed with the Second Squadron, but Rozhestvensky put him ashore at Vigo so that he could appear as a witness before the international commission investigating the Dogger Bank incident. Rozhestvensky no doubt felt relief—short-lived however—at Klado's departure.

Once ashore Klado began to agitate in *Novoe vremia* for the reinforcement of the Second Squadron. The naval ministry accused him of misrepresenting the facts and placed him under arrest. However, public pressure in favor of the popular Captain Klado forced the authorities to back down. The unreal debate between Klado, unrestrained by naval discipline, and his superiors continued until Rozhestvensky got more ships, which he neither wanted nor needed. But then Klado began to question the success of the mission that he himself had helped launch and reinforce. His campaign had two unintended results. Widely reported in the world press, the debate between Klado and the navy undermined the morale of the Second Squadron and it provided the Japanese with detailed information on the size, strength, and problems of the Russian fleet. After the war, Klado was dismissed from the navy in disgrace, but he later returned to favor and resumed his writing on tactics and strategy.

Klado's views on naval matters can be found in two works: Captain N.L. Klado, *The Russian Navy in the Russo-Japanese War*, trans. L.J.H. Dickinson (London, 1905) and *The Battle of the Sea of Japan*, trans. L.J.H. Dickinson (London, 1906). Klado is discussed favorably in Mitchell, *History of Russian and Soviet Seapower.*

26. Admiral Togo was waiting with his main battle fleet in the Korean port of Masan. The discovery of the Russian fleet was not quite the matter of chance that the author suggests. Togo did not know Rozhestvensky's route but he knew his alternatives. Early on the 25th of May, Rozhestvensky detached six supply ships, including colliers, and sent them to Shanghai. Their arrival late that same day was reported to Togo who then knew that the Russians were making for the Korean Straits—if Rozhestvensky planned to pass east of Japan, he would have kept the colliers to refuel the fleet. That was the first of his mistakes. At 3:30 on the morning of the 26th an armed merchantman spotted the *Orel*, a hospital ship trailing the Russian fleet. At 5:00 a.m. Togo's flagship *Mikasa* led the Japanese out of Masan. Wireless reports kept Togo informed of the course and speed of the Russian ships, then about forty miles away. Togo planned to close for battle at two in the afternoon. The action began at 1:55.

27. Rozhestvensky had no battle plan, except to reach Vladivostok. Togo, on the other hand, knew exactly what he wanted to do and in doing it he accomplished one of the great feats in naval history. The squadrons were headed in opposite directions on a parallel course when they first sighted each other, the Russians sailing northeast and the Japanese southwest. Rozhestvensky had deployed his squadron in two columns or line abreast with four battleships led by *Suvorov* to starboard while *Osliabia* led the second and third divisions of the older battleships and cruisers. While still out of range, Togo swung his column to the west and cut directly across the path of the approaching Russian ships. It appeared that he intended to pass down the line of the weaker Russian ships and rake them with his heavier broadsides while the newer battleships were screened by the other vessels and unable to use their guns. However, that maneuver might have allowed the Russian battleships to escape to the north. Togo had no such intention.

"I looked and looked and, not believing my eyes, could not put down my glasses," wrote Semenov in the *Suvorov*. Togo's *Mikasa* with the others in succession turned south and then east, tracing nearly a full circle that put them on a parallel course in the same direction as the Russians. That turn enabled the Japanese to enfilade the entire Russian line and use their superior speed once again to "cross the T." The maneuver was risky, for each ship turned at roughly the same point and thus offered an exposed and relatively stationary target for the Russian gunners. But the Russians fired without effect at the turning ships. Togo held his fire until all ships were again in line. Then the Japanese began to shoot, concentrating first on the *Osliabia* and the *Suvorov*. At 2:30 *Osliabia* rolled over, floated for fifteen minutes like a gigantic whale, and then went to the bottom. By 3:00 the Russians ships, many burning fiercely, were no longer a squadron but rather milling hulks that the Japanese pounded almost at will.

28. Several Japanese ships were damaged, including the cruiser *Asama*, which had to retire early in the battle. Ironically the greatest damage was inflicted on the Japanese by Nebogatov's scurrilous collection of "flat irons." All together Russia lost thirty-four warships; 4,380 seamen were killed, 5,917 were captured, and 1,862 were interned in neutral ports. Japan suffered 700 casualties, including 110 killed.

There are many first-hand accounts and other descriptions of Tsushima; in addition to works previously mentioned (Chapter IX, Notes 13 and 42), see Captain V.I. Semenov, *The Battle of Tsu-Shima* (London, 1906) and *The Price of Blood* (London, 1910); J.M. Westwood, *Witnesses of Tsushima* (Tokyo, 1970); an excellent account is in Herbert W. Wilson, *Battleships in Action*, vol. 1 (London, 1926); Captain Togo Kichitaro (nephew of the admiral), *Naval Battles of the Russo-Japanese War* (Tokyo, 1907); and Ogasawara Nagayo, *The Life of Admiral Togo* (Tokyo, 1934), which is based on official records.

The paragraph that follows this in Oldenburg's text (Vol. I, p. 281) has been moved below to the beginning of the section titled "Nicholas, Bloody but Unbowed."

29. The All-Russian Union of Unions was formed early in May. Its composition changed continuously but originally it represented fourteen unions of writers, engineers, professors, secondary and primary school teachers, zemstvo employees, veterinarians, and an All-Russian Peasant Union. Far from representing organized professions, however, these mainly were groups of self-appointed activists. (Oldenburg's note)

The origins and development of the liberal movement can be followed in numerous works, many previously cited. Find a concise account of the immediate revolutionary period in V. King, "The Liberal Movement in Russia, 1904-1905," *The Slavonic and East European Review*, 14 (1935), 124-37. For broader treatment see George Fischer, *Russian Liberalism from Gentry to Intelligentsia* (Cambridge, Mass., 1958) and Jacob Walkin, *The Rise of Democracy in Pre-Revolutionary Russia: Political and Social Institutions under the Last Three Czars* (New York, 1962).

30. The Shipov moderates and the zemstvo constitutionalists both wanted an elected national assembly. The difference was that the constitutionalists wanted it to have legislative powers like a parliament, while Shipov's group wanted only a consultative assembly. That, they felt, was more in keeping with Russian traditions and more workable under existing institutions and conditions.

31. Quoted from *Letters from the Kaiser to the Czar*, pp. 172-73.

32. The kaiser's "strictly confidential" memorandum is reprinted from the Papers of Theodore Roosevelt by Tyler Dennett in his *Roosevelt and the Russo-Japanese War* (New York, 1925; reprint, 1959), p. 220.

33. Meyer wrote: "While the Emperor is not a man of force I was impressed with his self-possession." On the point that Russian territory remained intact, Meyer reported Nicholas's words as follows: "You have come at a psychological moment; as yet no foot has been placed on Russian soil; but I realize that at almost any moment they can make an attack on Sakhalin [Island—north of Japan]. Therefore it is important that the meeting should take place before that occurs." Quoted ibid., p. 194. The letters and papers of Ambassador Meyer are included in the biography by M.A. DeWolfe Howe, *George von Lengerke Meyer: His Life and Public Services* (New York, 1919).

34. In an interview with the correspondent of the *Echo de Paris* on 2 January 1905, Admiral Dubasov declared that with the loss of Port

Arthur Admiral Rozhestvensky hardly could count on victory. "Offhand I would say that we are heading closer to peace; we will leave to Japan Port Arthur and that part of Manchuria that they now occupy." He concluded: "Russia will build a strong and invincible fleet. Then we will play the second round of this game, only this time we will hold all the trump." (Oldenburg's note)

35. Miliukov, *Russia and Its Crisis* (Chicago, 1905), p. xi.

36. At the end of March 1905, General Kodama Gentaro returned to Tokyo from the front to inform the government that no further advance by the army was possible. Kodama was chief of staff to the supreme commander, Marshal Oyama Iwao. He was recognized as Japan's finest tactician and the architect of its successes in the field. He had been a hawk before the war, but after Mukden he was anxious to make peace while Japan could negotiate from strength—"Don't you know that if you light a fire, you must also know how to put it out?" The question of war and peace is covered in detail in Shumpei Okamoto, *The Japanese Oligarchy and the Russo-Japanese War* (New York, 1970).

37. The Union of Unions' resolution of 25 May openly declared that it would "endeavor with all strength to remove the band of highwaymen who had usurped power and replace the bandits with a constituent assembly." (Oldenburg's note)

The Union of Unions met on 25 May; representatives of the zemstvos, municipalities, and gentry met from 24 to 27 May. The chief purpose of the May zemstvo congress was to smooth over the differences between liberals (constitutionalists) and moderates in the national crisis created by the annihilation of the Russian fleet at Tsushima.

38. The delegation consisted of the following persons, listed in order of the votes they received: Count Peter A. Heiden, Prince George E. Lvov, Nicholas N. Lvov, Ivan I. Petrunkevich, Dmitry N. Shipov, Prince Peter D. Dolgorukov, Nicholas N. Kovalevsky, Iu. A. Novosiltsev, Feodor I. Rodichev, and Prince Dmitry I. Shakhovskoy. The deputation was completed by the inclusion of the author of the petition, Prince Trubetskoy, and the chairman of the St. Petersburg Municipal Duma, M.P. [M.I.-?] Fedorov. (Oldenburg's note)

39. The Zemsky Sobor—assembly of the land or national assembly— was established formally by the Terrible Tsar, Ivan IV (1530-84). In 1566 Ivan summoned representatives of the princes, boyars, government, church, and merchantry in order to whip up support and assess the financial prospects for a war with Poland and Sweden. The Zemsky Sobor, which Ivan convened several times during his reign (1533-84), met at his pleasure, discussed what he allowed it to discuss, and offered advice, which he could accept or reject, when he asked for it. Tsar Boris Godunov (1598-1605) revived the Zemsky Sobor in 1598 on the eve of Russia's Time of Troubles. The reign of the Romanov's began in 1613 when the most broadly representative of all the Sobors elected Michael Romanov as tsar. The Zemsky Sobor was convened regularly in the next decade and exerted a fair degree of influence on the new monarchy. Thereafter, however, its meetings became less frequent and its influence diminished as the Romanovs reasserted the autocratic prerogatives of their predecessors. The last Sobor convened in 1653,

and the institution passed into oblivion, leaving no trace of its existence in the constitutional structure of Russia. The demise of the institution is explained by J.L.H. Keep, "The Decline of the Zemsky Sobor," *The Slavonic and East European Review*, 36 (December 1957), 100-22; reprinted in Sidney Harcave, ed., *Readings in Russian History*, Vol. I: *From Ancient Times to the Abolition of Serfdom* (New York, 1962), pp. 195-211.

40. The Union of Russian Men was a small organization of conservatives outside the government and administration and was separate, therefore, from the Patriotic Union formed by conservative officials. The two organizations met jointly in May to compose an address to the tsar. The Union of Russian Men (*Soiuz russkykh liudei*) should not be confused with the Union of Russian People (*Soiuz russkago naroda*), a mass organization of reactionaries and anti-Semites formed in October 1905.

41. With the defection of the *Georgy Pobedonosets* the fleet commander, Vice Admiral Alexander C. Krieger, hesitated. He was uncertain of the discipline of the crews among the remaining ships, and the *Potemkin* carried heavier guns than any ship under his command. *The Potemkin Mutiny* by Richard Hough (New York, 1961) tells the story vividly, as does Sergei Eisenstein's film classic, *The Battleship Potemkin* (1925). In Soviet historiography revolution was the supreme accomplishment of the Imperial navy, and the *Potemkin* is a favorite example; consult the bibliographies mentioned above, Note 7.

42. Apparently the victim was Paul Petrovich Shuvalov (1858-) who as a colonel once commanded a brigade of horse artillery and early in the 1890s became an aide-de-camp to Grand Duke Sergei Alexandrovich. The assassin was Peter Alexandrovich Kulikovsky, a member of the SR Battle Organization but acting independently at the time. Kulikovsky had lost his nerve before the assassination of the grand duke, and the murder of Shuvalov presumably proved to himself and the organization that he was, after all, a competent terrorist. A military tribunal sentenced him to death, and the sentence later was reduced to hard labor for an indeterminate term.

43. Maximillian Ilyich Schweizer (1881-1905) was expelled from Moscow University in 1899 for participating in student disorders. He joined the SRs as an exile in Yakutsk province and in 1903 went abroad and joined its terrorist organization. Schweizer headed a team preparing the assassination of the tsar's uncle, Grand Duke Vladimir Alexandrovich. On the night of 26 February 1905, while loading the bombs for the occasion, he made his last mistake.

Nicholas Yurievich Tatarov (c. 1870-1906), originally a member of the Polish Socialist Party—his father was the arch-priest of the Warsaw cathedral—was first arrested in 1892. After his fourth arrest in 1901, he was exiled to eastern Siberia. There he joined the Socialist Revolutionary Party and proved his worth in its activities among the exiles. He returned to St. Petersburg late in 1904 and was admitted to the Battle Organization. However, while in Siberia, the governor-general, a friend of the family, had persuaded him to work with the police. After Schweizer's accidental death, Tatarov betrayed the Petersburg organization. On

16-17 March the police arrested sixteen SR terrorists. In October 1905 they all were released as part of a general amnesty. As they retraced the steps that had led to their arrests, it was apparent that they had been betrayed and that the traitor was Tatarov. Tatarov worked for the police for eight months and earned over 16,000 rubles and one mortal wound. The last payment was delivered by an assassin from the Battle Organization on 22 March 1906.

One of the Russian newspapers referred to the arrests of 16-17/29-30 March 1905 as "the Mukden of the Russian Revolution." If not that, at least they marked the decline of the Battle Organization, which never recovered the prestige or power it had enjoyed since the assassination of Plehve. On that point and on the two terrorists, Schweizer and Tatarov, see Nikolaevsky, *Aseff the Spy*, 107-27; and Savinkov, *Memoirs*, 128-34.

44. An Imperial Ukaz of 21 June 1905 somewhat streamlined the old Army Main Staff (usually also called the general staff) and created a modern General Staff directed by a Chief. The "new" General Staff had eight divisions: three departments—Quartermaster General, Military Communications, and Military Topography; a Military History Commission; and four sections—Mobilization, Fortresses, Troops, and Airships. The General Staff also controlled the military attaches, the Nicholas (Military) Academy, and the School of Military Topography. From 1905 to 1908 the chief of the General Staff (General Palitsyn) reported directly to the tsar, by-passing the minister of war. In 1908 the chief was subordinated to the minister.

A little later, in April and June 1906, some of the functions of the Main Naval Staff (1885) were transferred to a new Naval General Staff. The chief of the Naval General Staff assumed direction of strategic planning, mobilization, bases, and naval attaches.

See Erik Amburger, *Geschichte der Behördenorganisation Russlands von Peter dem grossen bis 1917* [History of Russian Government Organization from Peter the Great to 1917] (Leiden, 1966), pp. 308-11 and 355-56.

45. The arrangements for this loan were such that the Russian government paid at a real rate of 6.33 percent; compare above, Note 2.

46. The author goes to some lengths here to defend the treaty signed at Björkö because the verdict of contemporaries and historians has been universally negative. Oldenburg's defense is unique in that Björkö is discussed invariably in a European context with little regard for Nicholas's apparent determination to press on with the war in Asia. That puts the treaty in a slightly different light, but it still remains unclear how the treaty would have served or strengthened Russia's position against Japan. Critics generally maintain that the treaty did not serve Russian national interests, because in a possible Anglo-Russian war Russia was most likely to be attacked in Asia but Germany's assistance was limited to Europe. Moreover, French adherence was an impossibility in view of the Anglo-French entente and the Franco-German crisis over Morocco. Although directed against an aggressor, the treaty would have neutralized the Franco-Russian Alliance which, of course, was one of the kaiser's goals. An act of aggression is not as clear-cut as the author implies—governments and then their historians have debated sixty years

without agreeing definitely on who the aggressor was in 1914 (though for some there never really was any question at all).

Existence of the treaty remained a secret until the new Soviet government revealed it in late 1917. The text of the treaty, which was quite similar to the kaiser's earlier proposal, can be found in *Krasnyi arkhiv*, 5 (1924), 25-26; and in *Sbornik dogovorov Rossii s drugimi gosudarstvami, 1856-1917 gg.* [Collection of Treaties of Russia with other States, 1856-1917] (Moscow, 1952), pp. 335-36.

47. For William's promise to Bülow and other exchanges see *Correspondance secrete de Bülow et de Guillaume II*, trans. Gilbert Lenoir (Paris, 1931), and in General Bülow's *Memoirs*, trans. Geoffrey Dunlop and F.A. Voight, 4 vols. (London, 1931-32).

48. For the text of the imperial manifesto and law see *Polnoe sobranie zakonov Rossiiskoi imperii* [Complete Collection of the Laws of the Russian Empire], 3rd ser., vol. XXV, pt. 1, No. 26,656; or F.I. Kalinychev, ed., *Gosudarstvennaia duma v Rossii v dokumentakh i materialakh* [The State Duma in Russia in Documents and Material] (Moscow, 1957), pp. 30-54.

49. Witte's instructions have been placed at the head of this paragraph; the rearranged material appears on page 297, Volume 1 of the original text.

50. Oldenburg indicates that he relied for his account of the Portsmouth negotiations at least partly on Tyler Dennett's *Roosevelt and the Russo-Japanese War*. That work reproduces Meyer's report of his 10/23 August conversation with Nicholas on page 270 (emphasis added): "He is *unwilling* to pay a substantial sum for half of Sakhalin as it would be interpreted as a war indemnity differently expressed." In his text, however, Dennett wrote: "Meyer argued with him for two hours and at length he [the tsar] agreed to the division of Sakhalin *and the payment of a 'substantial sum'* for the return to Russia of the northern part." (Page 255) That error had some bearing on the interpretation of Witte's role at Portsmouth by making him appear somewhat more willing to pay than he may have been.

51. The record of this final scene, held in secret of course, comes from the diary of Witte's secretary, Ivan Ia. Korostovetz. He recorded that "Witte calmly replied that the Japanese proposal was accepted and that the line of demarcation of Sakhalin would be reckoned the fiftieth degree." *Pre-War Diplomacy. The Russo-Japanese Problem. Treaty Signed at Portsmouth, U.S.A., 1905; Diary of J.J. Korostovetz* (London, 1920). Korostovetz's diary was published originally in *Byloe* in 1918, then in the English edition, and again finally by the Russian religious mission in China as *Stranitsa iz istorii russkoi diplomatii* [Pages from the History of Russian Diplomacy] (Peking, 1923). It is an indispensable source for the proceedings and for Russian policy at Portsmouth.

52. In a study of the financial side of the war the distinguished German economist and statesman, Karl Helffrich, concluded that by the war's end the Russian State Bank could cover 400,000,000 rubles in bank notes (paper money). That would have enabled Russia to sustain at least another six months of war without a new loan and without suspending the redemption of notes. If the government had decided—as

in 1854, or like France in 1870 (or like every government in World War I)—to draw on its gold reserve, that fund would have carried Russia for at least a year. Japan, on the other hand, possessed eight times less the financial reserve of Russia. "One can only acknowledge that the credit of the Russian state held up extremely well under the difficult strain of the East Asian war and the domestic turmoil. That is not an opinion subject to debate but an unquestionable fact that cannot be denied even by the blindest fanatic . . . . A great deal can be learned from much-abused Russia in the field of financial policy." Karl Helffrich, *Das Geld im russisch-japanischen Krieg* [Gold in the Russo-Japanese War] (Berlin, 1905). (Oldenburg's note)

More recent research is not quite so optimistic about the strength of Russia's finances;see A.L. Sidorov, "Finansovoe polozhenie tsarskogo samoderzhaviia v period russko-iaponskoi voiny i pervoi russkoi revoliutsii" [The Financial Position of the Tsarist Autocracy during the Russo-Japanese War and the First Russian Revolution], *Istoricheskii arkhiv* [Historical Archive], 2 (1955), 121-49; and by the same author, "Denezhnoe obrashchenie i finansovoe polozhenie Rossii (1904-07 gg.)" [Money Circulation and the Financial Position of Russia (1904-7)], ibid., 3 (1956), 88-123. Although not addressed specifically to Russian credit in 1904-5, John P. Sontag's recent article might be classified as revisionist and generally in agreement with Oldenburg's interpretation: "Tsarist Debts and Tsarist Foreign Policy," *Slavic Review*, 27 (December 1968), 529-41.

53. Dennett, *Roosevelt and the Russo-Japanese War*, p. 297. (Oldenburg's note)

54. Witte's telegram read: "Japan has accepted your terms for peace and thus peace will be re-established, thanks to your wise and firm decisions, in accord with Your Majesty's instructions. Russia remains a great power in the Far East, as she was and forever will be." (Oldenburg's note)

55. Ivan Tikhonovich Pososhkov (1652-1726) was a self-educated peasant-artisan who served in the administration of Peter the Great and became a master minter. He also wrote an amazing *Book on Poverty and Wealth* and other material. He praised Peter, who had all too few unqualified supporters, and condemned the sloth, illiteracy, inefficiency and corruption that he found everywhere in Russia. Pososhkov, imprisoned shortly after Peter's death in 1725, died there. His work was discovered in the nineteenth century and has been published in several editions. I.T. Pososhkov, *Kniga o skudosti i bogatstve i drugie sochineniia* [A Book on Poverty and Wealth and Other Works] (Moscow, 1951). A biographic sketch can be found in L.R. Lewitter, "Ivan Tikhonovich Pososhkov (1652-1726) and 'The Spirit of Capitalism'," *The Slavonic and East European Review*, 51 (October 1973), 524-53.

NOTES TO CHAPTER ELEVEN

1. *Encyclopedia Britannica*, 11th ed., s.v. "Russo-Japanese War."

2. Konni Zilliacus organized the voyage of the *John Grafton* with funds provided by Colonel Akashi, the Japanese intelligence officer; see

above Chapter X and Note 7. Efforts to establish regular material assistance to Russian revolutionaries is the subject of Futrell's *Northern Underground*; the *John Grafton* incident is covered on pages 66-80.

3. Erroneously the author gives the date of this congress as 13-15 September (Vol. I, p. 307). Political and constitutional conditions changed significantly between September and November 1905.

4. Guchkov specifically protested the convention's demand that martial law be revoked in Poland, "where, as everyone knows," he said, "there is an armed insurrection." He also urged the delegates to supplement their demand for the abolition of capital punishment with a "categorical denunciation of violence and assassination as methods of political struggle."

Alexander Ivanovich Guchkov (1862-1936) was a wealthy and prominent Moscow merchant. Having studied history and philosophy at Moscow University, he joined the family's enterprises while also serving on occasion in the municipal duma. He fought the British as a volunteer in the Boer War, and during the Russo-Japanese War he directed the Russian Red Cross in Manchuria, where he was captured. A political moderate, Guchkov was one of the principal organizers of the Union of October 17, and he consistently followed the policy that reform was impossible without order. Consequently he was a firm supporter of P.A. Stolypin's program of "first pacification, then reforms" (discussed below).

Guchkov served as chairman of the Third State Duma in 1910-11, was elected to the State Council, and during World War I headed the Central War Industries Committee and the Russian Red Cross. Bitterly critical of the government's war policies, he was one of the public figures who accepted the abdication of Nicholas II at Pskov in March 1917. Then from March to May Guchkov served as minister of war in the first coalition of the Provisional Government. After the Bolshevik coup in October, he joined the anti-Bolshevik resistance. In 1921 he emigrated to Paris and remained active in anti-Soviet movements until he died. Before his death, he began to dictate his memoirs, which were edited and published in 1936 in *Poslednie novosti* [The Latest News] (Paris) under the title "Iz vospominaniia A.I. Guchkova" [From the Memoirs of A.I. Guchkov].

5. At this point Oldenburg emphasizes with quotation marks the term *obshchestvennost*—"the public" or perhaps "public opinion," but in a special sense. The Russian word *obshchestvo* and its derivatives generally meant "society" in the sense of the upper classes—the nobility, the intelligentsia and professional elements, the wealthy merchantry and industrialists, and the state bureaucracy. But "society" had an even more particular (and also more abstract) meaning, and that is the sense that Oldenburg intends here. It also referred to that educated, articulate, and usually urban segment of the upper crust which was conscious of an identity and views *separate from the government*. That "public" or those "public men" believed that they stood and spoke for the real Russia, including the silent masses who could not speak for themselves, whereas the government represented something else—bureaucratic self-interest or autocratic or dynastic interests distinct from true Russian

national interests. In contrast, the term *narod*—"the people"—could include everyone, but more often referred to "the rest" of society, the illiterate or semi-literate masses, especially the peasantry but sometimes also the provincial gentry.

Those distinctions are followed throughout this translation. Terms such as "popular," "national," "people" and the like refer to the masses as distinct from "society"—the literate upper classes—and from "the public"—the articulate elite outside the government. Finally, Oldenburg consistently uses the word "intelligentsia" to designate *radical* elements within the "public."

6. This opening sentence appears as an isolated paragraph on page 306 of the original text; the following discussion of the universities begins on page 307.

7. The crest of Imperial Russia bears a double-headed eagle, symbolically confronting Europe and Asia. The Phrygian cap, from classical Greece, has a forward-curving peak; it often symbolizes Liberty.

8. Baron Michael A. de Taube dealt with this affair in his book "On the Way to the Great Catastrophe." He offered the probable explanation that Witte opposed the treaty because he was courting the support of Grand Duke Nicholas Nikolaevich, who strongly opposed the treaty. (Oldenburg's note)

Baron de Taube served for many years as legal advisor to the ministry of foreign affairs; from 1911 to 1915 he was an assistant minister of public education. The reference is to his *La Politique russe d'avant Guerre et la fin de l'Empire des Tsars (1904-1917). Memoires du baron M. de Taube* (Paris, 1928); enlarged German edition: *Der grossen Katastrophe entgegen: Die russische Politik der Vorkriegszeit und das Ende des Zarenreiches (1904-1917)* (Berlin and Leipzig, 1929).

More recent scholarship ties the fate of the Björkö treaty more closely to Russia's urgent need for a substantial foreign loan. Witte's apparent inconsistency is more understandable in that light. For details see the important recent study by Howard D. Mehlinger and John M. Thompson, *Count Witte and the Tsarist Government in the 1905 Revolution* (Bloomington, 1972), pp. 213-16; and also Girault, *Emprunts russes*, pp. 418-24. For documents and correspondence see "Russko-Germanskii dogovor 1905 goda [The Russo-German Treaty of 1905], *Krasnyi arkhiv*, 5 (1924), 1-49.

9. Witte's memorandum on *Autocracy and Zemstvo* (1899) is discussed above, Chapter VI. I.Ya. Gurland (1868-), a professor of constitutional law at the Yaroslavl Demidov Lyceum, entered the ministry of interior in 1904. In the department of general affairs he was responsible for drafting legislative projects and memoranda. Mehlinger and Thompson suggest that V.D. Kuzmin-Karavaev (1859-1928), a member of the 1904-5 zemstvo congresses, either or also may have authored the main lines of this memorandum: *Count Witte*, p. 34. For the text of the document see "Zapiska Vitte ot 9 oktiabria" [Witte's Memorandum of 9 October], *Krasnyi arkhiv*, 11-12 (1925), 51-57.

10. The October general strike was probably the most "general" general strike in history. On 10 October the entire work force struck in Moscow, Kharkov, and Reval. On the following day the strike hit Koslov,

Lodz, Smolensk, and Ekaterinoslav. On the 12th it paralyzed Kursk, Poltava, and Samara; on the next day Minsk, Kremenchug, Simferopol, and St. Petersburg, and it continued to spread. The key to the strike's success were the railway workers. In less than two weeks over 600,000 railway men walked off their jobs and tied up well over 25,000 miles of track.

The ministry of trade and industry estimated that during the entire year some 3,000,000 workers refused to work at some time, including 640,000 railway employees, 474,000 textile workers, and 301,000 metalworkers. That figure represented nearly 164 percent of the labor force within the purview of the ministry, and it indicated that many workers struck more than once. St. Petersburg, for example, had about 229,000 workers but nearly 628,000 strikers in 1905. There were about 14,000 individual strikes involving more than 5,000,000 workers. By contrast official statistics recorded only 420,000 strikers during the decade 1895-1904. See Andrei S. Amalrik, "K voprosu o chislennosti i geograficheskom razmeshchenii stachechnikov v evropeiskoi Rossii v 1905 g." [On the Problem of the Number and Geographic Distribution of Strikers in European Russia in 1905], *Istoricheskie zapiski*, 52 (1955), 142-85.

11. *Grazhdanin*, 10 October 1905. (Oldenburg's note)

12. *Novoe vremia*, 11 October 1905; *Slovo*, 13 October 1905; and Stolypin in *Novoe vremia*, 14 October 1905. (Oldenburg's note)

Alexander Arkadeevich Stolypin (1863-), a moderate journalist, edited *Peterburzhskie vedomosti* until 1903 when Plehve forced him to resign because of his "undesirable" editorial views. Stolypin then joined the staff of *Novoe vremia* and subsequently became an active member of the Union of October 17.

13. Witte, *Memoirs*, p. 239; *Vospominaniia*, 3:12.

14. Witte and his supporters argued that an imperial manifesto, essentially proclaiming a gift from the tsar, would bind Nicholas to a policy that might prove unsuccessful. Failure, therefore, would be attributed to the tsar. But if the tsar merely endorsed the proposals of his minister, the responsibility for failure (or success) would fall on the minister rather than the sovereign. Witte's critics have contended that he was trying to have reform associated exclusively with himself. In the latest study on this question Mehlinger and Thompson conclude that "Witte was not nearly as concerned with saving the tsar embarrassment or initiating a personal power play as he was with fighting for freedom in which to operate . . . . Witte wanted exactly what he had indicated in his report—a pledge which committed Russia in the direction of reform but which provided sufficient flexibility to permit initiation of specific reforms at a pace and in a form that seemed possible and desirable as circumstances dictated." *Count Witte*, p. 39.

15 Prince Obolensky drafted the manifesto on the night of 14 October at Witte's request and probably on the basis of their discussion of Witte's memorandum of the 9th. Obolensky accompanied Witte to Peterhof on the 15th.

Prince Alexis Dmitrievich Obolensky (1855-1933) began his administrative career in 1877 in the first department of the Senate. He held various provincial posts from 1881 to 1894, when he became manager of the Nobles Bank and the Peasant Land Bank, a post to which he returned briefly in 1905. He served in the ministry of interior as an assistant minister from 1897 to 1901, became a senator in 1901, and from 1902 to 1905 held the position (under Witte) of assistant minister of finance and director of the department of taxation. In June 1905 Nicholas appointed Obolensky to the State Council. On 20 October 1905 he became director-general of the holy synod in Witte's cabinet. He resigned with Witte and others in April 1906.

16. Count A.P. Ignatiev (1842-1906), an extreme conservative and anti-Semite, graduated from the Nicholas Academy of the General Staff in 1862 and subsequently held prestigious commands in the guards regiments. In 1885 he was appointed governor-general of Irkutsk. In 1889 he transferred to Kiev and governed that province until 1896, when he was named to the State Council. He headed the Conference to Examine Special Regulations on Preserving State Order and the Special Conference on Religious Toleration. Ignatiev was one of the emperor's closest advisors and frequently was summoned to important conferences. In Kiev in 1906 an SR terrorist killed him.

17. Cf. *The Secret Letters of the Last Tsar*, pp. 184-85.

18. The Black Hundreds were gangs of reactionary hoodlums whose patriotism expressed itself in violent assaults upon Jews, intellectuals, and socialists. Historians generally describe them as a proto-fascist movement. The Black Hundreds had no central organization but to a large extent expressed a spontaneous popular reaction to the domestic chaos inspired by liberal and radical agitation. Local authorities, both police and military, frequently connived with the Black Hundreds, and there is no question that officials of the central government and members of the imperial court approved and aided their activities, though not publicly. See Bertram Wolfe's unsurpassed description of the Black Hundreds in *Three Who Made a Revolution*, p. 327.

19. The first workers soviets or councils sprang up during local strikes in Ivanovo-Voznesensk (near Moscow) in May and nearby in Kostroma in July. The St. Petersburg Soviet—which became the revolutionary symbol of 1905—came into being at the height of the October general strike. It was different from the start in that it was formed with the idea of leading the general strike in the capital.

The move to organize the Soviet began on 10 October when the Menshevik group in Petersburg proposed the formation of a city-wide "workers committee" to direct the general strike. On the following day Menshevik agitators began to circulate this appeal among the workers. About forty elected deputies and revolutionaries met on the evening of the 13th. They issued another appeal for the election of representatives to provide unified direction to the strike. On the 14th more than eighty deputies from forty factories appeared, and on the following day 226 delegates representing 96 factories and five trade unions assembled. The deputies met again on 17 October and formally established the Soviet of Workers' Deputies. They elected a 22-member executive committee. Representatives of the three socialist parties (Mensheviks, Bolsheviks, and Socialist Revolutionaries) were admitted to the Soviet in an advisory capacity.

Oskar Anweiler, *The Soviets: The Russian Workers, Peasants, and Soldiers Councils, 1905-1921*, trans. Ruth Hein (New York, 1974), pp. 40-47. This, the standard work on the Russian soviets, first appeared as *Die Rätebewegung in Russland, 1905-1921* [The Soviet Movement in Russia 1905-1921] (Leiden, 1958).

20. "Okonchatelnyi tekst proekta manifesta Goremykina-Budberga" [Final Text of the Draft of the Goremykin-Budberg Manifesto], *Krasnyi arkhiv*, 11-12 (1925), 94-97.

21. *Secret Letters of the Last Tsar*, pp. 184-85.

22. Ibid. The headache he confided to his diary (17 October).

23. Witte, *Memoirs*, pp. 234, 235-36.

24. Speaking at a banquet on the evening of the 17th, Miliukov also minimized the manifesto: "Paying no attention to the elated mood of the public . . . I threw cold water on their merrymaking. . . . Yes, I told them, the victory is won, and it is not a small one. But, you see, this victory is not the first one; it is only a new link in the chain of our victories. "Rokovye Gody," *Russkie zapiski* (January 1939); [also, Miliukov, *Political Memoirs*, p. 51]. (Oldenburg's note)

25. In the two or three weeks following the manifesto, about 150 pogroms erupted throughout the country and claimed the lives of about 4,000 persons. Another 10,000 were injured and property damage was enormous. The most serious pogrom took place in Odessa on 18-21 October. There more than 500 persons were killed, of whom 400 were Jews. Nicholas explained the wave of terror to his mother: ". . . A whole mass of loyal people suddenly made their power felt. The result was obvious, and what one would expect in our country. The impertinence of the Socialists and revolutionaries had angered the people once more; and, because nine-tenths of the trouble makers are Jews, the people's anger turned against them. That's how the pogroms happened. It is amazing how they took place *simultaneously* in all the towns of Russia and Siberia. In England, of course, the press says that those disorders were organized by the police; they still go on repeating that worn-out fable. But not only Jews suffered; some of the Russian agitators, engineers, lawyers, and other such bad people suffered as well." *The Secret Letters of the Last Tsar*, pp. 191-92.

26. The deputy Sposobny from the city of Ekaterinoslav related this incident to the First Duma. (Oldenburg's note)

27. Western historians frequently allege that Bloody Sunday (9 January 1905) irrevocably destroyed the mystical bond between the tsar and his people. Closer examination of the peasant revolts, strikes, and mutinies of 1905 indicates that those outbursts often were directed against local conditions and against the usual targets—landlords and bureaucrats. During the strike at Ivanovo-Voznesensk, for example, "one lady agitator once called out: 'Down with autocracy!' and what a to-do there was then! Everybody got excited. 'What? Surely we are not against the czar? But we are only against the manufacturers, and the czar does us no harm. That's not how we want it!' " Quoted by Anweiler, *The Soviets*, p. 271, n. 84. See also a Social Democratic leader's experiences among the peasantry in 1905: W.S. Woytinsky, *Stormy Passage: A Personal History through Two Russian Revolutions*

to Democracy and Freedom, 1905-1960 (New York, 1961), pp. 67 ff., 180-87.

28. Nicholas Ernestovich Bauman (1873-1905), a relatively minor though active Bolshevik, became a major figure in the Soviet pantheon of revolutionary martyrs. Streets, schools, and even a district in the city of Moscow bear his name. Earlier party histories reckoned the participants in his funeral at 200,000; the Soviet Historical Encyclopedia (*Sovetskaia istoricheskaia entsiklopediia*, 1962) raised the celebrants to 300,000. The encyclopedia gives Bauman fifty-four lines and a photograph; Nikita Khrushchev gets twenty-seven lines and no photo.

29. An interesting exchange between Witte and Min took place in connection with this incident. Witte, at the request of certain "public figures," telephoned Min to suggest that he "not block the streets." I have no right to interfere with the orders of your superiors, and I am making this request not as prime minister but as a Russian citizen who loves his country." Colonel Min replied: "This is a Russian citizen who loves his fatherland as much if not more than you, and I am telling you . . . [that] I cannot allow part of my regiment to be surrounded by a mob and cut off from its barracks. . . . The best thing, Count, would be for you yourself to make an appearance at the square. You know only too well how to master a crowd. Talk to them, quiet them down, and convince them to disperse. . . . That would be the most dignified and effective solution." Witte, it should be understood, declined the invitation and concluded the interview by bidding Min to "do whatever you think necessary." (Oldenburg's note)

30. The resignees were Director-General of the Holy Synod Constantine Pobedonostsev, Minister of Finance Vladimir Kokovtsov, Minister of Public Education Vladimir Glazov, Minister of Ways and Communications Prince Michael Khilkov, Head of the Main Administration of Agriculture and State Domains Peter Schwanebach, State Comptroller General Paul Lobko, Minister of Internal Affairs Alexander Bulygin, and Grand Duke Alexander Mikhailovich, head of the Main Administration of Commercial Navigation and Ports. (Oldenburg's note)

31. *Novoe vremia,* 24 October 1905. (Oldenburg's note)

On 19 October Witte invited Shipov to join his government as state comptroller. Shipov, aware that he represented a minority within the zemstvo movement, insisted on the inclusion of other "public men" and especially those representing the leftist zemstvo majority. Witte agreed and began to negotiate with others, many of whom had joined the newly-formed Kadet Party (below and Note 55). In general the liberals presented demands and conditions, including a constituent assembly, which Witte could not accept. They appeared more interested in overthrowing the government than in cooperating with it in the reconstruction of Russia. As a result Witte was compelled to form his ministry from the bureaucracy.

The liberals insisted on their "principles," and western historians have either condoned or applauded their noble stand. This episode, however, fully revealed what Oldenburg maintained was the basic deficiency of Russian liberals, that they understood neither Russia nor the West. Their veneer of western liberalism was too shallow to permit them to appreciate the mechanics and virtue of compromise or to see the opportunities that Witte and the general situation then offered. They demanded all or nothing, they preferred opposition and revolution to the possibility of responsible constructive action, and eventually they got exactly what they bargained for.

The details of this negotiation can be followed in the memoirs of several participants: Witte, *Memoirs*, pp. 318-26; Shipov, *Vospominaniia*, pp. 334-49, which are translated in Gurko, *Features and Figures of the Past*, pp. 703-10, as well as Gurko's observations, pp. 403-7; V.A. Maklakov, *Vlast i obshchestvennost na zakate staroi Rossii: Vospominaniia sovremennika* [Government and Society in the Twilight of Old Russia: Reminiscences of a Contemporary] (Paris, 1939), pp. 420-35; Maxime Kovalevsky, *La crise russe: Notes et impressions d'un temoin* (Paris, 1906), pp. 230-34; N.S. Tagantsev, *Perezhitoe* [Experiences] (Petrograd, 1919), pp. 97-104; Miliukov, *Political Memoirs*, pp. 62-66. See also the critical analysis in Mehlinger and Thompson, *Count Witte* (pp. 76-84) and the studies based on the Soviet archives by E.D. Chermensky, *Burzhuaziia i tsarizm v revoliutsii 1905-07 gg.* [The Bourgeoisie and Tsarism during the Revolution of 1905-7] (Moscow, 1939), and also "Russkaia burzhuaziia oseniu 1905 goda" [The Russian Bourgeoisie in the Fall of 1905], *Voprosy istorii*, (1966) No. 6, 56-72.

32. Soviet historians have been enamored of "the revolutionary movement" in the tsarist armed forces: S.F. Naida, *Revoliutsionnoe dvizhenie v tsarskom flote, 1925-1917* [The Revolutionary Movement in the Tsarist Fleet, 1825-1917] (Moscow, 1948); Kh. Muratov, *Revoliutsionnoe dvizhenie v russkoi armii v 1905-1907 gg.* [The Revolutionary Movement in the Russian Army in 1905-1907] (Moscow, 1955); V.A. Petrov, *Ocherki po istorii revoliutsionnogo dvizhenie v russkoi armii v 1905 g.* [An Outline of the History of the Revolutionary Movement in the Russian Army in 1905] (Moscow-Leningrad, 1964). The subject has not attracted much attention in the West if for no other reason than the military archives have been available only to Soviet scholars.

33. Witte's cabinet included Prince Alexis D. Obolensky (Director-General of the Holy Synod), Klavdy S. Nemeshaev (Minister of Ways and Communications), Count Ivan I. Tolstoy (Minister of Public Education), Ivan P. Shipov (Minister of Finance), Nicholas N. Kutler (Minister of Agriculture), Vasily I. Timiriazev (Minister of Trade and Industry), and Dmitry A. Filosofov (State Comptroller). Of these only Prince Obolensky, through his efforts to convene a church council, attempted anything of significance. (Oldenburg's note)

The other members of the government were Count Lamsdorf (Foreign Affairs), Peter N. Durnovo (Acting Minister of Internal Affairs), Michael G. Akimov (Minister of Justice), Baron Frederichs (Minister of the Imperial Court) and the Ministers of War and Marine, General Rediger and Admiral Birilev. Witte could rely for complete support only on Kutler, Nemeshaev, and Shipov.

34. Among other things, the Union's program took the position that an eight-hour day was impractical. (Oldenburg's note)

35. The Union of October 17, or the Octobrist "party," represented a coalition of zemstvo moderates, led by D.N. Shipov, and a group of

industrialists and bankers mainly from Moscow, led by Alexander Guch-kov. The Union's central committee consisted of five intellectuals or professional men, six landowners, and eleven bankers and industrialists. The composition of its center probably was an accurate reflection of the organization's constituency in general. It was based on Moscow and the central industrial region. Although the Octobrists established nearly eighty branches in thirty-six provinces and published about thirty provincial papers, they attracted few peasants or workers and the Union never became a mass organization. Its support came mainly from the lower and middle bourgeoisie, the provincial gentry, and the bureaucracy.

The Union's program was deliberately general and imprecise, because the Octobrist leaders hoped to unite disparate groups and classes in a broad coalition of political moderates. Basically the Octobrists endorsed the October Manifesto and sought nothing more than it promised—civil liberties and an elected Duma. They were content to have the tsar remain an "autocrat" in a centralized but more modern and efficient state. The term "union" or "league" is the most apt description of the organization, since its program, adopted in February 1906, invariably avoided a specific position on most of the major questions of the day. On an issue like the right to strike, for example, the Union's charter took no position for fear of alienating either its more conservative or its more liberal members. It followed that policy on most controversial national or economic issues. Moreover, members of the Union could belong to another party as long as they subscribed to the principles of the October Manifesto.

36. *Novoe vremia*, 6 November 1905. (Oldenburg's note)

37. *The Secret Letters of the Last Tsar*, pp. 192-93.

38. S. Ye Kryzhanovsky, to whom Witte entrusted the drafting of new legislation, gave this opinion of the prime minister: "His head was filled with chaos, a multitude of impulses; he wanted to please everyone, but he had no definite plan of action. In general, the total effect of his personality was to create an impression not at all in accord with his reputation. In financial affairs, where he felt himself on solid ground, perhaps he was in control, but in politics and govern-ment he gave the impression of an adventurer rather than a statesman." Kryzhanovsky, *Vospominaniia* [Memoirs] (Berlin, 1938). (Oldenburg's note)

Sergei Kryzhanovsky (1862-1934) served in the ministry of interior from 1896 to 1911. He was instrumental in drafting the Law of 6 August 1905 (the Bulygin Duma) and later in formulating the electoral Law of 3 June 1907, which superseded the Law of 11 December 1905.

39. The navy had discharged Lt. Schmidt dishonorably only a few days before he assumed command of the Sevastapol mutiny. The reason was that he had placed himself at the head of a mob that forcibly freed a number of men imprisoned for their part in the *Potemkin* mutiny. His notoriety was partly a result of his status as the first officer to defect and openly challenge the government. His attorneys later pleaded that he was crazy, but the navy shot him anyway.

40. The Russian right found it difficult to form political organiza-tions because the idea of politics was alien to those who believed

fundamentally that political action was the monopoly of the state. The October Manifesto with its grant of civil liberties and solicitation of public participation in government compounded the dilemma of conservatives and reactionaries. Initially the right-wing parties conceived of themselves as pressure groups that might stiffen the resolve of the government and tsar to stand firm against the revolution.

The Union of Landowners, apparently founded sometime in 1905, though possibly earlier, was one of several rightist factions about which little is known. Gringmut's Monarchist Party took shape between March and October 1905. Through *Moskovskie vedomosti*, which he edited, Gringmut repeatedly called upon the Russian people to unite and proclaim their loyalty to tsar, church, and fatherland. The Monarchist program, adopted on 15 October, called upon the government to employ all lawful means in the suppression of the revolution. Gringmut himself, however, took an even more extreme position, advocating a military dictatorship and, in something of a contradiction, appealing to the people to rise in defense of law and order.

The largest right-wing organization was the Union of Russian People, a popular movement founded in October or November 1905. The URP was essentially a party of peasants, workers, and small businessmen committed to the principle of autocracy; it tended to view the Duma as a consultative body similar to the Zemsky Sobor. Estimates of the strength of the URP vary widely—from 10,000 to 3,000,000. It was distinct from the completely unorganized and elemental Black Hundreds, although the URP usually approved of their terror against liberals, socialists, and Jews. The Union of Russian People was somewhat akin to American populism insofar as it was anti-industrialist, anti-urban and anti-liberal. It was an extremist movement only in its willingness to use and condone violence. In 1908 the Union split first into two and then three factions.

The founder and chairman of the URP was Dr. Alexander I. Dubrovin (1855-1918), a St. Petersburg physician. He was in touch with officials in the ministry of interior, with Grand Duke Nicholas Nikolaevich and his aide General Rauch, and with other prominent bureaucratic and court officials. His organization apparently received funds from the police and from members of the tsar's entourage. In 1906 Dubrovin allegedly instigated and organized the murder of two Jewish deputies of the Duma. In association with Pavolaki Krushevan—the Jew-baiter identified with the 1903 Kishinev pogrom—he published the official organ of the URP, *Russkoe znamia* (The Russian Banner), and was fined several times for slandering members of the government and Duma. In 1918 he was shot by the Bolsheviks.

For a survey of rightist organizations and bibliography see Hans Rogger, "The Formation of the Russian Right, 1900-1906," *California Slavic Studies*, 3 (1964) and an analysis of the Union of Russian People by the same author: "Was There a Russian Fascism?" *Journal of Modern History*, 36 (December 1964), 398-415. The program and statutes of the Union of Russian People are reproduced in Basil Dmytryshyn ed., *Imperial Russia: A Source Book, 1700-1917*, 2nd ed. (Dryden Press, 1974), pp. 410-16.

41. *Novaia zhizn,* 26 November 1905. (Oldenburg's note)
42. Short-lived mutinies erupted in the latter three cities. (Oldenburg's note)
43. *Novaia zhizn,* 24 November 1905. (Oldenburg's note)
44. Khrustalev-Nosar, a lawyer by profession, was a leftist intellectual without party affiliation. During the elections to the Shidlovsky commission in February 1905, he borrowed the identity papers of a worker named Khrustalev in order to participate in the electoral assembly. Very popular among the workers, he was elected chairman of the Soviet. In November he joined the Social Democratic Party as a Menshevik. He was tried with other leaders of the Soviet in 1906 and exiled to Siberia. He escaped, fled abroad, and lived in France until 1914. When he returned to Russia, he was arrested and imprisoned until 1917. He then attempted to play a leading role in the Petrograd Soviet but failed and returned to his native Ukraine where he became chairman of the zemstvo board of Pereiaslavl. He supported Ukrainian independence after the Bolshevik coup and backed the nationalist regime of Skoropadsky and Petliura. When the Red Army overran the Ukraine in 1918, Nosar was arrested and shot. A biographical sketch is V. Kantorovich, "Khrustalev-Nosar," *Byloe,* 4:32 (1925), 117-53.
45. Peter A. Stolypin succeeded Goremykin as chairman of the council of ministers; he is introduced in Chapter XII. Victor Sakharov had been minister of war since February 1904. Bitsenko cannot be identified.
46. The author presumably refers here to the "Diary of A.A. Polovtsev"—"Dnevnik A.A. Polovtseva," *Krasnyi arkhiv,* 4 (1923), 63-128.

Alexander A. Polovtsev (1832-1909) served at or near the center of power for thirty-five years as a senator (1873-92) and member of the State Council (1892-1909). During this entire period he kept a diary (1877-1908) which has been published in two volumes covering the years 1883-92 and in several installments in the documentary collection, *Krasnyi arkhiv.* Polovtsev's diary is one of the most important records of the reigns of Alexander III and Nicholas II. He was also a founder of the Imperial Historical Society (1866) and its president from 1879 until his death in September 1909. *Dnevnik gosudarstvennogo sekretaria A.A. Polovtsova, 1883-1892* [The Diary of State Secretary A.A. Polovtsov, 1883-1892], ed. P.A. Zaionchkovsky, 2 vols. (Moscow, 1966); the editor has provided a biographical sketch in Volume I, pp. 5-18, and note 34, pp. 14-15 lists the location of the remainder of the diary in *Krasnyi arkhiv.*
47. The right-wing newspaper *Obedinenie* (Unification) subsequently published this interview and was taken to court for violating the regulations governing imperial audiences. The content of the emperor's speech never was denied, however. (Oldenburg's note)
48. The Moscow Soviet, unlike its counterpart in St. Petersburg, was essentially an apparatus of the Bolsheviks who gained control of the local worker movement after the October strike. Whereas the Petersburg Soviet was the more or less spontaneous creation of the workers, the deputies of the Moscow Soviet were chosen by indirect election, and the assembly was influenced strongly by the political leaders at the center. On 6 December the Moscow Soviet voted unanimously to begin

a general strike on the 7th. Ostensibly the strike was to protest the arrest of the Petersburg Soviet, but the Bolsheviks hoped that the strike would be transformed into an armed insurrection with the Moscow Soviet at the head of the revolution. The paralysis of the local authorities stemmed mainly from their concern over the reliability of the local garrison. See Keep, *Rise of Social Democracy*, pp. 242-52; Mehlinger and Thompson, *Count Witte*, pp. 146-48; and generally the account by N.N. Yakovlev, *Vooruzhennye vosstaniia v dekabre 1905 g.* [Armed Uprisings in December 1905] (Moscow, 1957).

49. Trotsky, *Die russiche Revolution 1905.* (Oldenburg's note)

50. In Russia, then as now, building porters were also quasi-police agents responsible for reporting any suspicious activity.

51. "Dnevnik A.N. Kuropatkina" [The Diary of A.N. Kuropatkin], *Krasnyi arkhiv*, 2 (1922), 9-112.

52. This *Poliarnaia zvezda* was published weekly from December 1905 to March 1906 in St. Petersburg under Struve's editorship. It took its name from an earlier *Polar Star* edited by Herzen in London from 1855 to 1862. Struve's journal reflected the views of the right wing of the Constitutional Democratic Party. It was succeeded in April-May 1906 by *Svoboda i kultura* (Freedom and Culture).

53. Maria Alexandrovna Spiridonova was a native of Tambov and of gentry background. While still a student at the Tambov gymnasium, she joined the SRs. In March 1906 a military tribunal sentenced her to death for the murder of Luzhenovsky. The sentence was commuted to life imprisonment, and she was incarcerated for eleven years. Released from prison after the February Revolution, she went to Petrograd and took up with the Left SRs who were allies of the Bolsheviks. She eventually became a member of the Soviet Central Executive Committee but split with the Bolsheviks over the treaty of Brest-Litovsk—the Russo-German peace. She was arrested and imprisoned once again for approving the Left SR terrorist campaign against the Bolsheviks. Released around 1930, she lived in retirement in Ufa until her death in 1941.

54. French bankers initially refused to grant Russia any further credit until the international situation was stabilized. However, the French president and premier intervened to secure a loan of 100,000,000 rubles at 5.5 percent for eleven months. Returning to Russia, Kokovtsov paused in Berlin and won an extension of the short-term German loan. Nevertheless, during December and January the Russian government still issued 150,000,000 rubles of notes without gold backing. Though contrary to statute, the authorities successfully concealed this operation from the public.

55. *The Secret Letters of the Last Tsar*, p. 211.

56. "Kadet" is an acronym derived from the initial letters "ka" and "deh" in *konstitutsionalnaia demokratiia*. The Kadet program called for the establishment of a constitutional monarchy along British lines with the Duma as a parliament similar to the British institution. Its platform advocated a variety of reforms: a general redistribution of land with compensation to landlords for confiscated property, an eight-hour day and legalization of the right to strike, Polish and Finnish autonomy; universal, free, and compulsory elementary education with education

accessible to all without regard to sex, nationality, or religion; abolition of the death penalty, and so on. The Kadet program of 1905-6 can be found in Dmytryshyn, ed., *Imperial Russia,* pp. 405-10.

57. The text of the February 20th manifesto is in *Gosudarstvennaia Duma,* pp. 102-4; and *Polnoe sobranie zakonov,* 3rd ser., XXVI, no. 27,423. The manifesto also stipulated that no law could take effect without the approval of the Duma, the State Council, and the tsar, although under certain conditions the latter could act without the prior approval of those two bodies. This provision formed the basis of Article 87 of the Fundamental Laws, discussed below. See "Tsarskoselskie soveshchaniia: Protokoly sekretnago soveshchaniia v fevrale 1906 goda pod predsedatelstvom byvshago imperatora po vyrabotke Uchrezhdenii Gosudarstvennoi Dumy i Gosudarstvennago Soveta" [The Tsarskoe Selo Conference: Protocols of the Secret Conference in February 1906, Under the Chairmanship of the Former Emperor, on the Development of the State Duma and the State Council], *Byloe,* 5-6 (27-28), (November-December 1917), 289-318.

58. The Russian Assembly, formed in 1900 by a handful of the Petersburg social elite and conservative intellectuals, attempted in 1905 to organize the Russian right-wing. It lacked the inclination or capacity to become an organization with mass appeal and it was superseded as the major organization on the right by the less respectable Union of Russian People. Rogger, "Formation of the Russian Right," 70-72.

59. Although Kokovtsov claimed the lion's share of the credit for the loan, Russia got the money mainly through the efforts of Witte and Eduard Noetzlin, who headed the Parisian syndicate of bankers. On 15 April 1906, two days after the loan was concluded, Nicholas wrote to Witte: "The successful conclusion of the loan forms the best page in the history of your ministerial activity. It is for the Government a great moral triumph and a pledge of Russia's undisturbed and peaceful development in the future." Witte, *Memoirs,* p. 309. At the same time, Nicholas accepted Witte's resignation and a few weeks later awarded Kokovtsov (at his request, according to Witte) the Order of Alexander Nevsky. See also *The Memoirs of Count Kokovtsov,* pp. 119-24; and for the complex course of the negotiation Mehlinger and Thompson, *Count Witte,* pp. 220-40. On the question of the liberal opposition to the loan see Olga Crisp, "The Russian Liberals and the 1906 Anglo-French Loan to Russia," *Slavonic and East European Review,* 39 (June 1961), 497-511; and B.V. Ananich, "Vneshnie zaimy tsarizma i dumskii vopros v 1906-07 gg." [Tsarist Foreign Loans and the Duma Question in 1906-7], *Istoricheskie zapiski,* 81 (1968), 172-98.

60. The Russians actually obtained about 150,000,000 rubles less than they wanted. The loan totaled 843,750,000 rubles, carried a five percent coupon, and was offered to the public at 88. Moreover, the French government added a proviso that banned the Russian government from the French market for two years. As a result and despite a great need for more funds, Russia had to adopt austerity budgets in 1907 and 1908 before raising a new loan in Paris in 1909.

61. The *Trudovaia gruppa* or Trudovik group (a *trudovik* is a toiler) formed a substantial bloc of about one hundred peasant deputies in the

First Duma. Their leaders were intelligentsia with populist or Socialist Revolutionary leanings. Politically the Trudoviks were left of the Kadets and right of the Social Democrats. They had one common goal: land redistribution to be achieved through compulsory expropriation of landlords' property with compensation.

62. Mehlinger and Thompson estimate that only 30-40 percent of the franchised electorate actually voted. Although the apathy of the Russian electorate is unexplained, they suggest that Russians generally were "sick of the turmoil and violence of the revolution and longed for a return to civil peace and order . . . . Several contemporary observers noted that if the elections to the Duma had been held in January, that body would have had a far more conservative hue than it eventually had." *Count Witte*, pp. 169 and 273.

Because of the indirect system of election—voters, voting by class, elected electors who in turn elected deputies—it is impossible to reconstruct the popular vote in this first national election. However, the composition of the First Duma by party affiliation was roughly as follows:

Rightists	7	(1%)
Union of October 17	38	(8%)
National and Religious groups	32	(6%)
Kadets	184	(37%)
Leftists (including Trudoviks)	124	(25%)
No affiliation (mainly peasants)	112	(22%)
Total	497	

From Warren B. Walsh, "Political Parties in the Russian Dumas," *Journal of Modern History*, 22 (June 1950), 144-50; reprinted in Warren B. Walsh, comp. and ed., *Readings in Russian History*, vol. III: *The Revolutionary Era and the Soviet Period*, 4th rev. ed. (Syracuse University Press, 1963), pp. 611-20, esp. 612-13. But see also the tabular analysis in Mehlinger and Thompson, *Count Witte*, p. 279 and their description of the campaign and election, pp. 251-88.

Basic Soviet studies are Chermensky, *Burzhuaziia i tsarism*, and S.M. Sidelnikov. *Obrazovanie i deiatelnost pervoi Gosudarstvennoi dumy* [The Formation and Activity of the First State Duma] (Moscow, 1962).

63. Count Constantine Ivanovich Pahlen (1833-1912) was an ancient fixture in the State Council. He began his career in the chancellery of that organization in 1855. Then, having served for a decade in the ministry of justice, he was appointed to the State Council in 1878.

64. Andrei Alexandrovich Saburov (1838-1916) entered the state administration in 1857 in the chancellery of the committee of ministers. He subsequently held various positions in the senate and justice and education ministries, serving as director of the latter in 1880-81. He was appointed to the State Council in 1899.

Edward Vasilievich Frisch (1833-1907) was only slightly junior to Pahlen as a tenured member of the State Council. He was appointed in 1883 and had held several major positions, including most recently the post of chairman of the legislative department (1900-6). In May 1906 he succeeded Count Solsky (above, Chapter X, Note 16) as president of the State Council.

65. The author probably took this dialogue from "Tsarskoselskie soveshchaniia: Protokoly sekretnago soveshchaniia v aprele 1906 goda pod predsedatelstvom byvshago imperatora po peresmotru osnovnykh zakonov [The Tsarskoe Selo Conference: Protocols of a Secret Conference in April 1906, Under the Chairmanship of the Former Emperor, on the Revision of the Fundamental Laws], ed. V. Vodovozov, *Byloe*, 4 (26), (October 1917), 183-245.

CHAPTER TWELVE

1. Kryzhanovsky, *Vospominaniia*, pp. 66-67.
2. The Prussian constitution, promulgated by the monarchy in December 1848, asserted the ultimate authority of the king. It established a bicameral legislature in which the lower house, the Landtag, was popularly though indirectly elected by universal suffrage. The Landtag could vote new laws and taxes, but the ministers remained responsible to the crown. When the parliament was not in session the government had the right to issue decrees with the force of law.

The Russian government published the Fundamental Laws of 1906 three days before the opening of the Duma in order to prevent that body from transforming itself into a constituent assembly. That move emphasized the sovereignty of the crown and added more fuel to the hostility and suspicion that the deputies felt for the regime.
3. Catherine the Great Built the Taurida Palace in 1783 and presented it to her favorite, Prince Gregory Potemkin (1739-91) in commemoration of his conquest of the Crimea. When Potemkin died, the palace reverted to the crown. It housed the State Duma from 1906 to 1917 and the Provisional Government in 1917. The Soviet government converted it into a university and renamed it the Uritsky Palace in honor of Moisei S. Uritsky, a revolutionary degenerate who headed the Petrograd CHEKA until his assassination in August 1918.
4. Deputies from the Caucasus and Central Asia arrived after the Duma had begun its work. Party alignments were fractionalized throughout the Duma. There were about 170 Kadets, 100 Trudoviks, 15 Social Democrats, 70 "autonomists" (Poles, Lithuanians, and other national representatives), 30 moderates and rightists (26 of whom formed the Party of Peaceful Reconstruction in June), and 100 non-affiliated deputies. (Oldenburg's note)
5. Toward the end of April the Social Democratic leadership repealed their boycott of the Duma, and several workers founded a Social Democratic fraction. Later several Georgian deputies joined them. (Oldenburg's note)
6. Nicholas was serving in the elite Preobrazhensky Guards Regiment at the time of his father's death. Alexander III had promoted him to the rank of colonel, and Nicholas often appeared at important public ceremonies in the uniform of a Preobrazhensky colonel.
7. V.I. Gurko, a conservative with little patience for the imperial establishment, maintained that this display of wealth had an unintended effect: "Naively believing that the people's representatives, many of

whom were peasants, would be awed by the splendor of the Imperial court, the ladies of the Imperial family had worn nearly all their jewels; they were literally covered with pearls and diamonds. But the effect was altogether different. This Oriental method of impressing upon spectators a reverence for the bearers of supreme power was quite unsuited to the occasion. What it did achieve was to set in juxtaposition the boundless Imperial luxury and the poverty of the people. The demagogues did not fail to comment upon this ominous contrast." *Features and Figures of the Past,* p. 470.

8. These impressions were recorded by State Councillor Count D.A. Olsufiev and published in the Saratov paper, *Golos pravdy* [Voice of Truth]. (Oldenburg's note)

Prince Dmitry Adamovich Olsufiev (1862-) was a prominent figure among the United Nobility (below, Note 26), one of the principal organizers of the Union of October 17 in Saratov, and founder of the Octobrist newspaper *Volga.* He was elected to the State Council in 1906, 1909 and 1912. As a state councillor, Olsufiev opposed the Octobrists in the naval staffs crisis (Volume III, Chapter XIV) and vigorously defended the principle of monarchical supremacy in military affairs.

The Olsufiev family owned great estates in Moscow and Saratov provinces. After his graduation from Moscow University, D.A. Olsufiev attended the Mikhailovsky Artillery School and served in the Horse Guards Artillery Regiment. From 1891 to 1894 he was a land captain (zemskii nachalnik) in Moscow province. In 1894 he was appointed marshal of the Saratov nobility. From 1902 to 1904 he served as chairman of the Saratov provincial zemstvo board, which he represented at the 1907 zemstvo congress.

9. S.A. Muromtsev (1850-1910) was one of the founders of the Kadet Party and a member of its central committee. He had been active since the early nineties as a liberal leader in zemstvo affairs. Miliukov in his memoirs accused Muromtsev of behaving "pompously" as president of the Duma, considering himself to be "the second person in the state after the tsar." (*Political Memoirs*, p. 103) As one of the signers of the Vyborg manifesto, Muromtsev had to retire from political life. He lost his position at Moscow University and spent his last years at Shaniavsky University.

10. In this and subsequent chapters the author draws extensively on the verbatim record of the transactions of the State Dumas, published in 32 volumes. For the First Duma the bibliographic entry is: Gosudarstvennaia duma, *Stenograficheskie otchety. 1906 god. Sessiia 1* [State Duma, Stenographic Reports. 1906. Session 1], 2 vols. (St. Petersburg, 1906). There are two important companion works to the stenograhic reports for each Duma.

An index gives a profile of each member of the Duma and a guide to his activities with references to the stenographic reports. It provides a complete guide to the fractions of the Duma and its committees and also indexes the interpellations and other activities, including speeches and legislative proposals, of each official who had dealings with the Duma: Gosudarstvennaia duma, *Ukazatel k stenograficheskim otchetam*

[Index to the Stenographic Reports (of the State Duma)], followed by appropriate data for each session (St. Petersburg, 1907-).

On the basis of extensive questionnaires completed by each deputy, the ministry of internal affairs published a comprehensive guide to the membership of the Dumas. The guide lists all deputies by party or fractional affiliation; indicates the representation throughout the empire by province, district, and city; and provides biographies and portraits of each deputy. There is a volume for each of the four Dumas, and each volume contains a floor plan of the Duma indicating the seat of each member. Each of the volumes was compiled by M.M. Boiovich, *Chleny Gosudarstvennoi dumy. (Portrety i biografii)* [Members of the State Duma (Portraits and Biographies)] . . . (St. Petersburg, 1907, 1907, 1910, 1913). This work is quite rare; a more accessible brief biographical guide to the members of the first three Dumas is the *Entsiklopedicheskii slovar Granat* [The Granat Encyclopedic Dictionary], ed. I.E. Andreevsky, vol. 17, s. v. "Chleny Gosudarstvennoi dumy pervogo, vtorogo i tretego sozyva" [Members of the First, Second, and Third State Dumas]. Additional biographical material on the Dumas is listed in *Spravochniki po istorii dorevoliutsionnoi Rossii* [References for the History of Prerevolutionary Russia], ed. P.A. Zaionchkovsky (Moscow, 1971), pp. 172-75.

11. Michael A. Stakhovich (1861-1923) was elected marshal of the nobility (1895-97) of Orel province, where he was a substantial landowner. A prominent conservative leader, he served in the First and Second Dumas and was elected to the State Council in 1907 and 1912.

12. Prince Eugene Trubetskoy (1863-1920), a younger brother of Sergei Trubetskoy, was professor of legal philosophy at Kiev University. He joined the Kadet Party in 1905-6 and then left it to become one of the founders of the Party of Peaceful Reconstruction.

13. In 1236 Batu Khan (died 1255), a grandson of Genghis Khan, led the Mongol conquest of Russia.

14. Through October 1906, the political struggle in Russia had claimed nearly 17,000 victims of whom more than 7,000 were killed. Semiofficial statistics indicated that 3,611 government officials had been killed or wounded while 13,381 citizens had been executed by courtsmartial or killed by troops or terrorists. Alfred Levin, *The Second Duma: A Study of the Social Democratic Party and the Russian Constitutional Experiment*, 2nd ed. (Archon Books, 1966), p. 21, n. 28.

15. Alexander S. Stishinsky (1852-1920), a man of extremely conservative views, briefly headed the agricultural ministry (the main administration of land organization and agriculture) from April to June 1906. When Stolypin became chairman of the council of ministers, he insisted on Stishinsky's resignation, because the minister was an inveterate opponent of agrarian reform. Stishinsky's bureaucratic career began in 1872, and he had served in the ministry of internal affairs from 1886 until 1904, when he was appointed to the State Council.

16. Ivan V. Shcheglovitov (1861-1918) served as minister of justice from April 1906 until July 1915. He was appointed to the State Council in 1907 and was the last president of that body (January-February 1917). The Provisional Government arrested him after the February Revolution, and the Bolsheviks executed him in August 1918.

17. Prince Alexis A. Shirinsky-Shikhmatov (1862-1930) was a noted reactionary and anti-Semite, well-known for his endorsement of the Black Hundreds. According to Witte, he gained the undying friendship of the emperor when he took charge of the arrangements for the canonization of St. Seraphim in 1903. He directed the holy synod in April-July 1905 and then the tsar appointed him to the State Council.

18. Peter A. Stolypin (1862-1911) brought a wholly new perspective to the government in that he was the only member of the bureaucratic cabinet whose career was outside the central administration. Stolypin was a substantial landowner in the western province of Kovno, where he served as marshal of the nobility from 1887 to 1902. In 1902 he was made governor of Grodno and in 1903 of Saratov. His fair but firm policies and ruthless suppression of peasant revolts in that province brought him to the attention of the central government and led to his appointment as minister of interior in Goremykin's cabinet. Stolypin was a courageous, conservative, Russian nationalist, and those traits characterized the policy of the government that he eventually came to lead. There is a substantial literature on Stolypin but the outstanding political study is Geoffrey A. Hosking, *The Russian Constitutional Experiment: Government and Duma, 1907-1914* (Cambridge, 1973). The best brief studies are: Alfred Levin, "Peter Arkad'evich Stolypin: a Political Re-appraisal," *Journal of Modern History*, 37 (1965), 445-63; and L.I. Strakhovsky, "The Statesmanship of Peter Stolypin: A Re-appraisal," *Slavonic and East European Review*, 37 (1959), 348-70.

19. Alexander P. Izvolsky (1856-1919) served as minister of foreign affairs from 1906 to 1910. Under his direction Russian foreign policy was characterized by reconciliation with Japan and rapprochement with England. Especially after the Bosnian crisis (below), Izvolsky became bitterly anti-German and worked strenuously to strengthen the Triple Entente. His was a liberal voice in the council of ministers, and his memoirs are an important source not only for the history of Russian foreign policy but also for the workings of the Russian government during the first revolutionary period—*The Memoirs of Alexander Iswolsky* (London, 1920; Academic International Press, 1974).

20. V.D. Nabokov (1869-1922) was a prominent criminologist, one of the founders of the Kadet party, chairman of its central committee, and one of the editors of *Rech*, the organ of the left-Kadets. Nabokov played a leading role in the First Duma. As one of the signers of the Vyborg manifesto (below), he eventually served a three-month prison term and was barred from politics. In 1917 he became the executive secretary of the Provisional Government. After the Bolshevik coup, he became minister of justice in Wrangel's government in southern Russia, and when the anti-Bolshevik resistance collapsed he fled to Berlin. He was murdered there in 1922 by a Russian reactionary who was trying to shoot Miliukov.

21. In a parliamentary system, where the government is formed by and responsible to the legislature, a vote of no-confidence normally leads to the government's resignation. In Russia the tsar appointed the ministers, and they were responsible to him.

22. General Nepliuev was slated for assassination because of his role in the suppression of the Sevastopol mutinies. Although this attempt

was the work of the local Socialist Revolutionaries, a detachment of the
Battle Organization was also in town working on the assassination of
Admiral Chukhnin. According to Savinkov's account, the assassin, a
local sailor named Ivan Frolov, was among the victims. Thirty-seven
people were injured, but Nepliuev escaped. *Memoirs of a Terrorist*, p.
254.

23. *Narodnyi vestnik* [The People's Messenger], 20 May 1906. Late in
July in Sevastopol terrorists murdered the commander of the Black Sea
Fleet, Vice Admiral Gregory P. Chukhnin. (Oldenburg's note)

24. Cf. Gurko, *Features and Figures of the Past*, pp. 474-78.

25. *Novoe vremia*, 12 December 1906, gave the following tally of
revolutionary murders during the first six months of 1906: January-80;
February-64; March-50; April-56; May-122; June-127. (Oldenburg's note)

26. The United Nobility was formed early in 1906 because many
nobles felt that Russia's noblemen collectively were doing too little to
oppose the revolutionary movement and stiffen the resolve of the government. The initial impetus came from two ultra-conservatives, Alexander N. Naumov of Samara and Prince V.M. Volkonsky of Tambov. As
one of the leading nobles of the empire, Prince Peter N. Trubetskoy,
marshal of the nobility of Moscow, summoned a congress of provincial
marshals which met in Moscow on 7-11 January 1906. One of the
decisions of that meeting was to organize the nobility nationwide.
Trubetskoy, an aristocratic liberal, wanted to continue the constitutional
tradition of submitting loyal petitions. Reactionaries wanted to establish a strong conservative organization, backed by the empire's nobility,
to exert constant pressure on the government at the center of power.
Before the May congress assembled, the rightists managed to replace
Trubetskoy as leading organizer with Prince N.F. Kasatkin-Rostovsky
of Kursk, a province distinguished by its reactionary zemstvo and noble
assemblies.

Six provincial assemblies boycotted the May congress, and nine failed
to send delegates. Conservatives and ultra-rightists dominated the proceedings, established a Permanent Council with strong executive powers,
and elected Count A.A. Bobrinsky as its chairman. While the government welcomed the support of the United Nobility in 1906, it became
something of an embarrassment when the government under Stolypin
embarked on a program of reform. Then the United Nobility, dedicated
to the narrow defense of its class interests, became more an obstacle
than a positive force in Russian politics. Hosking, *Russian Constitutional Experiment*, pp. 31-34.

27. Miliukov was not eligible for election to the Duma, since he did
not meet the residency requirement (one year); however, he remained
at the head of the party and directed its activities in the First Duma
from behind the scene. (Oldenburg's note)

Whether the government was serious about a Kadet ministry is unsettled. Trepov and Baron Frederichs apparently were. Miliukov believed that the government's intentions were serious or not serious,
depending on when he was writing or speaking. Oldenburg's interpretation basically follows Kokovtsov, who quotes the tsar as having said,
when the matter was settled: "I can tell you now that I never intended

to venture into the remote unknown which people were advising me to test. I did not mention this to those who, with the best of intentions, of course, suggested the idea to me . . . . I no longer have any doubts—nor indeed did I ever have any doubts, since I do not have the right to renounce that which has been bequeathed to me by my ancestors and which I must bequeath for safe-keeping to my son." In the course of the negotiation—or inquiries—Miliukov demanded all or nothing: adoption of the Kadet program and a Kadet ministry with himself at its head. Sir Bernard Pares, an admirer of Miliukov and all that he stood for, called this "one of the most crucial mistakes of his career."

Kokovtsov, *Iz moego proshlago*, I: 195-202 ff.; Sir Bernard Pares, *The Fall of the Russian Monarchy* (New York, 1939, 1961), pp. 96-97; Miliukov, *Political Memoirs*, pp. 106-16; and *Tri popytki: k istorii russkogo lzhekonstitutsionalizma* [Three Attempts: Toward a History of Russian Pseudo-Constitutionalism] (Paris, 1921), pp. 31-33.

28. Late in October 1905 Lenin left Geneva and traveled to Russia by way of Stockholm. In the fall of 1906 he took up residence across the border in Finland, and in December 1907 he returned to Switzerland. He remained abroad until April 1917.

29. *Novoe vremia*, 24 June 1906. (Oldenburg's note)

30. The appeal, drafted by Miliukov, was debated for two days (9-10 July 1906); the people's "passive resistance" was to end with the convocation of the Second Duma.

31. The government brought indictments against the signers on 16 July 1906. The trial followed after more than a year, and on 18 December 1907 they were sentenced to three months in prison. Since about two-thirds of the signatures belonged to Kadets, the government's action crippled the party's leadership.

32. Stolypin also interviewed Count Peter Heiden, who was elected to the First Duma as an Octobrist and subsequently helped to found the somewhat less conservative Party of Peaceful Reconstruction; Anatoly Koni, a prominent jurist and academician; and Prince George Lvov, who served in the First Duma as a right-wing Kadet. All the men consulted by Stolypin were moderate liberals—somewhat to the right of the Kadets. Their conditions were the most moderate yet received by the government, but not moderate enough: land reform including, if necessary, the compulsory expropriation of private land; an amnesty for crimes committed in the liberation movement that did not involve loss of life or property; annulment of the emergency decrees; suspension of the death penalty until the Second Duma could be convened; and the immediate legislative enactment of the civil liberties promised by the October Manifesto. Hosking, *Russian Constitutional Experiment*, p. 24.

33. In June 1907 Stalin participated (in a role never clarified) in a sensational robbery of the Tiflis State Bank. This operation netted the Bolsheviks nearly 350,000 rubles. The raid was illegal not only in a "bourgeois" sense but also as a violation of a Menshevik resolution approved by the Social Democratic Party at its fourth ("unity") congress in 1906 in Stockholm. Lenin, however, approved of "exes," as they were known to the revolutionaries, and the Bolsheviks ignored the party's ban against armed robbery.

Joseph Stalin (Joseph Vissarionovich Dzhugashvili) (1879-1953) joined the SDs in Tiflis in 1898. Repeatedly arrested and exiled, he repeatedly escaped. He was arrested and exiled for the last time in February
1913. After four years in Eastern Siberia, he returned to Petrograd
(Petersburg) just after the February Revolution, and thereafter he was
always at the center of party and state affairs. By 1928 he had defeated
all the claimants to Lenin's mantle, and for the next twenty-five years
he was the unassailable personification of the Soviet state and the un-
questioned leader of the communist movement. See the widely acclaimed biography by Robert C. Tucker, *Stalin as Revolutionary, 1879-
1929: A Study in History and Personality* (New York, 1974), the first
of a projected two-volume study.

34. The proceeds of the Tiflis bank job were all in 500-ruble notes and
had to be smuggled out of Russia and disposed of abroad. Lenin entrusted the coordination of the project to Dr. Jacob Zhitomirsky, a trusted
associate in Berlin—who was also a police spy. Through Zhitomirsky the
police and state banks throughout Europe received the serial numbers
of the hot money and a description of the several people who would be
attempting to cash or deposit them. One of those with a suitcase full
of money was Maxim M. Litvinov (Meyer Wallach) (1876-1951). He was
arrested in Paris. Fortunately for him, the French government decided
that his crime was "political," and it therefore refused his extradition
to Russia. On the robbery and aftermath see Wolfe, *Three Who Made a
Revolution,* pp. 393-97.

Litvinov became a Social Democrat in 1898 and a Bolshevik in 1903.
He traveled frequently in Western Europe on party business, mainly as a
procurer of arms and gun-runner. After the revolution he became deputy
commissar for foreign affairs and from 1930 to 1939, commissar. As
foreign minister, he was known principally as an advocate of collective
security against fascist aggression. He was the Soviet ambassador to the
United States during the early part (1941-43) of World War II.

35. In 1917 leaders of the Union of Russian People confessed to the
Provisional Government's Extraordinary Investigating Commission that
Dr. Dubrovin, the founder and head of the URP, had organized Herzenstein's murder in June 1906 and in March 1907 that of G.B. Iollos, the
liberal editor of *Russkiia vedomosti* and also a Kadet deputy in the
First Duma. In January and May 1907 Dubrovin instigated two unsuccessful attempts to assassinate Count Witte. One of Dubrovin's chief
confederates was A.E. Kazantsev, an officer in the Okhrana, the tsarist
secret police. It is unlikely that this information escaped the author's
scrutiny.

36. On the day of General Min's funeral the commander of the Corps
of Guards, Adjutant General Vladimir N. Danilov, issued the following
order: "I swear, and I call upon all of the ancient Imperial Guard to
swear with me, to remain loyal to our legitimate Sovereign and our
motherland as bravely and fearlessly as you did. If any of us should
waver, let him come to the chapel of the Semenovsky Regiment to pray
beside your remains, there to regain renewed and indestructible courage
for the performance of his duty. For us the chapel of the Semenovsky
has acquired special significance as the shrine for curing the most terrible
of all diseases—irresolution." (Oldenburg's note)

37. The initiative for the Ukaz of 19 August establishing the field courts-martial originated with the tsar. According to Stolypin's assistant, Gurko, the tsar's command came as a surprise to Stolypin and horrified him. In any event he allowed it to expire without pressing for its extension. One of the new features of the law was the establishment of a hostage system: persons condemned to death for political crimes were not executed; instead they were held as hostages against the commission of further crimes by their associates or terrorists in general. Gurko, *Features and Figures of the Past*, p. 499.

38. The Party of Peaceful Reconstruction drew its adherents from the Kadet right and the Octobrist left. Its founders were Nicholas Lvov, Michael Stakhovich, Dmitry Shipov, and Count Peter Heiden. The party favored a constitutional monarchy; it opposed Stolypin's violent repression and his agrarian program. On the question of land reform the Party of Peaceful Reconstruction favored the compulsory expropriation of private property with just compensation.

39. Dubasov asked the emperor to pardon the man who made the attempt on his life, but Stolypin objected, and on 4 December 1906 the emperor replied: "The courts-martial function independently of you and me; let them carry on in the full severity of the law. There is and can be no other means of struggle against those who have become brutalized. You know me and know that I am not spiteful: I write to you fully convinced of the correctness of my opinion. It is painful and difficult but true, much to our sorrow and shame, that only the execution of a few can prevent seas of blood, and indeed have prevented them already." (The expression, "much to our sorrow and shame," came from a letter of Stolypin to the emperor.) (Oldenburg's note)

Some of the correspondence between Nicholas and Stolypin is published in "Perepiska N.A. Romanova i P.A. Stolypina" [The Correspondence of N.A. Romanov and P.A. Stolypin], *Krasnyi arkhiv*, 5 (1924), 102-28.

40. The emperor referred to a railway accident [which nearly killed the imperial family] at Borky in 1888. (Oldenburg's note)

41. The reader may wish to refer to the text of this article in connection with the author's defense of the Law of 3 June 1907 at the end of this chapter:

"When the State Duma is not in session, if extraordinary circumstances require legislative action, the Council of Ministers may present a measure directly to the Emperor. This measure cannot, however, introduce changes either in the Fundamental State Laws, or in the institutions of the State Council and State Duma, or in regulations governing elections to the Council and Duma. Such a measure becomes void if a draft law corresponding to the measure is not submitted to the Duma by a Minister or responsible department head within the first two months after the Duma reconvenes, or if the draft law is not passed by the Duma and State Council."

Translated by Mehlinger and Thompson, *Count Witte*, pp. 340-41; see also their discussion of the improper identification of this article, p. 395, n. 59.

42. The author's characterization of the agricultural policy of the SDs is an anachronism in that neither Bolsheviks nor Mensheviks had

any definite agrarian program at that time. Soviet agricultural policy hammered out in the late twenties and early thirties finally settled on large-scale collectivized agriculture, a program that was neither inherently Marxist or Leninist. Before 1917 the peasantry interested the SDs mainly as revolutionary allies of the more advanced proletariat. The slogan "All Land to the Tillers" was a call to arms not an economic program nor, as it turned out, a promise.

43. The two most important limitations removed by this decree were the authority of village officials to control passports (without which a peasant could not leave his residence for more than a few days) and the power of the land captain to punish peasants without a trial. *Polnoe sobranie*, 3rd ser., XXVI, No. 28,392. For a discussion of the law see Robinson, *Rural Russia*, pp. 209-11.

44. *Polnoe sobranie*, 3rd. ser., XXVI, No. 28,528.

45. Ibid., Articles 12-14. The complexities of the law and the problems of repartition and consolidation are described and analyzed in Robinson, *Rural Russia*, pp. 212-42.

46. A.V. Krivoshein (1858-1923) joined the agricultrual ministry in 1896, after more than a decade in the interior and justice ministries. He long had championed the breakup of the communes in order to create independent individual farmsteads. From 1908 to 1915 Krivoshein directed the main administration of land organization and agriculture.

47. A.I. Lykoshin (1861-1918) had served, since 1882, principally in the ministry of justice. However, in 1907 he was appointed an assistant minister of interior and made head of the peasant section, positions that he held until 1914. At that time the tsar appointed him to the State Council.

48. A.A. Rittikh (1868-1930) spent his entire government career in the main administration of land organization and agriculture (formerly the ministry of agriculture and state domains, 1894-1905). In 1905 he became director of the department of state domains and also manager of affairs of the committee for land organization. He succeeded to the second post in the ministry in 1912 and on the eve of the collapse of the monarchy, in November 1916, he became minister of agriculture.

49. Election results in St. Petersburg were as follows (the figures in parentheses are the votes cast in the election to the First Duma): Socialist bloc—16,000 (——); Kadets—18,000 (40,000); Octobrists—16,000 (18,000); Rightists—5,000 (3,000).

In Moscow: Socialist bloc—5,000 (——); Kadets—21,000 (26,000); Octobrists—10,000 (12,000); and Rightists—3,000 (2,000). (Oldenburg's note)

50. Oldenburg's note (original text, p. 377) on the composition of the Second Duma omits over a hundred deputies (Kadets and Muslims), and the following summary is adapted from Levin, *The Second Duma*, p. 67. Oldenburg states that most of the rightist deputies, especially clergy and peasants, were designated "non-party." The parties are listed roughly by political persuasion from right to left:

Rightists	10	(2%)
Octobrists	44	(8%)
No party affiliation.	51	(10%)

Cossack fraction	17	(3%)
Kadets	98	(19%)
Muslim fraction	30	(6%)
Polish fraction	46	(9%)
Trudoviks and Popular Socialists	120	(23%)
Socialist Revolutionaries	37	(7%)
Social Democrats	65	(13%)
Total	518	

51. A digression by the author into the West European elections of 1906-7, which had little similarity and no bearing on the Russian election, has been omitted. The deleted paragraph is found on page 378 of the original text.

52. Count V.A. Bobrinsky (1867-1927), a panslavist, had been active since the early nineties in zemstvo affairs in the district of Bogoroditsk and was the district marshal of nobility. He was a voice of conservatism in the Second, Third, and Fourth Dumas and played a significant role in all three.

53. V.M. Purishkevich (1870-1920), a wealthy landowner and reactionary fanatic of great ability and energy, personified most of the worst in Old Russia. In 1904 he became a special advisor on Jewish affairs to V.K. Plehve, the minister of interior. With A.I. Dubrovin he helped create the Union of Russian People and served as its vice-president. Then in 1908 he broke with Dubrovin and formed a rival pogrom-promoting organization, the Union of Michael the Archangel. His last service to his country was to conspire in the murder of Rasputin in December 1916.

54. V.V. Shulgin (187 -1945?), a conservative nationalist from the Ukraine, became editor of *Kievlianin* in 1911. Shulgin served continually after 1907 in the Dumas, and in March 1917 the last Duma sent him with Guchkov to obtain the abdication of Nicholas II.

55. P.N. Krupensky (1863-) was a wealthy landowner in Bessarabia and a district marshal of nobility. Krupensky was elected to the Second, Third, and Fourth Dumas, where he was a prominent figure on the right. Related by marriage to I.L. Goremykin, he served as a legislative double-agent. The ministry of interior paid him to keep it informed of the non-public activity of the Duma, and Krupensky also organized a number of political clubs with government funds, which he used to his private advantage.

56. F.I. Rodichev (1854-1933) was well-known in and out of zemstvo circles as a liberal activist. He was one of the authors of the Tver zemstvo petition of 1894 which had prompted the tsar to warn against "senseless dreams." A Liberationist and one of the founders of the Kadet Party, Rodichev was one of its foremost orators in all four Dumas.

57. A prospering attorney in St. Petersburg and Moscow, V.A. Maklakov (1870-1959) gained national prominence in 1905-7 as a defense attorney in a number of political cases. Maklakov joined the Kadets in 1906 and was elected to its central committee. He was associated with the Kadet right and was one of Miliukov's most relentless opponents within the party. Maklakov served in the last three Dumas as a deputy from Moscow.

58. A.A. Kizevetter (1866-1933) was an active member of the Liberation movement before the 1905 revolution. He edited a couple of liberal

reviews but was by profession an historian and held positions on the faculties of Moscow University and the Moscow Women's University. He was one of the founders of the Kadet Party, a member of its central committee, but a deputy only in the Second Duma.

59. I.G. Tseretelli (1882-1960) was one of the most prominent leaders of the socialist opposition in the Second Duma. When the Duma was prorogued, he was arrested with the other SDs and sentenced to five years at hard labor and loss of rights. Amnestied after the 1917 revolution, he returned to Petrograd and became one of the leaders in the executive committee of the Petrograd Soviet and a minister in the Provisional Government.

60. G.A. Aleksinsky (1879-) became a Bolshevik during the 1905 revolution. In 1909, however, he broke with Lenin and joined others in forming the *Vpered* (Forward) group. During World War I, he identified with the "defensists." In 1917 he allied himself with Plekhanov in the Unity group and then, having run out of anti-Leninist organizations, he emigrated to France.

61. Stolypin's major speeches are published in *Sbornik rechei P.A. Stolypina (1906-1911 gg.)* [Collection of P.A. Stolypin's Speeches (1906-1911)], ed. V.V. Logachev (St. Petersburg, 1911). The record of the Second Duma is: *Stenograficheskie otchety. 1907. Sessiia 1* [Stenographic Reports. 1907. Session 1], 2 vols. (St. Petersburg, 1907); and the *Ukazatel* [Index] (St. Petersburg, 1907) (see above, Note 10).

62. Socialists later used this remark to allege that "130,000 landlords really rule Russia." (Oldenburg's note—from the text)

63. Zurabov was an Armenian born in Tiflis in 1873. As a result of his revolutionary activities, he was expelled from a teacher's seminary and subsequently was imprisoned several times. When free, he edited Armenian revolutionary newspapers.

64. F.A. Golovin (1867-), though not a nobleman, was descended from nobility. He had been a member since 1898 of the Moscow provincial zemstvo board and was its chairman from 1904 to 1906. He was one of the founders of the Union of Liberation, the congress of zemstvos, and the Moscow committee of the Kadet Party. Elected to the Third Duma, he resigned in October 1910. During the world war, he was active in the Union of Towns. Golovin remained in Russia after the revolution and worked in the Soviet administration.

65. *Russkaia mysl*, a Petersburg monthly, was established in 1880 as a slavophile journal. In the 1890s it became a vehicle for liberal populist thought. Struve became its editor in 1906 and from then until its suppression in 1918 it reflected the line of the Kadet right.

66. In late March the police arrested thirty persons who were preparing to assassinate the tsar as well as Grand Duke Nicholas Nikolaevich, Stolypin, and Shcheglovitov! (Oldenburg's note) See Nikolajewsky, *Aseff the Spy*, pp. 215-23.

67. The tsar and government had decided that the Duma had to be dissolved, but they needed a legal basis to do so. The Duma's refusal to surrender its "conspirators" provided the pretext, even though the government could implicate only one or two SDs in the alleged conspiracy, which consisted of soliciting and receiving a petition from a soldiers'

organization (which was illegal). This last crisis of the Second Duma is described by Levin, *Second Duma*, pp. 307-49.

68. A translation and analysis of the Law of 3 June 1907 can be found in Samuel N. Harper, *The New Electoral Law for The Russian Empire* (Chicago, 1908).

69. *Novoe vremia*, 22 September 1906. (Oldenburg's note)

"*Roma locuta . . .*"—Rome has spoken, the matter is closed.

70. Oldenburg's italics, here and below. The manifesto and the author's discussion were meant to rationalize the government's action. See above Note 41.

ᔪᕽᕽᔫ

CONVERSION TABLE

Linear Measure
  1 *versta* (plur., *verst*) = 0.663 mile
  1 *arshin* = 28 inches

Land Area
  1 *desiatina* (plur., *desiatin*) = 2.7 acres
  1 *kvadratnaia versta* = 0.43957 square miles

Weight
  1 *pud* = 36.113 pounds
  1 *berkovets* (10 puds) = 361.13 pounds

Volume, Dry Measure
  1 *chetvert* = 6 bushels (approx.)

Volume, Liquid Measure
  1 *vedro* (plur., *vedra*) = 3.25 gallons
  1 *bochka* (40 *vedra*) = 131.5 gallons

Currency
  1 *rubl* (gold ruble, 1896-1914) = $ 0.50 (approx.)
    (The "Witte" or gold-standard ruble of 1896-97 was equal to two-thirds the value of the old silver ruble.)
  1 *kopeika* (kopeck) = 1/100th ruble